A Kodansha Comics Trade Paperback Original
Hitorijime My Hero 12 copyright © 2021 Memeco Arii
English translation copyright © 2022 Memeco Arii

Published in the United States by Kodansha Comics, an imprint of Kodansha USA Publishing, LLC, New York.

Publication rights for this English edition arranged through Kodansha Ltd., Tokyo.

First published in Japan in 2021 by Ichijinsha Inc., Tokyo.

ISBN 978-1-64651-409-0

Printed in the United States of America.

www.kodanshacomics.us

1st Printing
Translation: Kevin Gifford
Lettering: Michael Martin
Editing: Greg Moore
Kodansha Comics edition cover design by Phil Balsman

Publisher: Kiichiro Sugawara

Director of publishing services: Ben Applegate
Associate director of operations: Stephen Pakula
Publishing services managing editors: Madison Salters, Alanna Ruse
Production managers: Emi Lotto, Angela Zurlo

The beloved characters from *Cardcaptor Sakura* return in a brand new, reimagined fantasy adventure!

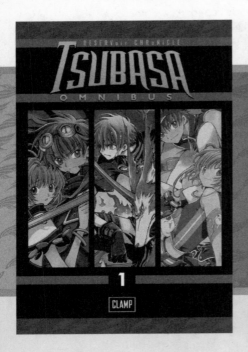

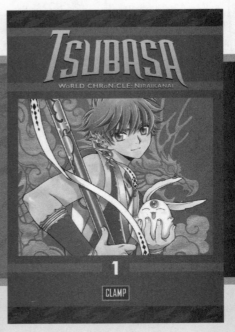

"[*Tsubasa*] takes readers on a fantastic ride that only gets more exhilarating with each successive chapter." —Anime News Network

In the Kingdom of Clow, an archaeological dig unleashes an incredible power, causing Princess Sakura to lose her memories. To save her, her childhood friend Syaoran must follow the orders of the Dimension Witch and travel alongside Kurogane, an unrivaled warrior; Fai, a powerful magician; and Mokona, a curiously strange creature, to retrieve Sakura's dispersed memories!

The art-deco cyberpunk classic from the creators of *xxxHOLiC* and *Cardcaptor Sakura*!

CLOVER © CLAMP·ShigatsuTsuitachi CO.,LTD./Kodansha Ltd.

Su was born into a bleak future, where the government keeps
tight control over children with magical powers—codenamed
"Clovers." With Su being the only "four-leaf" Clover in the
world, she has been kept isolated nearly her whole life. Can
ex-military agent Kazuhiko deliver her to the happiness she
seeks? Experience the complete series in this hardcover
edition, which also includes over twenty pages of ravishing
color art!

KC
KODANSHA
COMICS

THE WORLD OF CLAMP!

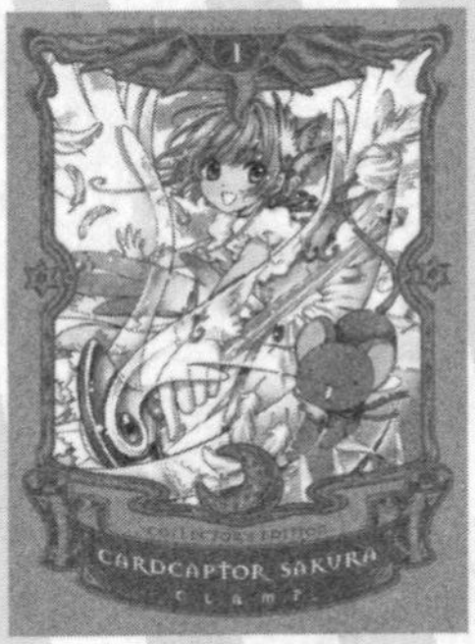
CARDCAPTOR SAKURA
CLAMP

Cardcaptor Sakura
Collector's Edition

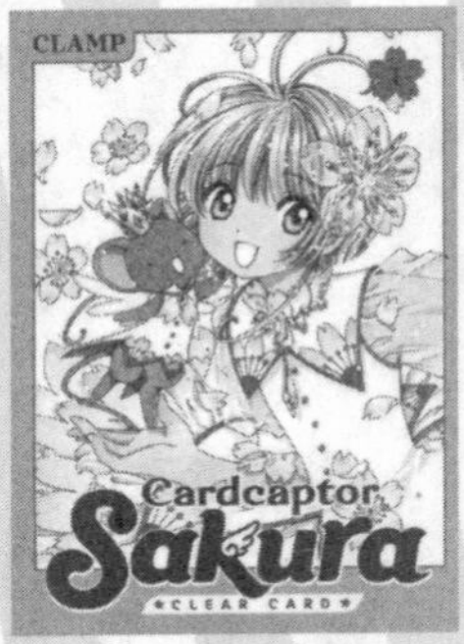
CLAMP
Cardcaptor Sakura
CLEAR CARD

Cardcaptor Sakura:
Clear Card

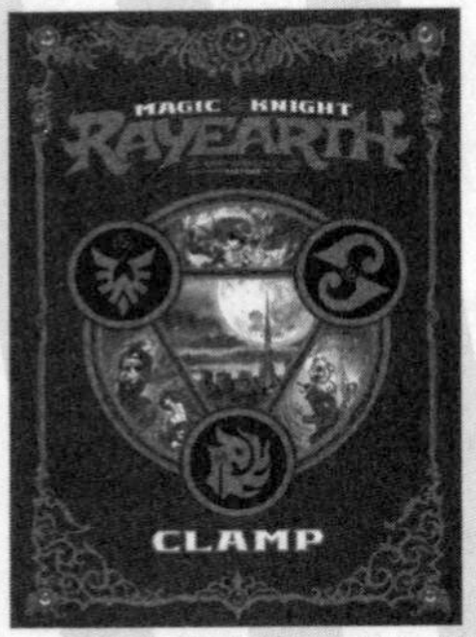
MAGIC KNIGHT
RAYEARTH
CLAMP

Magic Knight Rayearth
25th Anniversary Box Set

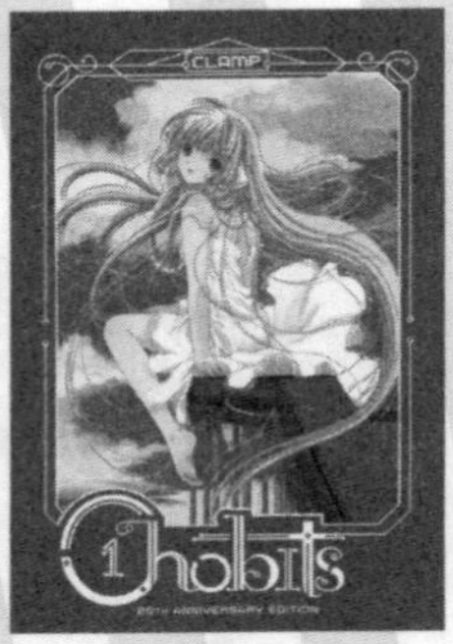
CLAMP
1 Chobits

Chobits

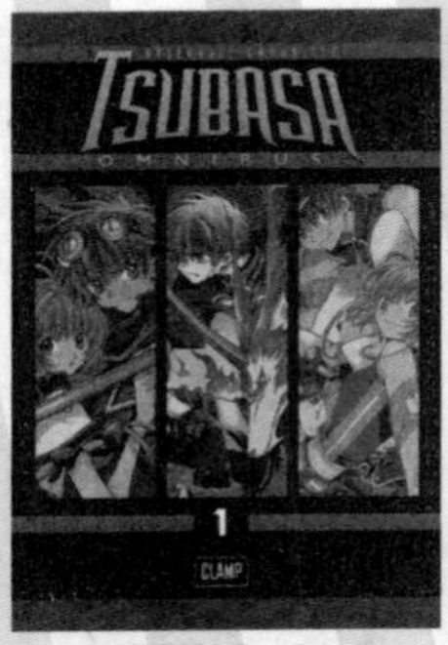
TSUBASA
OMNIBUS
1
CLAMP

TSUBASA Omnibus

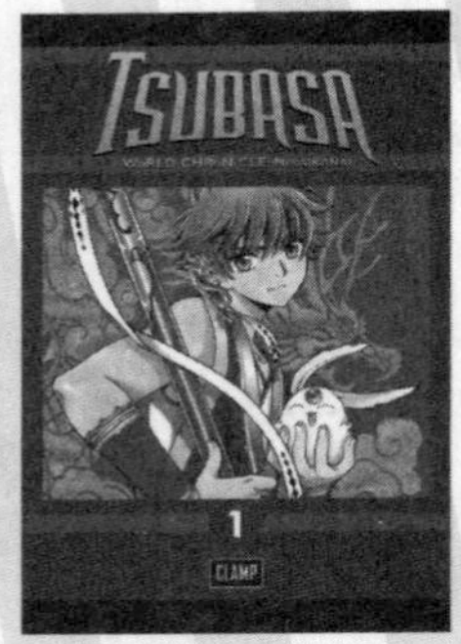
TSUBASA
1
CLAMP

TSUBASA WoRLD CHRoNiCLE

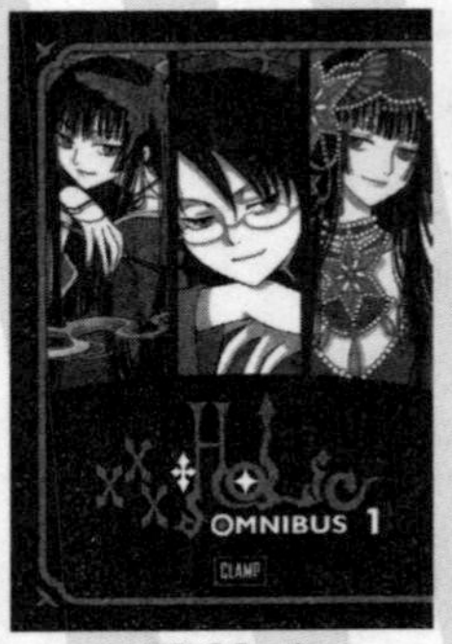
xxxHOLiC
OMNIBUS 1
CLAMP

xxxHOLiC Omnibus

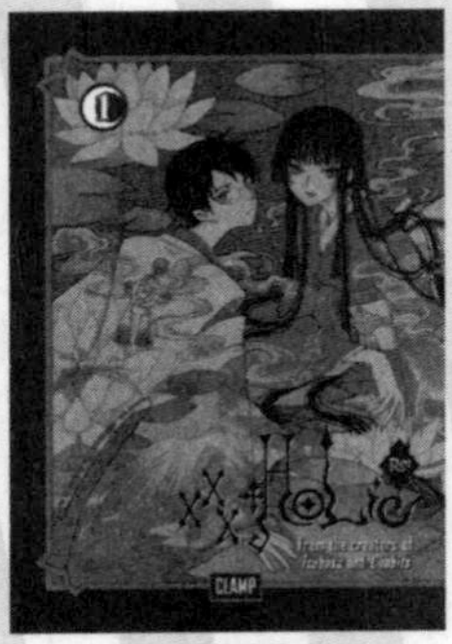
xxxHOLiC
CLAMP

xxxHOLiC Rei

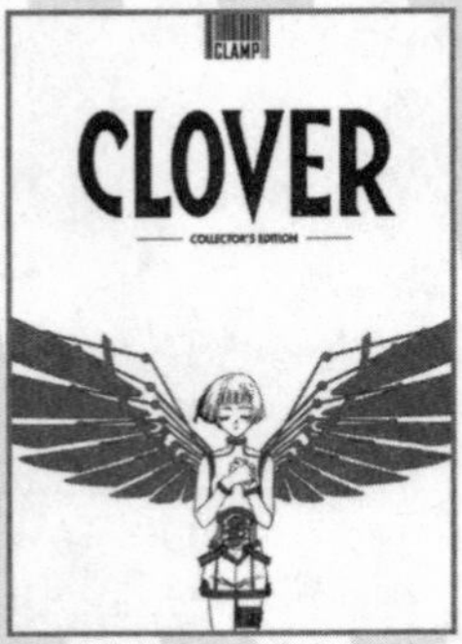
CLAMP
CLOVER
COLLECTOR'S EDITION

CLOVER Collector's Edition

Kodansha Comics welcomes you to explore the expansive world of CLAMP, the all-female artist collective that has produced some of the most acclaimed manga of the century. Our growing catalog includes icons like *Cardcaptor Sakura* and *Magic Knight Rayearth*, each crafted with CLAMP's one-of-a-kind style and characters!

THE SWEET SCENT OF LOVE IS IN THE AIR! FOR FANS OF OFFBEAT ROMANCES LIKE *WOTAKOI*

VOL. 1
SWEAT AND SOAP
KINTETSU YAMADA

Sweat and Soap © Kintetsu Yamada / Kodansha Ltd.

In an office romance, there's a fine line between sexy and awkward... and that line is where Asako — a woman who sweats copiously — meets Koutarou — a perfume developer who can't get enough of Asako's, er, scent. Don't miss a romcom manga like no other!

KC KODANSHA COMICS

The adorable new odd-couple cat comedy manga from the creator of the beloved *Chi's Sweet Home*, in full color!

Praise for Chi's Sweet Home

"Nearly impossible to turn away... a true all-ages title that anyone, young or old, cat lover or not, will enjoy. The stories will bring a smile to your face and warm your heart."

—School Library Journal

Sue & Tai-chan
Konami Kanata

Sue is an aging housecat who's looking forward to living out her life in peace... but her plans change when the mischievous black tomcat Tai-chan enters the picture! Hey! Sue never signed up to be a catsitter! *Sue & Tai-chan* is the latest from the reigning meow-narch of cute kitty comics, Konami Kanata.

KC KODANSHA COMICS

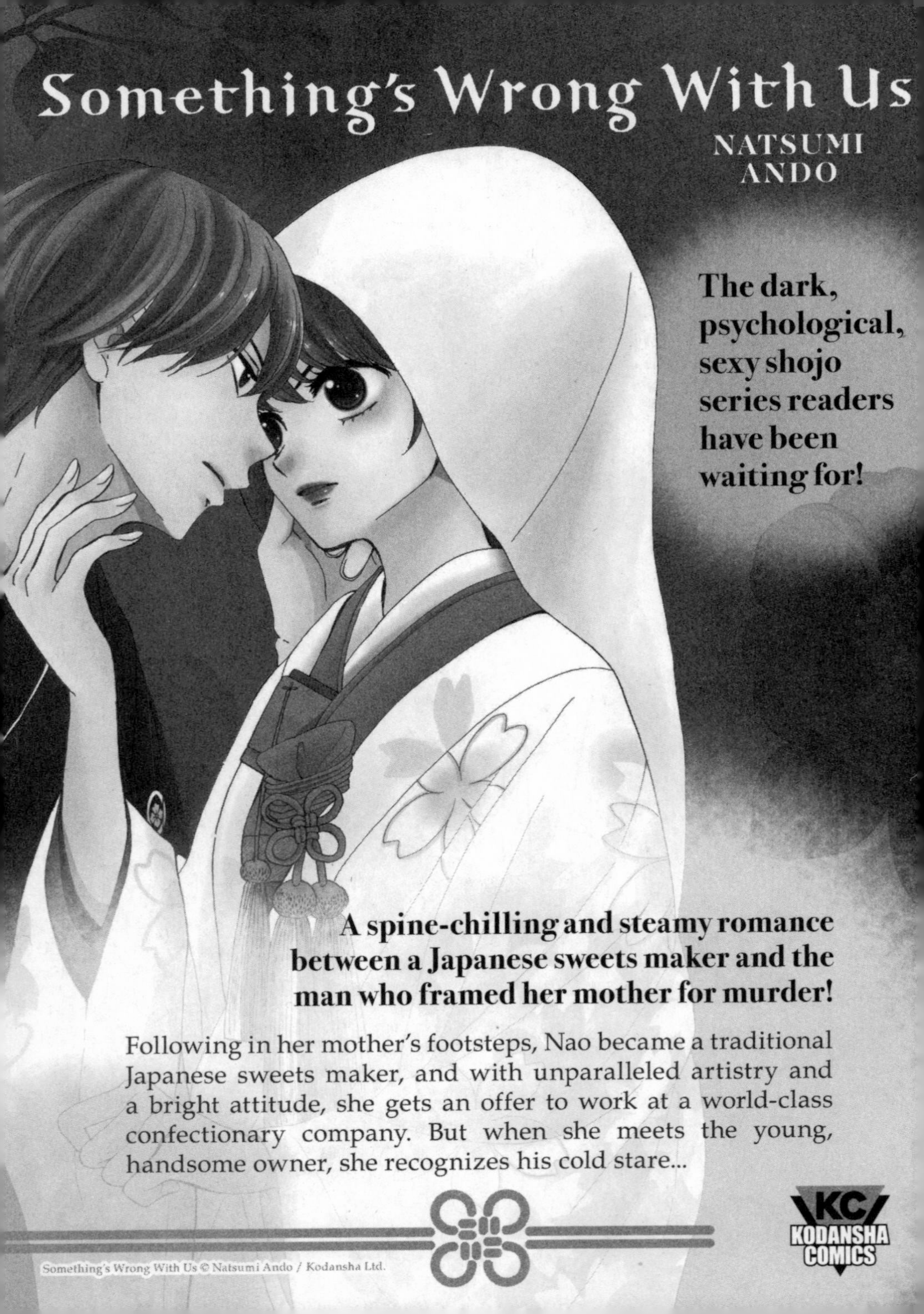
Something's Wrong With Us
NATSUMI ANDO
The dark, psychological, sexy shojo series readers have been waiting for!
A spine-chilling and steamy romance between a Japanese sweets maker and the man who framed her mother for murder!
Following in her mother's footsteps, Nao became a traditional Japanese sweets maker, and with unparalleled artistry and a bright attitude, she gets an offer to work at a world-class confectionary company. But when she meets the young, handsome owner, she recognizes his cold stare...
KC KODANSHA COMICS
Something's Wrong With Us © Natsumi Ando / Kodansha Ltd.

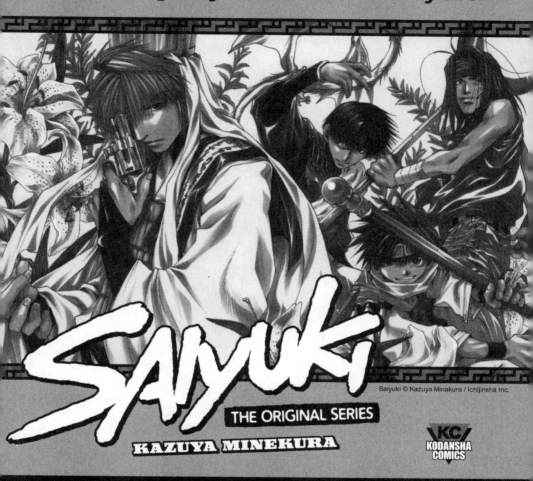

PERFECT WORLD

Rie Aruga

A TOUCHING
NEW SERIES
ABOUT LOVE AND
COPING WITH
DISABILITY

An office party reunites Tsugumi with her high school crush Itsuki. He's realized his dream of becoming an architect, but along the way, he experienced a spinal injury that put him in a wheelchair. Now Tsugumi's rekindled feelings will butt up against prejudices she never considered — and Itsuki will have to decide if he's ready to let someone into his heart...

"Depicts with great delicacy and courage the difficulties some with disabilities experience getting involved in romantic relationships... Rie Aruga refuses to romanticize, pushing her heroine to face the reality of disability. She invites her readers to the same tasks of empathy, knowledge and recognition."
—Slate.fr

"An important entry [in manga romance]... The emotional core of both plot and characters indicates thoughtfulness... [Aruga's] research is readily apparent in the text and artwork, making this feel like a real story."
—Anime News Network

KC/
KODANSHA
COMICS

A SMART, NEW ROMANTIC COMEDY FOR FANS OF *SHORTCAKE CAKE* AND *TERRACE HOUSE*!

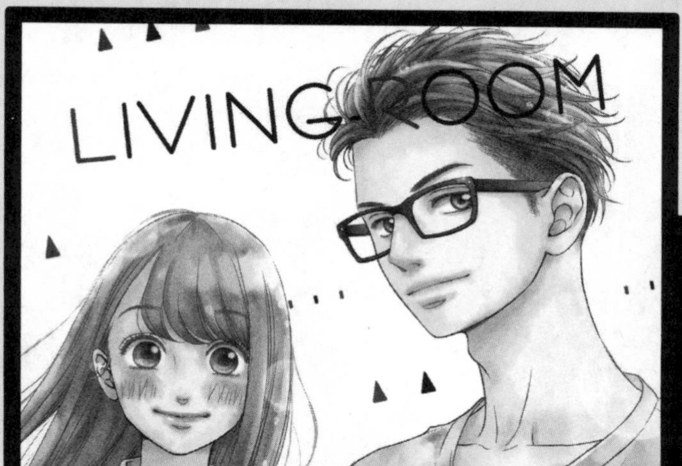
LIVING-ROOM
1
Keiko Iwashita
MATSUNAGA-SAN

KC KODANSHA COMICS

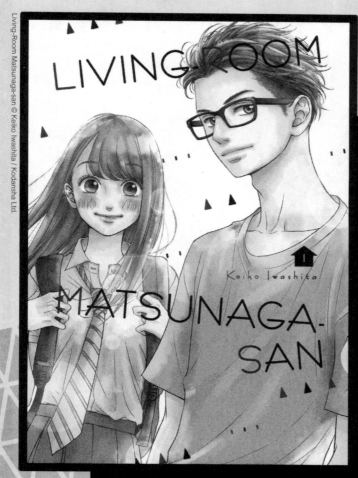

A romance manga starring high school girl Meeko, who learns to live on her own in a boarding house whose living room is home to the odd (but handsome) Matsunaga-san. She begins to adjust to her new life away from her parents, but Meeko soon learns that no matter how far away from home she is, she's still a young girl at heart — especially when she finds herself falling for Matsunaga-san.

Knight of the Ice ©Yayoi Ogawa/Kodansha Ltd.

SKATING THRILLS AND ICY CHILLS WITH THIS NEW TINGLY ROMANCE SERIES!

A rom-com on ice, perfect for fans of *Princess Jellyfish* and *Wotakoi*. Kokoro is the talk of the figure-skating world, winning trophies and hearts. But little do they know... he's actually a huge nerd! From the beloved creator of *You're My Pet* (*Tramps Like Us*).

Chitose is a serious young woman, working for the health magazine *SASSO*. Or at least, she would be, if she wasn't constantly getting distracted by her childhood friend, international figure skating star Kokoro Kijinami! In the public eye and on the ice, Kokoro is a gallant, flawless knight, but behind his glittery costumes and breathtaking spins lies a secret: He's actually a hopelessly romantic otaku, who can only land his quad jumps when Chitose is on hand to recite a spell from his favorite magical ice anime!

KC KODANSHA COMICS

Hitorijime
My Hero
CONTENTS

Hitorijime My Hero 6

Memeco Arii

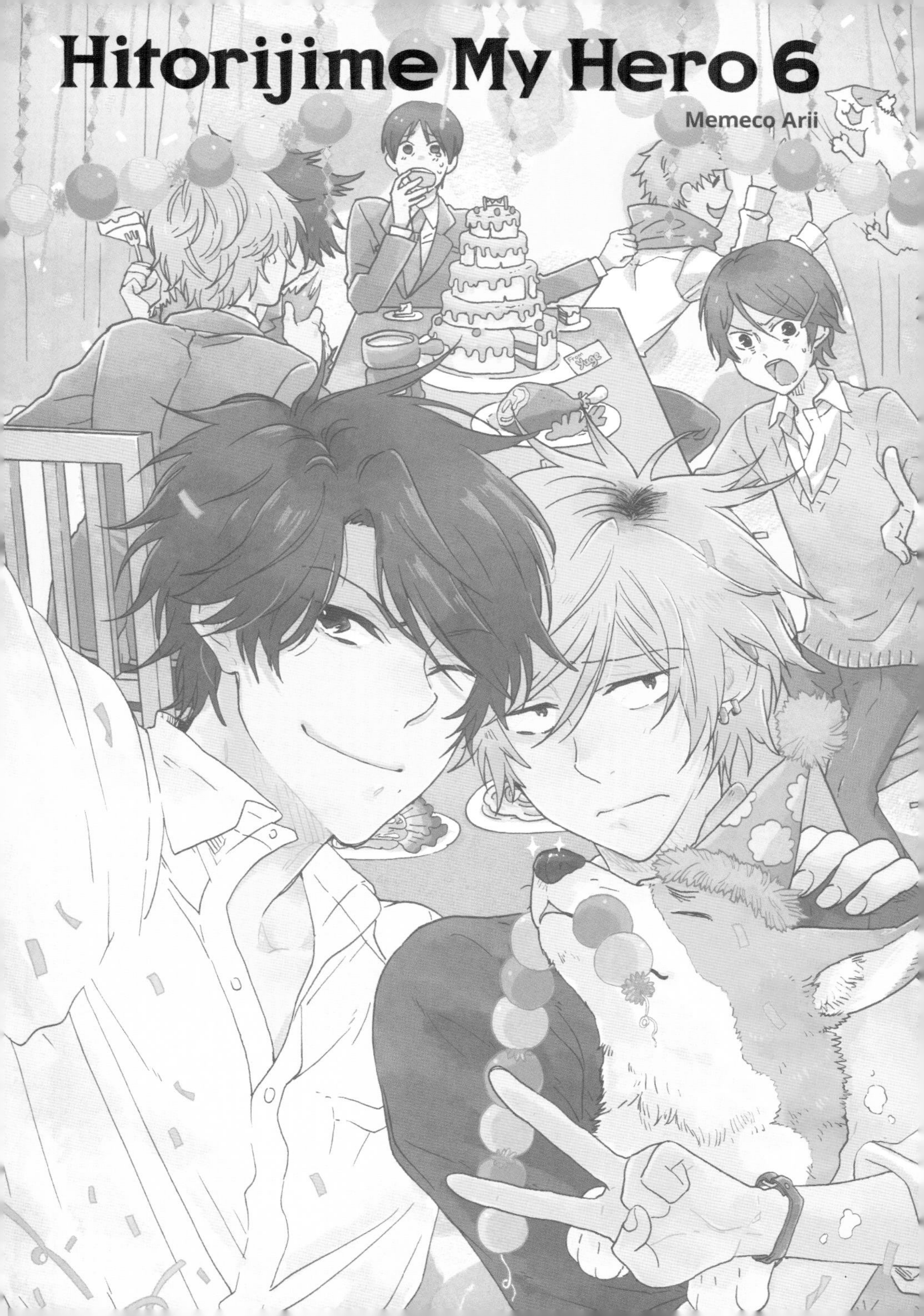
From Yuge

Hitorijime My Hero

Memeco Arii

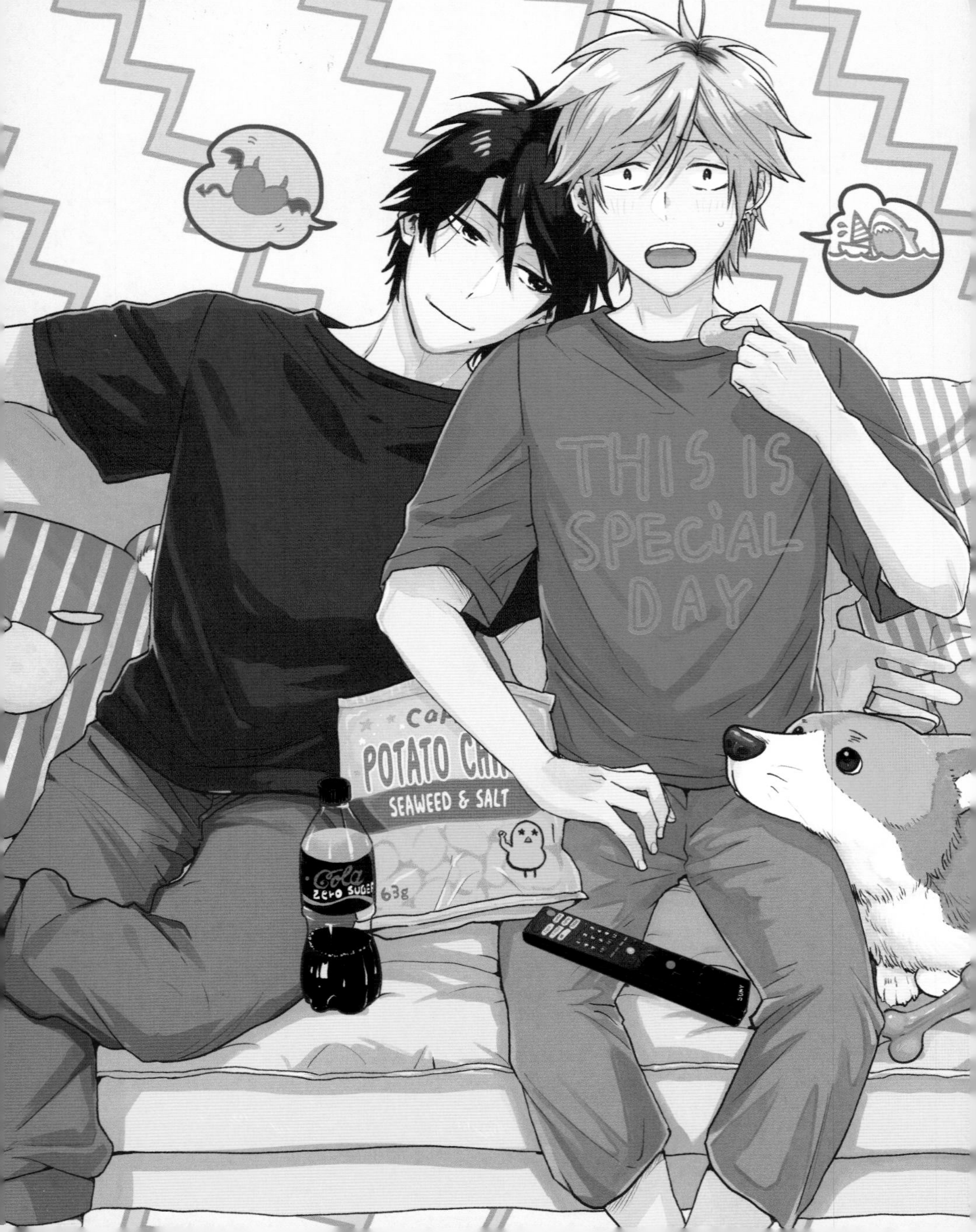
THIS IS SPECIAL DAY
SEAWEED & SALT
Cola
63g

Hitorijime My Hero
CONTENTS

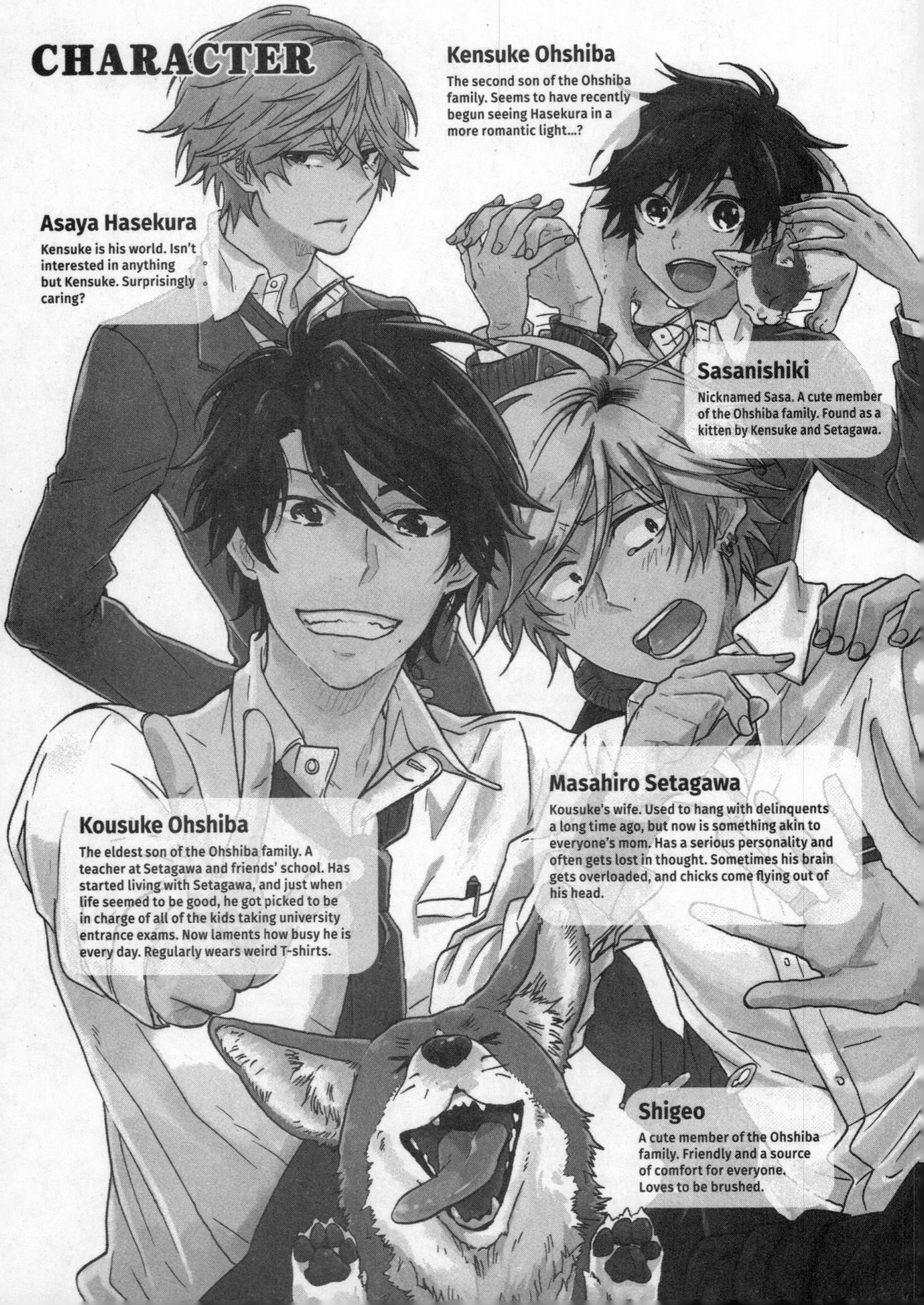

CHARACTER

Kensuke Ohshiba

The second son of the Ohshiba family. Seems to have recently begun seeing Hasekura in a more romantic light...?

Asaya Hasekura

Kensuke is his world. Isn't interested in anything but Kensuke. Surprisingly caring?

Sasanishiki

Nicknamed Sasa. A cute member of the Ohshiba family. Found as a kitten by Kensuke and Setagawa.

Masahiro Setagawa

Kousuke's wife. Used to hang with delinquents a long time ago, but now is something akin to everyone's mom. Has a serious personality and often gets lost in thought. Sometimes his brain gets overloaded, and chicks come flying out of his head.

Kousuke Ohshiba

The eldest son of the Ohshiba family. A teacher at Setagawa and friends' school. Has started living with Setagawa, and just when life seemed to be good, he got picked to be in charge of all of the kids taking university entrance exams. Now laments how busy he is every day. Regularly wears weird T-shirts.

Shigeo

A cute member of the Ohshiba family. Friendly and a source of comfort for everyone. Loves to be brushed.

Cast of Characters

Jirou Yoshida
Chairman. Tends to bear witness to things. Has some feelings for Monika.

Tsuyoshi Yamabe
Yamabe. The scarf he wears around his neck is his trademark.

Mitsuru Fukushige
Shige. Loves Setagawa as a friend and sometimes finds Kousuke irritating.

Ayaka and Tsunehito Houjou
Married couple. Ayaka is Hasekura's older sister. They're both Kousuke's friends.

Shirou Shinkai
Yakuza. Kousuke's friend. Works hard at getting contracts for new homes signed.

Natsuo Nanaoka
Bar owner. Has been in love with Kousuke for a long time, but his feelings are unrequited.

Yuusei Yuge
Setagawa and friends' friend. Likes Natsuo.

Miho Ohshiba
The mom of the Ohshiba family. Loves going to karaoke.

Hasekura cult
Hasekura's obsessive fans. Secretly acting before others is taboo.

Kaide-sensei
Assistant teacher for Kousuke's class. Loves gossip.

Summary

Setagawa has finally introduced himself to Ohshiba's parents, although he's a little concerned that the dad thinks he's a woman. Regardless, he's now living with Kousuke and the rest of the Ohshiba family—but lately, Setagawa's found himself at a loss for words whenever he's around Kousuke. It's a nice problem to have, maybe...but now Hasekura and Kensuke have been having reservations of their own?

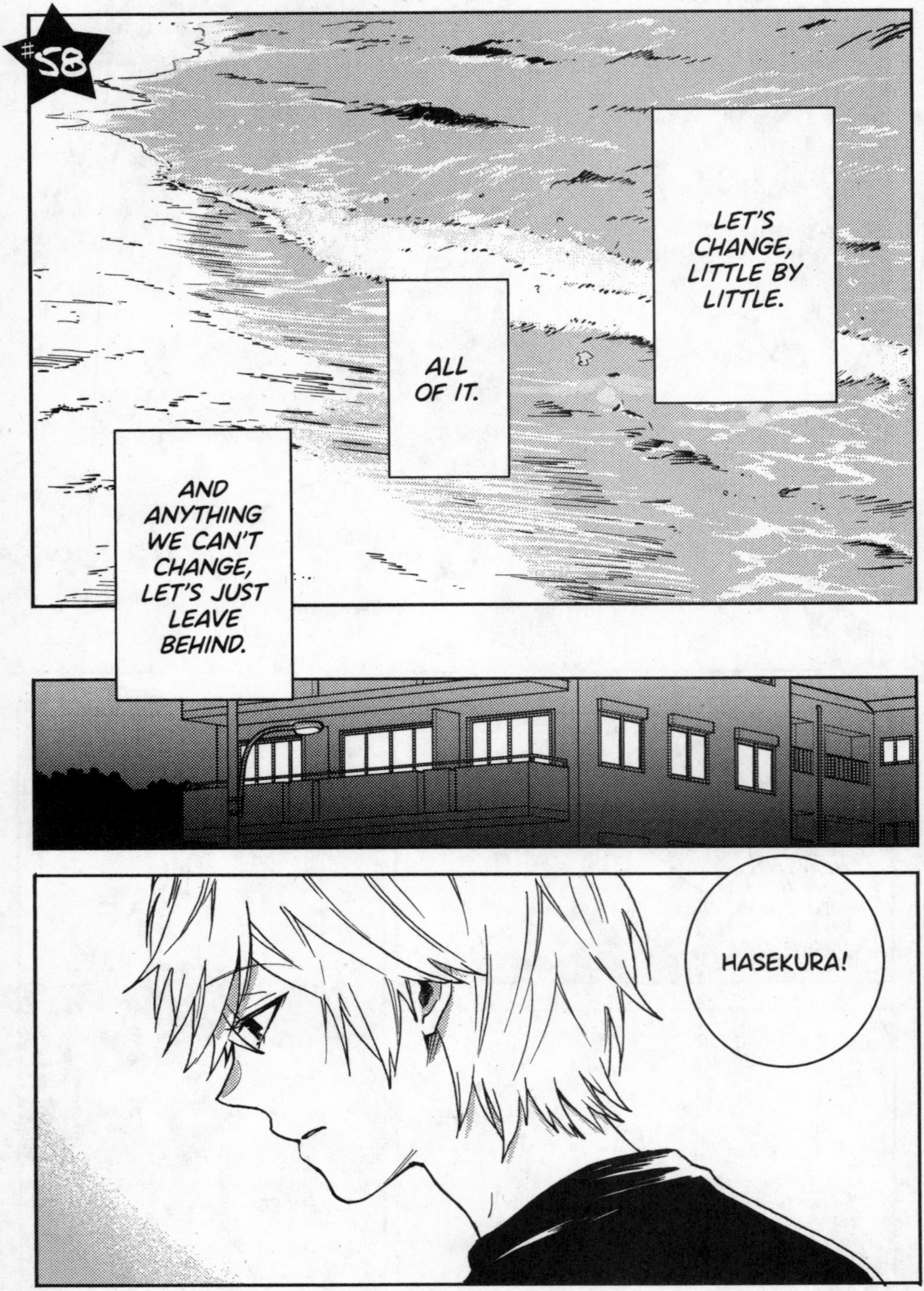
#58
LET'S CHANGE, LITTLE BY LITTLE.
ALL OF IT.
AND ANYTHING WE CAN'T CHANGE, LET'S JUST LEAVE BEHIND.
HASEKURA!

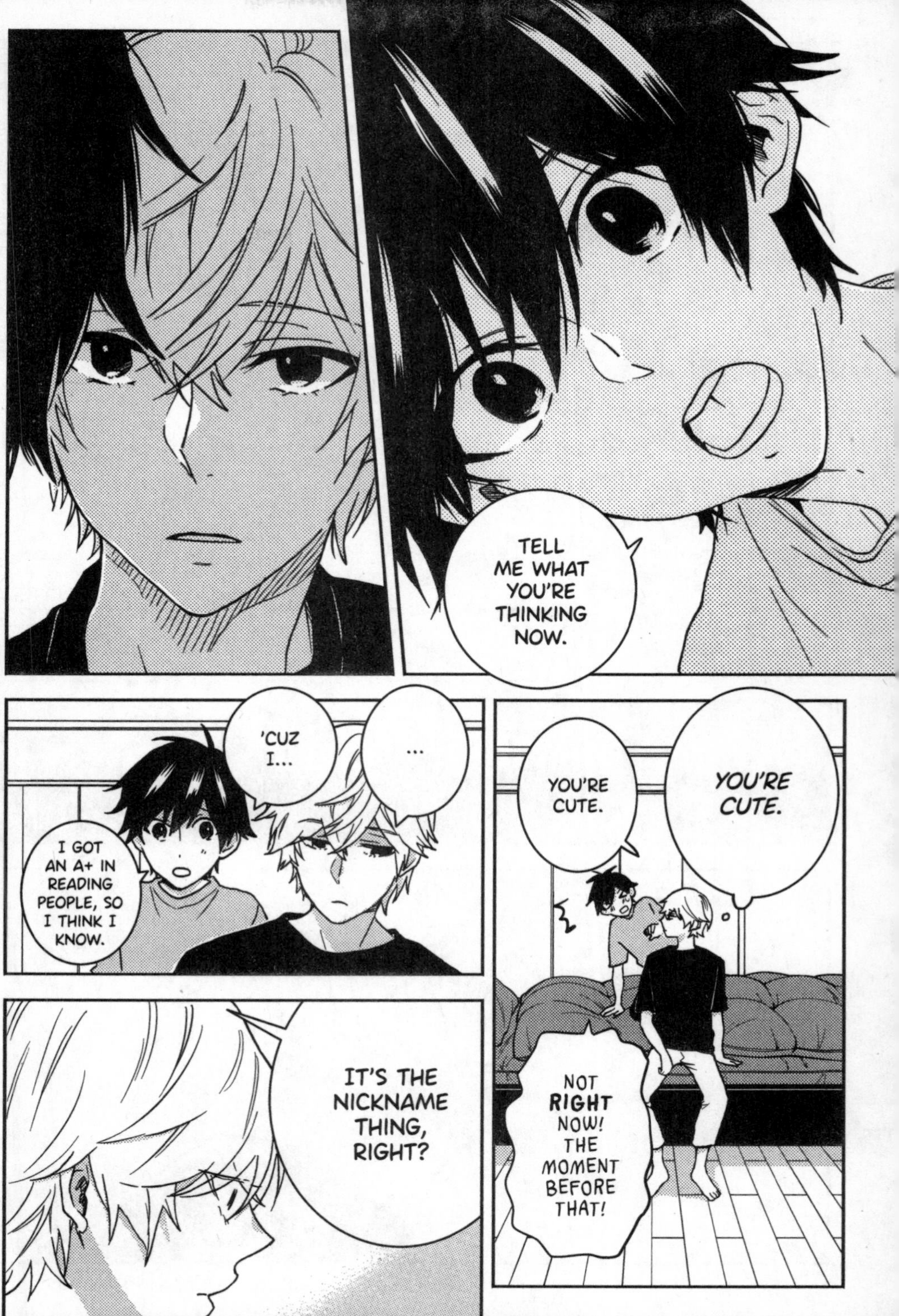
TELL ME WHAT YOU'RE THINKING NOW.
YOU'RE CUTE.
YOU'RE CUTE.
NOT RIGHT NOW! THE MOMENT BEFORE THAT!
...
'CUZ I...
I GOT AN A+ IN READING PEOPLE, SO I THINK I KNOW.
IT'S THE NICKNAME THING, RIGHT?

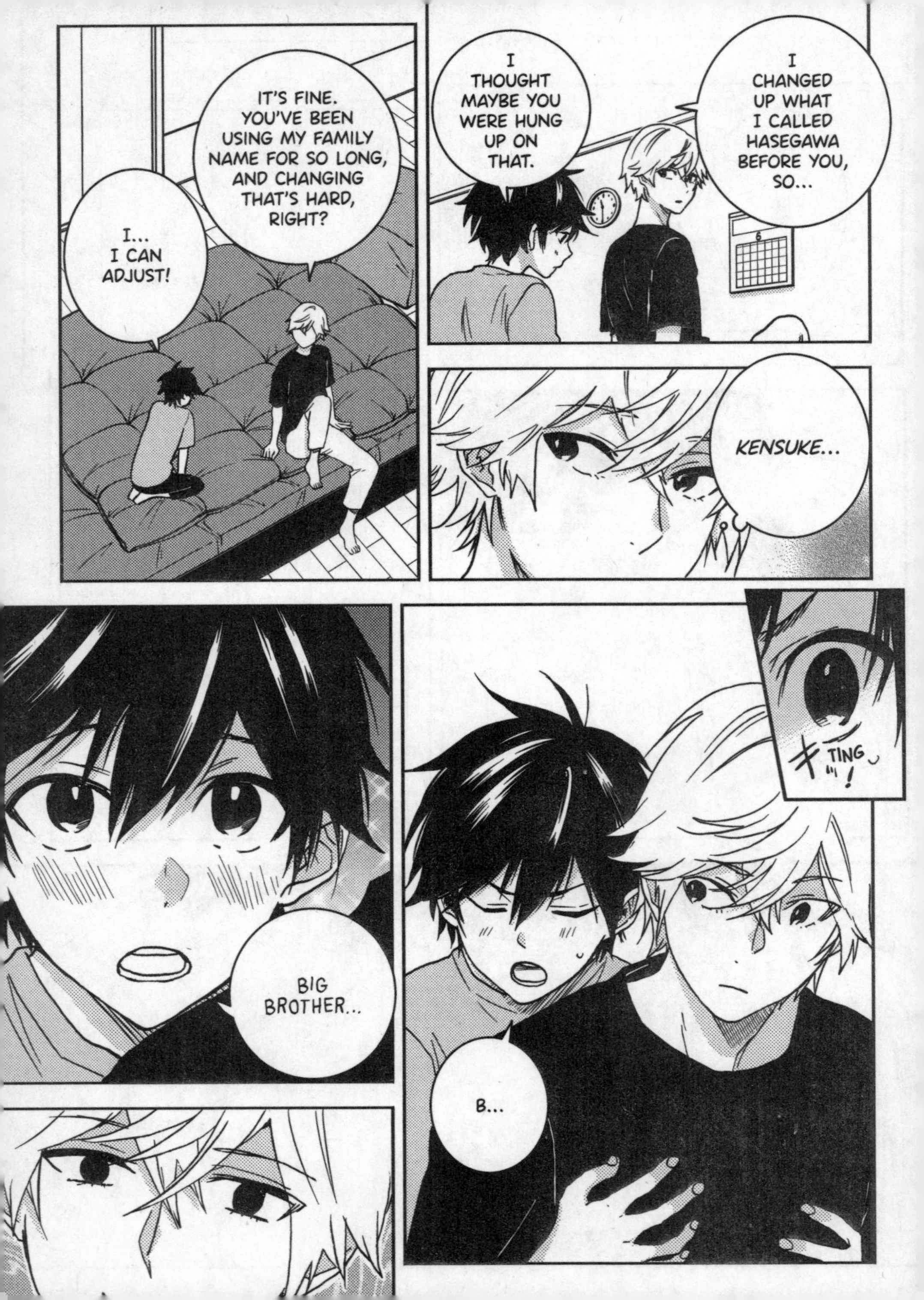
I CHANGED UP WHAT I CALLED HASEGAWA BEFORE YOU, SO...
I THOUGHT MAYBE YOU WERE HUNG UP ON THAT.
KENSUKE...
IT'S FINE. YOU'VE BEEN USING MY FAMILY NAME FOR SO LONG, AND CHANGING THAT'S HARD, RIGHT?
I... I CAN ADJUST!
TING
B...
BIG BROTHER...

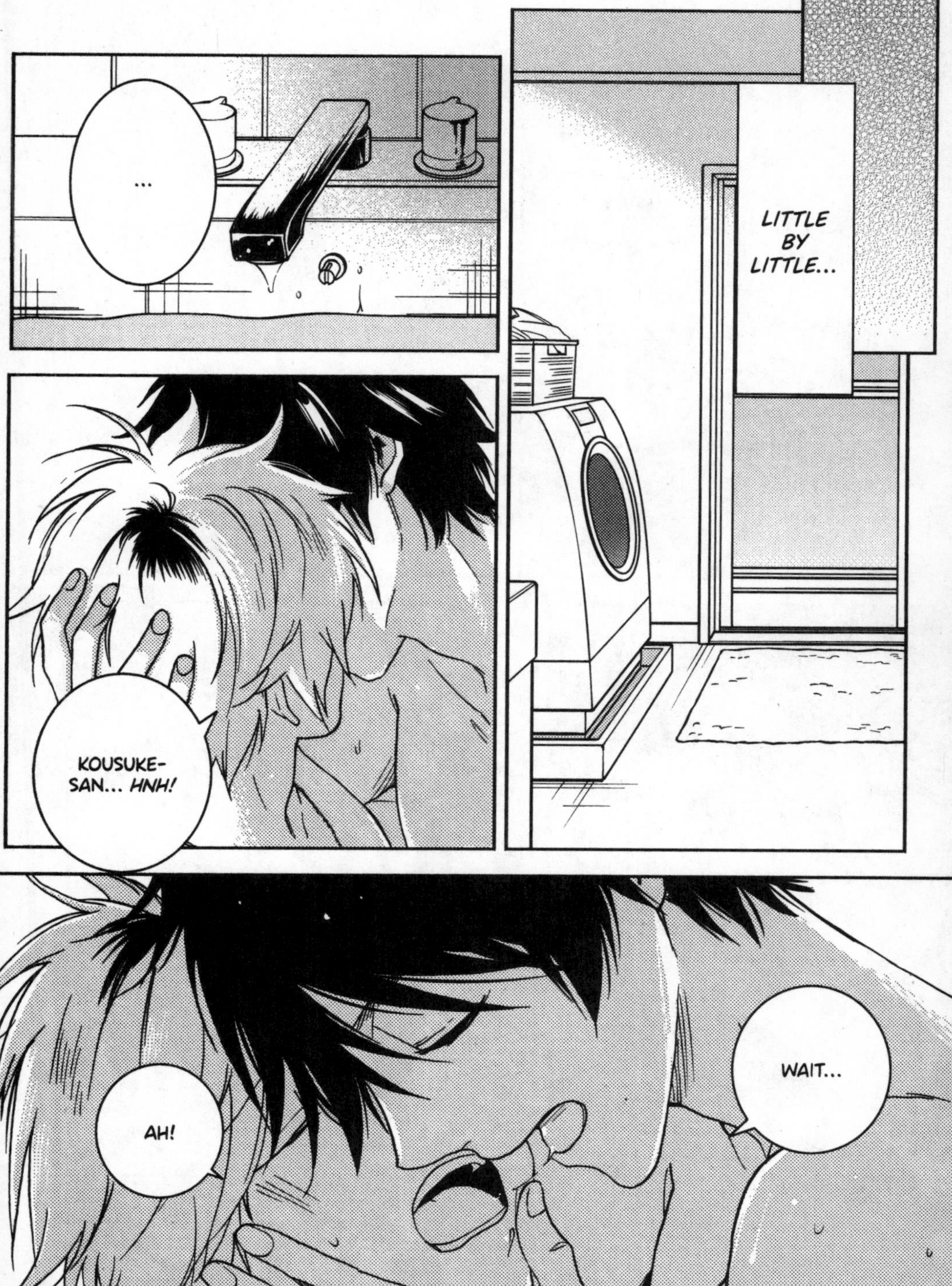
LITTLE BY LITTLE...
...
KOUSUKE-SAN... *HNH!*
WAIT...
AH!

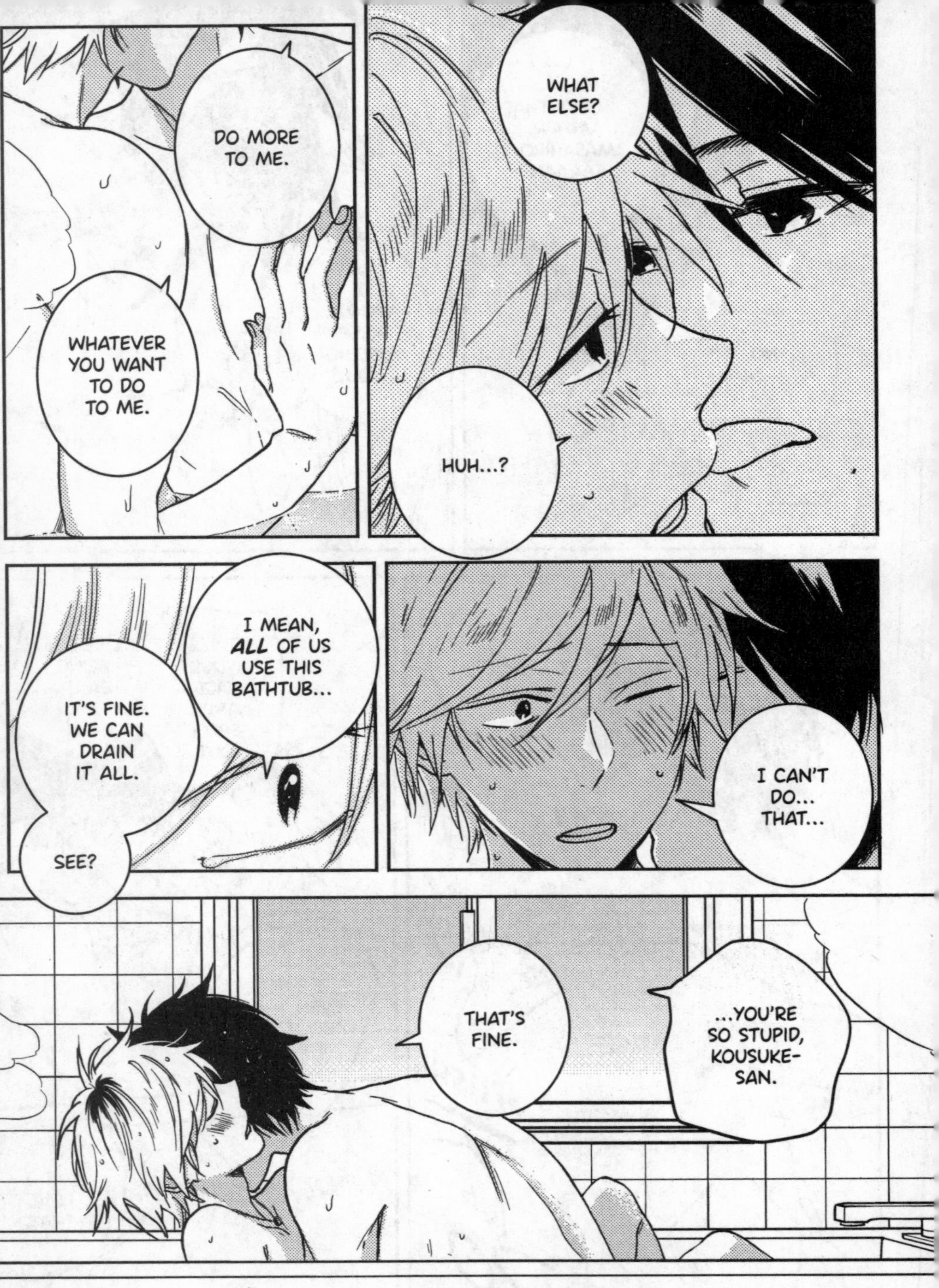
WHAT ELSE?
HUH...?
DO MORE TO ME.
WHATEVER YOU WANT TO DO TO ME.
I CAN'T DO... THAT...
I MEAN, *ALL* OF US USE THIS BATHTUB...
IT'S FINE. WE CAN DRAIN IT ALL.
SEE?
...YOU'RE SO STUPID, KOUSUKE-SAN.
THAT'S FINE.

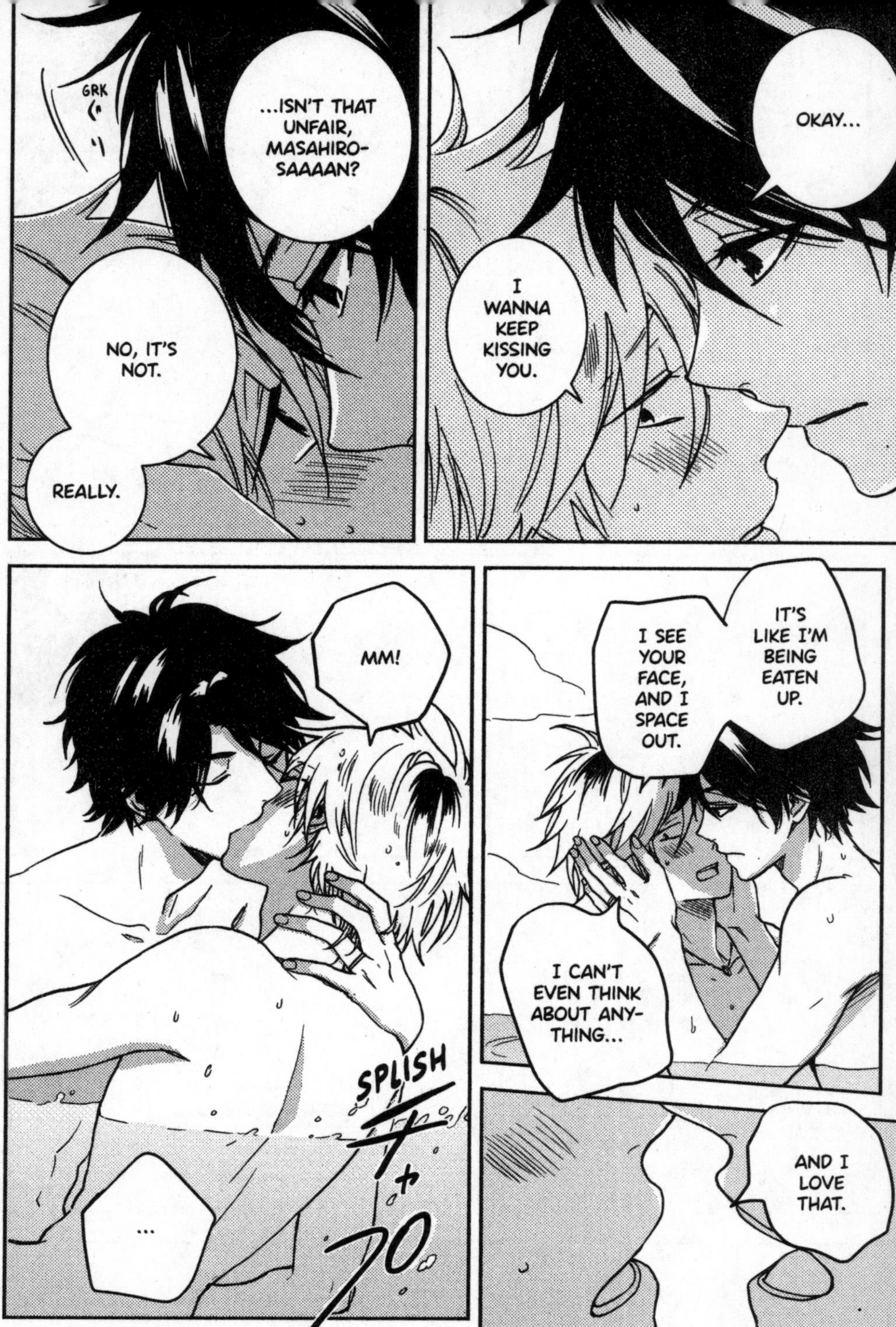
OKAY...
I WANNA KEEP KISSING YOU.
...ISN'T THAT UNFAIR, MASAHIRO-SAAAAN?
GRK
NO, IT'S NOT.
REALLY.
IT'S LIKE I'M BEING EATEN UP.
I SEE YOUR FACE, AND I SPACE OUT.
I CAN'T EVEN THINK ABOUT ANY-THING...
AND I LOVE THAT.
MM!
SPLISH
...

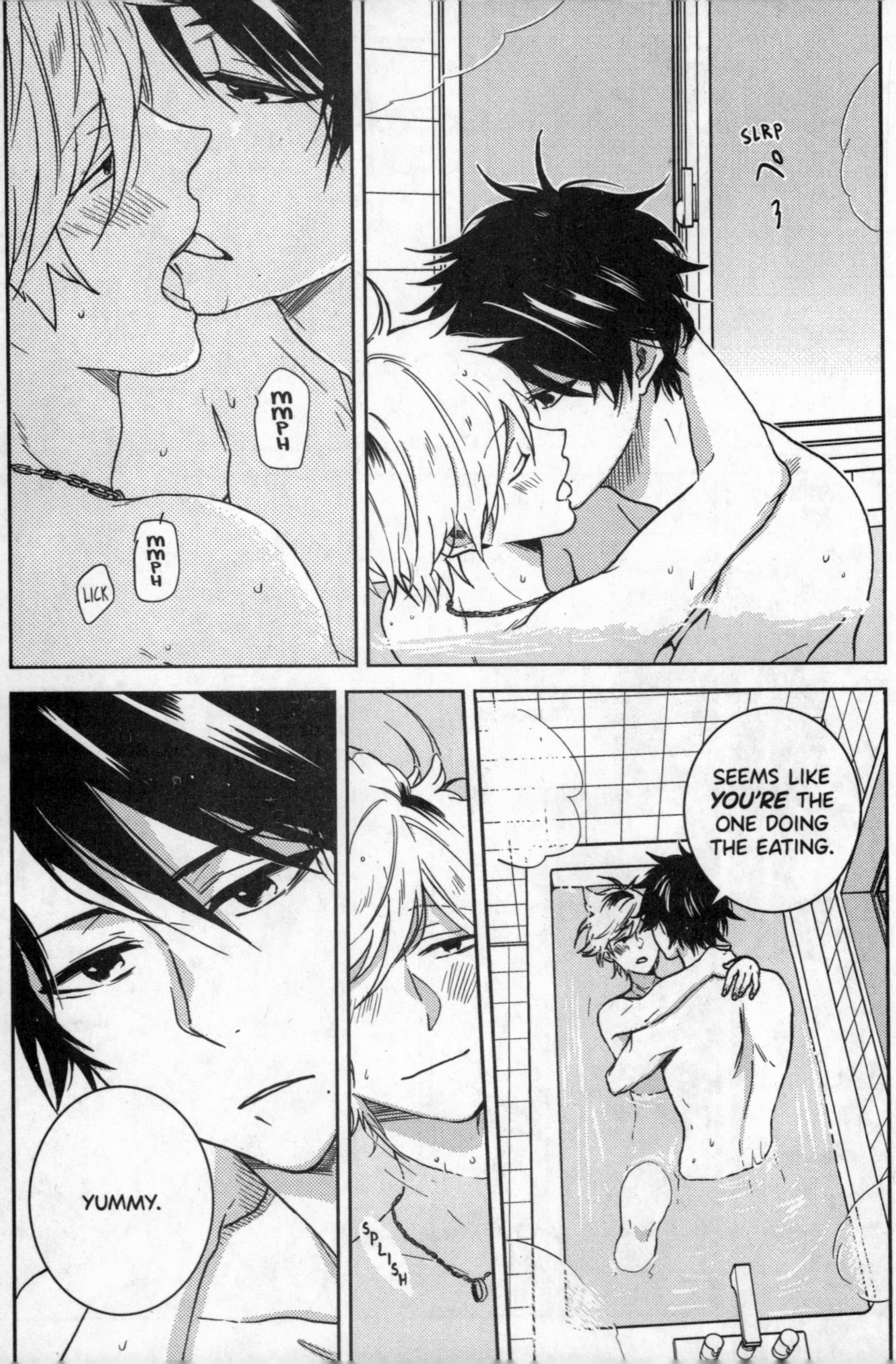
SLRP
MMPH
MMPH
LICK
SEEMS LIKE *YOU'RE* THE ONE DOING THE EATING.
SPLISH
YUMMY.

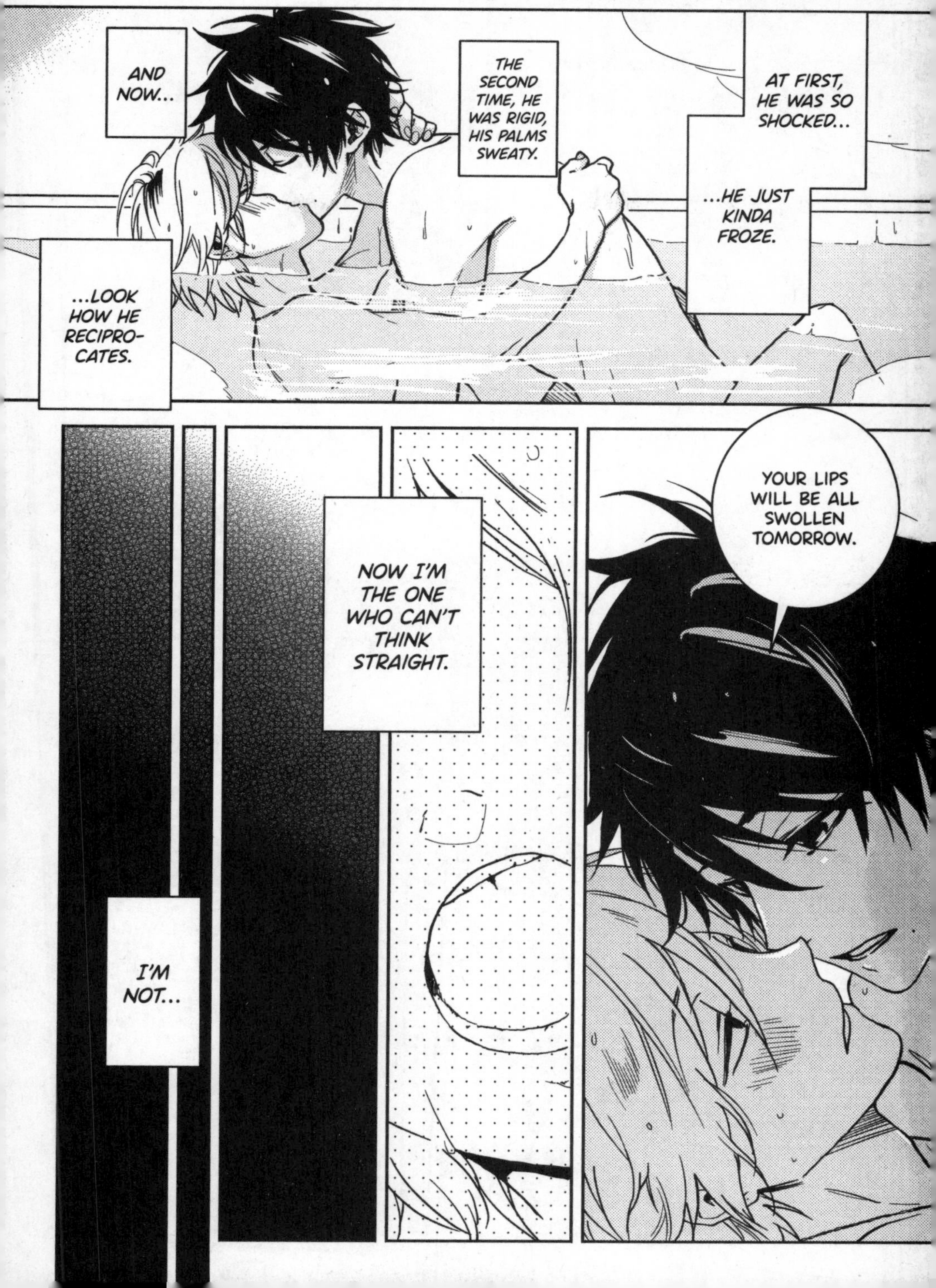
AT FIRST, HE WAS SO SHOCKED...
...HE JUST KINDA FROZE.
THE SECOND TIME, HE WAS RIGID, HIS PALMS SWEATY.
AND NOW...
...LOOK HOW HE RECIPROCATES.
YOUR LIPS WILL BE ALL SWOLLEN TOMORROW.
NOW I'M THE ONE WHO CAN'T THINK STRAIGHT.
I'M NOT...

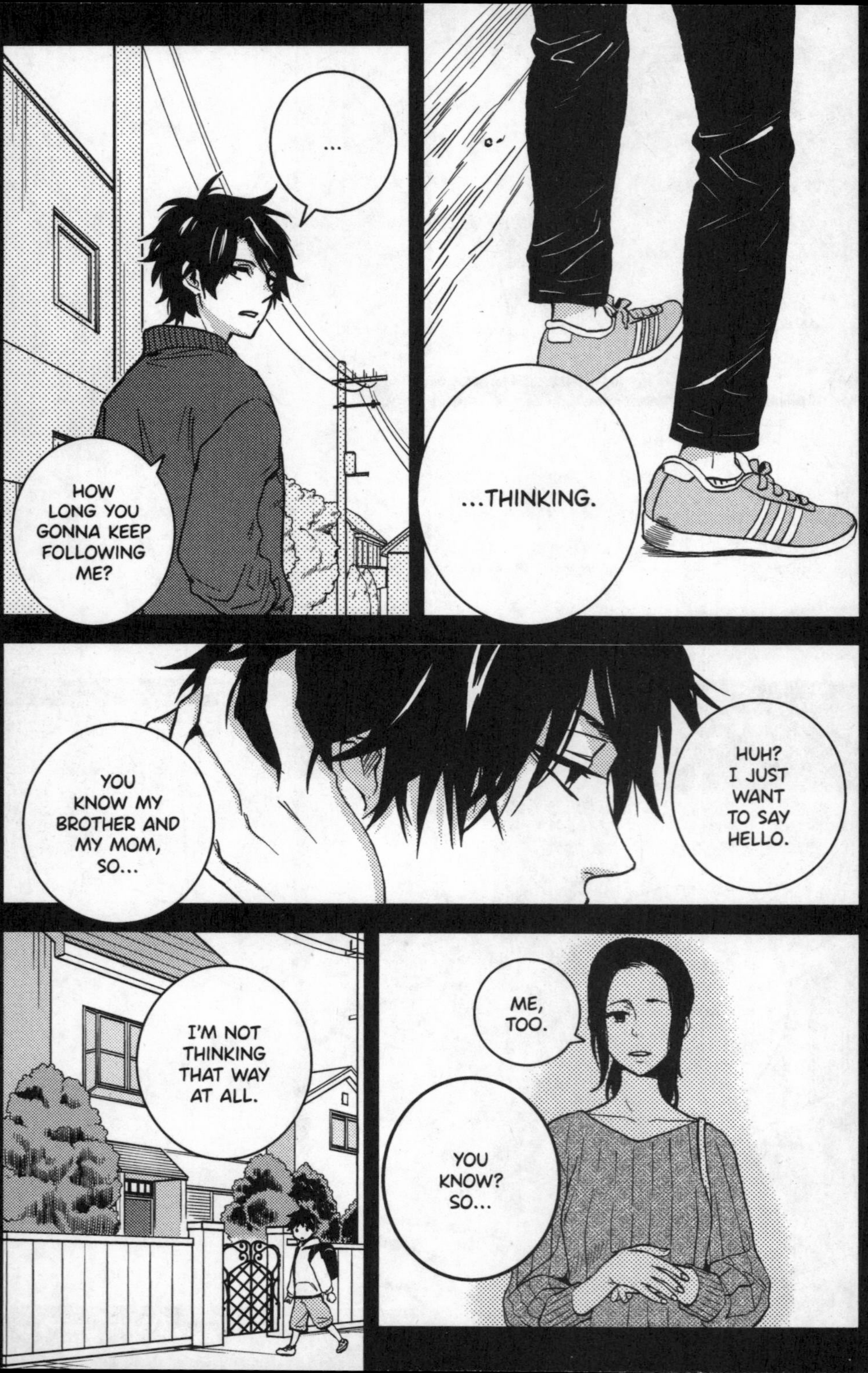
...THINKING.
...
HOW LONG YOU GONNA KEEP FOLLOWING ME?
HUH? I JUST WANT TO SAY HELLO.
YOU KNOW MY BROTHER AND MY MOM, SO...
ME, TOO.
YOU KNOW? SO...
I'M NOT THINKING THAT WAY AT ALL.

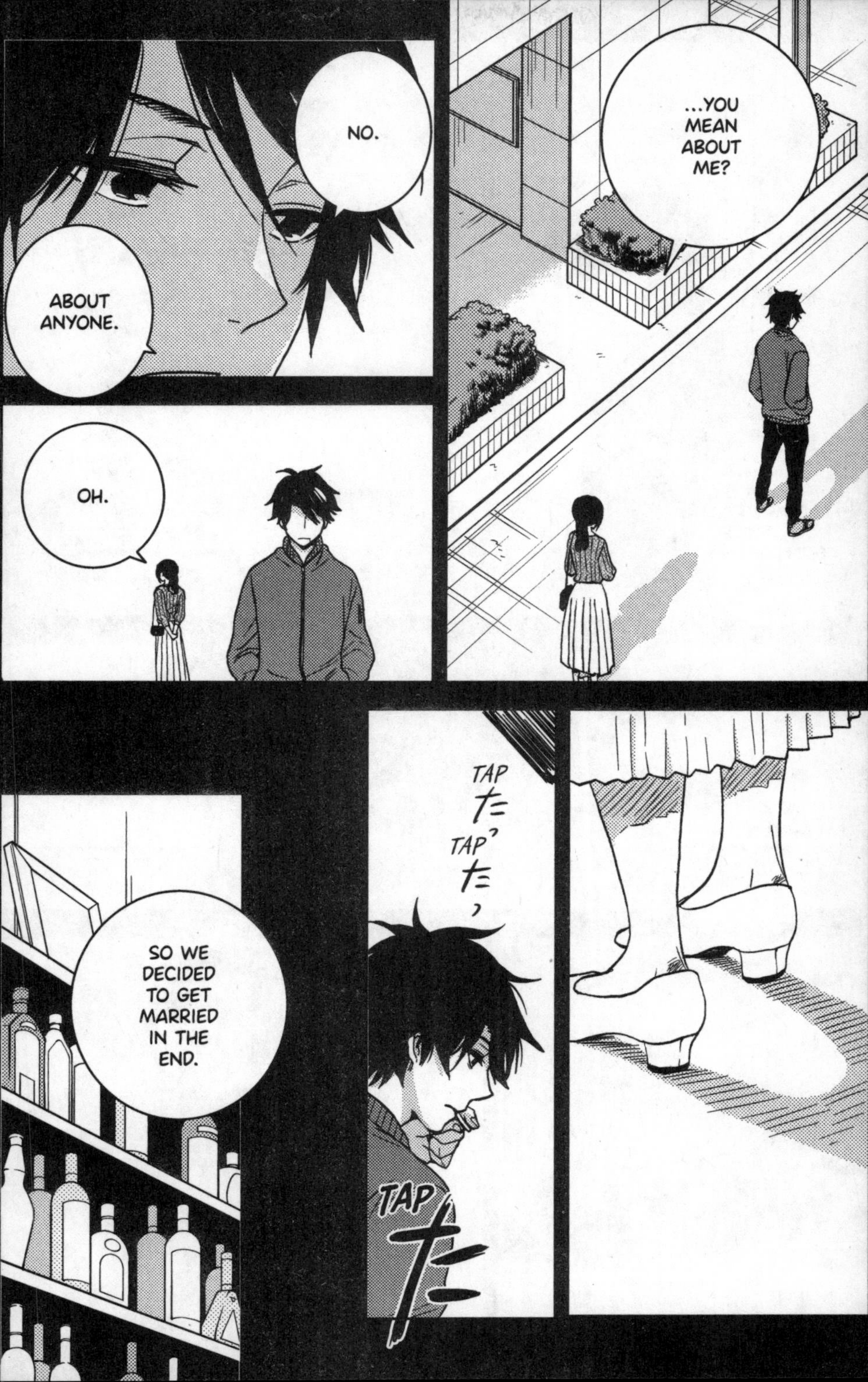
...YOU MEAN ABOUT ME?
NO.
ABOUT ANYONE.
OH.
TAP
たっ
TAP
たっ
TAP
たー
SO WE DECIDED TO GET MARRIED IN THE END.

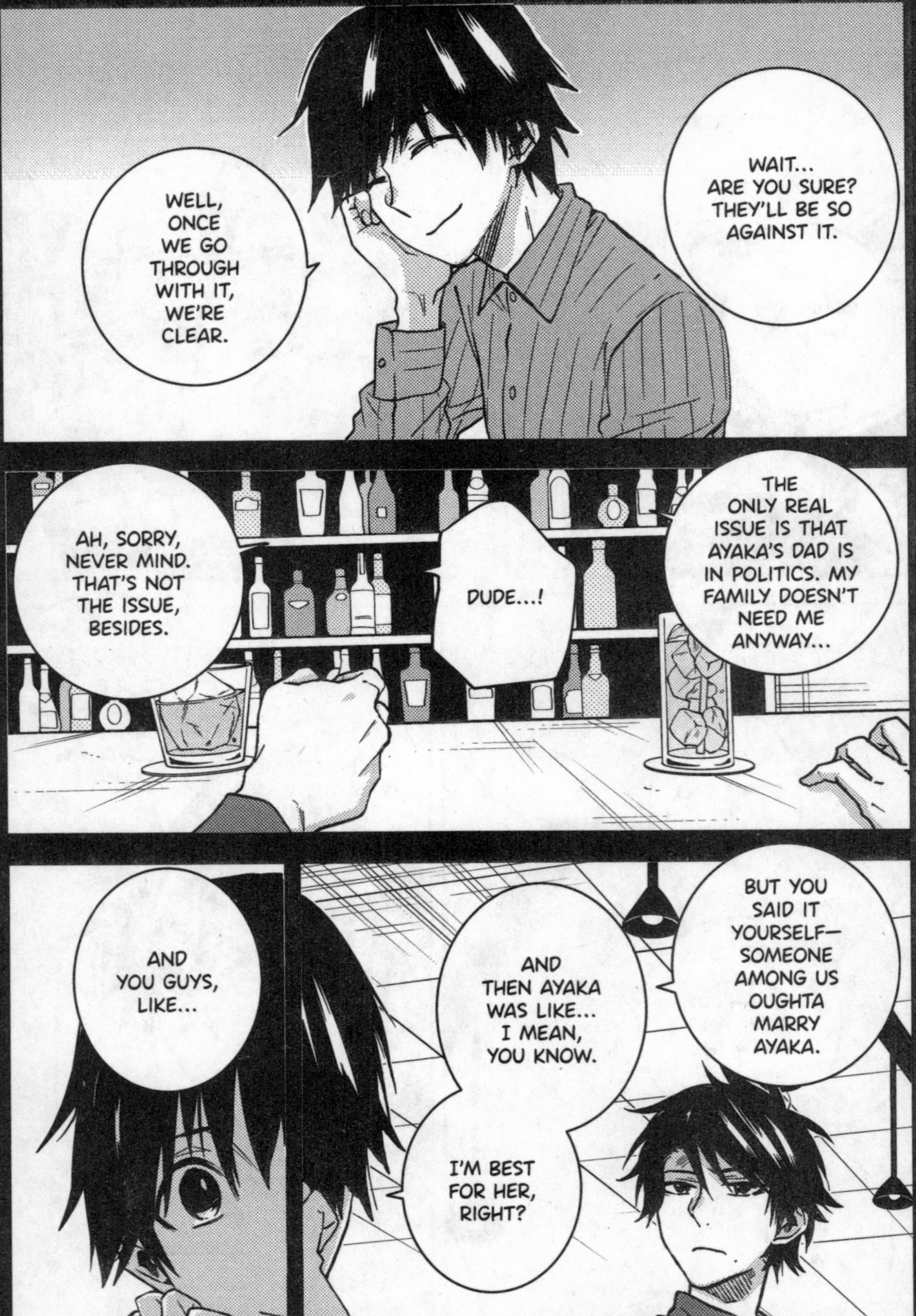
WAIT... ARE YOU SURE? THEY'LL BE SO AGAINST IT.
WELL, ONCE WE GO THROUGH WITH IT, WE'RE CLEAR.
THE ONLY REAL ISSUE IS THAT AYAKA'S DAD IS IN POLITICS. MY FAMILY DOESN'T NEED ME ANYWAY...
DUDE...!
AH, SORRY, NEVER MIND. THAT'S NOT THE ISSUE, BESIDES.
BUT YOU SAID IT YOURSELF—SOMEONE AMONG US OUGHTA MARRY AYAKA.
AND THEN AYAKA WAS LIKE... I MEAN, YOU KNOW.
I'M BEST FOR HER, RIGHT?
AND YOU GUYS, LIKE...

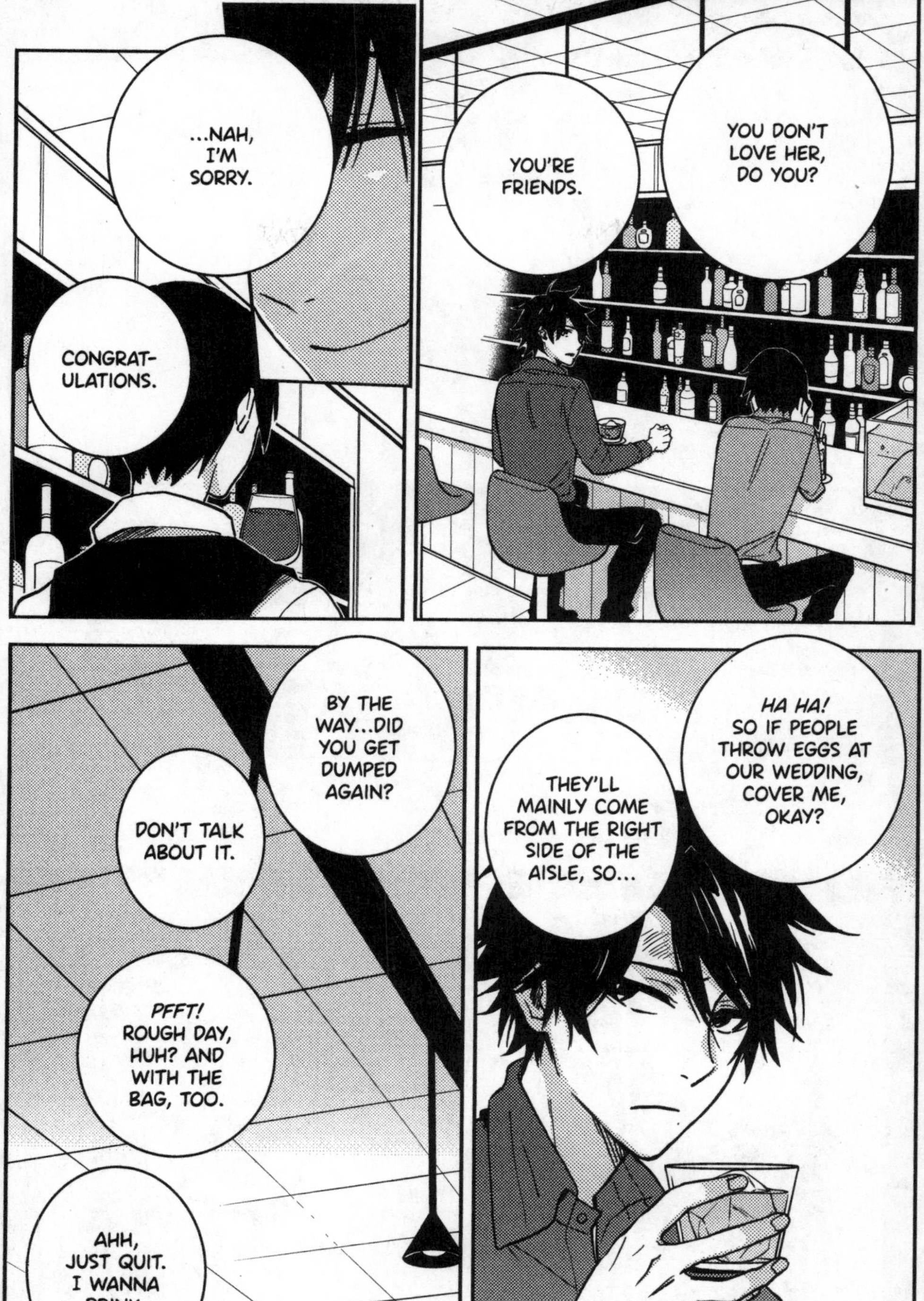
YOU DON'T LOVE HER, DO YOU?
YOU'RE FRIENDS.
...NAH, I'M SORRY.
CONGRAT-ULATIONS.
HA HA! SO IF PEOPLE THROW EGGS AT OUR WEDDING, COVER ME, OKAY?
THEY'LL MAINLY COME FROM THE RIGHT SIDE OF THE AISLE, SO...
BY THE WAY...DID YOU GET DUMPED AGAIN?
DON'T TALK ABOUT IT.
PFFT! ROUGH DAY, HUH? AND WITH THE BAG, TOO.
AHH, JUST QUIT. I WANNA DRINK.

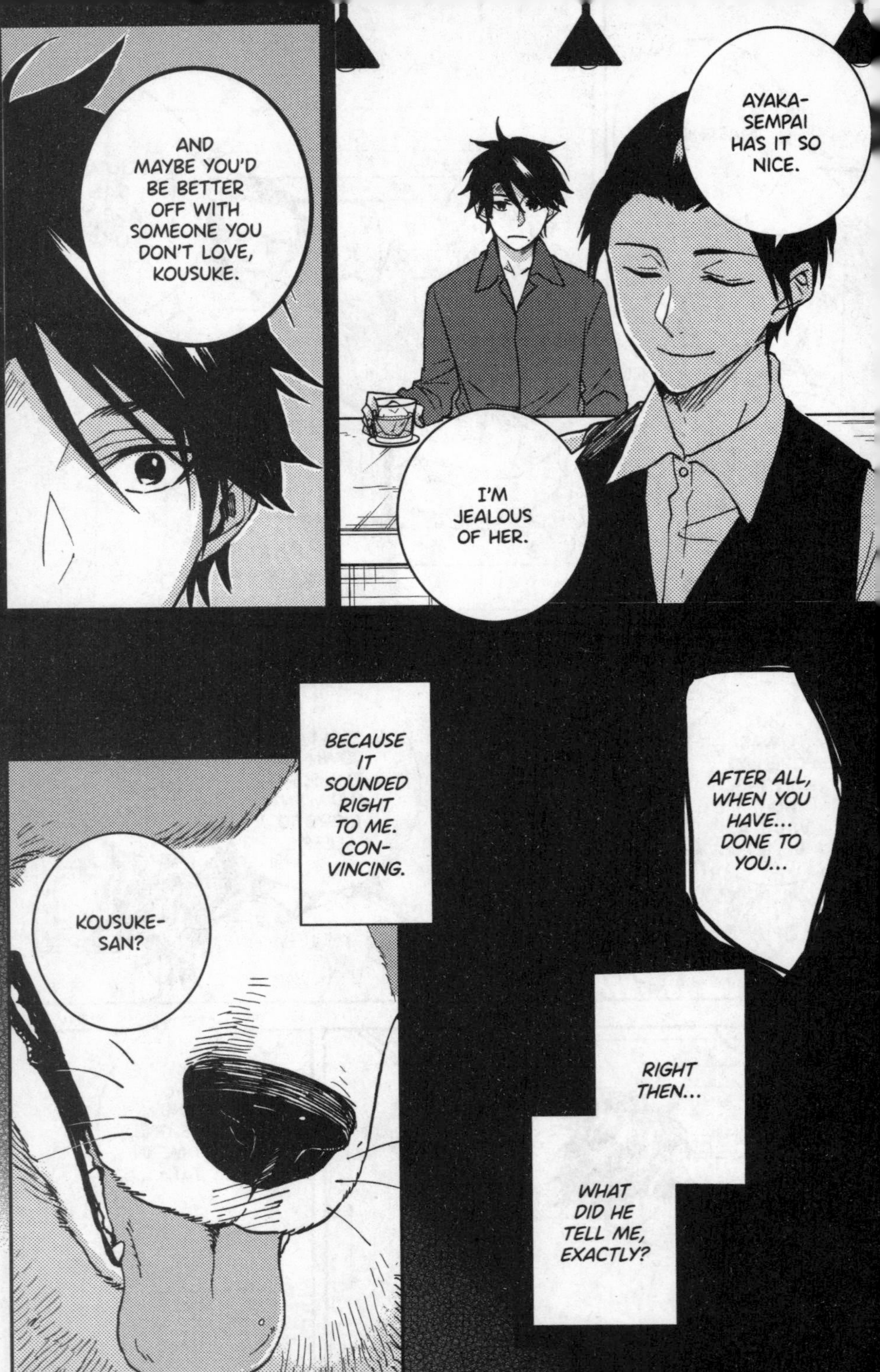
AYAKA-SEMPAI HAS IT SO NICE.
I'M JEALOUS OF HER.
AND MAYBE YOU'D BE BETTER OFF WITH SOMEONE YOU DON'T LOVE, KOUSUKE.
AFTER ALL, WHEN YOU HAVE... DONE TO YOU...
RIGHT THEN...
WHAT DID HE TELL ME, EXACTLY?
BECAUSE IT SOUNDED RIGHT TO ME. CON-VINCING.
KOUSUKE-SAN?

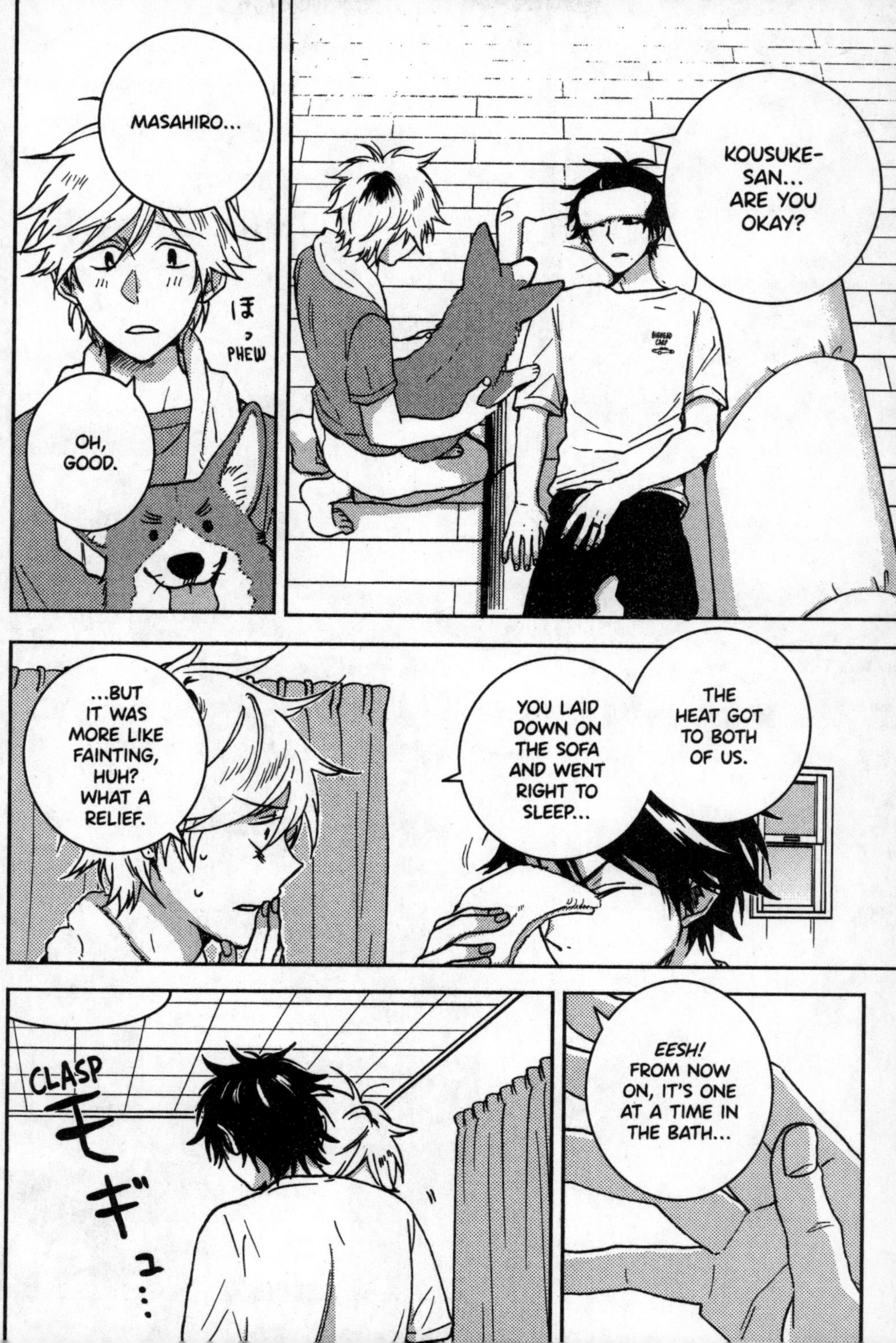
KOUSUKE-SAN... ARE YOU OKAY?
MASAHIRO...
ほっ
PHEW
OH, GOOD.
THE HEAT GOT TO BOTH OF US.
YOU LAID DOWN ON THE SOFA AND WENT RIGHT TO SLEEP...
...BUT IT WAS MORE LIKE FAINTING, HUH? WHAT A RELIEF.
EESH! FROM NOW ON, IT'S ONE AT A TIME IN THE BATH...
CLASP
モギュ...

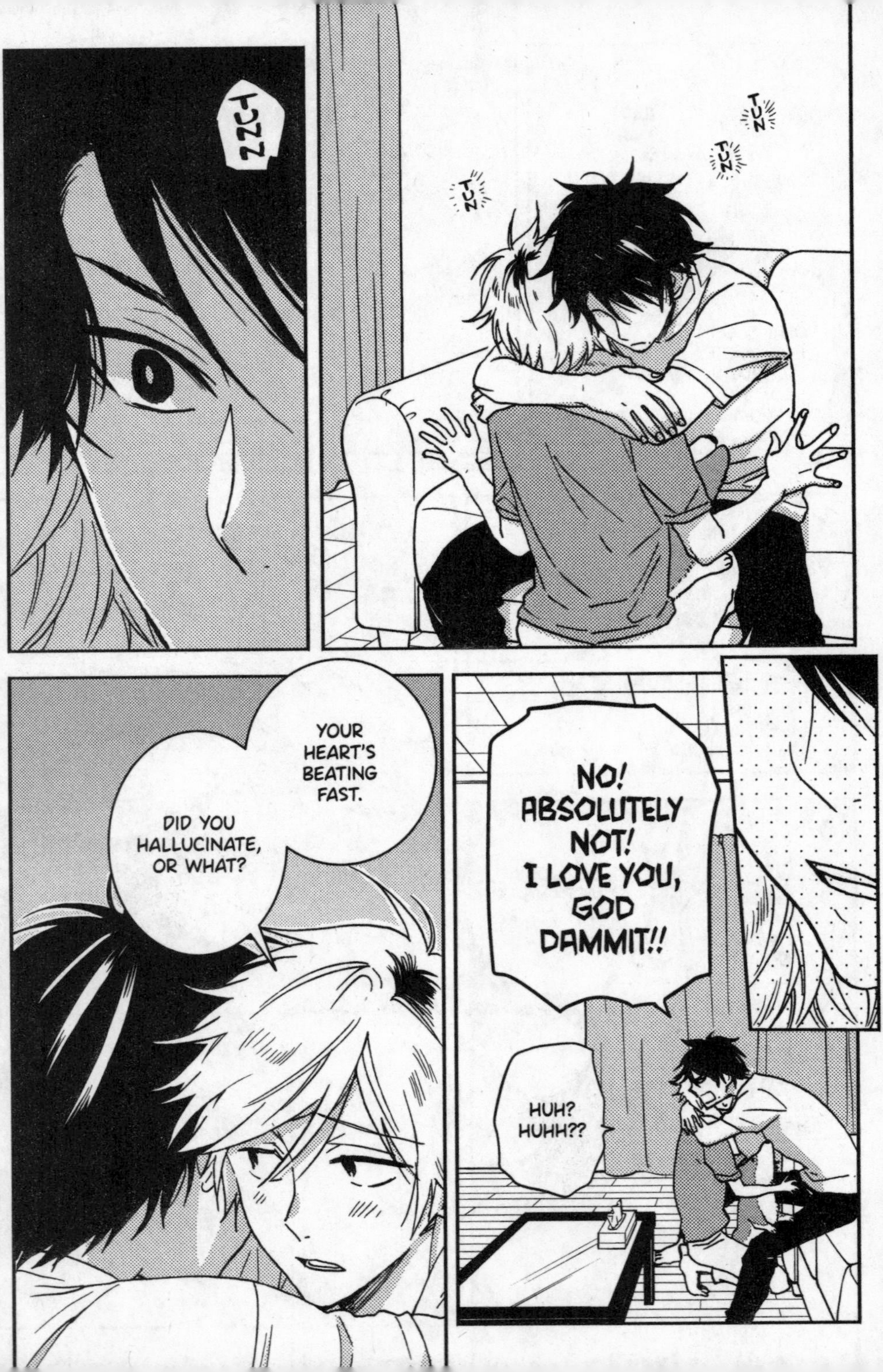
TUN
TUN
TUN
NO! ABSOLUTELY NOT! I LOVE YOU, GOD DAMMIT!!
HUH? HUHH??
YOUR HEART'S BEATING FAST.
DID YOU HALLUCINATE, OR WHAT?

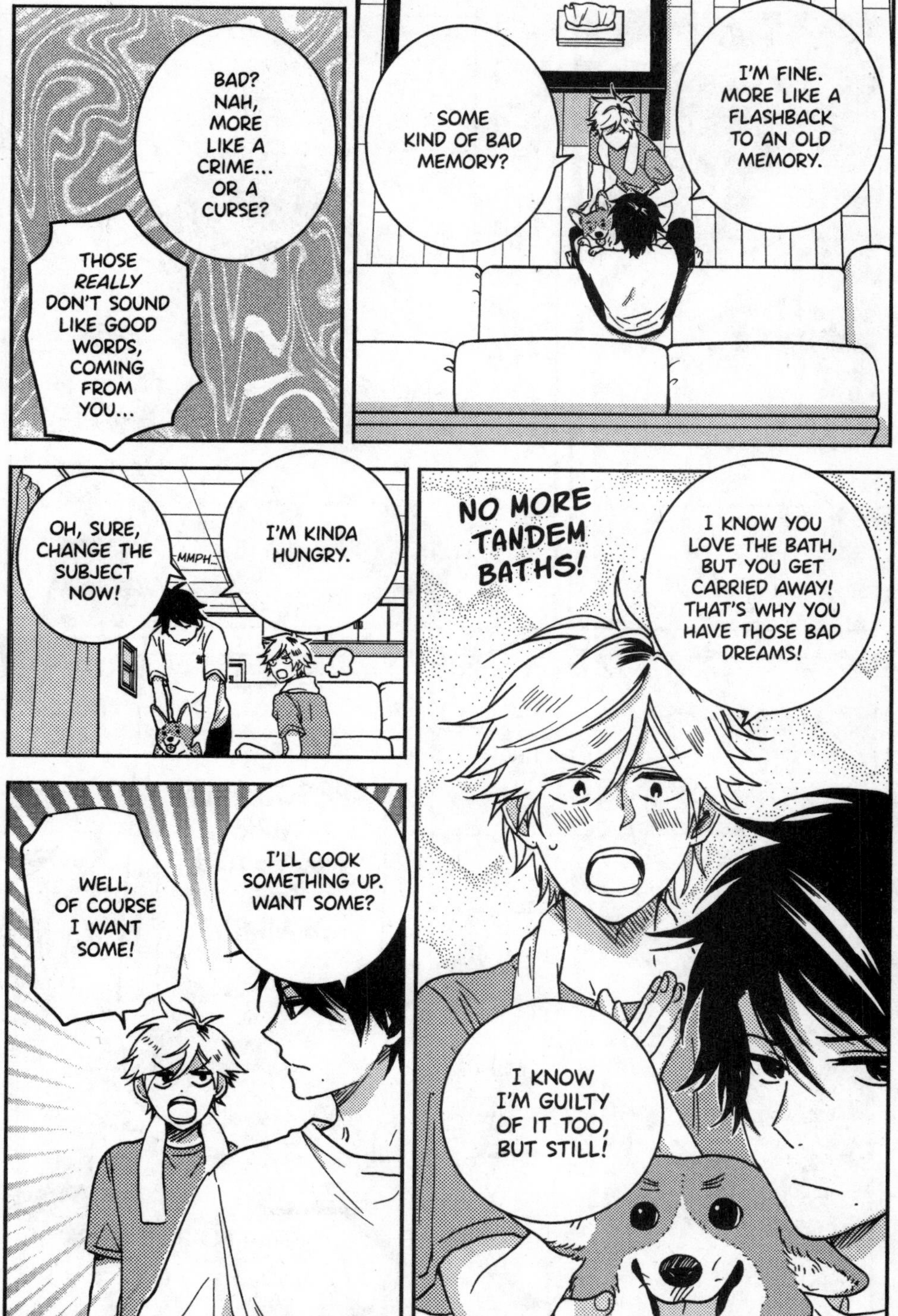
I'M FINE. MORE LIKE A FLASHBACK TO AN OLD MEMORY.
SOME KIND OF BAD MEMORY?
BAD? NAH, MORE LIKE A CRIME... OR A CURSE?
THOSE *REALLY* DON'T SOUND LIKE GOOD WORDS, COMING FROM YOU...
NO MORE TANDEM BATHS!
I KNOW YOU LOVE THE BATH, BUT YOU GET CARRIED AWAY! THAT'S WHY YOU HAVE THOSE BAD DREAMS!
I KNOW I'M GUILTY OF IT TOO, BUT STILL!
I'M KINDA HUNGRY.
MMPH...
OH, SURE, CHANGE THE SUBJECT NOW!
I'LL COOK SOMETHING UP. WANT SOME?
WELL, OF COURSE I WANT SOME!

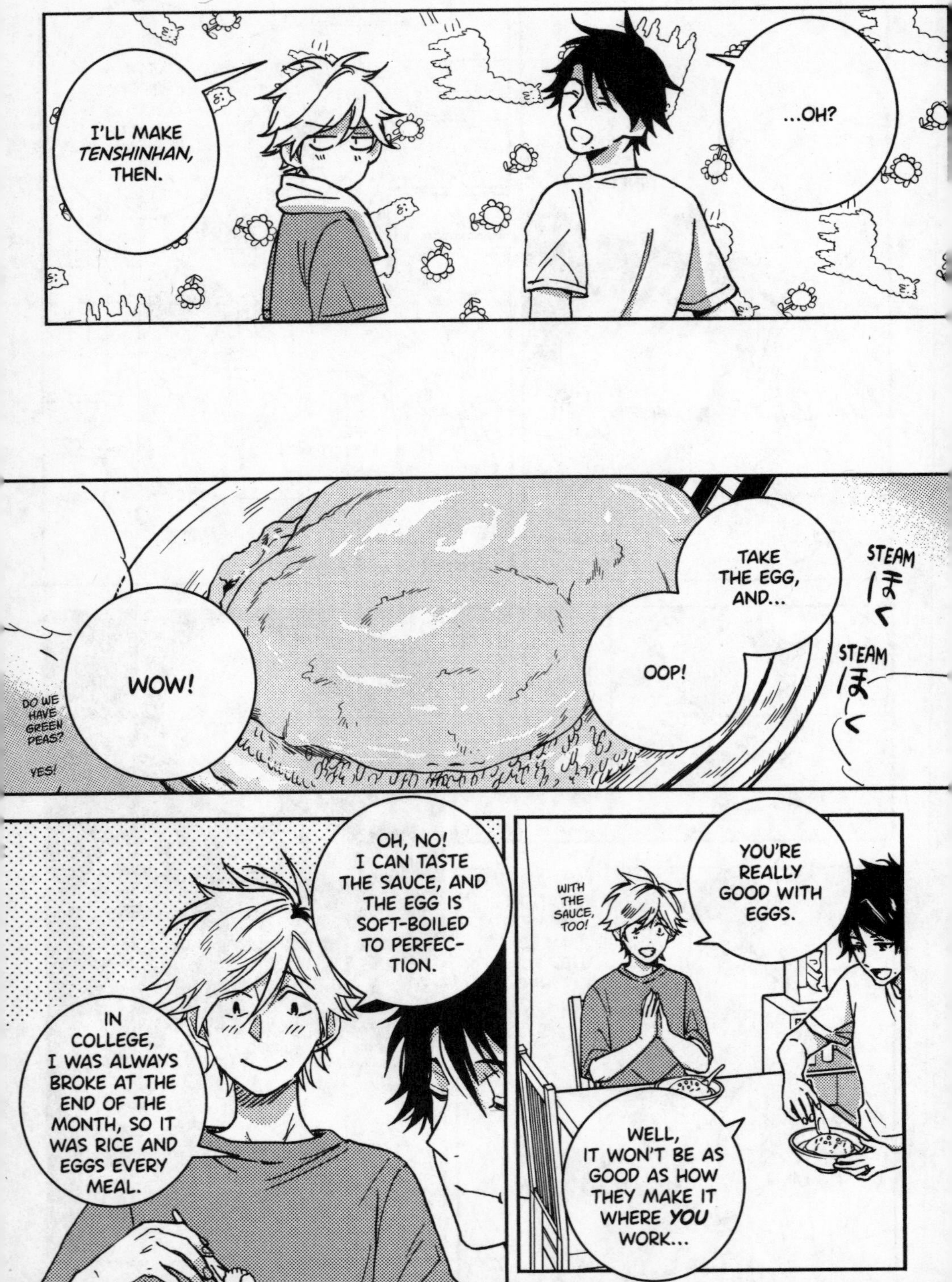
...OH?
I'LL MAKE *TENSHINHAN*, THEN.
STEAM ほく
STEAM ほく
TAKE THE EGG, AND...
OOP!
WOW!
DO WE HAVE GREEN PEAS?
YES!
YOU'RE REALLY GOOD WITH EGGS.
WITH THE SAUCE, TOO!
WELL, IT WON'T BE AS GOOD AS HOW THEY MAKE IT WHERE ***YOU*** WORK...
OH, NO! I CAN TASTE THE SAUCE, AND THE EGG IS SOFT-BOILED TO PERFEC-TION.
IN COLLEGE, I WAS ALWAYS BROKE AT THE END OF THE MONTH, SO IT WAS RICE AND EGGS EVERY MEAL.

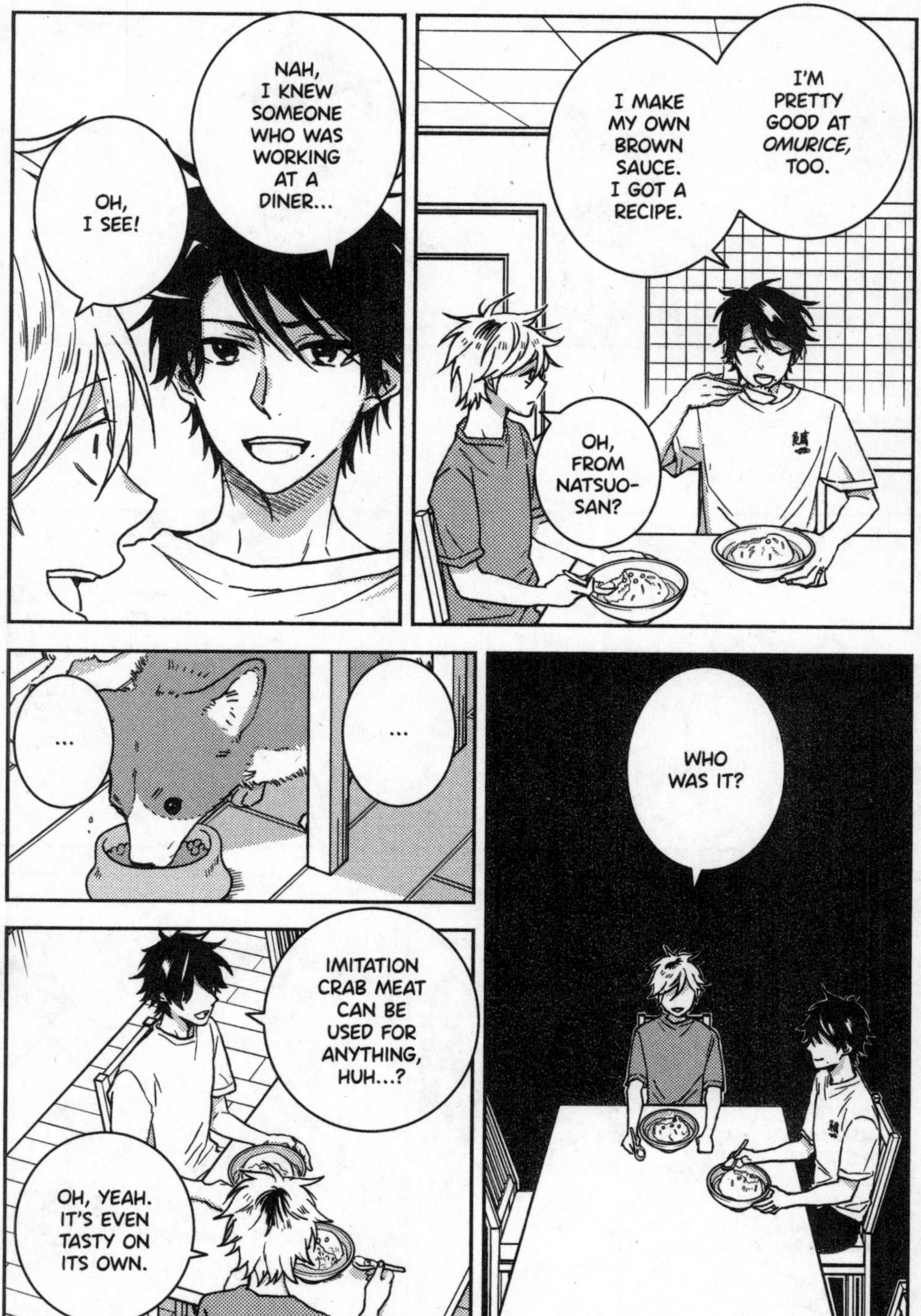
I'M PRETTY GOOD AT *OMURICE*, TOO.
I MAKE MY OWN BROWN SAUCE. I GOT A RECIPE.
OH, FROM NATSUO-SAN?
NAH, I KNEW SOMEONE WHO WAS WORKING AT A DINER...
OH, I SEE!
WHO WAS IT?
...
...
IMITATION CRAB MEAT CAN BE USED FOR ANYTHING, HUH...?
OH, YEAH. IT'S EVEN TASTY ON ITS OWN.

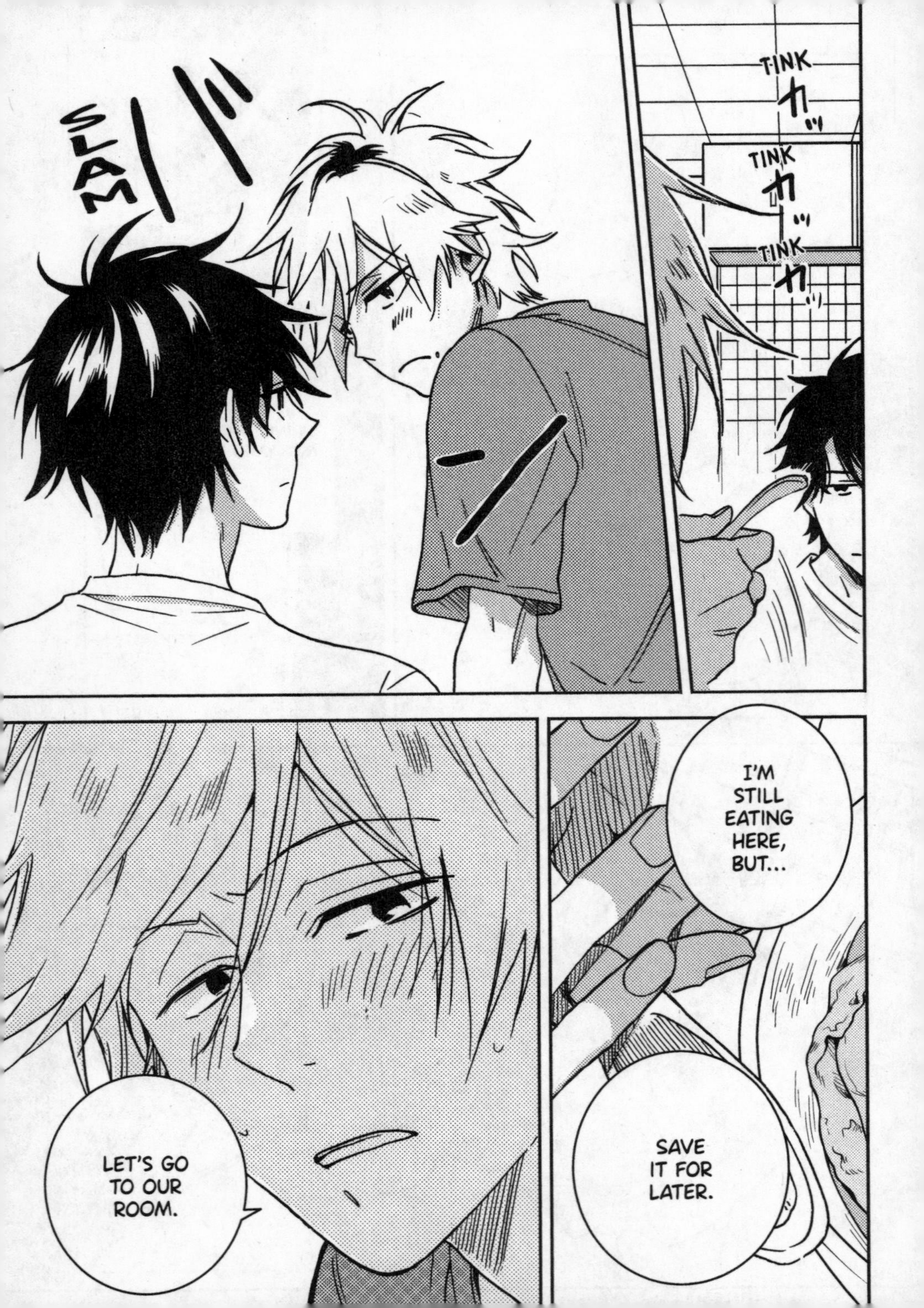
TINK
TINK
TINK
SLAM
I'M STILL EATING HERE, BUT...
SAVE IT FOR LATER.
LET'S GO TO OUR ROOM.

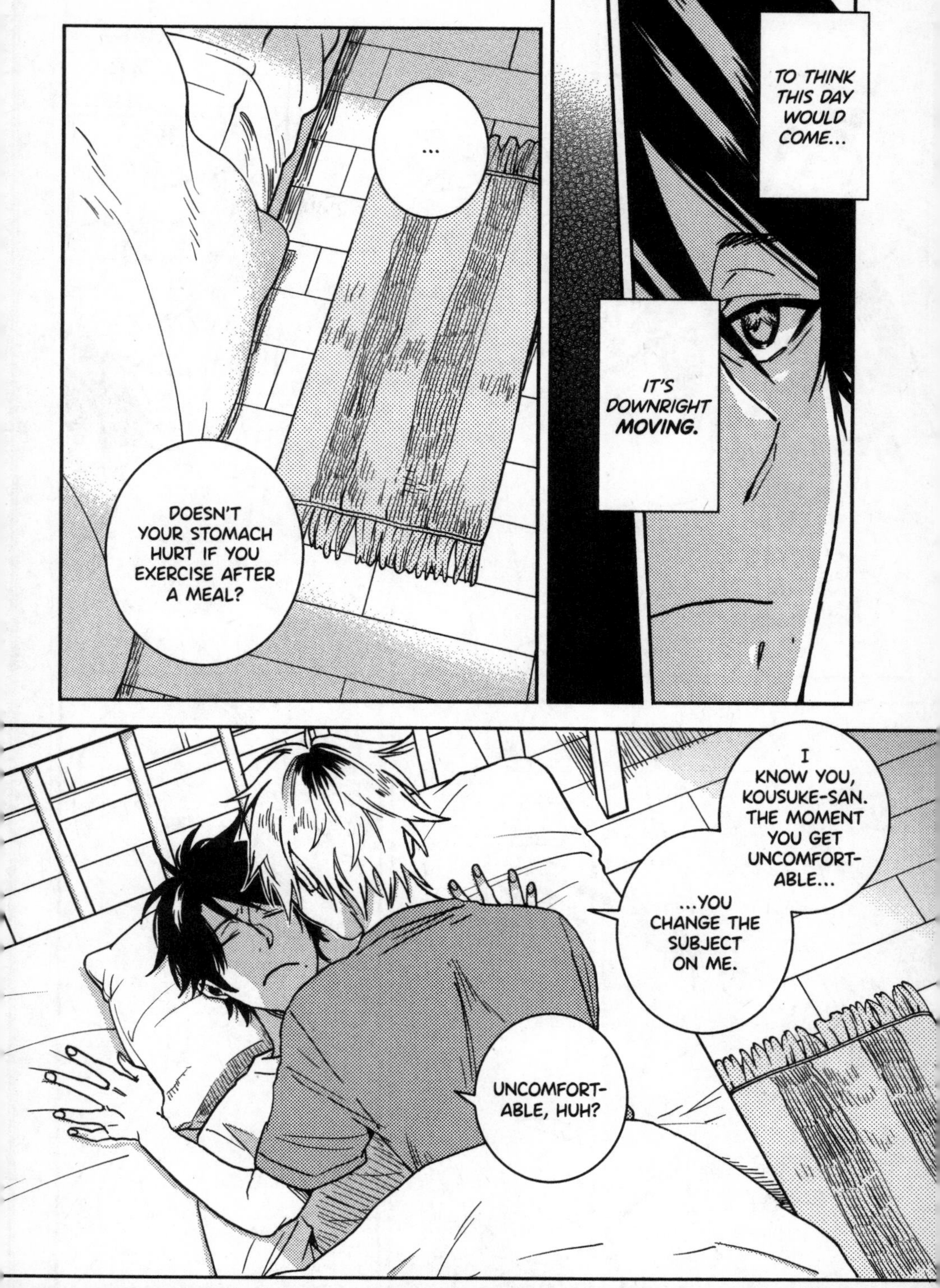
TO THINK THIS DAY WOULD COME...
IT'S DOWNRIGHT **MOVING.**
...
DOESN'T YOUR STOMACH HURT IF YOU EXERCISE AFTER A MEAL?
I KNOW YOU, KOUSUKE-SAN. THE MOMENT YOU GET UNCOMFORT-ABLE...
...YOU CHANGE THE SUBJECT ON ME.
UNCOMFORT-ABLE, HUH?

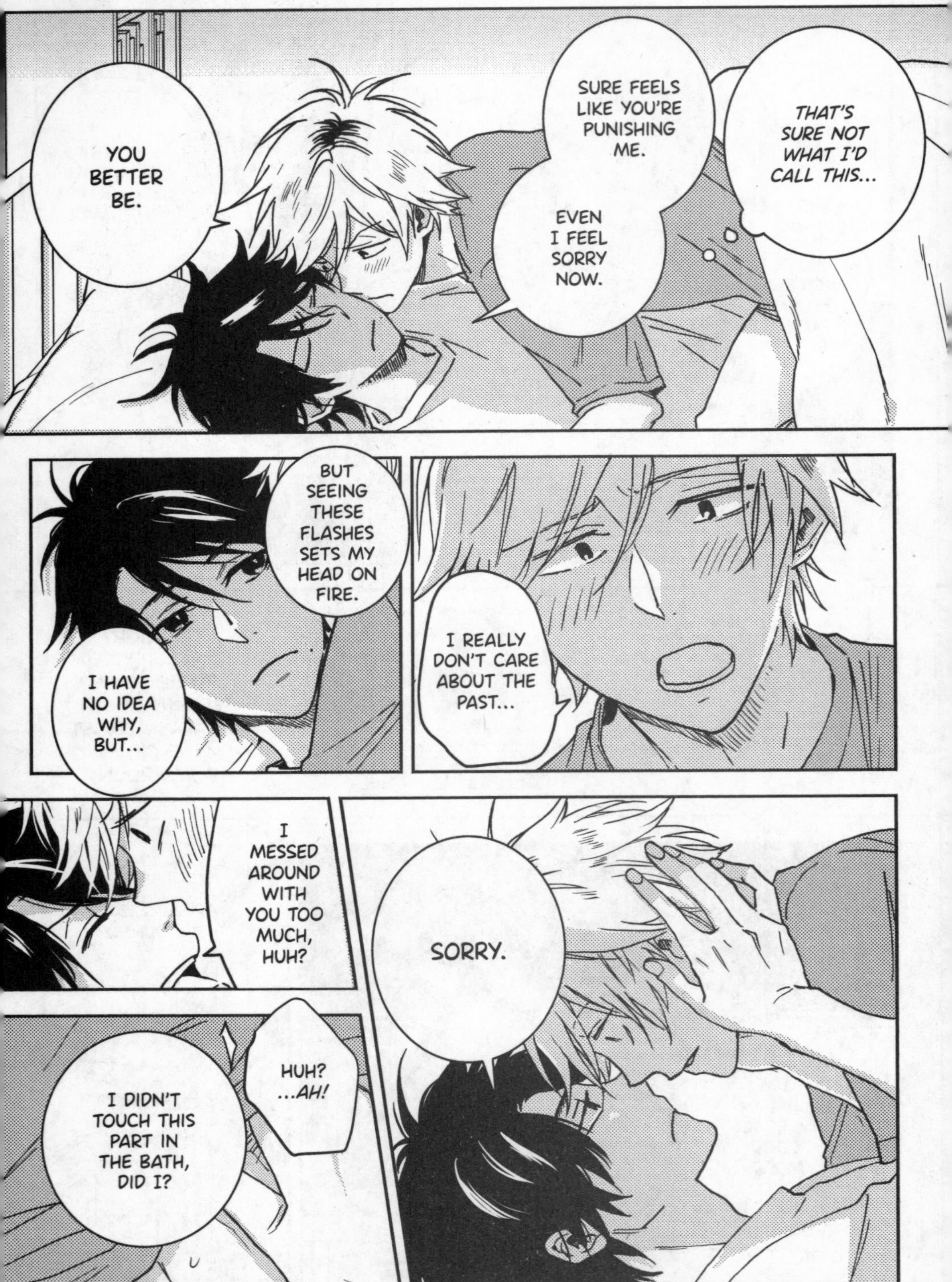
THAT'S SURE NOT WHAT I'D CALL THIS...
SURE FEELS LIKE YOU'RE PUNISHING ME.
EVEN I FEEL SORRY NOW.
YOU BETTER BE.
I REALLY DON'T CARE ABOUT THE PAST...
BUT SEEING THESE FLASHES SETS MY HEAD ON FIRE.
I HAVE NO IDEA WHY, BUT...
SORRY.
I MESSED AROUND WITH YOU TOO MUCH, HUH?
HUH? ...*AH!*
I DIDN'T TOUCH THIS PART IN THE BATH, DID I?

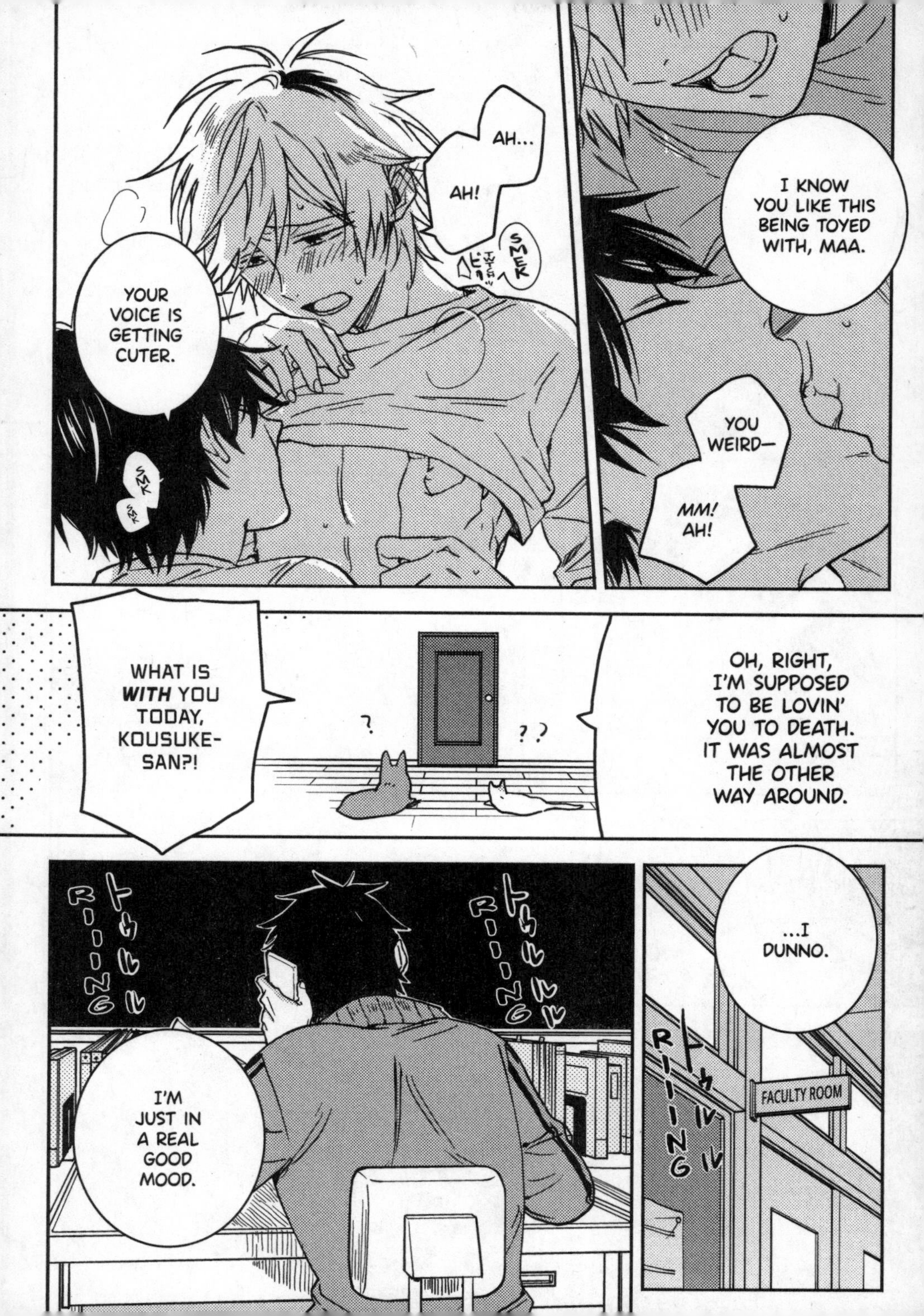
I KNOW YOU LIKE THIS BEING TOYED WITH, MAA.
YOU WEIRD—
MM! AH!
AH...
AH!
SMEK
YOUR VOICE IS GETTING CUTER.
SMK
SMK
OH, RIGHT, I'M SUPPOSED TO BE LOVIN' YOU TO DEATH. IT WAS ALMOST THE OTHER WAY AROUND.
??
?
WHAT IS *WITH* YOU TODAY, KOUSUKE-SAN?!
...I DUNNO.
RIIING
FACULTY ROOM
RIIING
RIIING
I'M JUST IN A REAL GOOD MOOD.

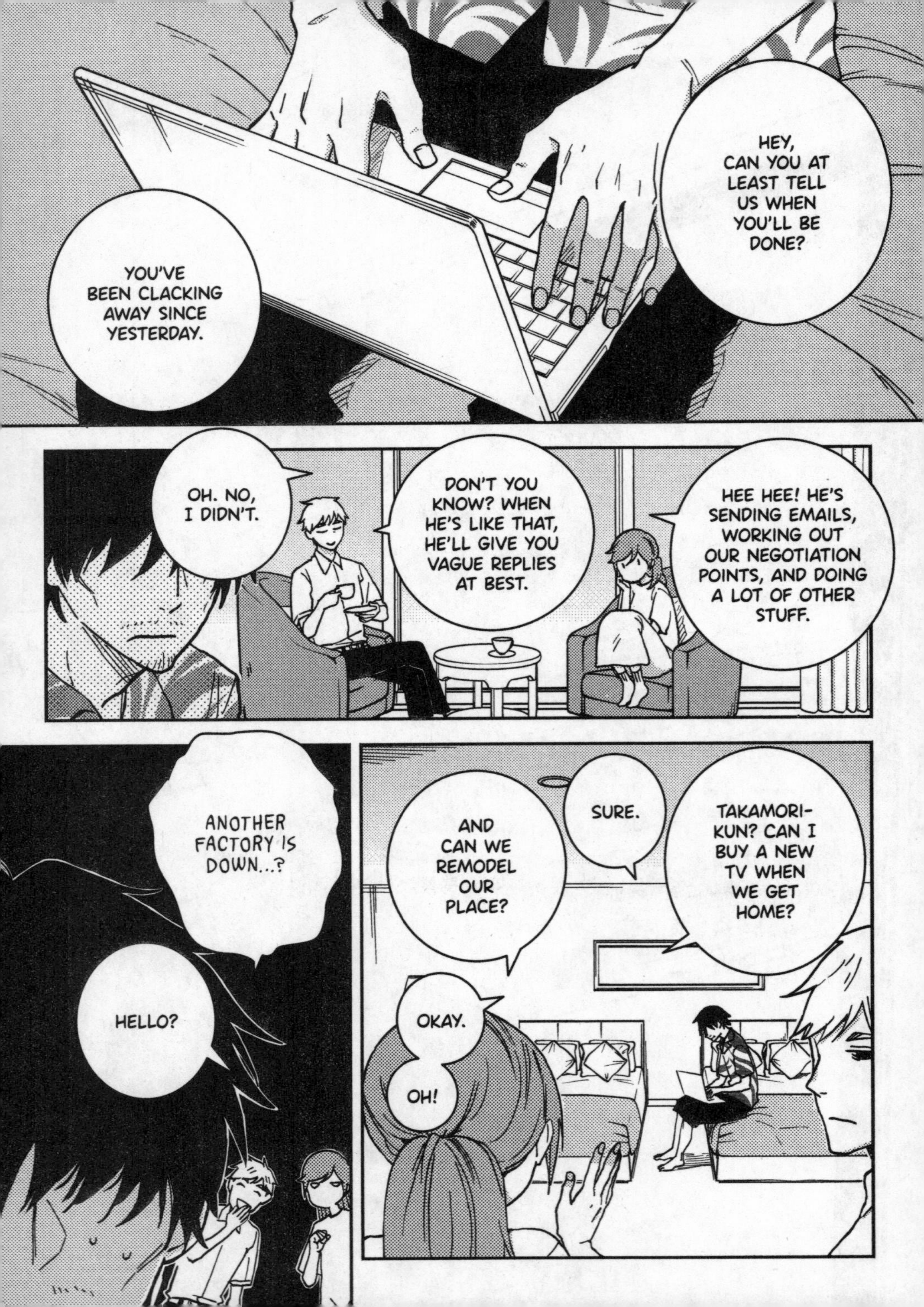
HEY, CAN YOU AT LEAST TELL US WHEN YOU'LL BE DONE?
YOU'VE BEEN CLACKING AWAY SINCE YESTERDAY.
HEE HEE! HE'S SENDING EMAILS, WORKING OUT OUR NEGOTIATION POINTS, AND DOING A LOT OF OTHER STUFF.
DON'T YOU KNOW? WHEN HE'S LIKE THAT, HE'LL GIVE YOU VAGUE REPLIES AT BEST.
OH. NO, I DIDN'T.
TAKAMORI-KUN? CAN I BUY A NEW TV WHEN WE GET HOME?
SURE.
AND CAN WE REMODEL OUR PLACE?
OKAY.
OH!
ANOTHER FACTORY IS DOWN...?
HELLO?

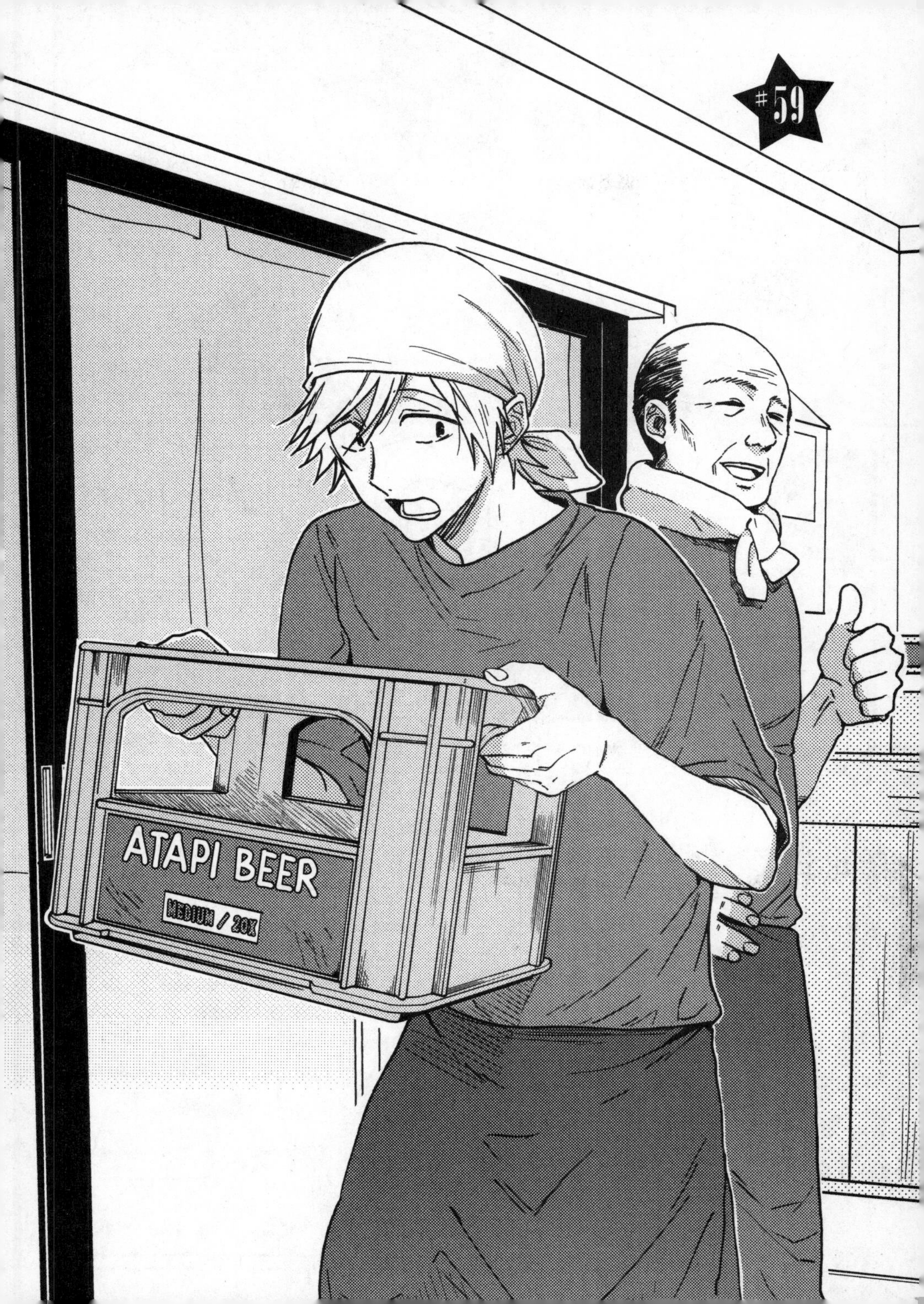
#59
ATAPI BEER
MEDIUM / 20X

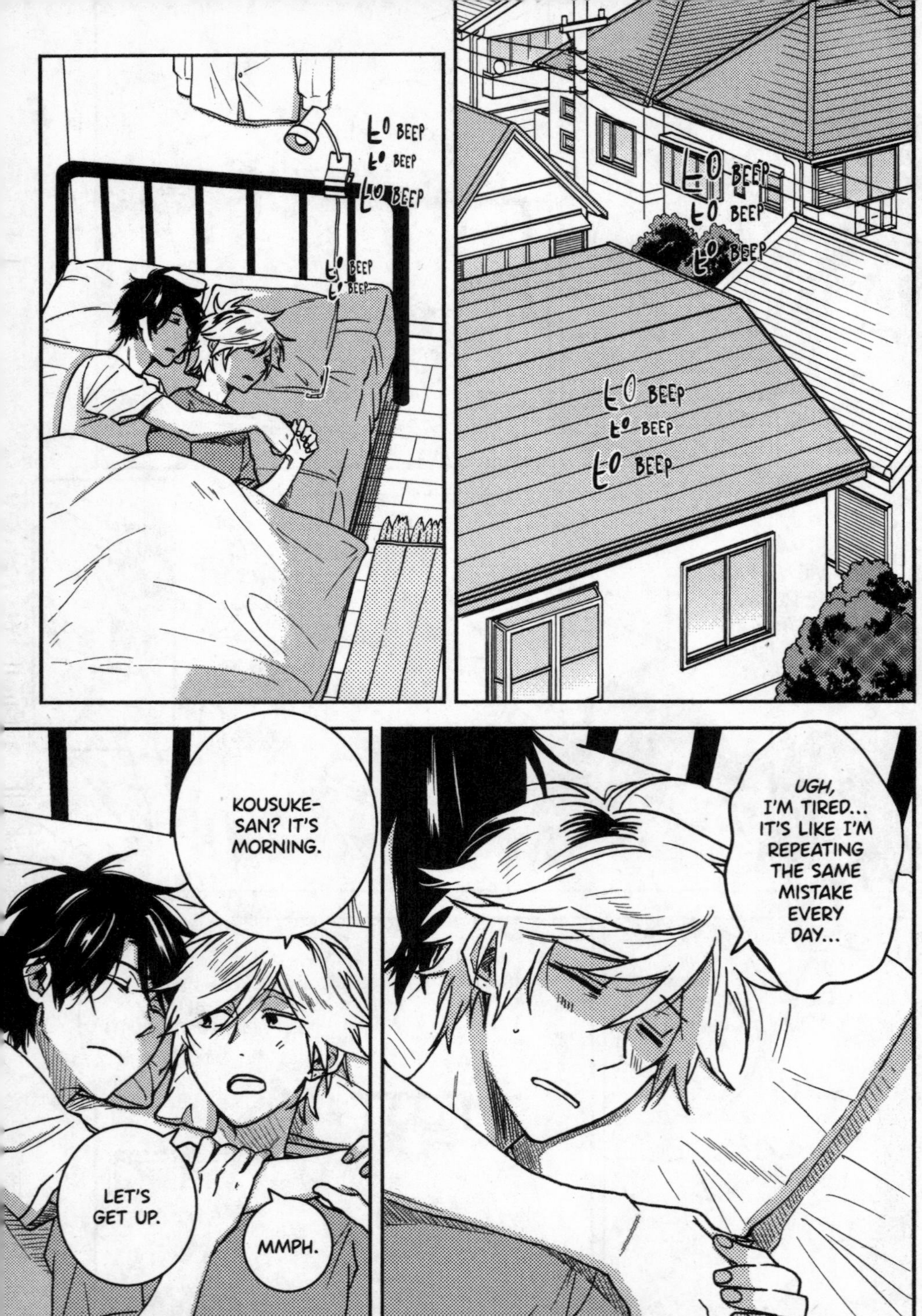
BEEP
BEEP
BEEP
BEEP
BEEP
BEEP
BEEP
BEEP
BEEP
BEEP
BEEP
UGH, I'M TIRED... IT'S LIKE I'M REPEATING THE SAME MISTAKE EVERY DAY...
KOUSUKE-SAN? IT'S MORNING.
LET'S GET UP.
MMPH.

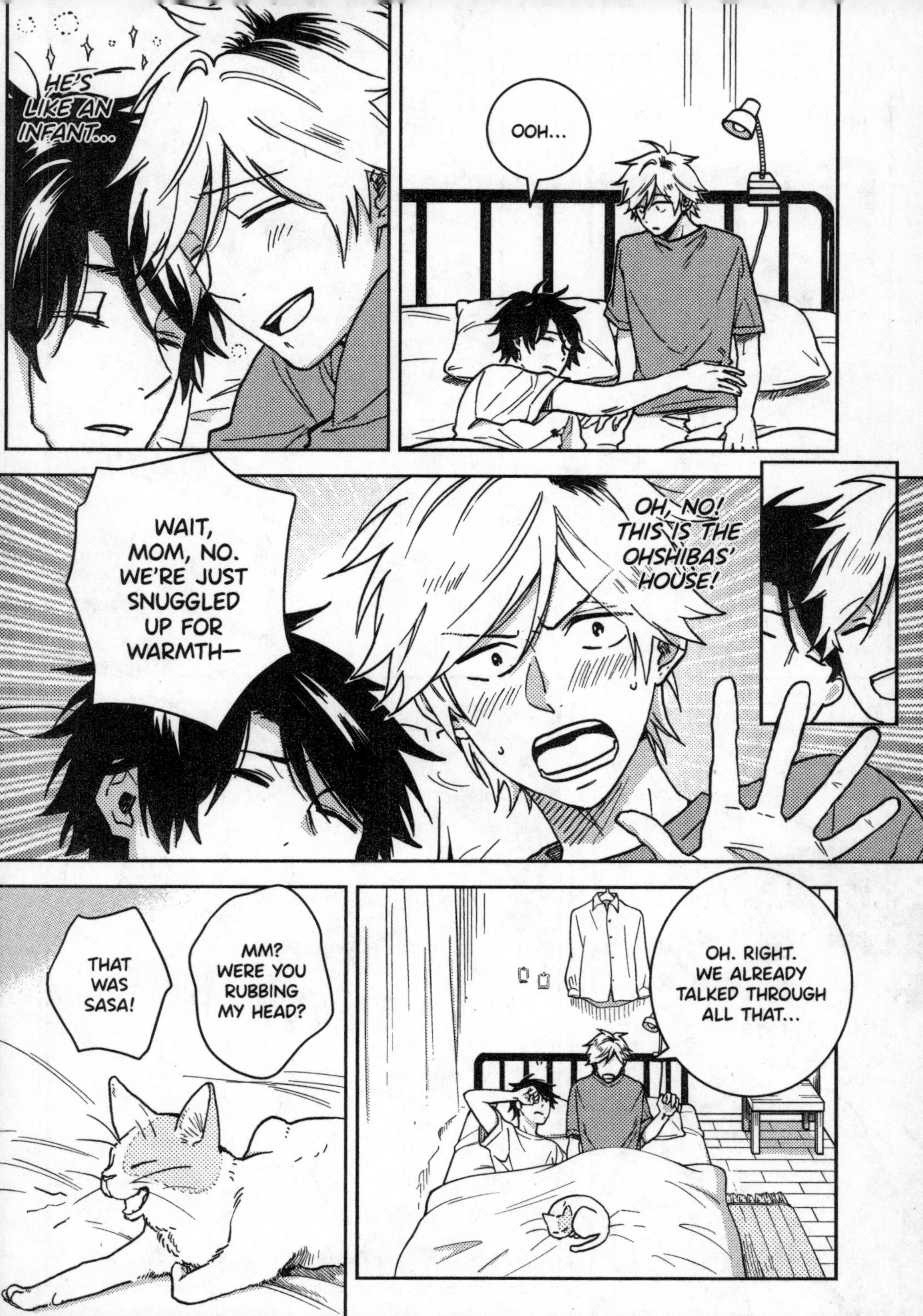
OOH...
HE'S LIKE AN INFANT...
OH, NO! THIS IS THE OHSHIBAS' HOUSE!
WAIT, MOM, NO. WE'RE JUST SNUGGLED UP FOR WARMTH—
OH. RIGHT. WE ALREADY TALKED THROUGH ALL THAT...
MM? WERE YOU RUBBING MY HEAD?
THAT WAS SASA!

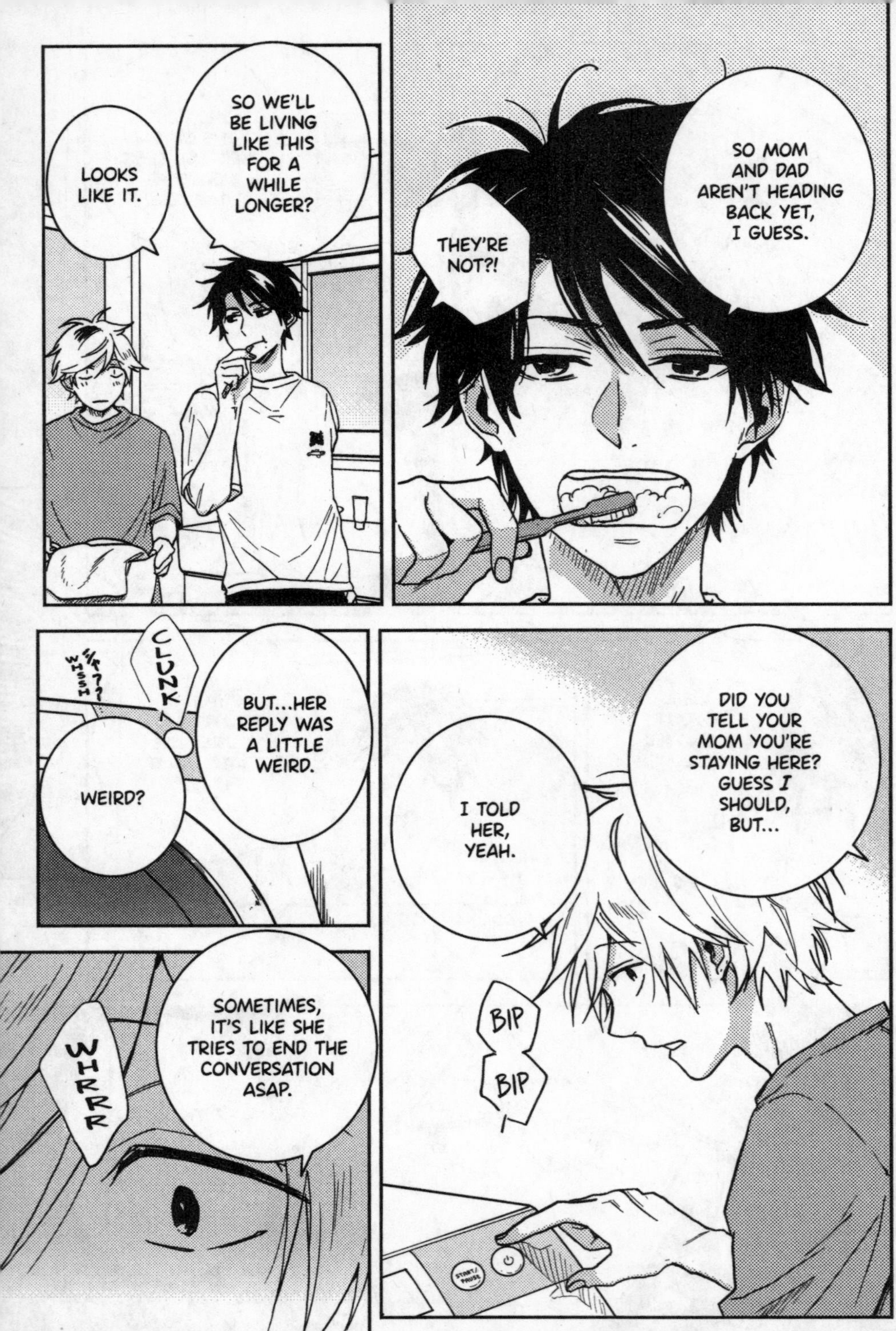
SO MOM AND DAD AREN'T HEADING BACK YET, I GUESS.
THEY'RE NOT?!
SO WE'LL BE LIVING LIKE THIS FOR A WHILE LONGER?
LOOKS LIKE IT.
DID YOU TELL YOUR MOM YOU'RE STAYING HERE? GUESS *I* SHOULD, BUT...
I TOLD HER, YEAH.
BIP
BIP
START/PAUSE
WHSH
CLUNK
BUT...HER REPLY WAS A LITTLE WEIRD.
WEIRD?
WHRRR
SOMETIMES, IT'S LIKE SHE TRIES TO END THE CONVERSATION ASAP.

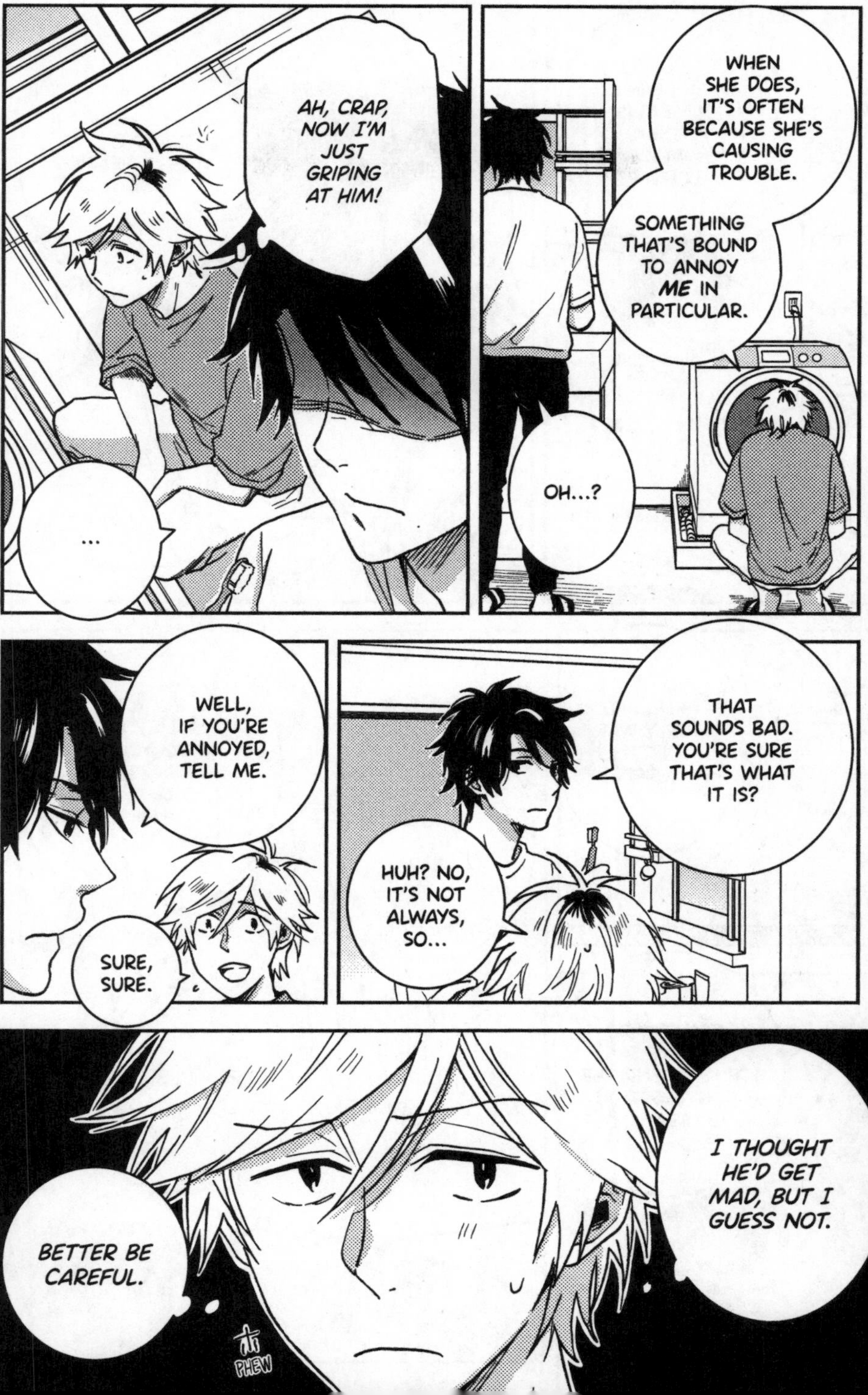
WHEN SHE DOES, IT'S OFTEN BECAUSE SHE'S CAUSING TROUBLE.
SOMETHING THAT'S BOUND TO ANNOY *ME* IN PARTICULAR.
OH...?
AH, CRAP, NOW I'M JUST GRIPING AT HIM!
...
THAT SOUNDS BAD. YOU'RE SURE THAT'S WHAT IT IS?
HUH? NO, IT'S NOT ALWAYS, SO...
WELL, IF YOU'RE ANNOYED, TELL ME.
SURE, SURE.
I THOUGHT HE'D GET MAD, BUT I GUESS NOT.
BETTER BE CAREFUL.
PHEW

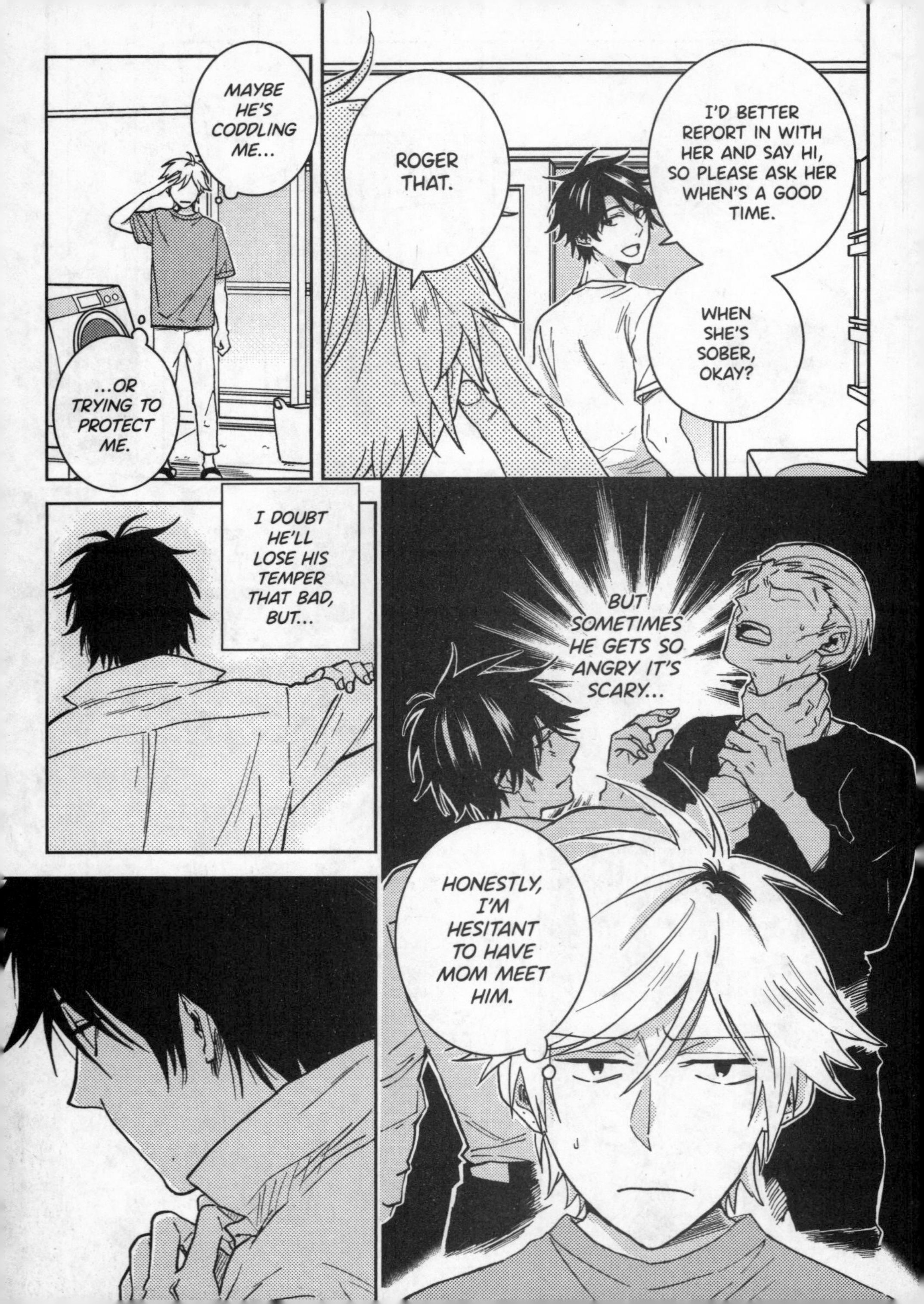
I'D BETTER REPORT IN WITH HER AND SAY HI, SO PLEASE ASK HER WHEN'S A GOOD TIME.
WHEN SHE'S SOBER, OKAY?
ROGER THAT.
MAYBE HE'S CODDLING ME...
...OR TRYING TO PROTECT ME.
I DOUBT HE'LL LOSE HIS TEMPER THAT BAD, BUT...
BUT SOMETIMES HE GETS SO ANGRY IT'S SCARY...
HONESTLY, I'M HESITANT TO HAVE MOM MEET HIM.

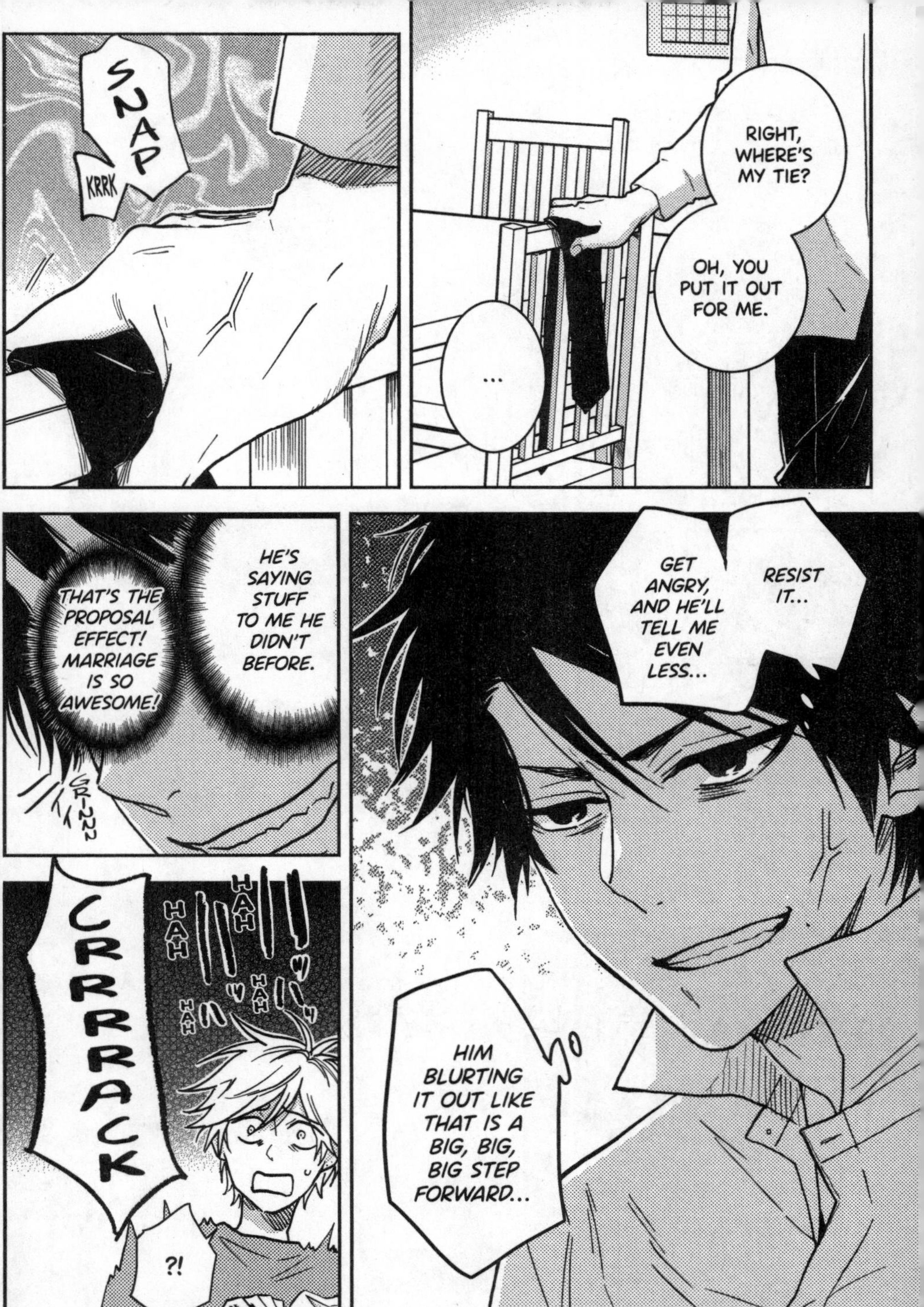
RIGHT, WHERE'S MY TIE?
OH, YOU PUT IT OUT FOR ME.
...
SNAP
KRRK
RESIST IT...
GET ANGRY, AND HE'LL TELL ME EVEN LESS...
HIM BLURTING IT OUT LIKE THAT IS A BIG, BIG, BIG STEP FORWARD...
HE'S SAYING STUFF TO ME HE DIDN'T BEFORE.
THAT'S THE PROPOSAL EFFECT! MARRIAGE IS SO AWESOME!
GRINNN
HAH HAH HAH HAH HAH
CRRRACK
?!

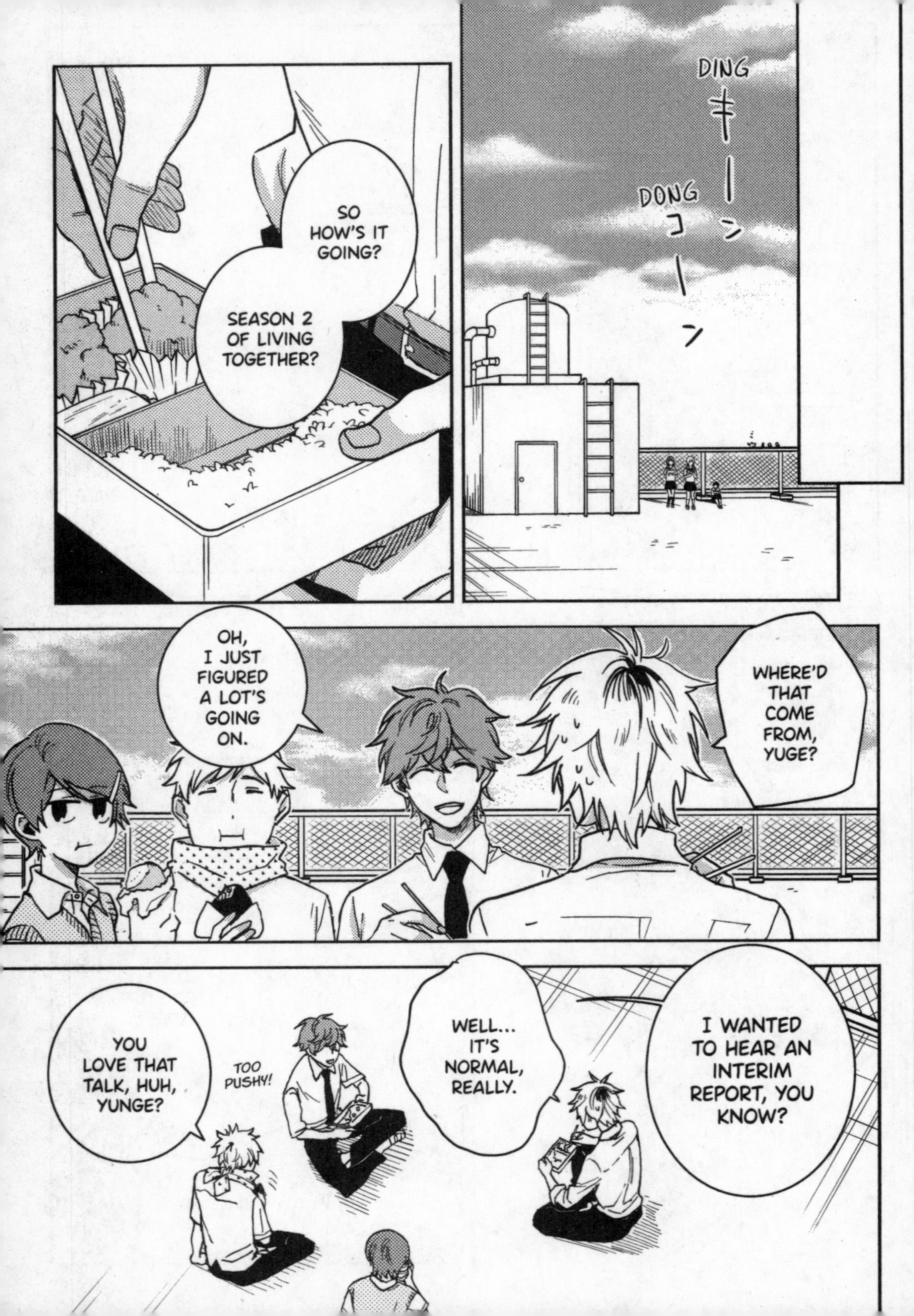
DING
キーン
DONG
コーン
SO HOW'S IT GOING?
SEASON 2 OF LIVING TOGETHER?
WHERE'D THAT COME FROM, YUGE?
OH, I JUST FIGURED A LOT'S GOING ON.
I WANTED TO HEAR AN INTERIM REPORT, YOU KNOW?
WELL... IT'S NORMAL, REALLY.
TOO PUSHY!
YOU LOVE THAT TALK, HUH, YUNGE?

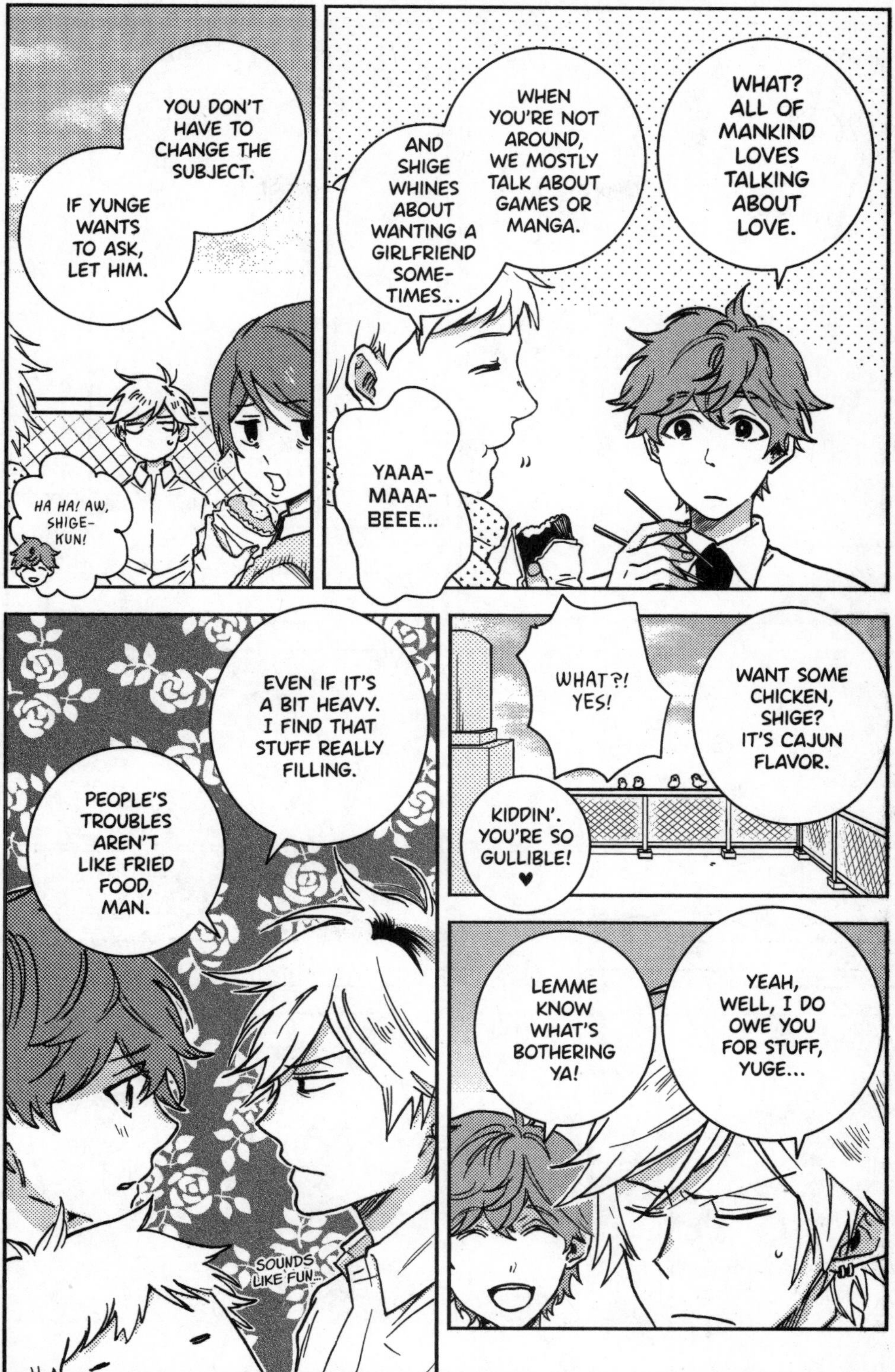
WHAT? ALL OF MANKIND LOVES TALKING ABOUT LOVE.
WHEN YOU'RE NOT AROUND, WE MOSTLY TALK ABOUT GAMES OR MANGA.
AND SHIGE WHINES ABOUT WANTING A GIRLFRIEND SOME-TIMES...
YAAA-MAAA-BEEE...
YOU DON'T HAVE TO CHANGE THE SUBJECT.
IF YUNGE WANTS TO ASK, LET HIM.
HA HA! AW, SHIGE-KUN!
WANT SOME CHICKEN, SHIGE? IT'S CAJUN FLAVOR.
WHAT?! YES!
KIDDIN'. YOU'RE SO GULLIBLE! ♥
YEAH, WELL, I DO OWE YOU FOR STUFF, YUGE...
LEMME KNOW WHAT'S BOTHERING YA!
EVEN IF IT'S A BIT HEAVY. I FIND THAT STUFF REALLY FILLING.
PEOPLE'S TROUBLES AREN'T LIKE FRIED FOOD, MAN.
SOUNDS LIKE FUN...

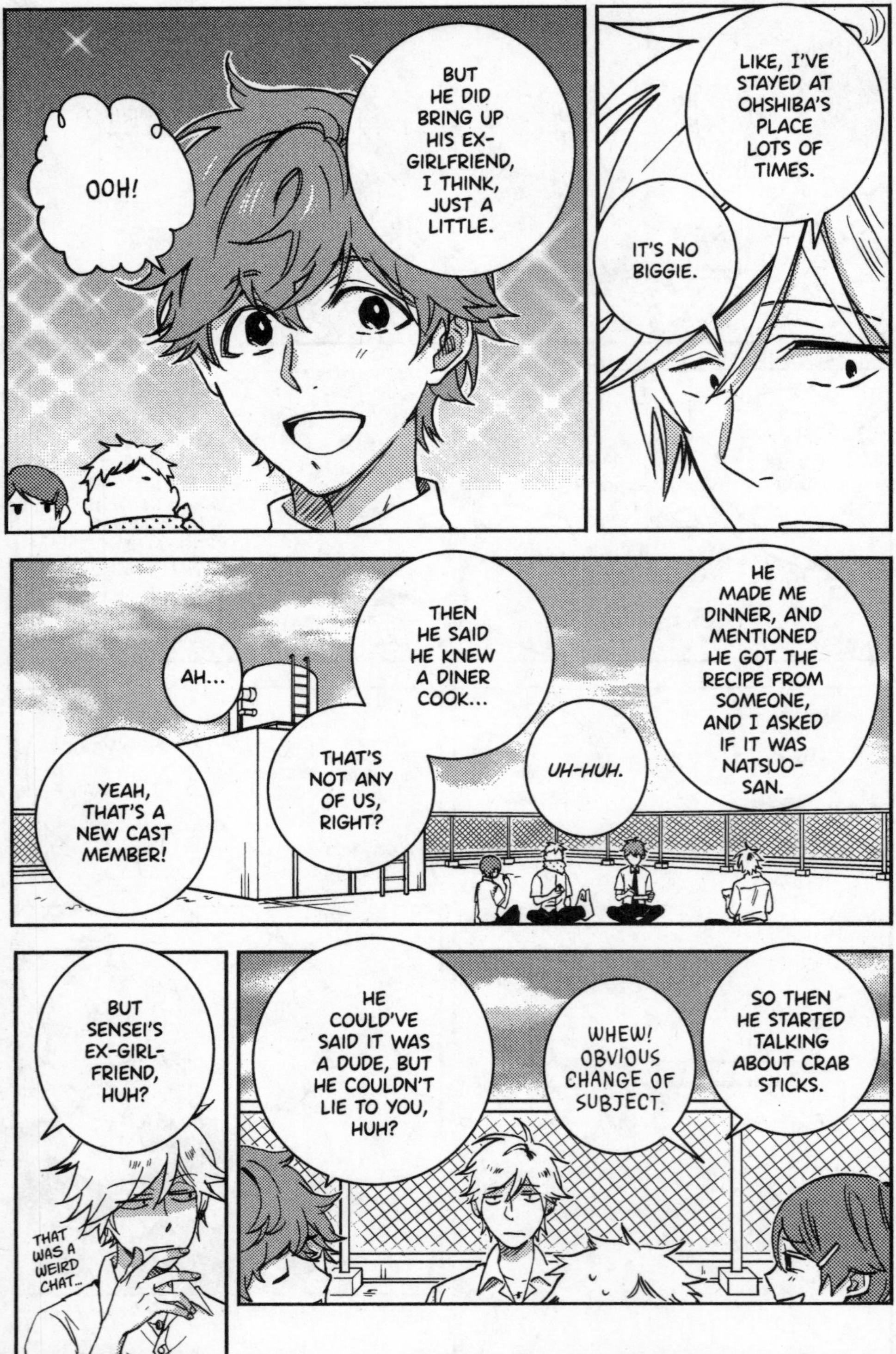
LIKE, I'VE STAYED AT OHSHIBA'S PLACE LOTS OF TIMES.
IT'S NO BIGGIE.
BUT HE DID BRING UP HIS EX-GIRLFRIEND, I THINK, JUST A LITTLE.
OOH!
HE MADE ME DINNER, AND MENTIONED HE GOT THE RECIPE FROM SOMEONE, AND I ASKED IF IT WAS NATSUO-SAN.
UH-HUH.
THEN HE SAID HE KNEW A DINER COOK...
AH...
THAT'S NOT ANY OF US, RIGHT?
YEAH, THAT'S A NEW CAST MEMBER!
SO THEN HE STARTED TALKING ABOUT CRAB STICKS.
WHEW! OBVIOUS CHANGE OF SUBJECT.
HE COULD'VE SAID IT WAS A DUDE, BUT HE COULDN'T LIE TO YOU, HUH?
BUT SENSEI'S EX-GIRL-FRIEND, HUH?
THAT WAS A WEIRD CHAT...

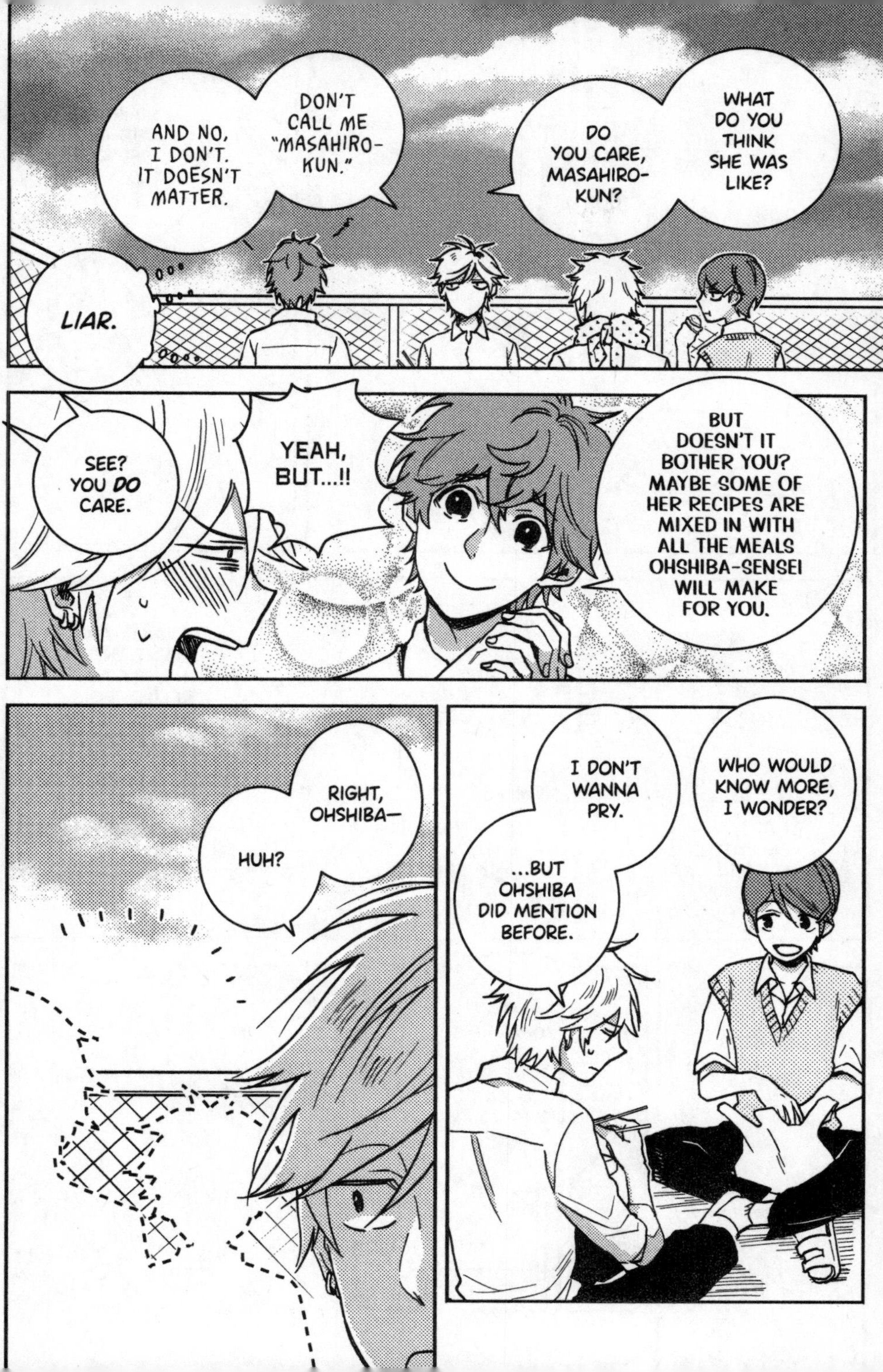
WHAT DO YOU THINK SHE WAS LIKE?
DO YOU CARE, MASAHIRO-KUN?
DON'T CALL ME "MASAHIRO-KUN."
AND NO, I DON'T. IT DOESN'T MATTER.
LIAR.
BUT DOESN'T IT BOTHER YOU? MAYBE SOME OF HER RECIPES ARE MIXED IN WITH ALL THE MEALS OHSHIBA-SENSEI WILL MAKE FOR YOU.
YEAH, BUT...!!
SEE? YOU DO CARE.
WHO WOULD KNOW MORE, I WONDER?
I DON'T WANNA PRY.
...BUT OHSHIBA DID MENTION BEFORE.
RIGHT, OHSHIBA—
HUH?

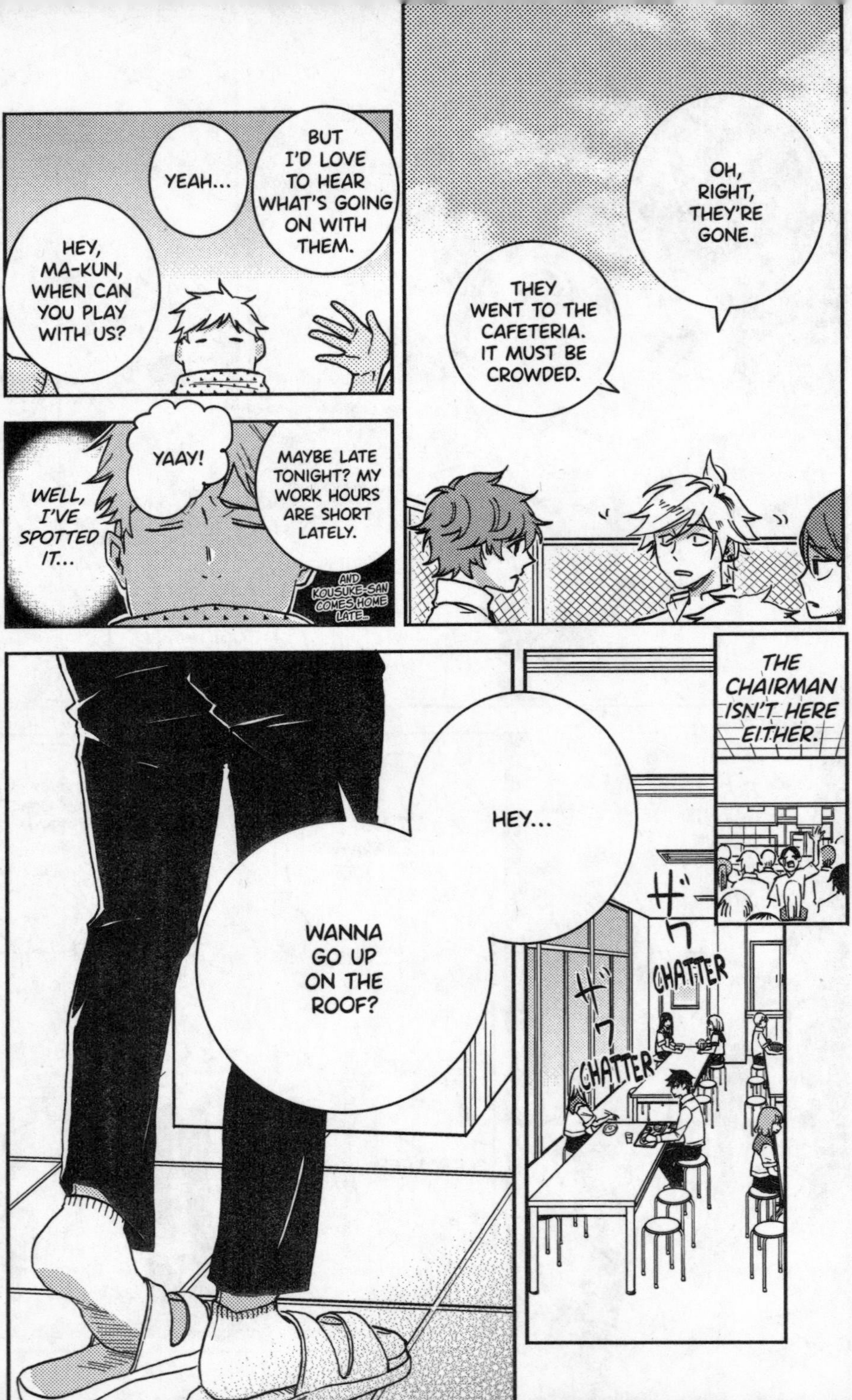
OH, RIGHT, THEY'RE GONE.
THEY WENT TO THE CAFETERIA. IT MUST BE CROWDED.
BUT I'D LOVE TO HEAR WHAT'S GOING ON WITH THEM.
YEAH...
HEY, MA-KUN, WHEN CAN YOU PLAY WITH US?
MAYBE LATE TONIGHT? MY WORK HOURS ARE SHORT LATELY.
AND KOUSUKE-SAN COMES HOME LATE...
YAAY!
WELL, I'VE SPOTTED IT...
THE CHAIRMAN ISN'T HERE EITHER.
ザワ
CHATTER
ザワ
CHATTER
HEY...
WANNA GO UP ON THE ROOF?

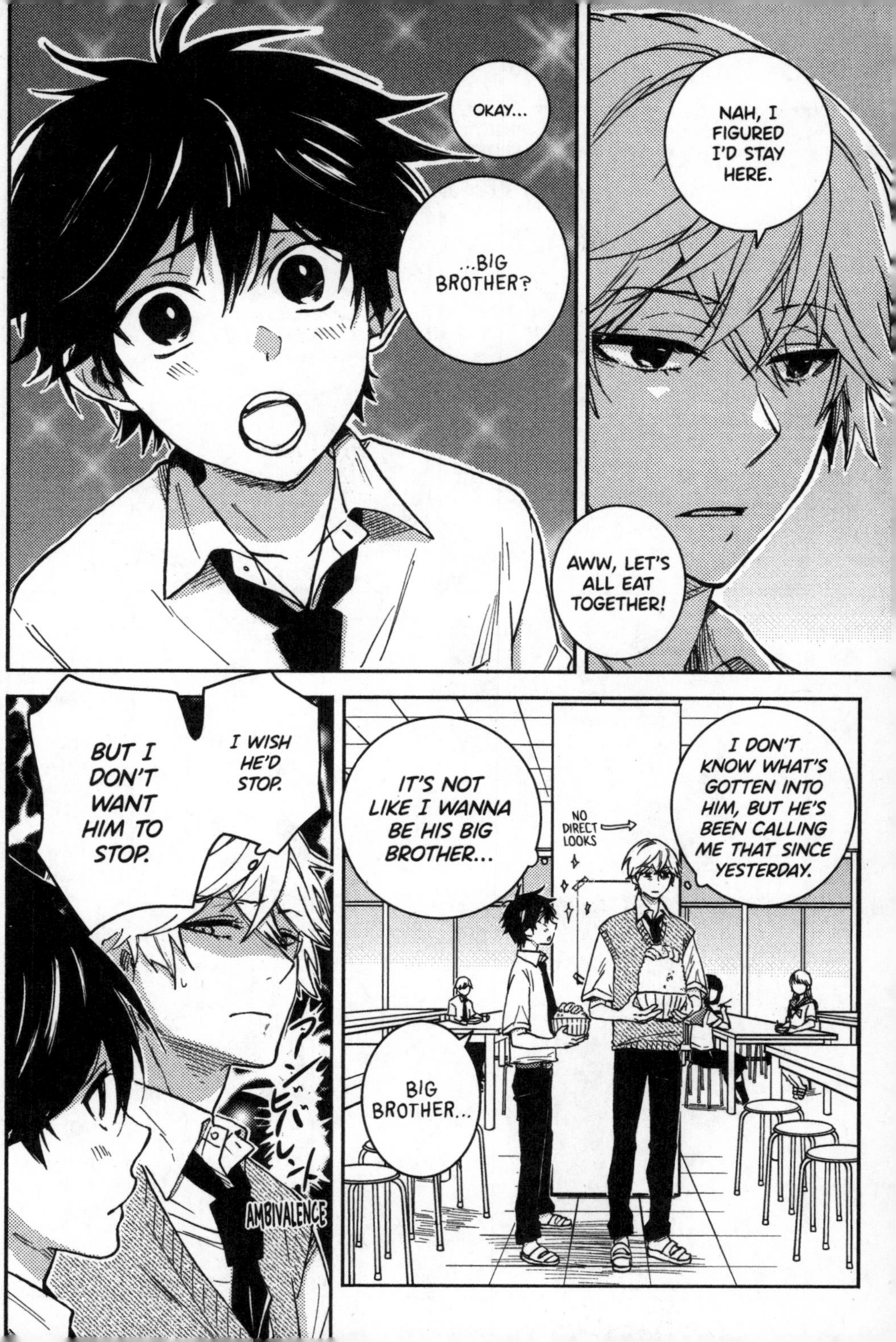
NAH, I FIGURED I'D STAY HERE.
AWW, LET'S ALL EAT TOGETHER!
OKAY...
...BIG BROTHER?
I DON'T KNOW WHAT'S GOTTEN INTO HIM, BUT HE'S BEEN CALLING ME THAT SINCE YESTERDAY.
NO DIRECT LOOKS
IT'S NOT LIKE I WANNA BE HIS BIG BROTHER...
BIG BROTHER...
I WISH HE'D STOP.
BUT I DON'T WANT HIM TO STOP.
アンビバレント
AMBIVALENCE

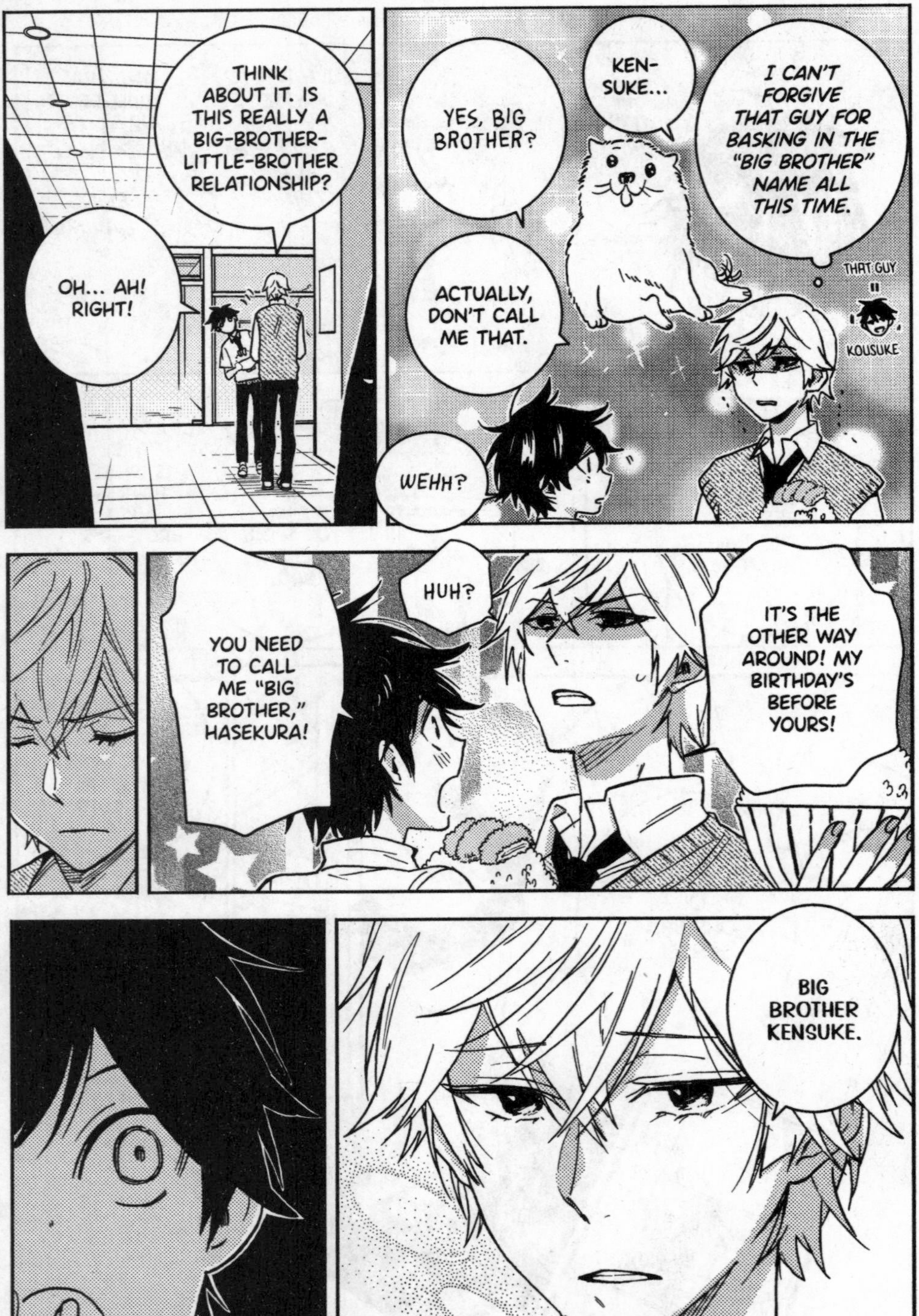
I CAN'T FORGIVE THAT GUY FOR BASKING IN THE "BIG BROTHER" NAME ALL THIS TIME.
THAT GUY = KOUSUKE
KEN-SUKE...
YES, BIG BROTHER?
ACTUALLY, DON'T CALL ME THAT.
WEHH?
THINK ABOUT IT. IS THIS REALLY A BIG-BROTHER-LITTLE-BROTHER RELATIONSHIP?
OH... AH! RIGHT!
IT'S THE OTHER WAY AROUND! MY BIRTHDAY'S BEFORE YOURS!
HUH?
YOU NEED TO CALL ME "BIG BROTHER," HASEKURA!
BIG BROTHER KENSUKE.

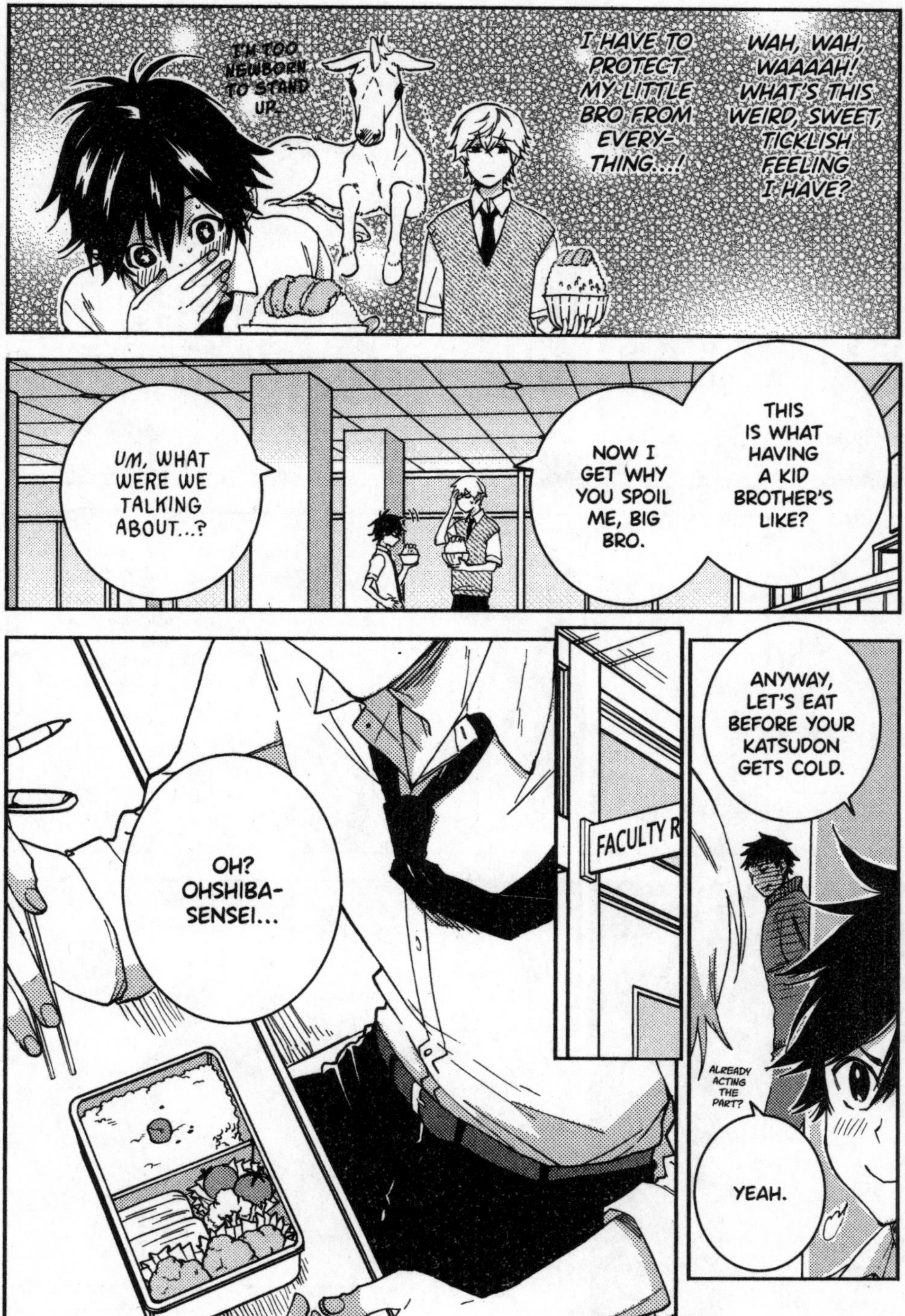
WAH, WAH, WAAAAH! WHAT'S THIS WEIRD, SWEET, TICKLISH FEELING I HAVE?
I HAVE TO PROTECT MY LITTLE BRO FROM EVERY-THING...!
I'M TOO NEWBORN TO STAND UP.
THIS IS WHAT HAVING A KID BROTHER'S LIKE?
NOW I GET WHY YOU SPOIL ME, BIG BRO.
UM, WHAT WERE WE TALKING ABOUT...?
ANYWAY, LET'S EAT BEFORE YOUR KATSUDON GETS COLD.
ALREADY ACTING THE PART?
YEAH.
FACULTY R
OH? OHSHIBA-SENSEI...

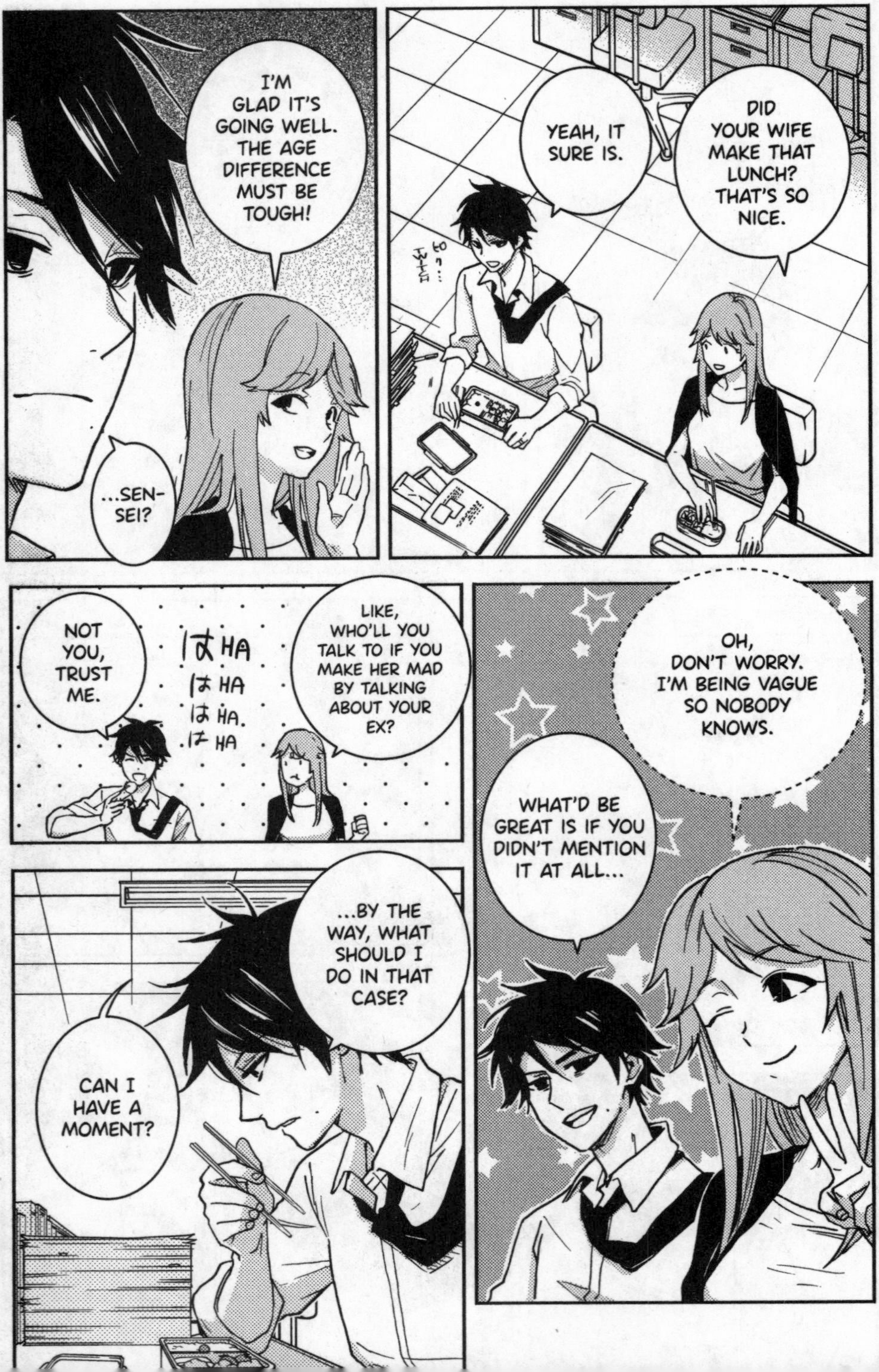
DID YOUR WIFE MAKE THAT LUNCH? THAT'S SO NICE.
YEAH, IT SURE IS.
ピク…
TWITCH
I'M GLAD IT'S GOING WELL. THE AGE DIFFERENCE MUST BE TOUGH!
...SEN-SEI?
OH, DON'T WORRY. I'M BEING VAGUE SO NOBODY KNOWS.
WHAT'D BE GREAT IS IF YOU DIDN'T MENTION IT AT ALL...
LIKE, WHO'LL YOU TALK TO IF YOU MAKE HER MAD BY TALKING ABOUT YOUR EX?
は HA は HA は HA は HA
NOT YOU, TRUST ME.
...BY THE WAY, WHAT SHOULD I DO IN THAT CASE?
CAN I HAVE A MOMENT?

SOMETHING UP?

NO, IT'S...THE PHONE.

SORRY TO BOTHER YOU DURING LUNCH.

GOZUTA-SENSEI...

I CAN STILL CATCH HIM DURING LUNCH... 'SCUSE ME!

ズン

ズン

I HAVE A QUESTION... I MEAN I NEED ADVICE. THIS IS NEW TO ME, SO...

WHAT'S IT ABOUT?

HE SURE WAS WORKED UP.

I'M SORRY, I'LL ASK THE KID HIMSELF.

UH-HUH...

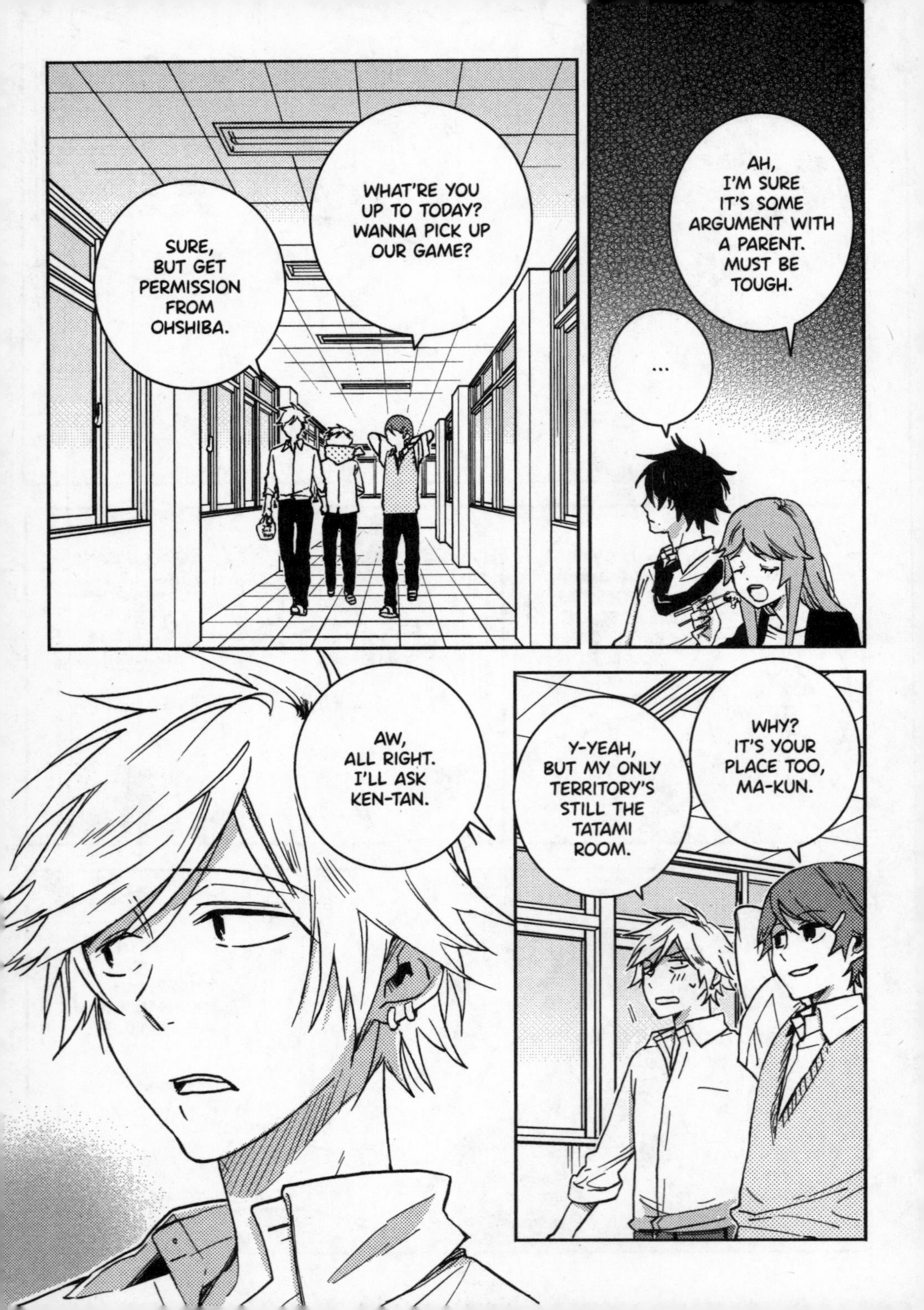
AH, I'M SURE IT'S SOME ARGUMENT WITH A PARENT. MUST BE TOUGH.
...
WHAT'RE YOU UP TO TODAY? WANNA PICK UP OUR GAME?
SURE, BUT GET PERMISSION FROM OHSHIBA.
WHY? IT'S YOUR PLACE TOO, MA-KUN.
Y-YEAH, BUT MY ONLY TERRITORY'S STILL THE TATAMI ROOM.
AW, ALL RIGHT. I'LL ASK KEN-TAN.

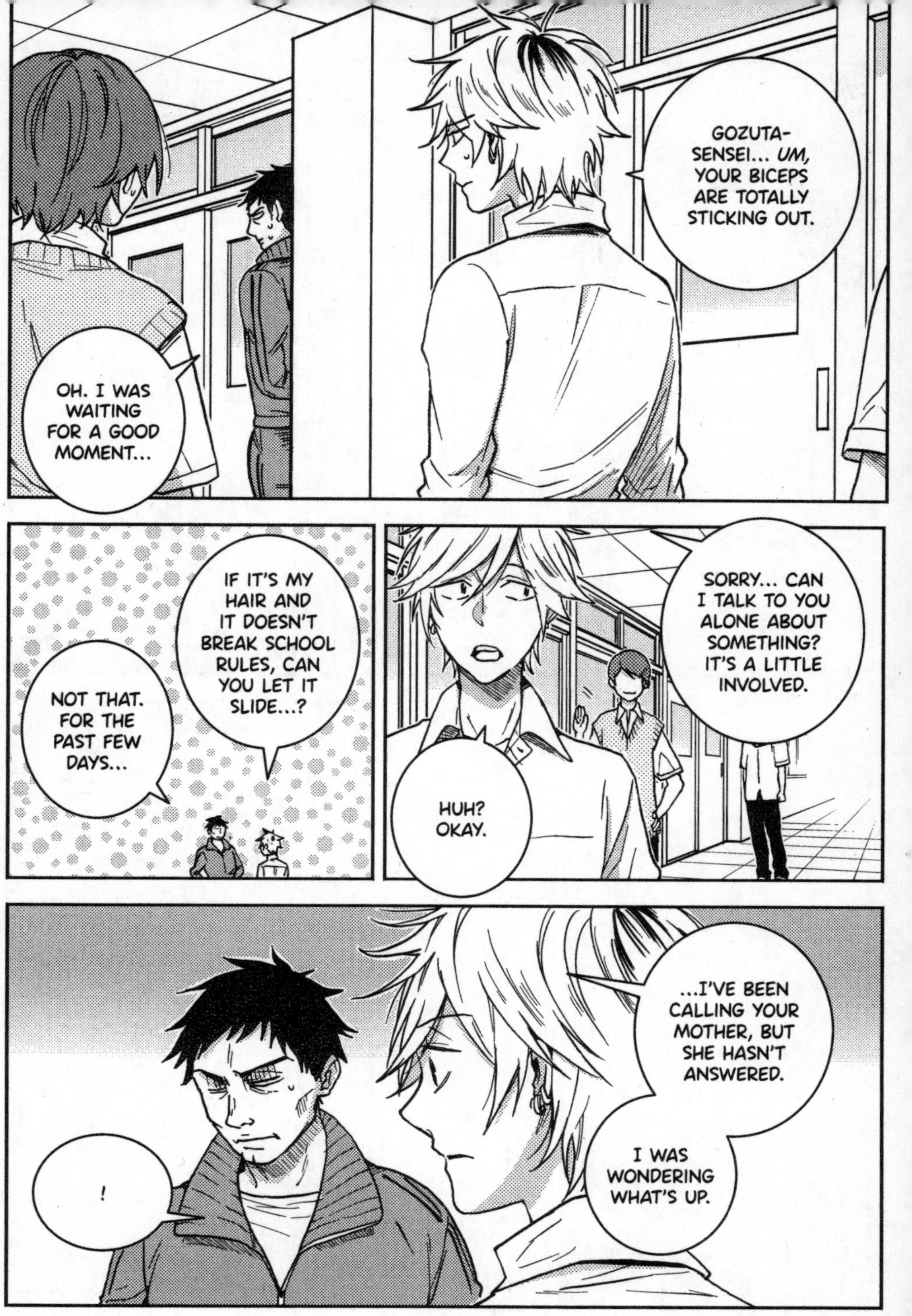
GOZUTA-SENSEI... *UM*, YOUR BICEPS ARE TOTALLY STICKING OUT.
OH. I WAS WAITING FOR A GOOD MOMENT...
SORRY... CAN I TALK TO YOU ALONE ABOUT SOMETHING? IT'S A LITTLE INVOLVED.
HUH? OKAY.
IF IT'S MY HAIR AND IT DOESN'T BREAK SCHOOL RULES, CAN YOU LET IT SLIDE...?
NOT THAT. FOR THE PAST FEW DAYS...
...I'VE BEEN CALLING YOUR MOTHER, BUT SHE HASN'T ANSWERED.
I WAS WONDERING WHAT'S UP.
!

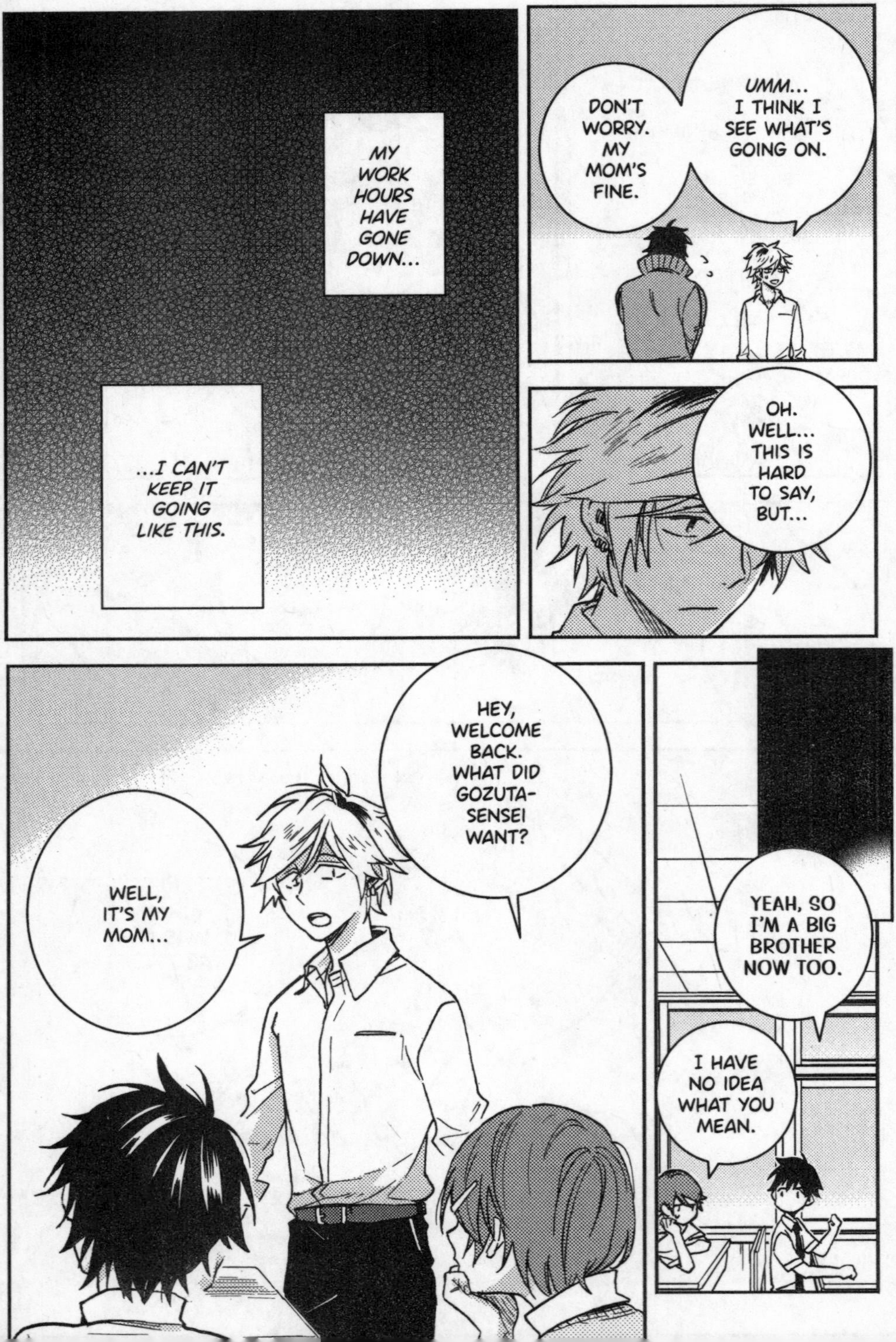
UMM... I THINK I SEE WHAT'S GOING ON.
DON'T WORRY. MY MOM'S FINE.
OH. WELL... THIS IS HARD TO SAY, BUT...
MY WORK HOURS HAVE GONE DOWN...
...I CAN'T KEEP IT GOING LIKE THIS.
YEAH, SO I'M A BIG BROTHER NOW TOO.
I HAVE NO IDEA WHAT YOU MEAN.
HEY, WELCOME BACK. WHAT DID GOZUTA-SENSEI WANT?
WELL, IT'S MY MOM...

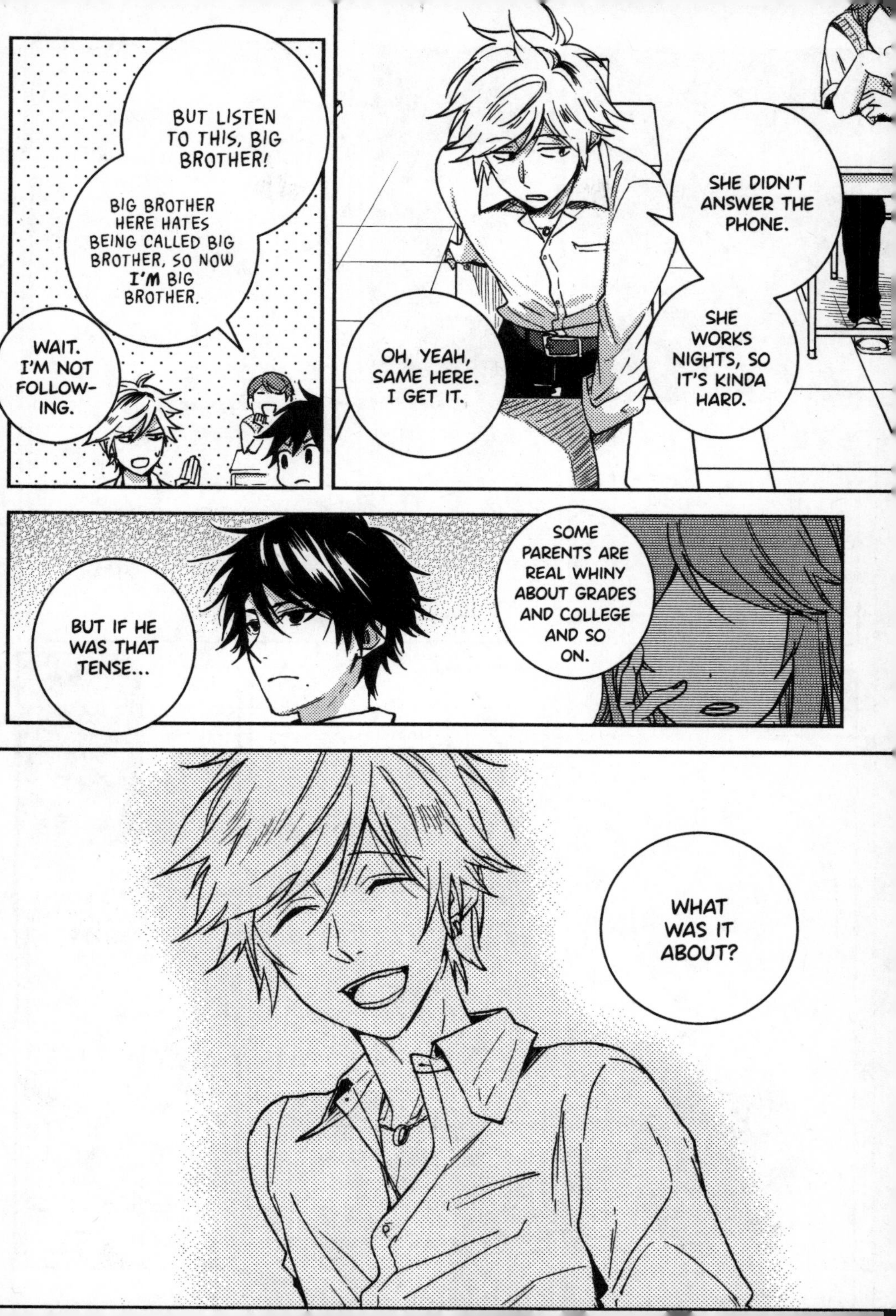
SHE DIDN'T ANSWER THE PHONE.
SHE WORKS NIGHTS, SO IT'S KINDA HARD.
OH, YEAH, SAME HERE. I GET IT.
BUT LISTEN TO THIS, BIG BROTHER!
BIG BROTHER HERE HATES BEING CALLED BIG BROTHER, SO NOW **I'M** BIG BROTHER.
WAIT. I'M NOT FOLLOW-ING.
SOME PARENTS ARE REAL WHINY ABOUT GRADES AND COLLEGE AND SO ON.
BUT IF HE WAS THAT TENSE...
WHAT WAS IT ABOUT?

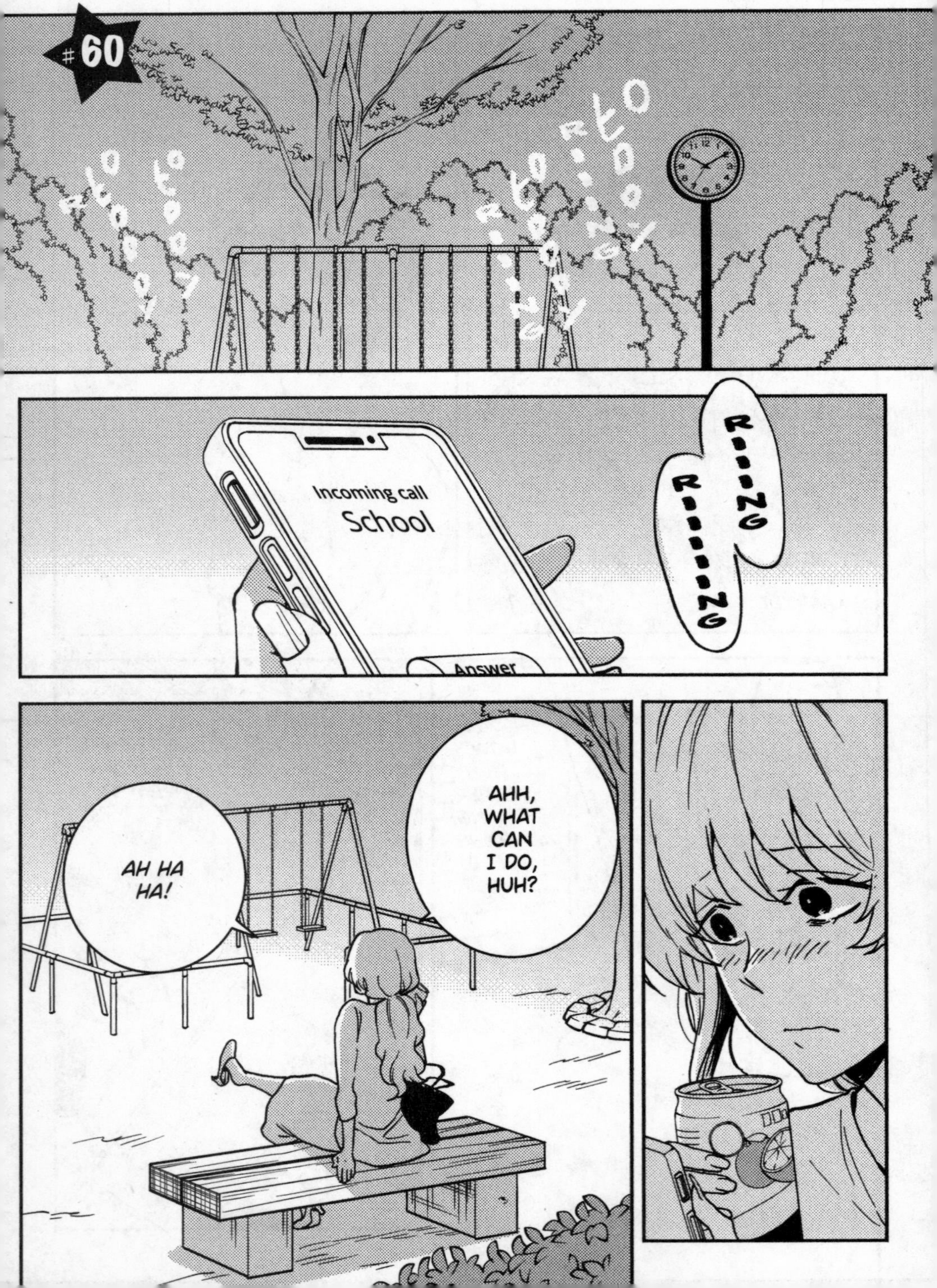
#60
Incoming call
School
Answer
RIIIING
RIIIIIIING
AHH, WHAT CAN I DO, HUH?
AH HA HA!

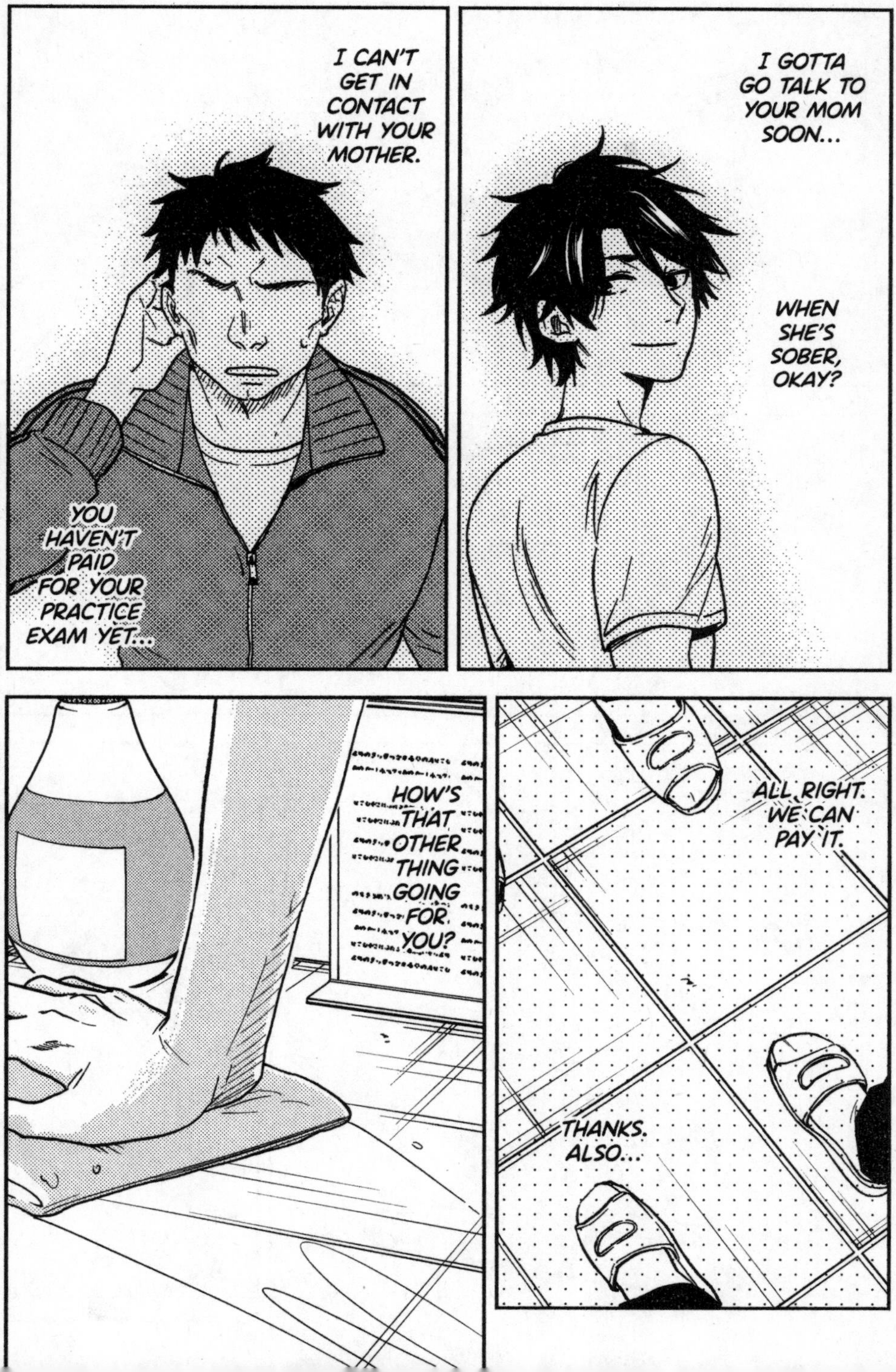
I GOTTA GO TALK TO YOUR MOM SOON...
WHEN SHE'S SOBER, OKAY?
I CAN'T GET IN CONTACT WITH YOUR MOTHER.
YOU HAVEN'T PAID FOR YOUR PRACTICE EXAM YET...
ALL RIGHT. WE CAN PAY IT.
THANKS. ALSO...
HOW'S THAT OTHER THING GOING FOR YOU?

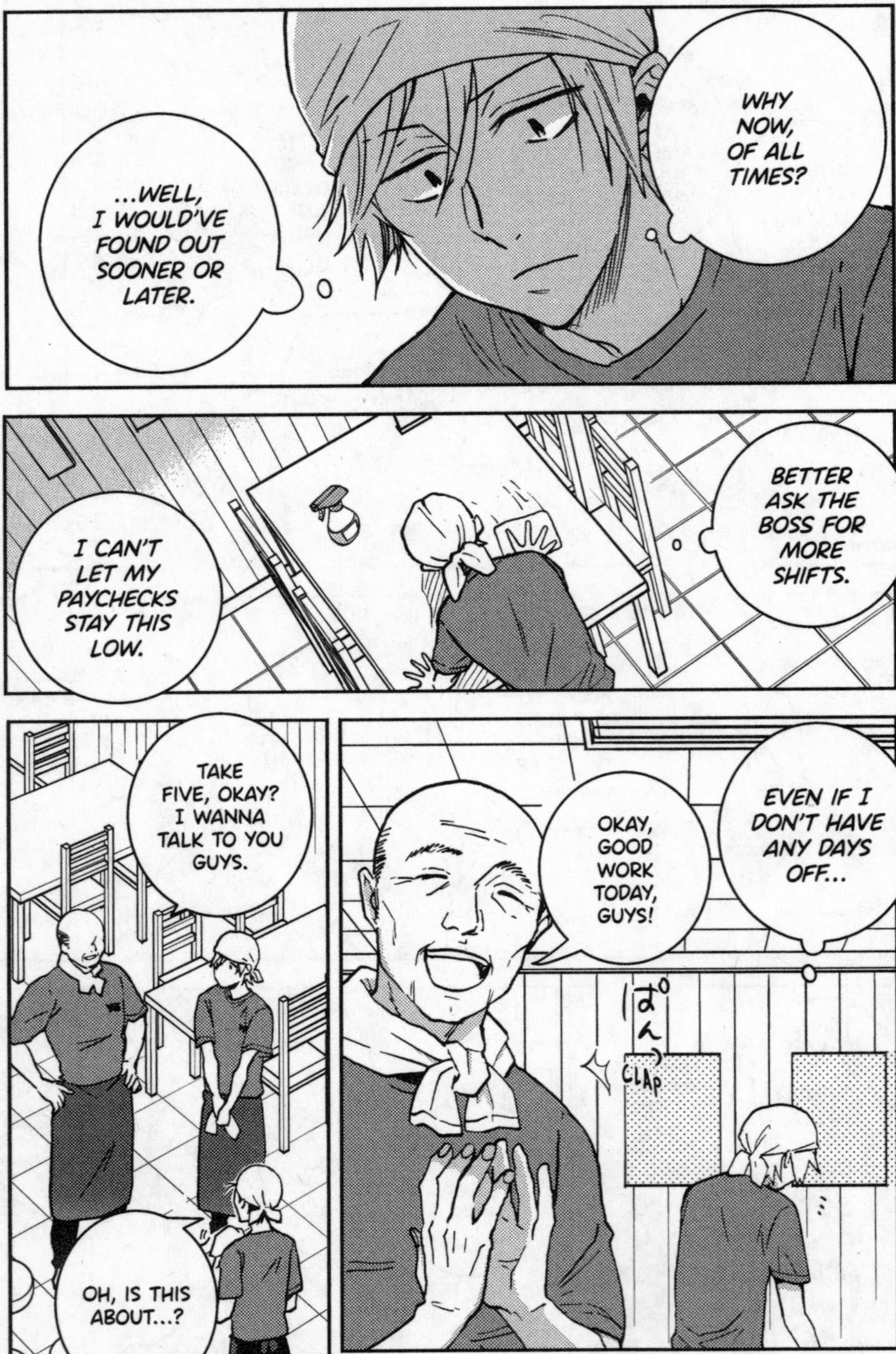
WHY NOW, OF ALL TIMES?
...WELL, I WOULD'VE FOUND OUT SOONER OR LATER.
BETTER ASK THE BOSS FOR MORE SHIFTS.
I CAN'T LET MY PAYCHECKS STAY THIS LOW.
EVEN IF I DON'T HAVE ANY DAYS OFF...
OKAY, GOOD WORK TODAY, GUYS!
ぱん
CLAP
TAKE FIVE, OKAY? I WANNA TALK TO YOU GUYS.
OH, IS THIS ABOUT...?

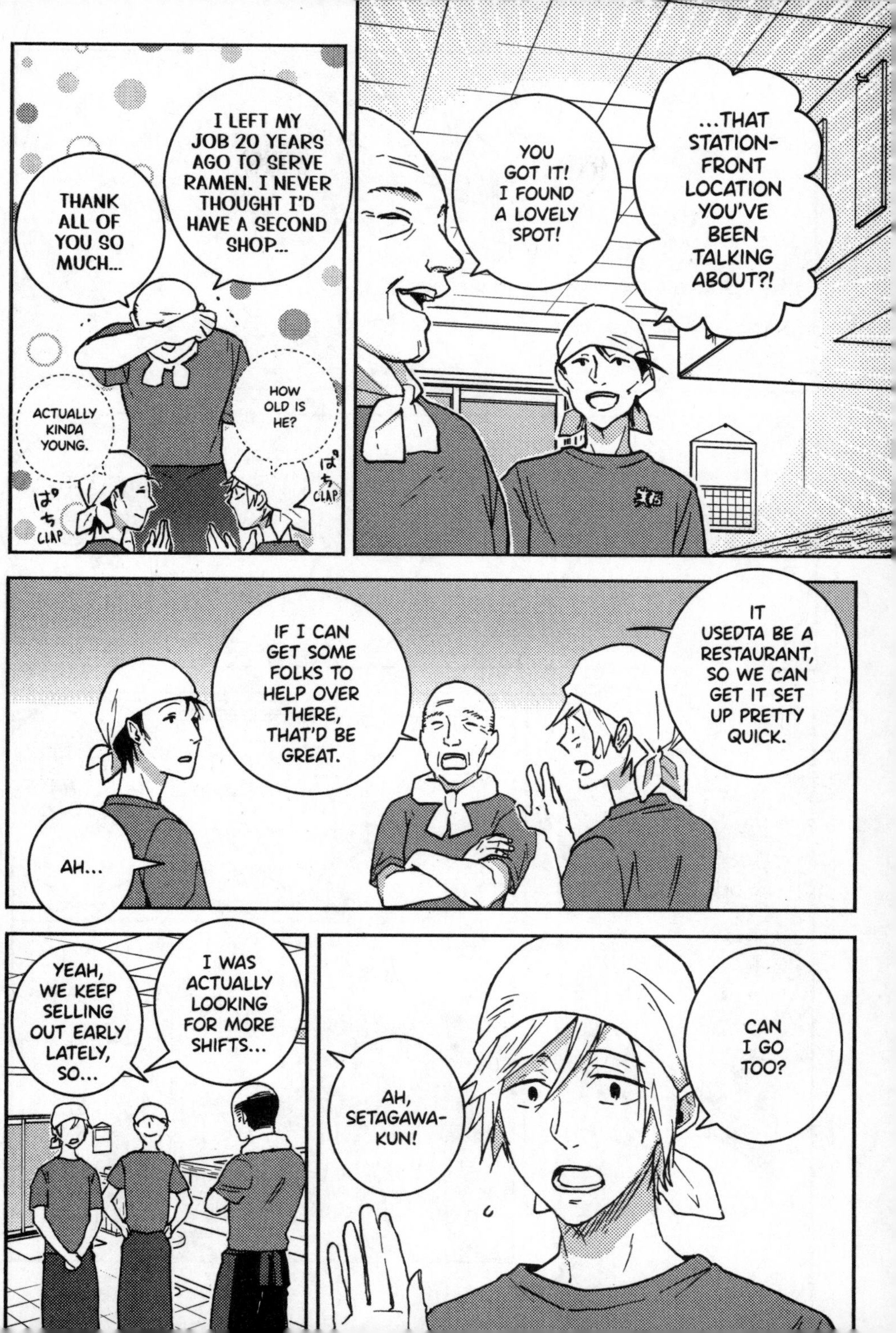
...THAT STATION-FRONT LOCATION YOU'VE BEEN TALKING ABOUT?!
YOU GOT IT! I FOUND A LOVELY SPOT!
I LEFT MY JOB 20 YEARS AGO TO SERVE RAMEN. I NEVER THOUGHT I'D HAVE A SECOND SHOP...
THANK ALL OF YOU SO MUCH...
HOW OLD IS HE?
ACTUALLY KINDA YOUNG.
ぱち CLAP
ぱち CLAP
IT USEDTA BE A RESTAURANT, SO WE CAN GET IT SET UP PRETTY QUICK.
IF I CAN GET SOME FOLKS TO HELP OVER THERE, THAT'D BE GREAT.
AH...
CAN I GO TOO?
AH, SETAGAWA-KUN!
I WAS ACTUALLY LOOKING FOR MORE SHIFTS...
YEAH, WE KEEP SELLING OUT EARLY LATELY, SO...

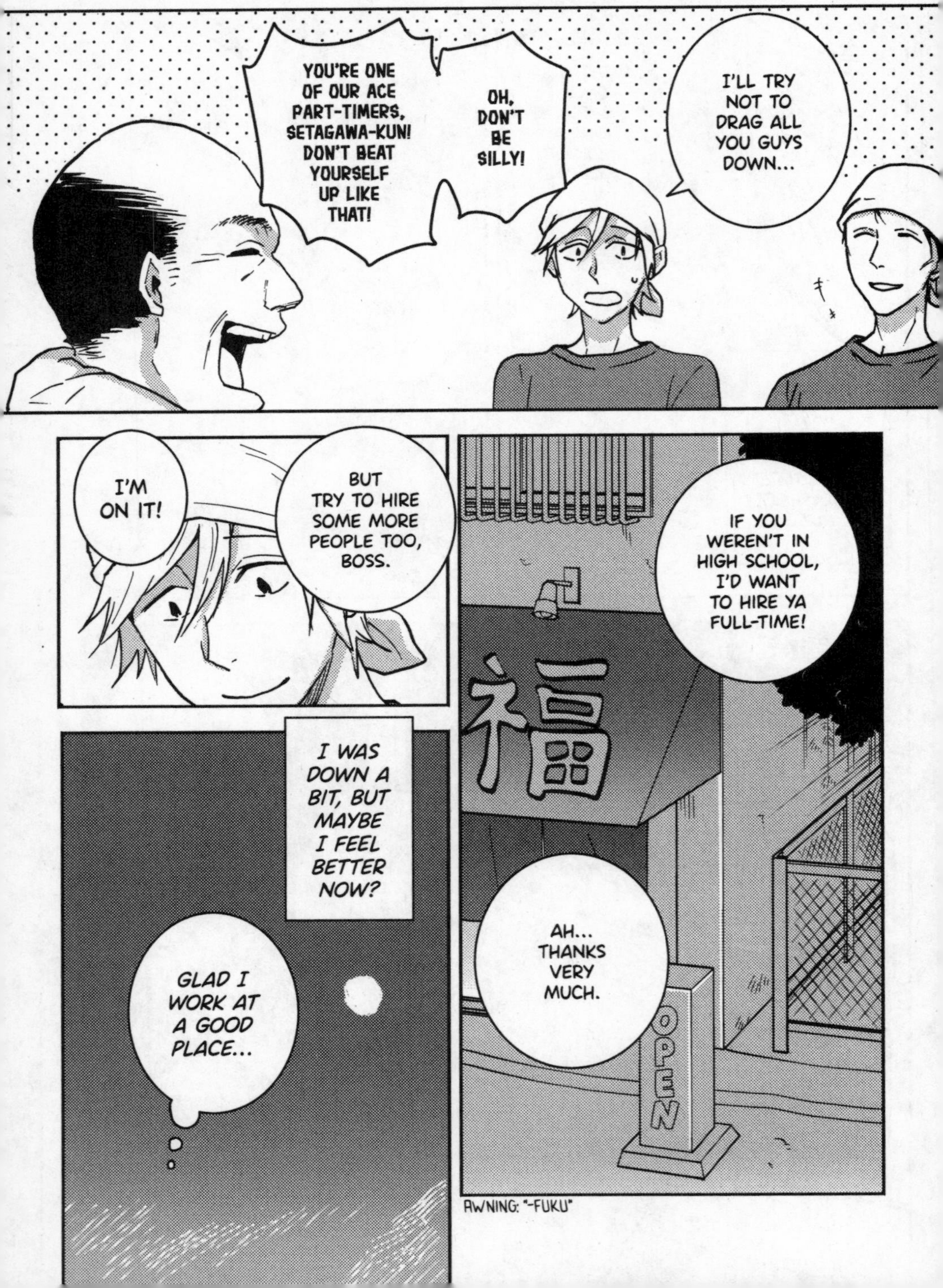
I'LL TRY NOT TO DRAG ALL YOU GUYS DOWN...
OH, DON'T BE SILLY!
YOU'RE ONE OF OUR ACE PART-TIMERS, SETAGAWA-KUN! DON'T BEAT YOURSELF UP LIKE THAT!
IF YOU WEREN'T IN HIGH SCHOOL, I'D WANT TO HIRE YA FULL-TIME!
福
AH... THANKS VERY MUCH.
OPEN
BUT TRY TO HIRE SOME MORE PEOPLE TOO, BOSS.
I'M ON IT!
I WAS DOWN A BIT, BUT MAYBE I FEEL BETTER NOW?
GLAD I WORK AT A GOOD PLACE...
AWNING: "-FUKU"

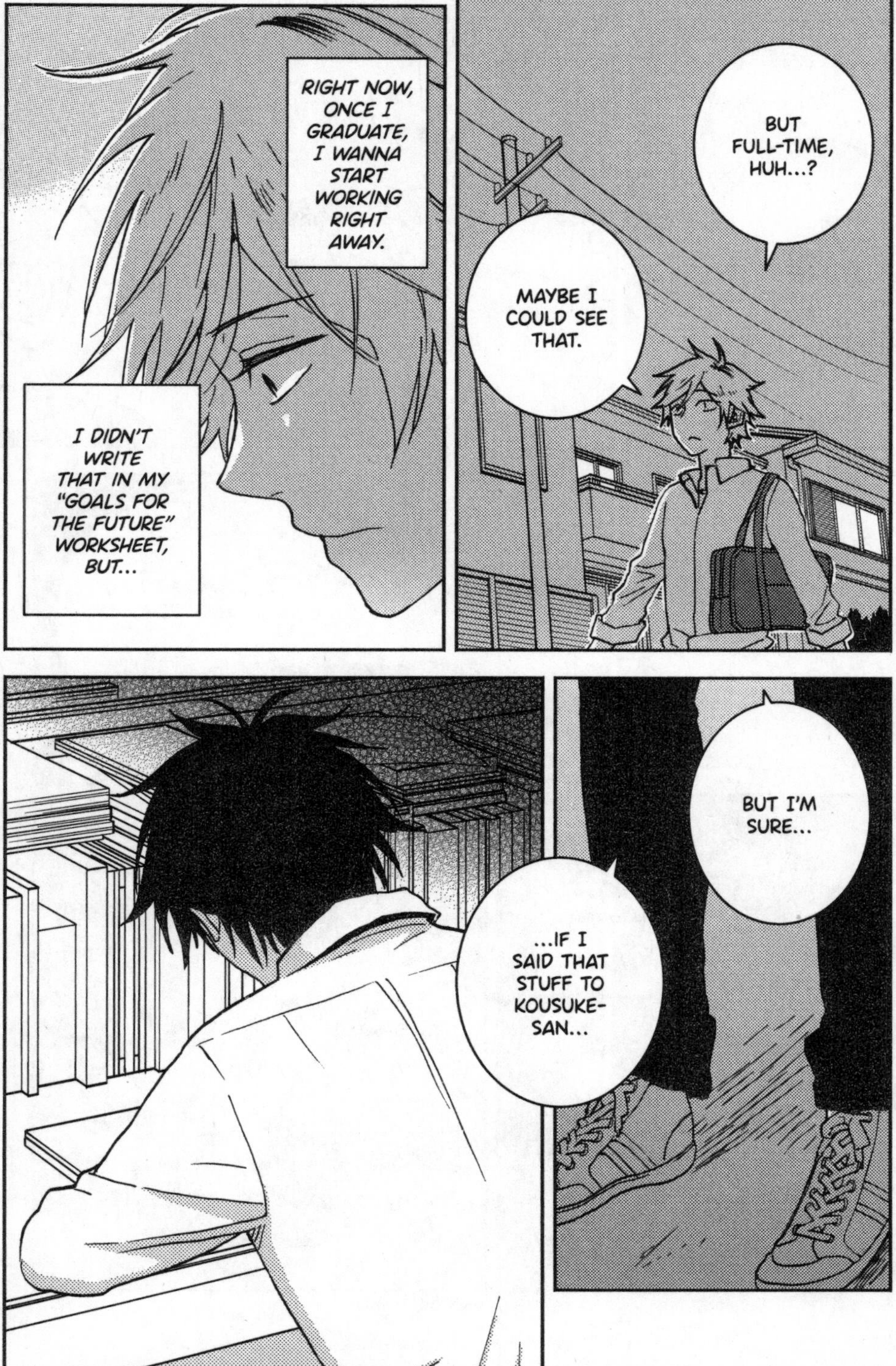
BUT FULL-TIME, HUH...?
MAYBE I COULD SEE THAT.
RIGHT NOW, ONCE I GRADUATE, I WANNA START WORKING RIGHT AWAY.
I DIDN'T WRITE THAT IN MY "GOALS FOR THE FUTURE" WORKSHEET, BUT...
BUT I'M SURE...
...IF I SAID THAT STUFF TO KOUSUKE-SAN...

WHAT GOZUTA-SENSEI SAID TODAY...

WAS IT ABOUT MASA-HIRO?

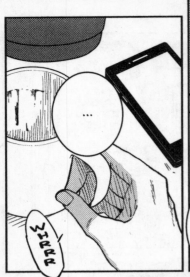

...

WHRRR

MY PHONE?

AH, WELL, NOBODY'S HERE...

HEY, KOU-CHAN! IT'S ME.

OH, HI, HOUJOU.

YELLO?

OH!

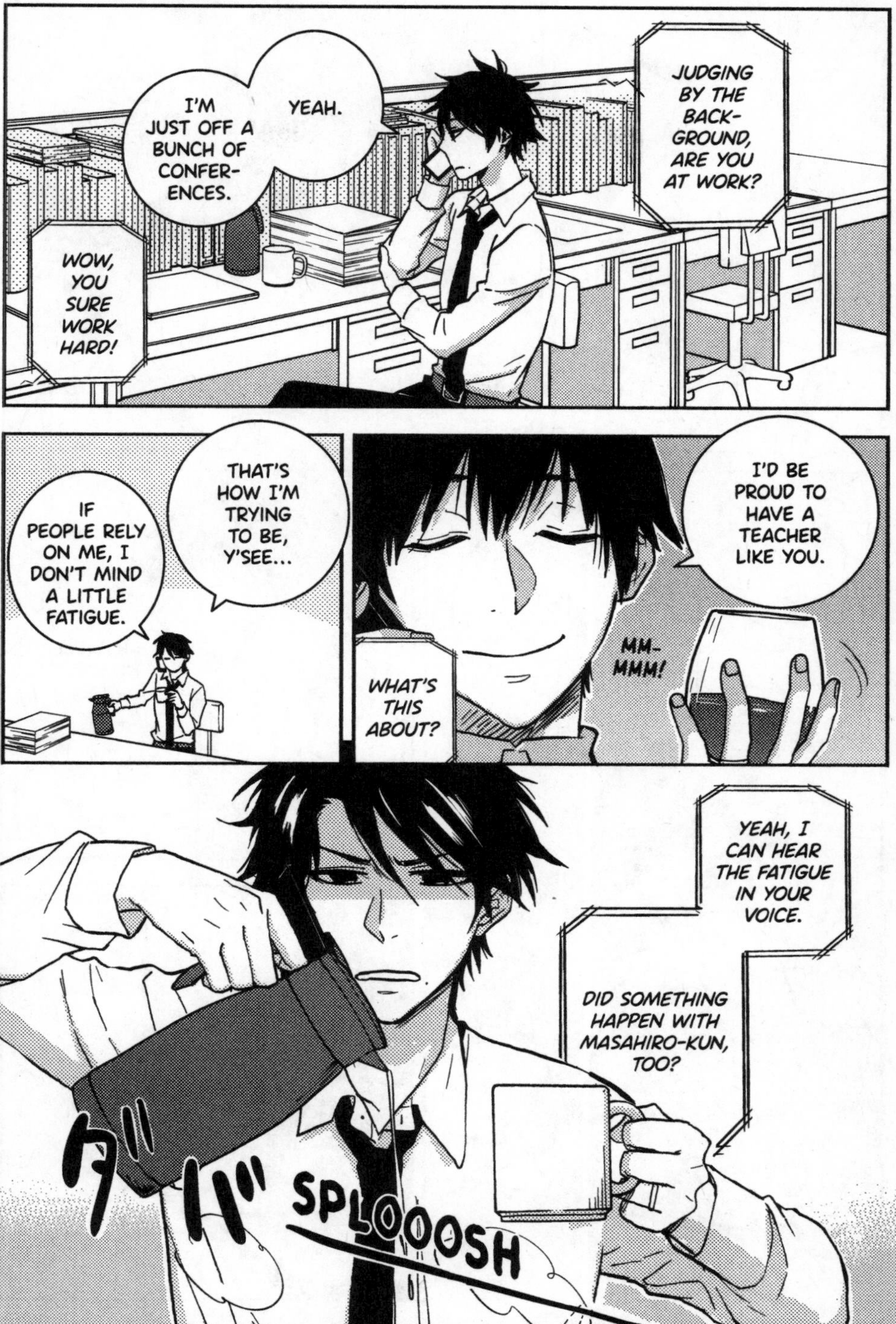
JUDGING BY THE BACK-GROUND, ARE YOU AT WORK?
YEAH.
I'M JUST OFF A BUNCH OF CONFER-ENCES.
WOW, YOU SURE WORK HARD!
I'D BE PROUD TO HAVE A TEACHER LIKE YOU.
MM-MMM!
WHAT'S THIS ABOUT?
THAT'S HOW I'M TRYING TO BE, Y'SEE...
IF PEOPLE RELY ON ME, I DON'T MIND A LITTLE FATIGUE.
YEAH, I CAN HEAR THE FATIGUE IN YOUR VOICE.
DID SOMETHING HAPPEN WITH MASAHIRO-KUN, TOO?
SPLOOOSH

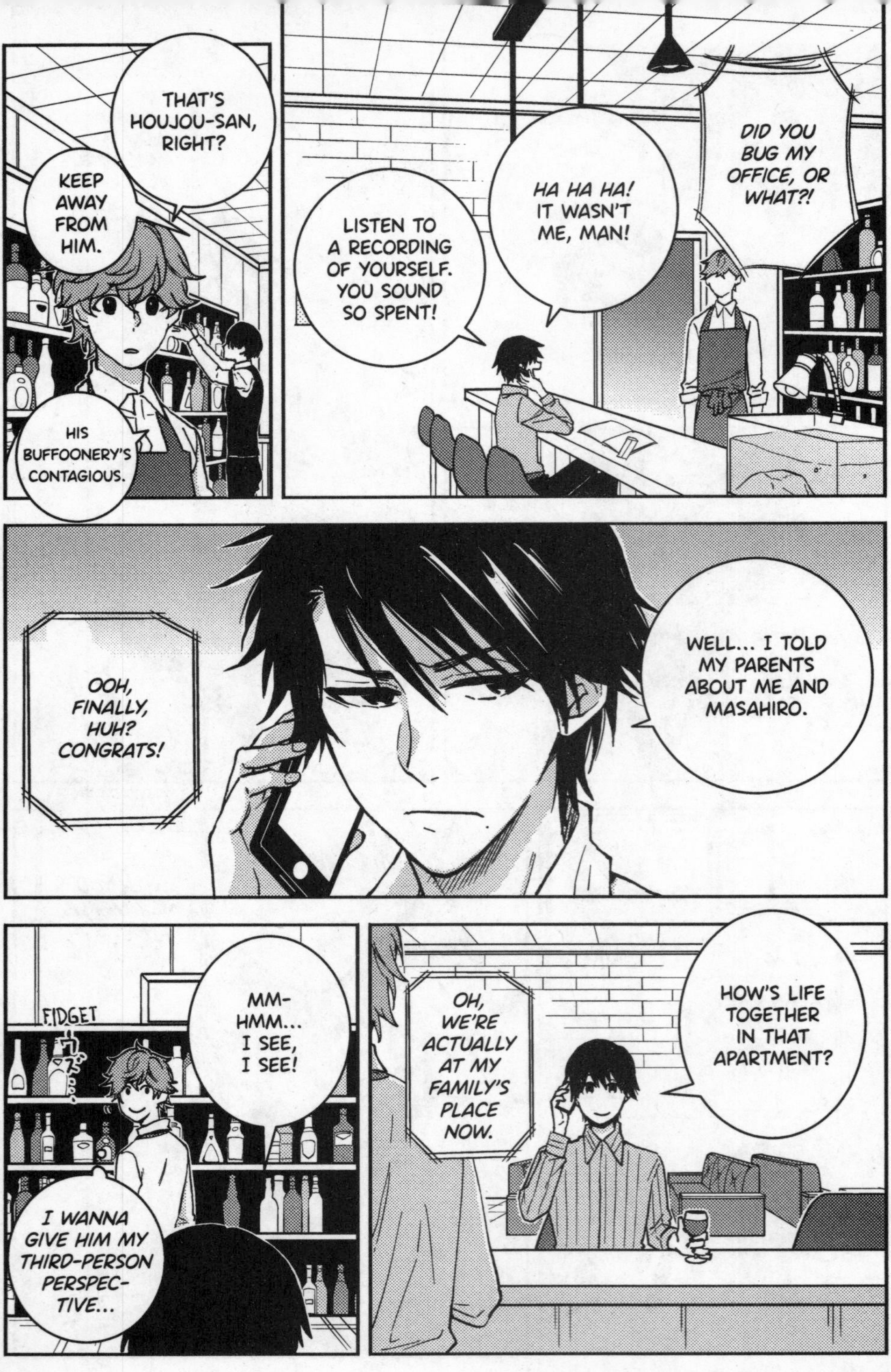
DID YOU BUG MY OFFICE, OR WHAT?!
HA HA HA! IT WASN'T ME, MAN!
LISTEN TO A RECORDING OF YOURSELF. YOU SOUND SO SPENT!
THAT'S HOUJOU-SAN, RIGHT?
KEEP AWAY FROM HIM.
HIS BUFFOONERY'S CONTAGIOUS.
WELL... I TOLD MY PARENTS ABOUT ME AND MASAHIRO.
OOH, FINALLY, HUH? CONGRATS!
HOW'S LIFE TOGETHER IN THAT APARTMENT?
OH, WE'RE ACTUALLY AT MY FAMILY'S PLACE NOW.
FIDGET
MM-HMM... I SEE, I SEE!
I WANNA GIVE HIM MY THIRD-PERSON PERSPEC-TIVE...

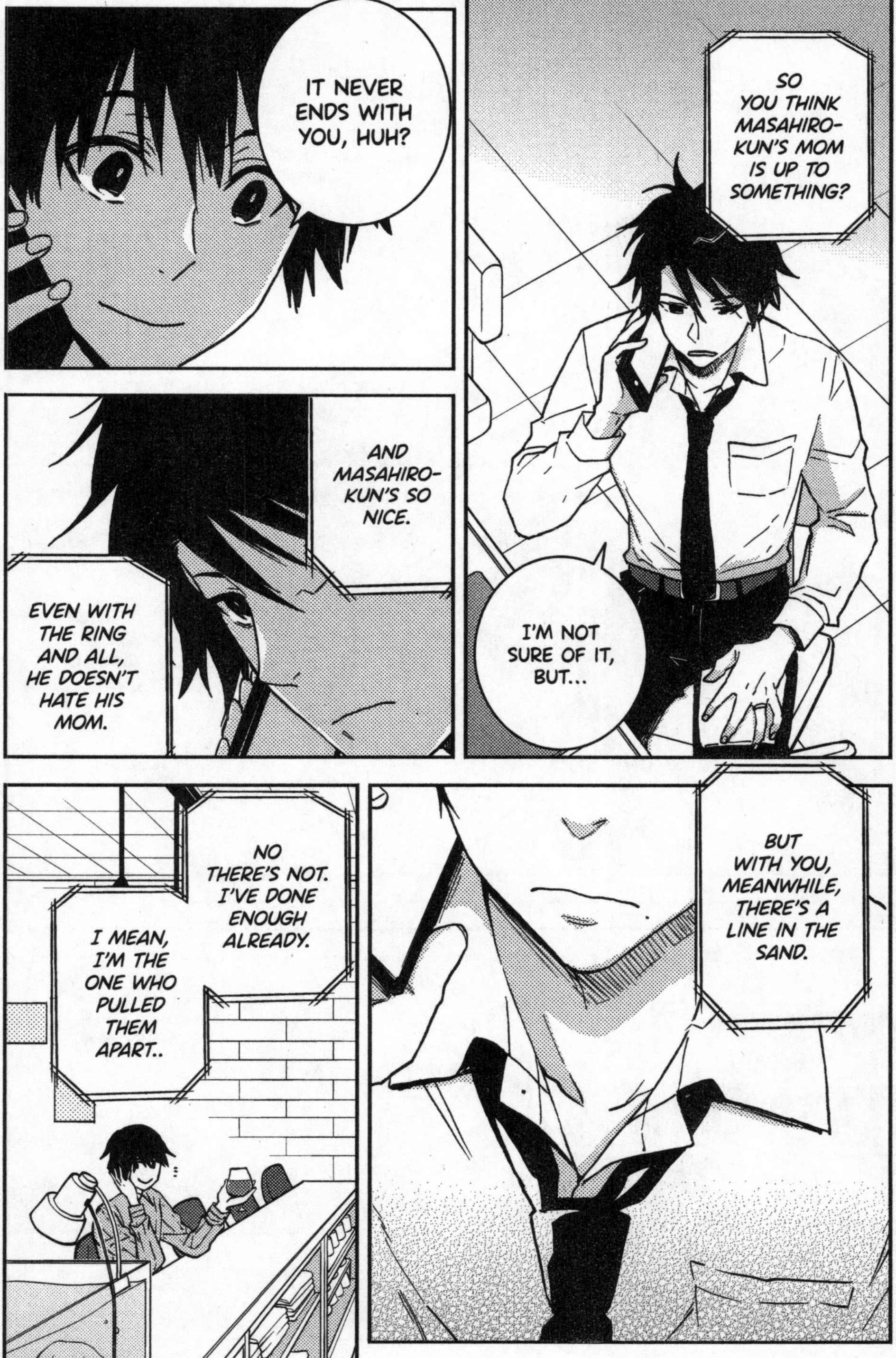
SO YOU THINK MASAHIRO-KUN'S MOM IS UP TO SOMETHING?
I'M NOT SURE OF IT, BUT...
IT NEVER ENDS WITH YOU, HUH?
AND MASAHIRO-KUN'S SO NICE.
EVEN WITH THE RING AND ALL, HE DOESN'T HATE HIS MOM.
BUT WITH YOU, MEANWHILE, THERE'S A LINE IN THE SAND.
NO THERE'S NOT. I'VE DONE ENOUGH ALREADY.
I MEAN, I'M THE ONE WHO PULLED THEM APART..

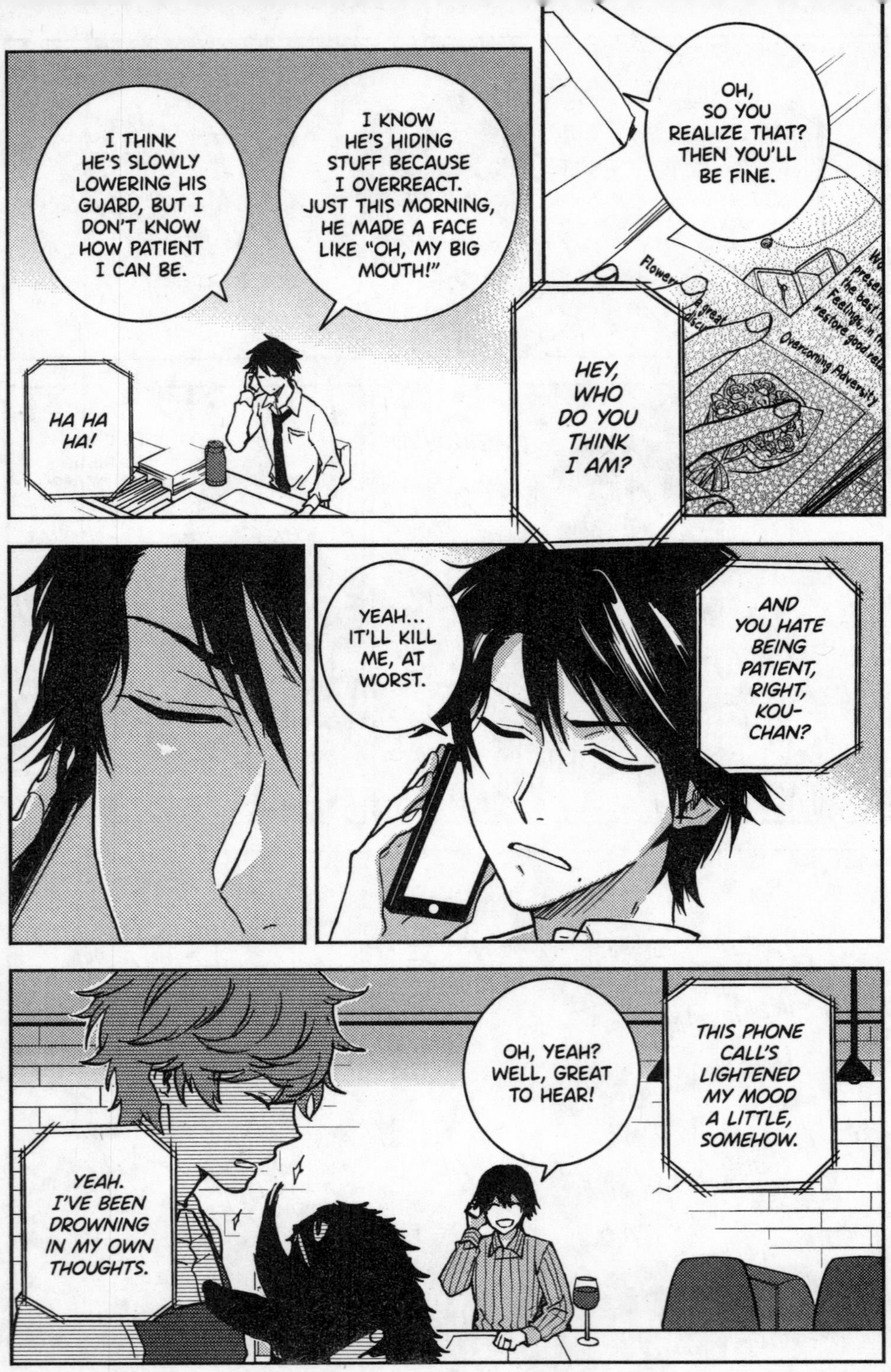
OH, SO YOU REALIZE THAT? THEN YOU'LL BE FINE.
Overcoming Adversity
HEY, WHO DO YOU THINK I AM?
I KNOW HE'S HIDING STUFF BECAUSE I OVERREACT. JUST THIS MORNING, HE MADE A FACE LIKE "OH, MY BIG MOUTH!"
I THINK HE'S SLOWLY LOWERING HIS GUARD, BUT I DON'T KNOW HOW PATIENT I CAN BE.
HA HA HA!
AND YOU HATE BEING PATIENT, RIGHT, KOU-CHAN?
YEAH... IT'LL KILL ME, AT WORST.
THIS PHONE CALL'S LIGHTENED MY MOOD A LITTLE, SOMEHOW.
OH, YEAH? WELL, GREAT TO HEAR!
YEAH. I'VE BEEN DROWNING IN MY OWN THOUGHTS.

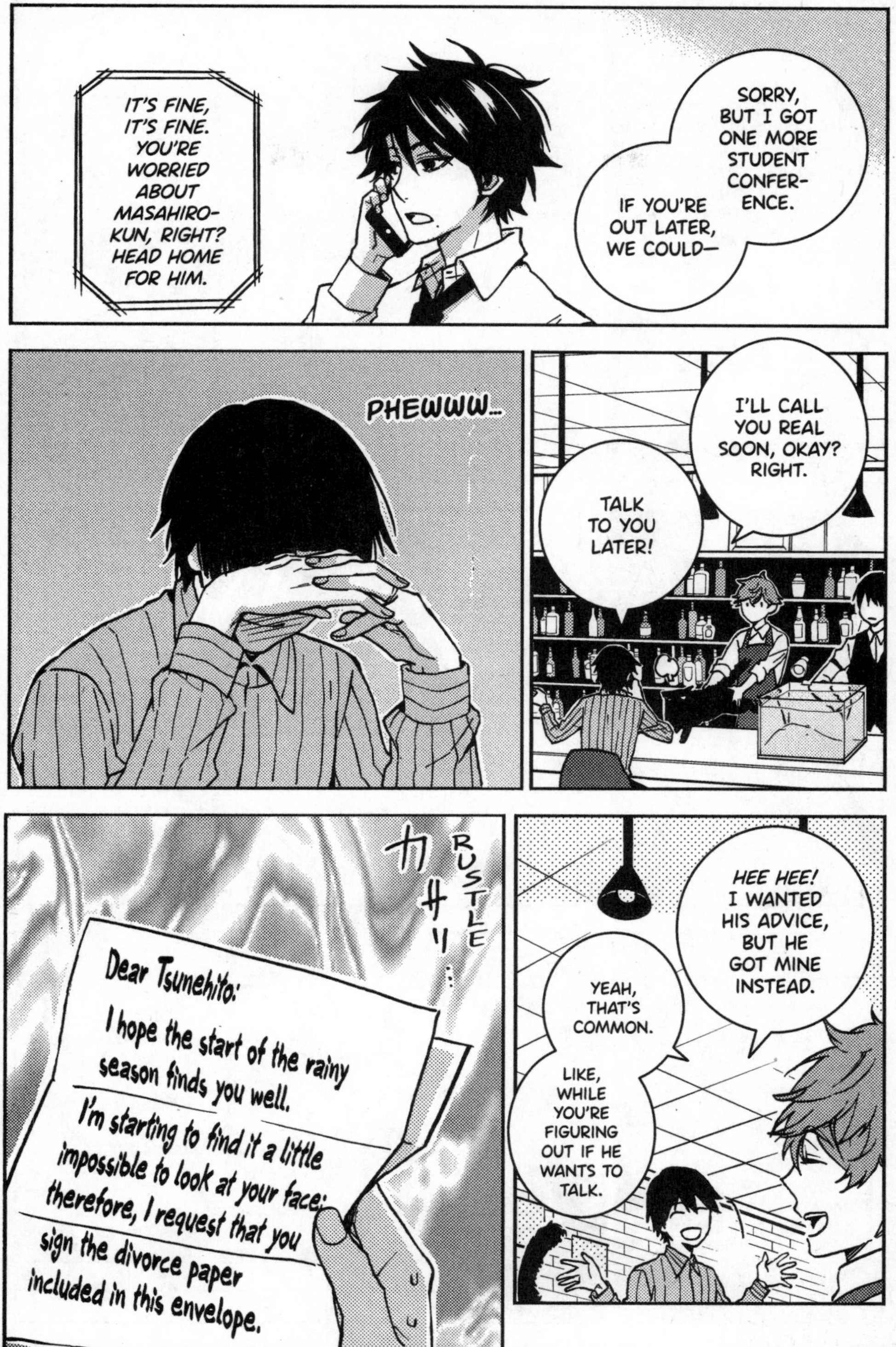
SORRY, BUT I GOT ONE MORE STUDENT CONFERENCE.
IF YOU'RE OUT LATER, WE COULD—
IT'S FINE, IT'S FINE. YOU'RE WORRIED ABOUT MASAHIRO-KUN, RIGHT? HEAD HOME FOR HIM.
I'LL CALL YOU REAL SOON, OKAY? RIGHT.
TALK TO YOU LATER!
PHEWWW...
HEE HEE! I WANTED HIS ADVICE, BUT HE GOT MINE INSTEAD.
YEAH, THAT'S COMMON.
LIKE, WHILE YOU'RE FIGURING OUT IF HE WANTS TO TALK.
カサリ
RUSTLE
Dear Tsunehito:
I hope the start of the rainy season finds you well.
I'm starting to find it a little impossible to look at your face; therefore, I request that you sign the divorce paper included in this envelope.

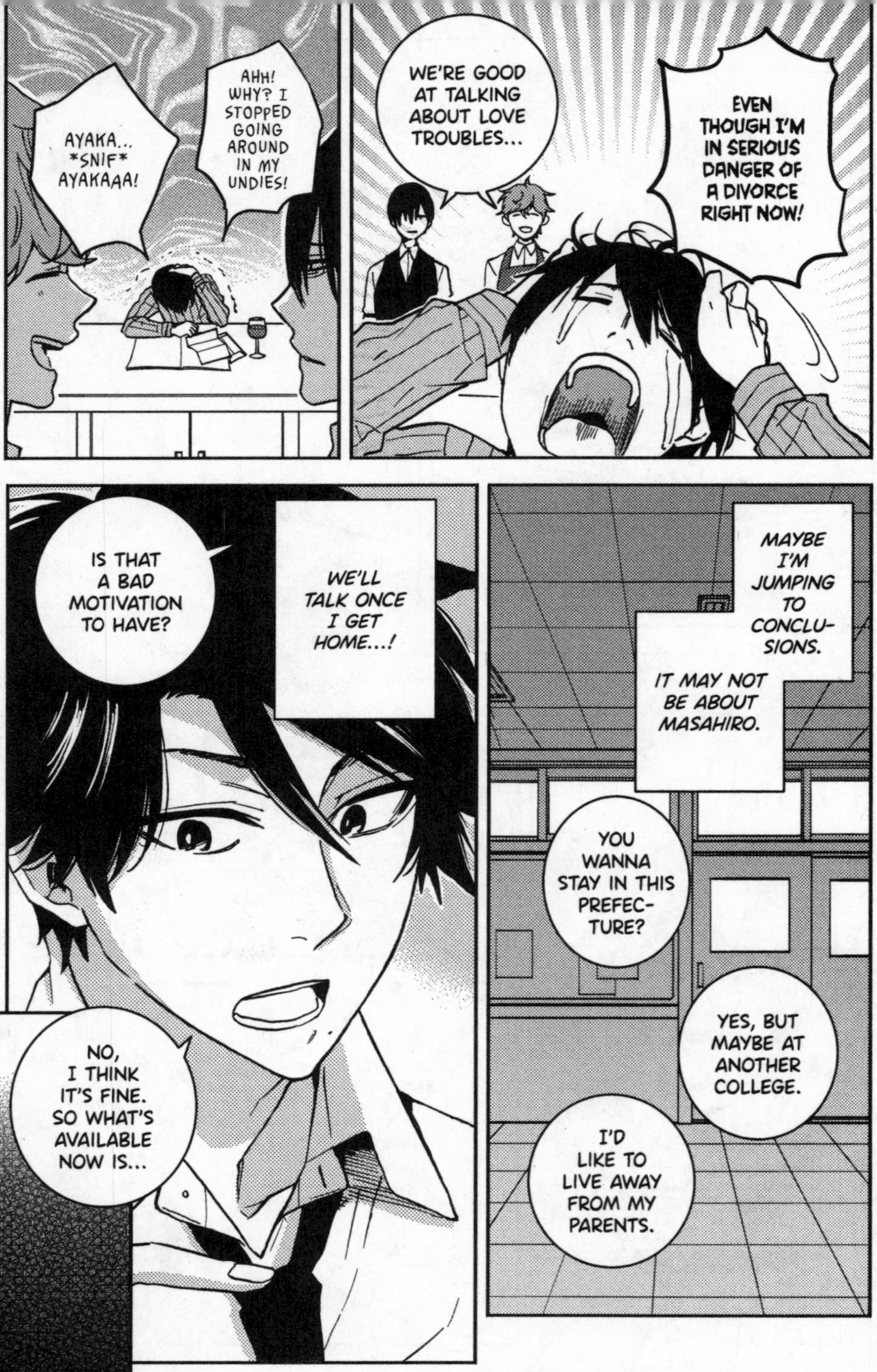
WE'RE GOOD AT TALKING ABOUT LOVE TROUBLES...
EVEN THOUGH I'M IN SERIOUS DANGER OF A DIVORCE RIGHT NOW!
AHH! WHY? I STOPPED GOING AROUND IN MY UNDIES!
AYAKA... *SNIF* AYAKAAA!
MAYBE I'M JUMPING TO CONCLUSIONS.
IT MAY NOT BE ABOUT MASAHIRO.
YOU WANNA STAY IN THIS PREFECTURE?
YES, BUT MAYBE AT ANOTHER COLLEGE.
I'D LIKE TO LIVE AWAY FROM MY PARENTS.
WE'LL TALK ONCE I GET HOME...!
IS THAT A BAD MOTIVATION TO HAVE?
NO, I THINK IT'S FINE. SO WHAT'S AVAILABLE NOW IS...

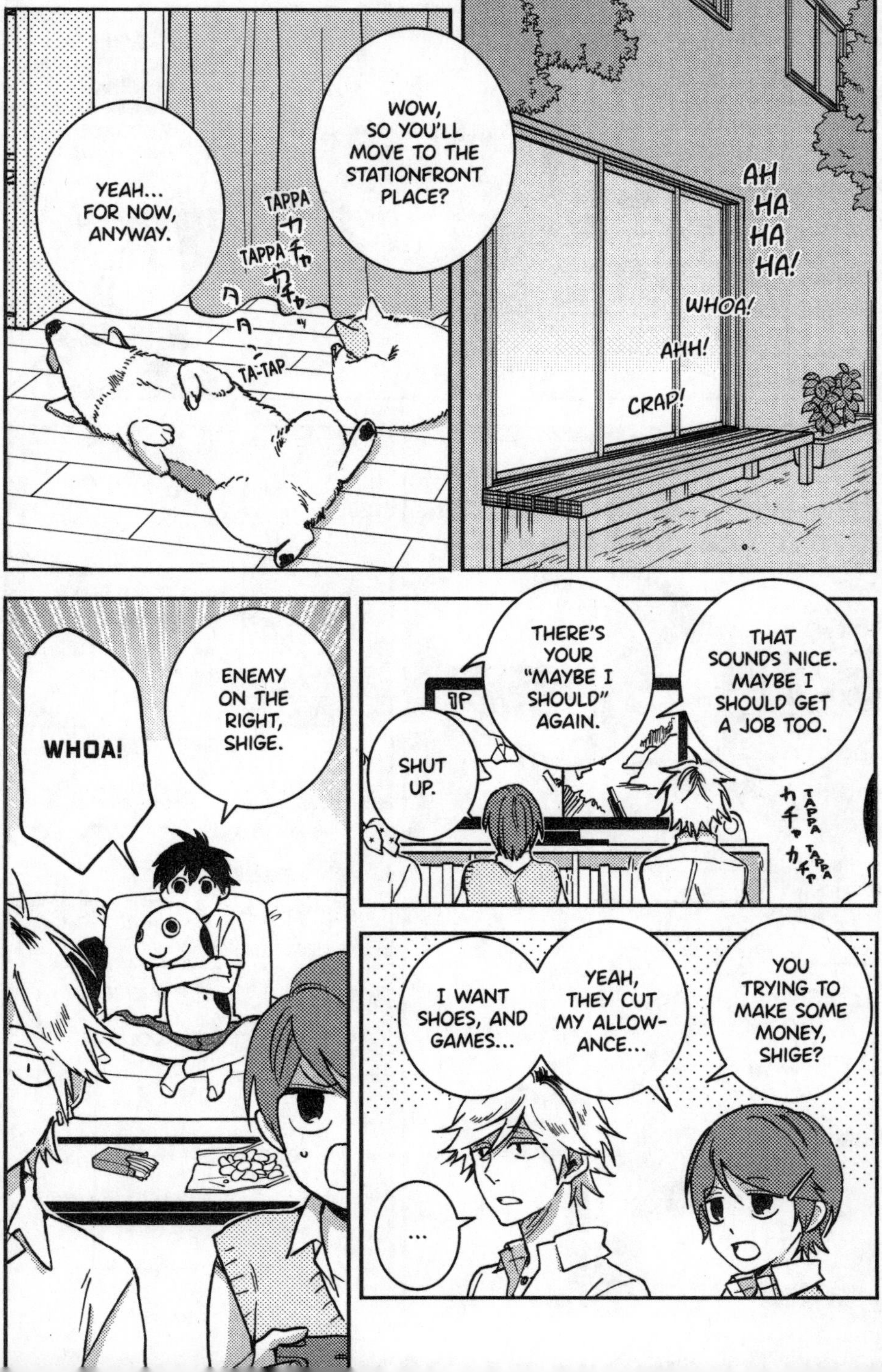
AH HA HA HA!
WHOA!
AHH!
CRAP!
WOW, SO YOU'LL MOVE TO THE STATIONFRONT PLACE?
YEAH... FOR NOW, ANYWAY.
TAPPA カチャ
TAPPA カチャ
TA-TAP
THAT SOUNDS NICE. MAYBE I SHOULD GET A JOB TOO.
THERE'S YOUR "MAYBE I SHOULD" AGAIN.
SHUT UP.
TAPPA カチャ TAPPA カチャ
YOU TRYING TO MAKE SOME MONEY, SHIGE?
YEAH, THEY CUT MY ALLOW-ANCE...
I WANT SHOES, AND GAMES...
...
ENEMY ON THE RIGHT, SHIGE.
WHOA!

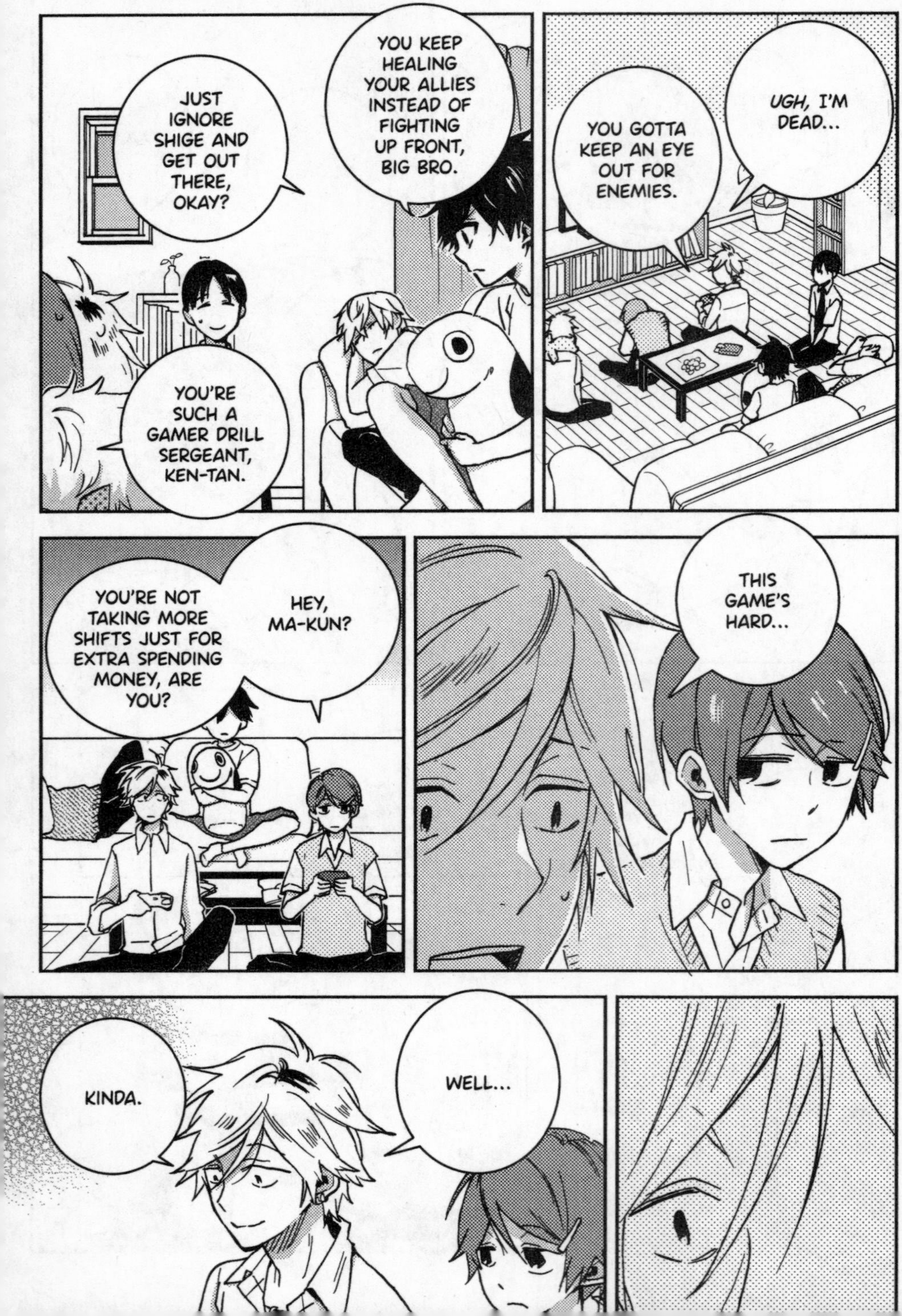
UGH, I'M DEAD...
YOU GOTTA KEEP AN EYE OUT FOR ENEMIES.
YOU KEEP HEALING YOUR ALLIES INSTEAD OF FIGHTING UP FRONT, BIG BRO.
JUST IGNORE SHIGE AND GET OUT THERE, OKAY?
YOU'RE SUCH A GAMER DRILL SERGEANT, KEN-TAN.
THIS GAME'S HARD...
HEY, MA-KUN?
YOU'RE NOT TAKING MORE SHIFTS JUST FOR EXTRA SPENDING MONEY, ARE YOU?
WELL...
KINDA.

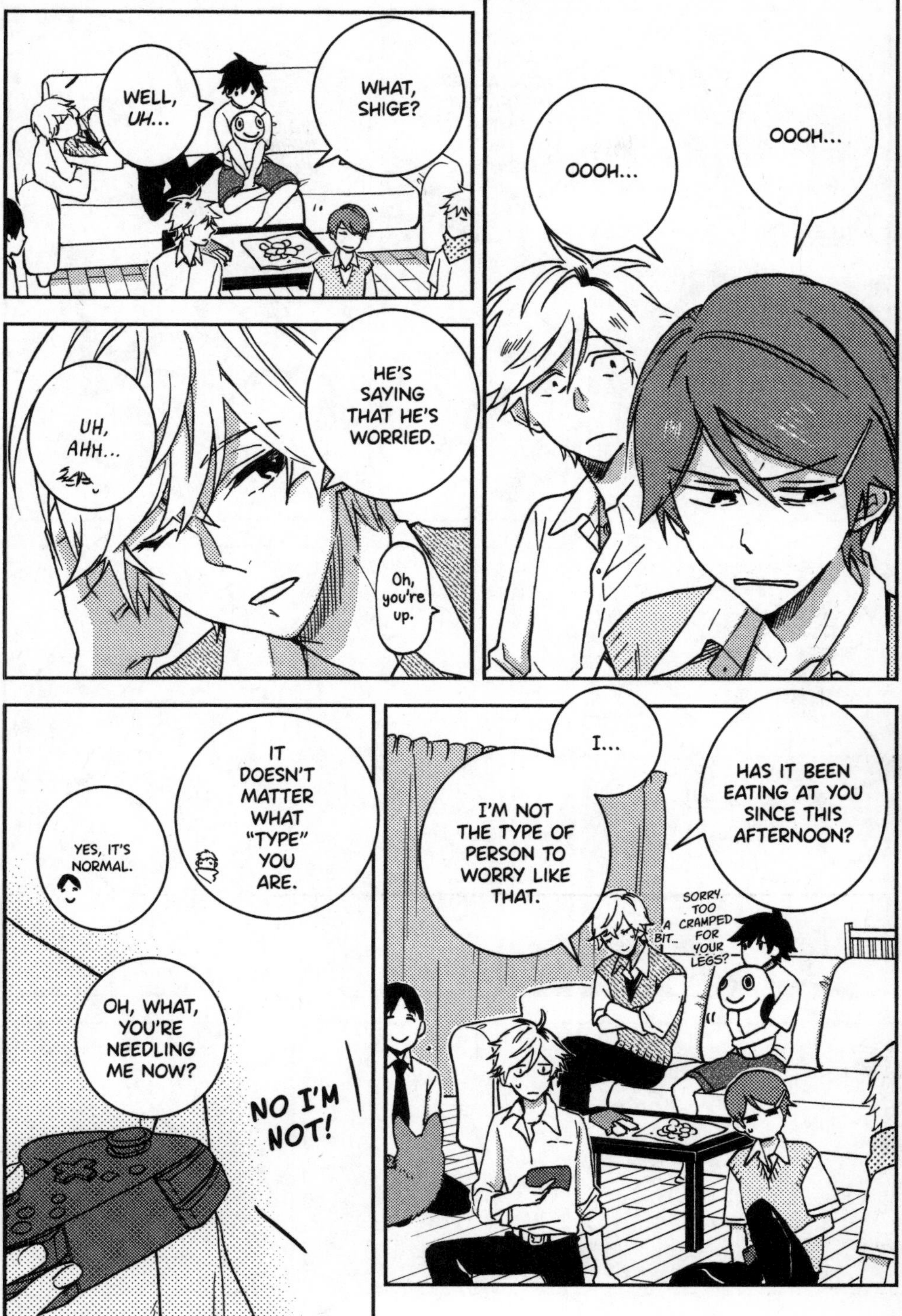
OOOH...
OOOH...
WHAT, SHIGE?
WELL, UH...
HE'S SAYING THAT HE'S WORRIED.
UH, AHH...
Oh, you're up.
HAS IT BEEN EATING AT YOU SINCE THIS AFTERNOON?
I...
I'M NOT THE TYPE OF PERSON TO WORRY LIKE THAT.
SORRY. TOO CRAMPED FOR YOUR LEGS?
A BIT...
IT DOESN'T MATTER WHAT "TYPE" YOU ARE.
YES, IT'S NORMAL.
OH, WHAT, YOU'RE NEEDLING ME NOW?
NO I'M NOT!

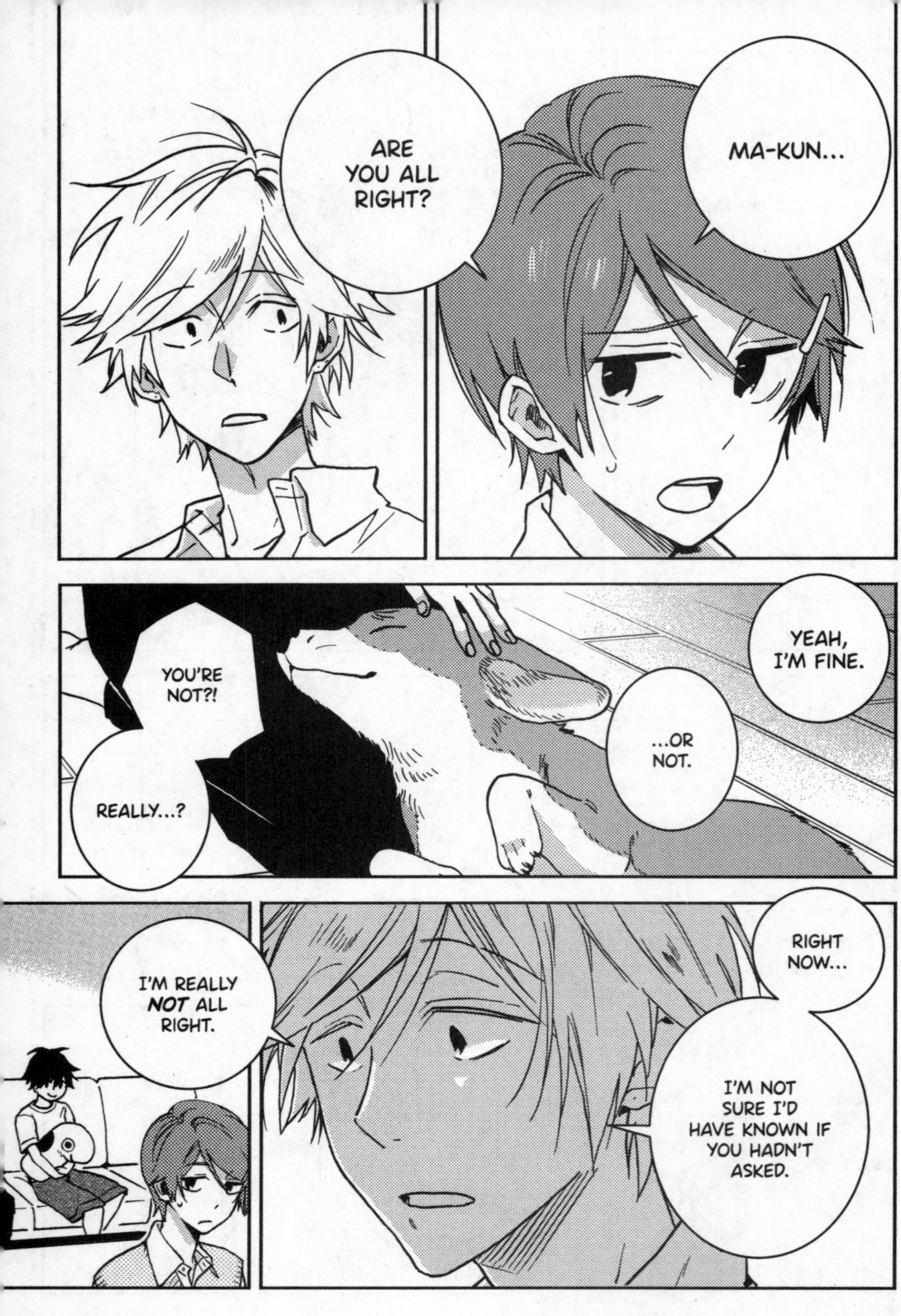

MA-KUN...
ARE YOU ALL RIGHT?
YEAH, I'M FINE.
...OR NOT.
YOU'RE NOT?!
REALLY...?
RIGHT NOW...
I'M REALLY *NOT* ALL RIGHT.
I'M NOT SURE I'D HAVE KNOWN IF YOU HADN'T ASKED.

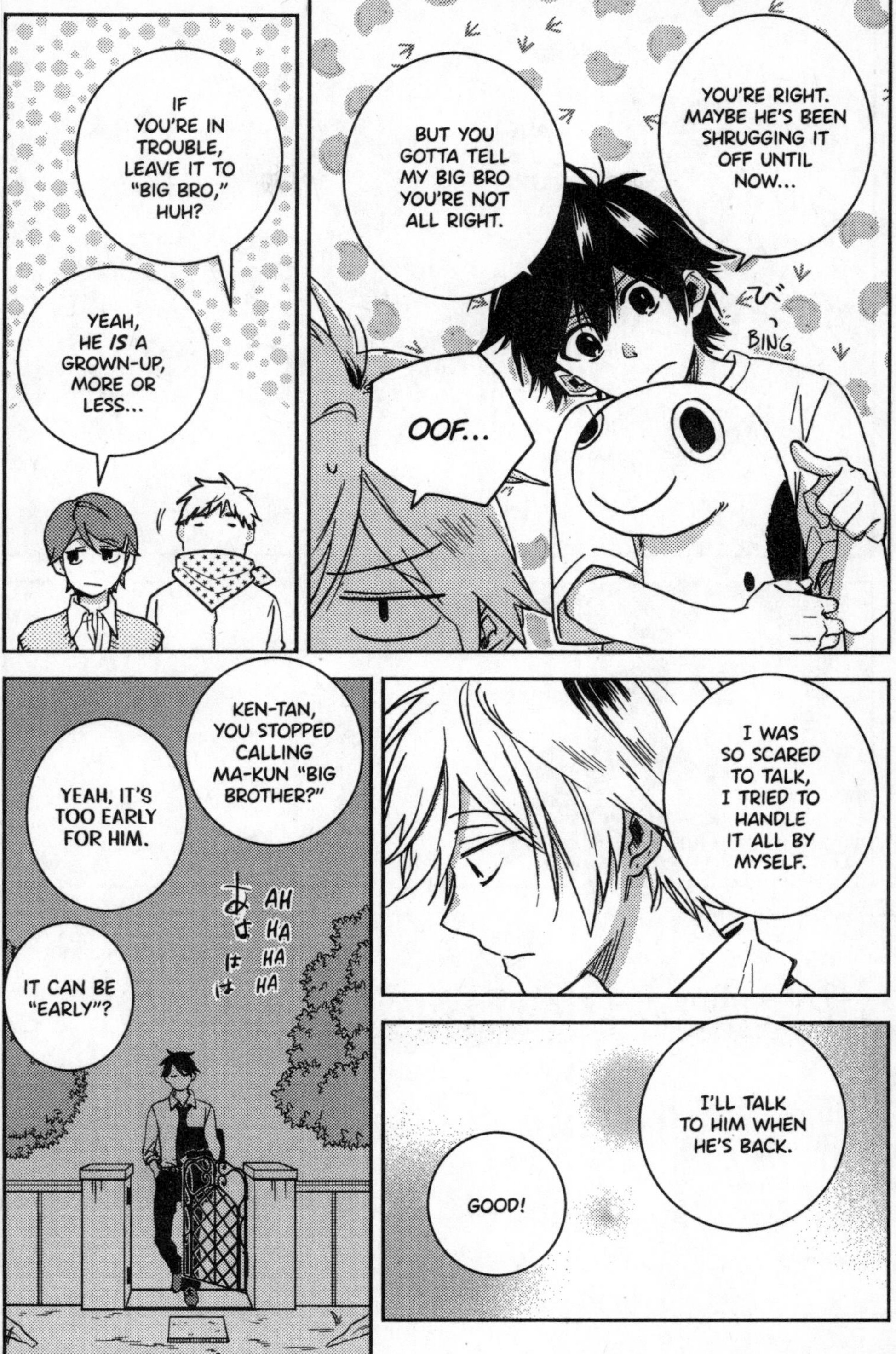
YOU'RE RIGHT. MAYBE HE'S BEEN SHRUGGING IT OFF UNTIL NOW...
BUT YOU GOTTA TELL MY BIG BRO YOU'RE NOT ALL RIGHT.
びっ BING
OOF...
IF YOU'RE IN TROUBLE, LEAVE IT TO "BIG BRO," HUH?
YEAH, HE *IS* A GROWN-UP, MORE OR LESS...
I WAS SO SCARED TO TALK, I TRIED TO HANDLE IT ALL BY MYSELF.
I'LL TALK TO HIM WHEN HE'S BACK.
GOOD!
KEN-TAN, YOU STOPPED CALLING MA-KUN "BIG BROTHER?"
YEAH, IT'S TOO EARLY FOR HIM.
あははは AH HA HA HA
IT CAN BE "EARLY"?

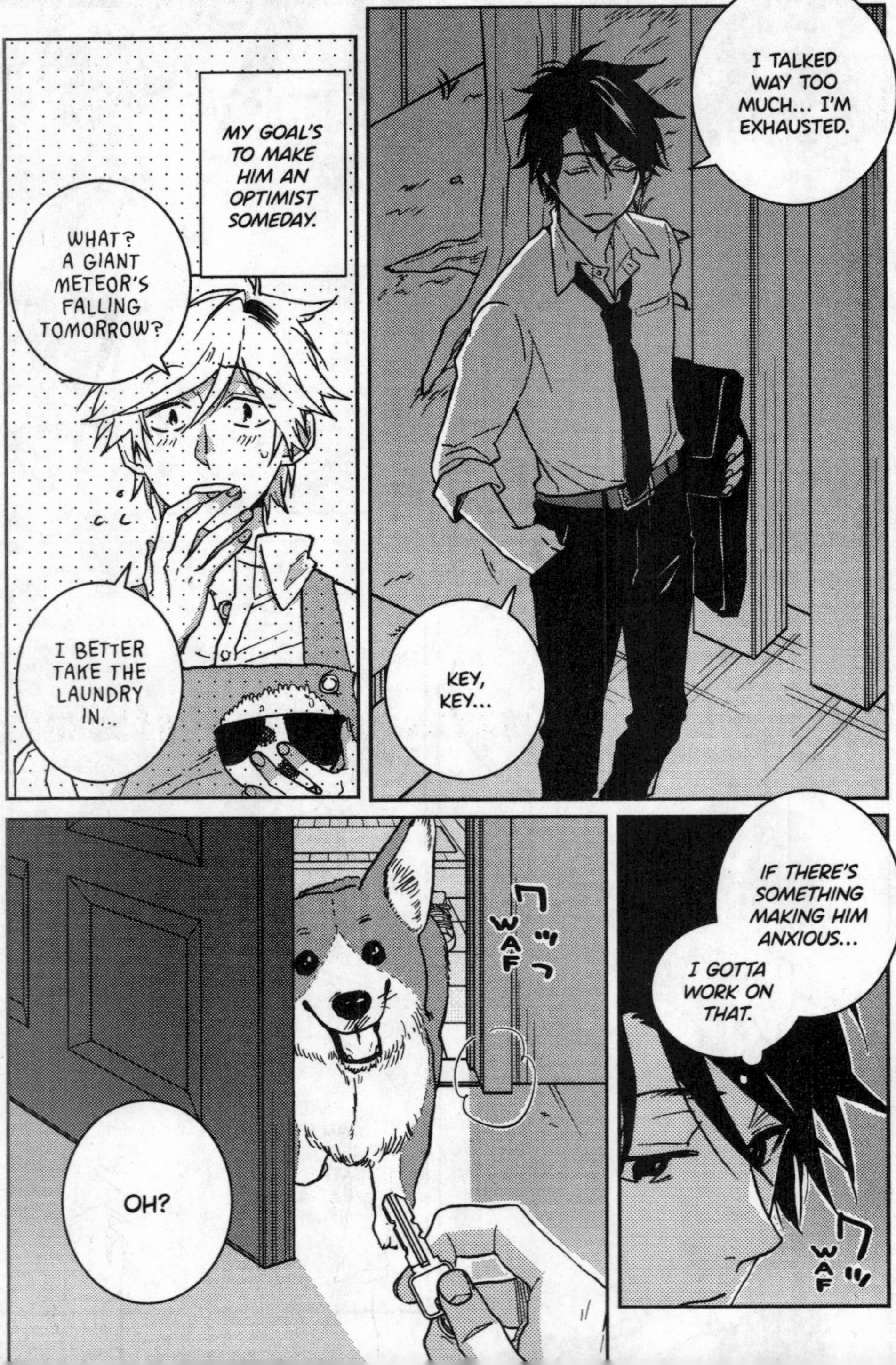
I TALKED WAY TOO MUCH... I'M EXHAUSTED.
KEY, KEY...
MY GOAL'S TO MAKE HIM AN OPTIMIST SOMEDAY.
WHAT? A GIANT METEOR'S FALLING TOMORROW?
I BETTER TAKE THE LAUNDRY IN...
IF THERE'S SOMETHING MAKING HIM ANXIOUS...
I GOTTA WORK ON THAT.
WAF
WAF
OH?

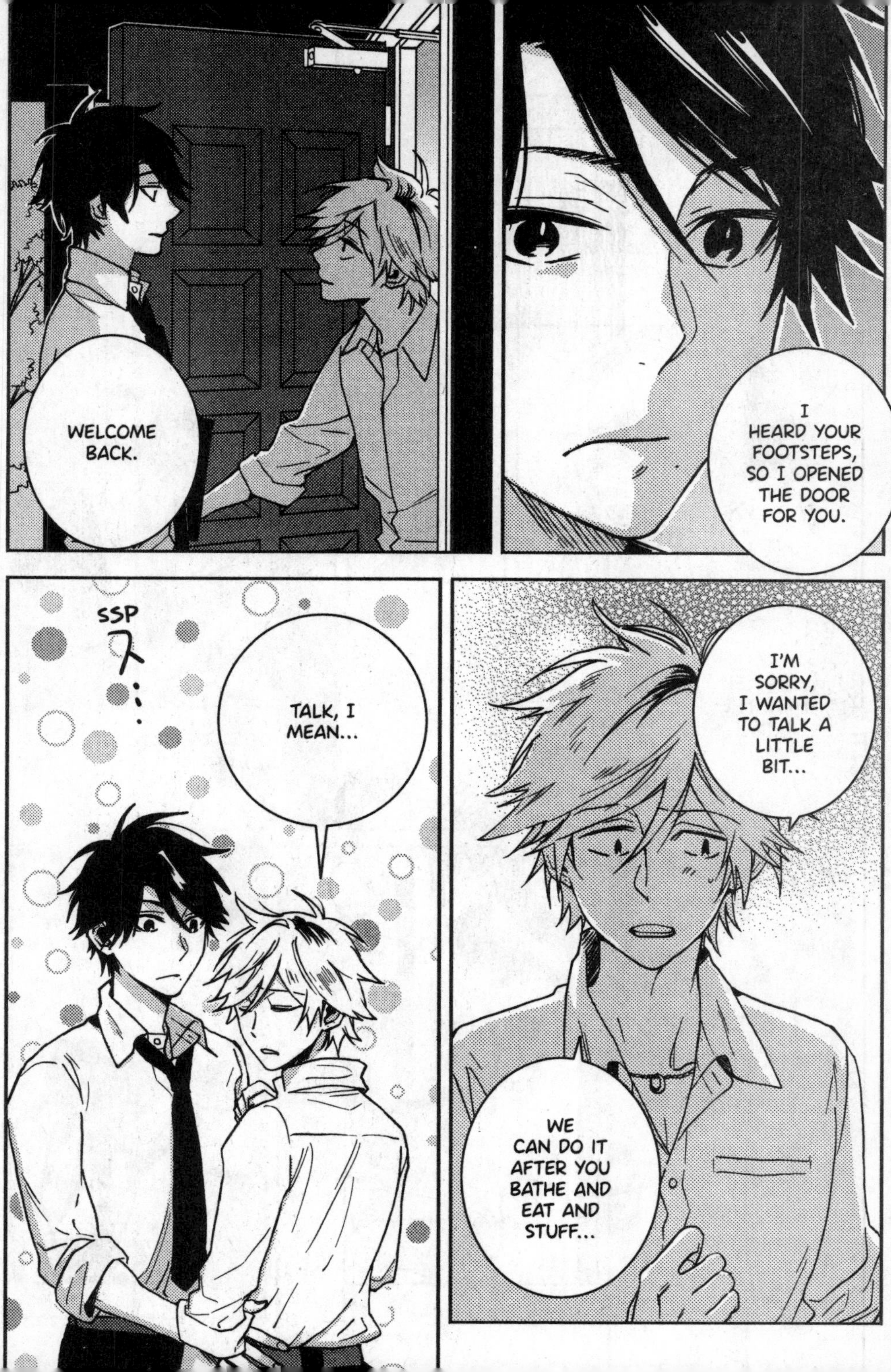
I HEARD YOUR FOOTSTEPS, SO I OPENED THE DOOR FOR YOU.
WELCOME BACK.
I'M SORRY, I WANTED TO TALK A LITTLE BIT...
WE CAN DO IT AFTER YOU BATHE AND EAT AND STUFF...
SSP
TALK, I MEAN...

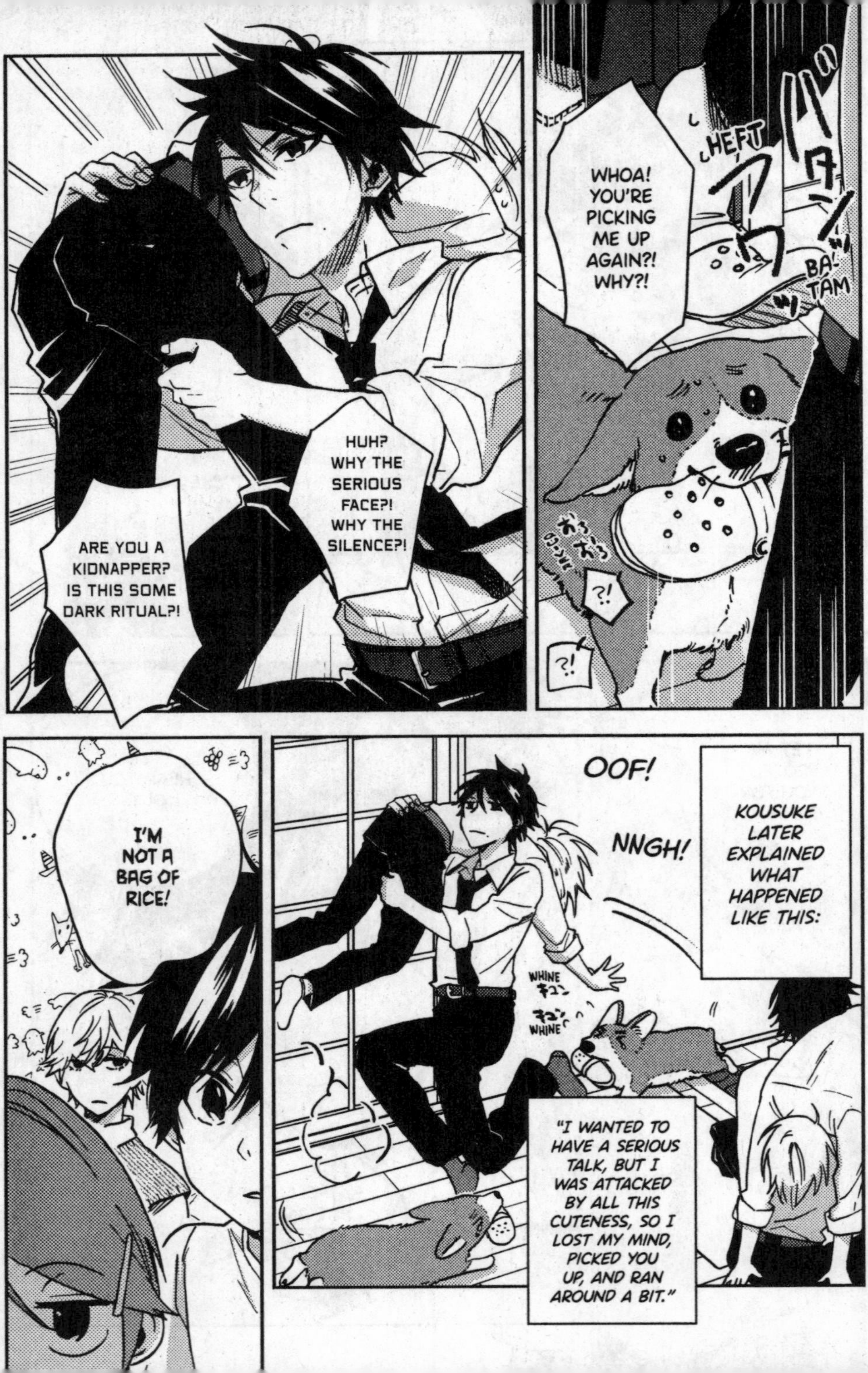
HEFT
WHOA! YOU'RE PICKING ME UP AGAIN?! WHY?!
BA-TAM
?!
?!
HUH? WHY THE SERIOUS FACE?! WHY THE SILENCE?!
ARE YOU A KIDNAPPER? IS THIS SOME DARK RITUAL?!
KOUSUKE LATER EXPLAINED WHAT HAPPENED LIKE THIS:
OOF!
NNGH!
WHINE
WHINE
"I WANTED TO HAVE A SERIOUS TALK, BUT I WAS ATTACKED BY ALL THIS CUTENESS, SO I LOST MY MIND, PICKED YOU UP, AND RAN AROUND A BIT."
I'M NOT A BAG OF RICE!

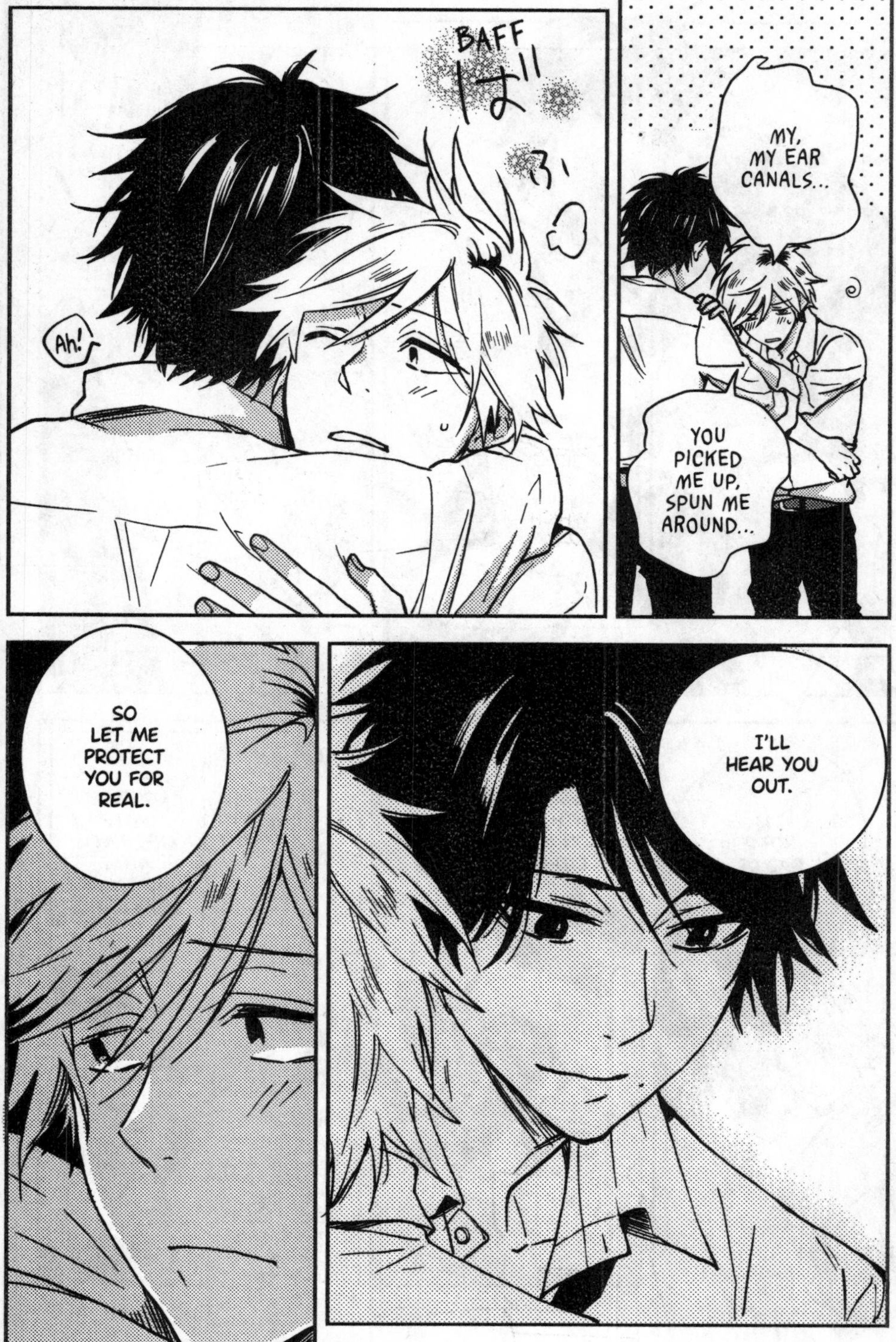
MY, MY EAR CANALS...
YOU PICKED ME UP, SPUN ME AROUND...
BAFF
Ah!
I'LL HEAR YOU OUT.
SO LET ME PROTECT YOU FOR REAL.

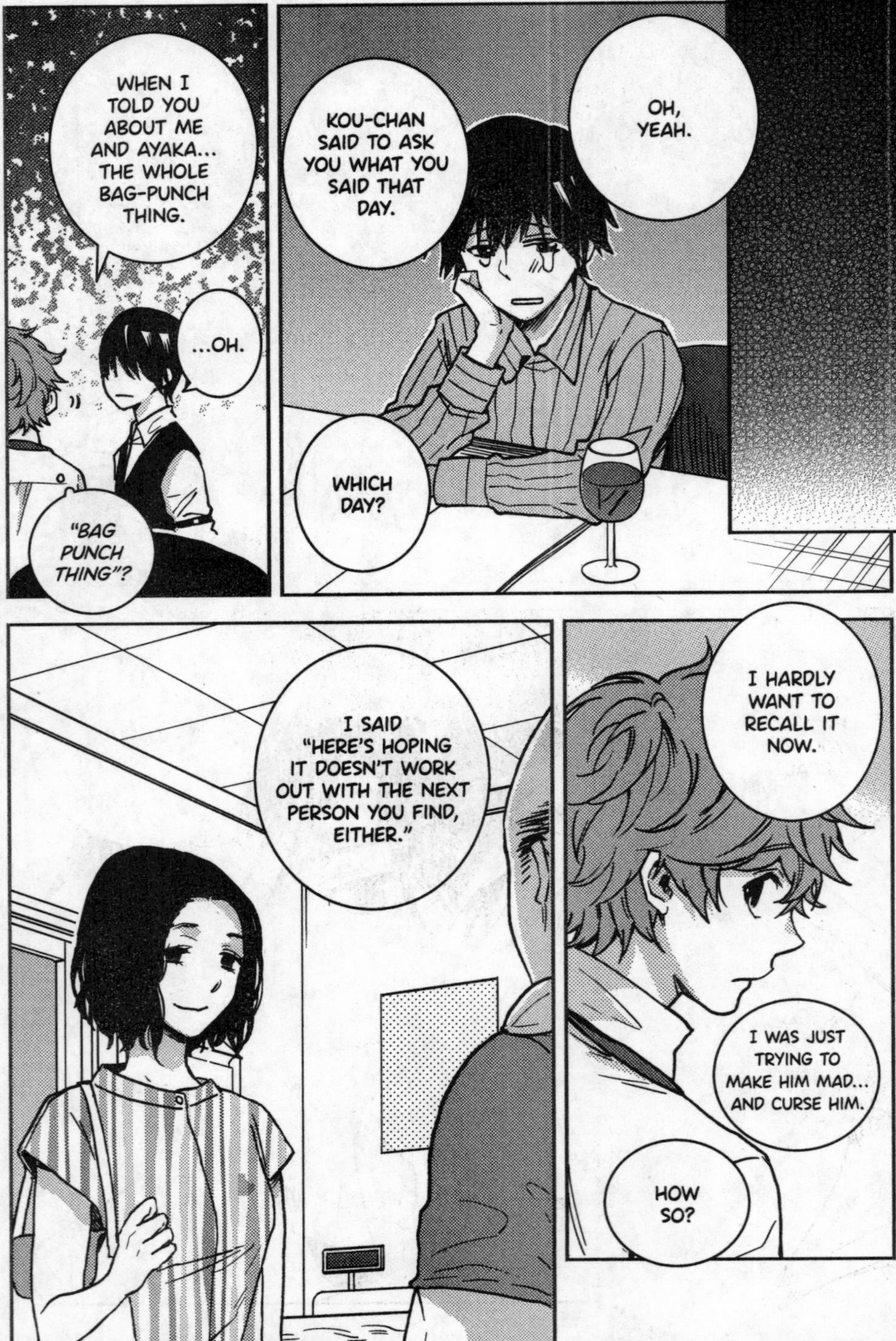
OH, YEAH.
KOU-CHAN SAID TO ASK YOU WHAT YOU SAID THAT DAY.
WHICH DAY?
WHEN I TOLD YOU ABOUT ME AND AYAKA... THE WHOLE BAG-PUNCH THING.
...OH.
"BAG PUNCH THING"?
I HARDLY WANT TO RECALL IT NOW.
I WAS JUST TRYING TO MAKE HIM MAD... AND CURSE HIM.
HOW SO?
I SAID "HERE'S HOPING IT DOESN'T WORK OUT WITH THE NEXT PERSON YOU FIND, EITHER."

Hitorijime My Hero

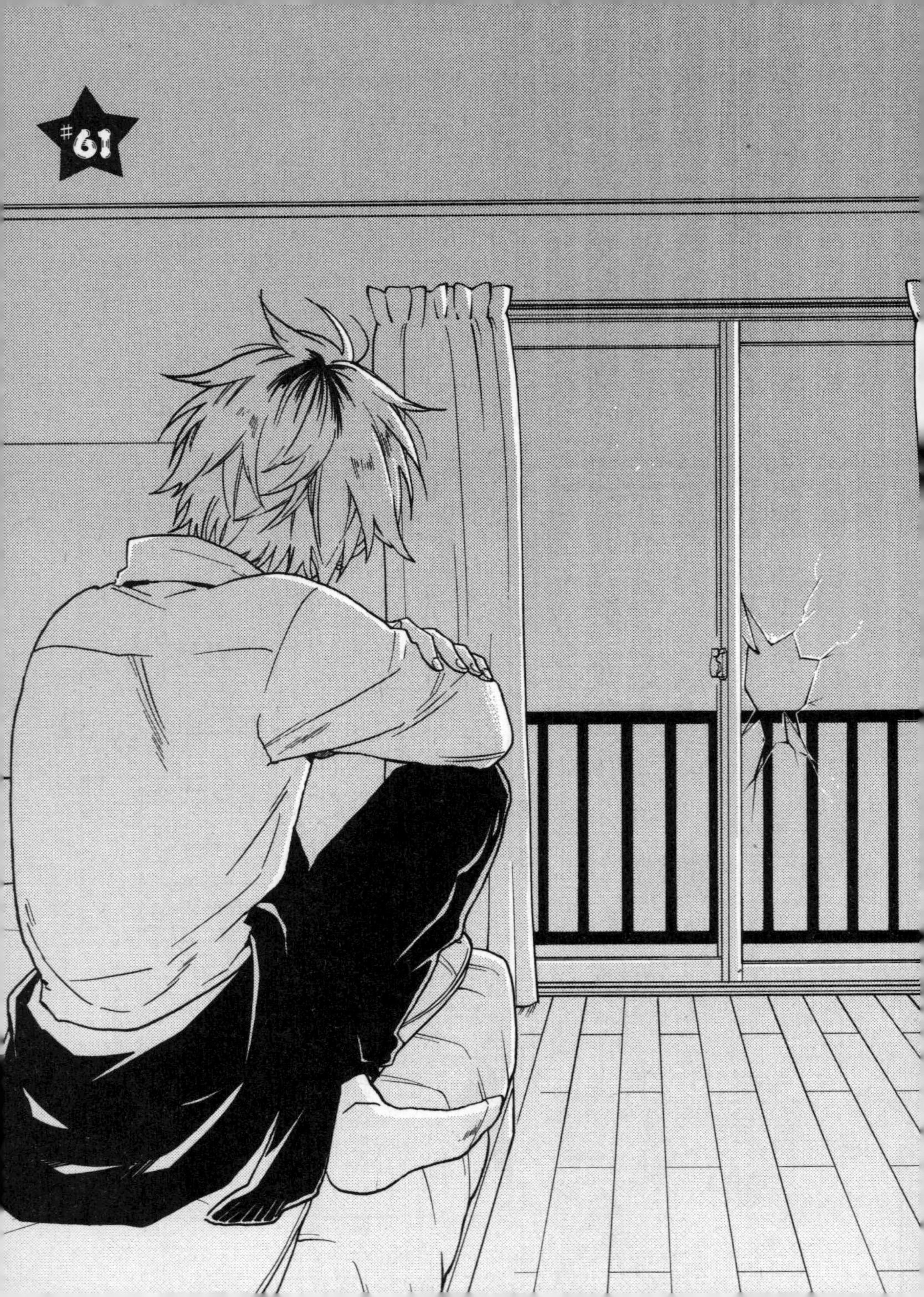
#61

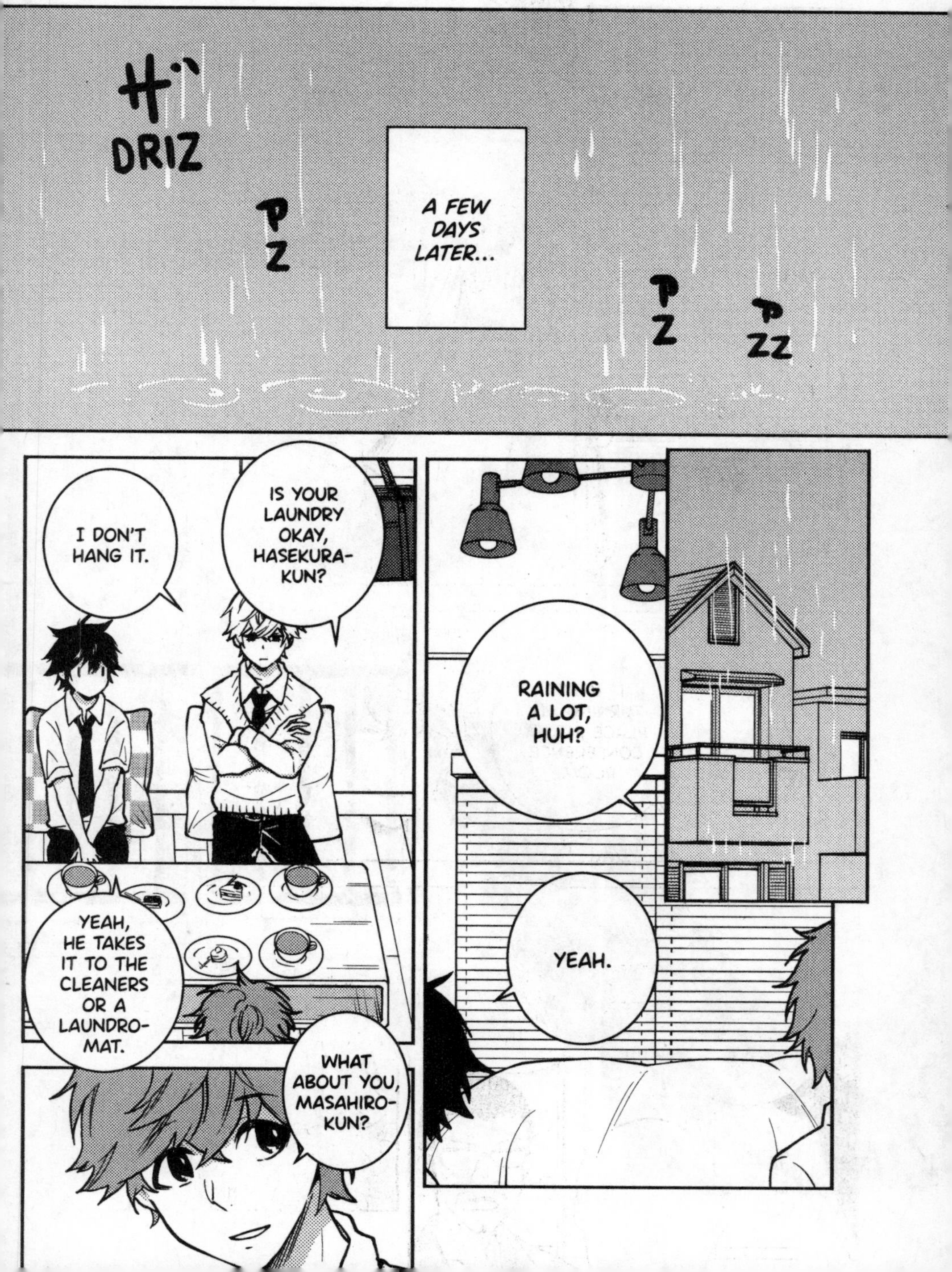
PZZ
PZ
A FEW DAYS LATER...
PZ
DRIZ
RAINING A LOT, HUH?
YEAH.
IS YOUR LAUNDRY OKAY, HASEKURA-KUN?
I DON'T HANG IT.
YEAH, HE TAKES IT TO THE CLEANERS OR A LAUNDROMAT.
WHAT ABOUT YOU, MASAHIRO-KUN?

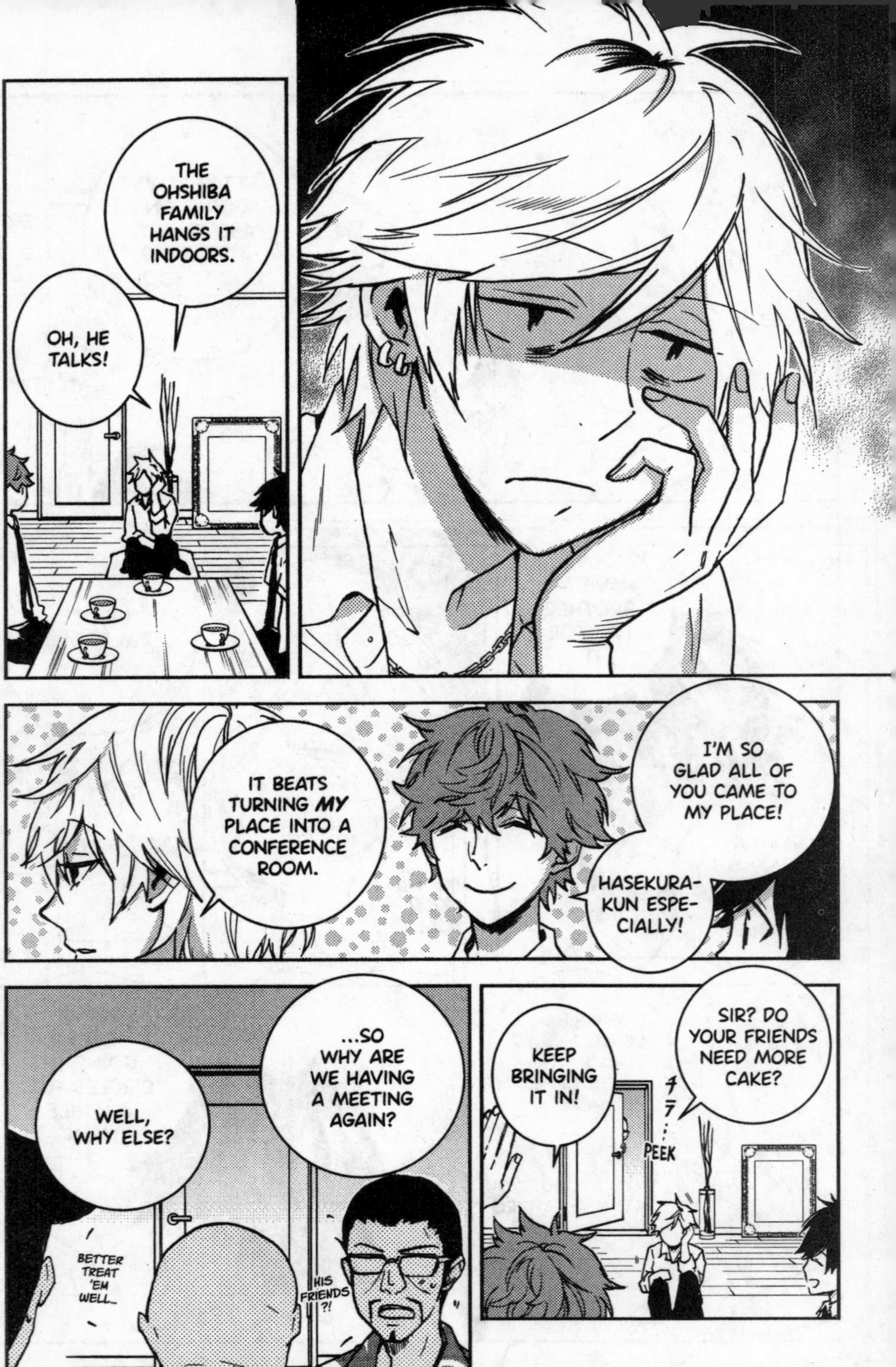
THE OHSHIBA FAMILY HANGS IT INDOORS.
OH, HE TALKS!
I'M SO GLAD ALL OF YOU CAME TO MY PLACE!
HASEKURA-KUN ESPECIALLY!
IT BEATS TURNING *MY* PLACE INTO A CONFERENCE ROOM.
SIR? DO YOUR FRIENDS NEED MORE CAKE?
チラ…
PEEK
KEEP BRINGING IT IN!
...SO WHY ARE WE HAVING A MEETING AGAIN?
WELL, WHY ELSE?
HIS FRIENDS?!
BETTER TREAT 'EM WELL...

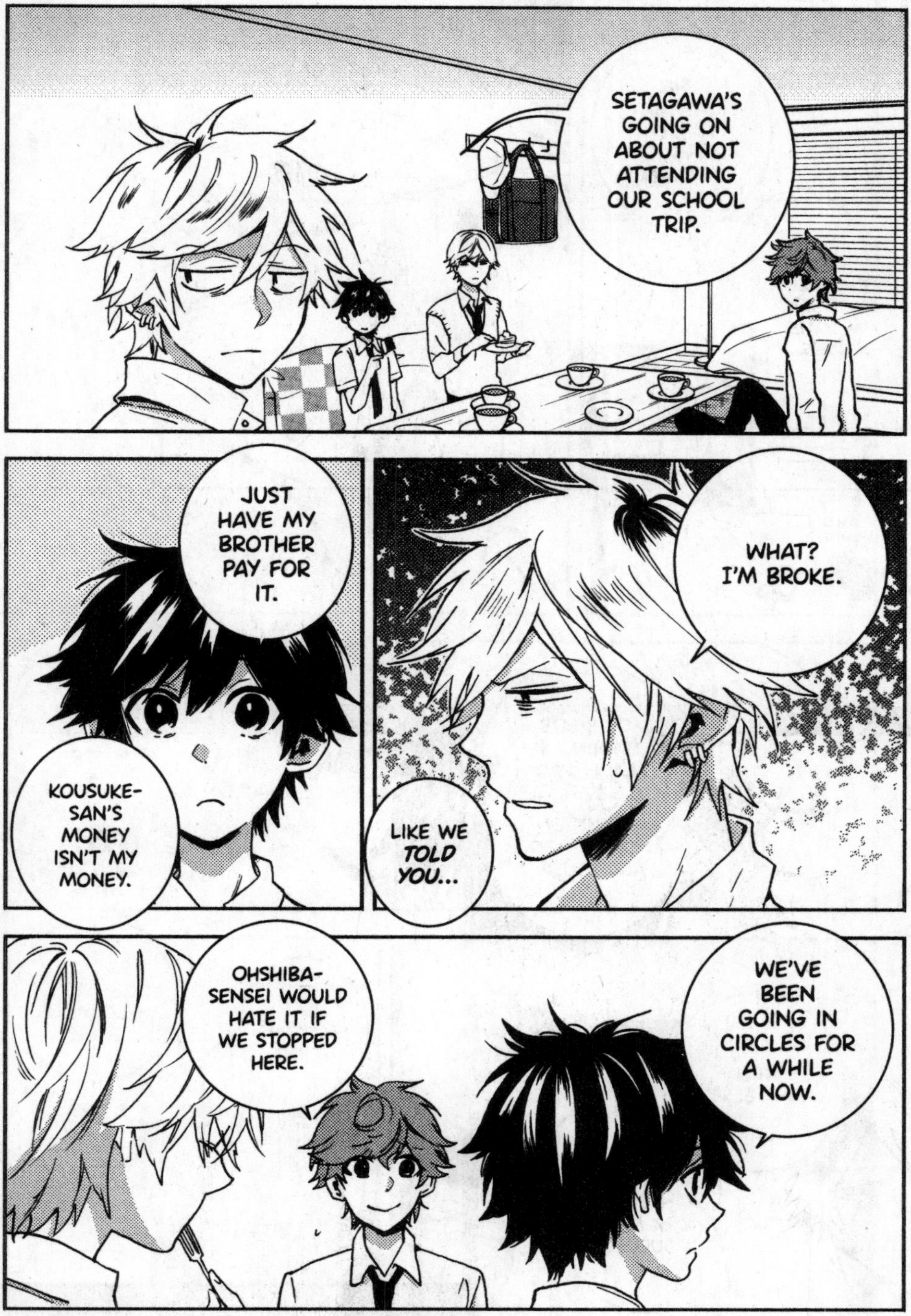
SETAGAWA'S GOING ON ABOUT NOT ATTENDING OUR SCHOOL TRIP.
WHAT? I'M BROKE.
LIKE WE *TOLD YOU*...
JUST HAVE MY BROTHER PAY FOR IT.
KOUSUKE-SAN'S MONEY ISN'T MY MONEY.
WE'VE BEEN GOING IN CIRCLES FOR A WHILE NOW.
OHSHIBA-SENSEI WOULD HATE IT IF WE STOPPED HERE.

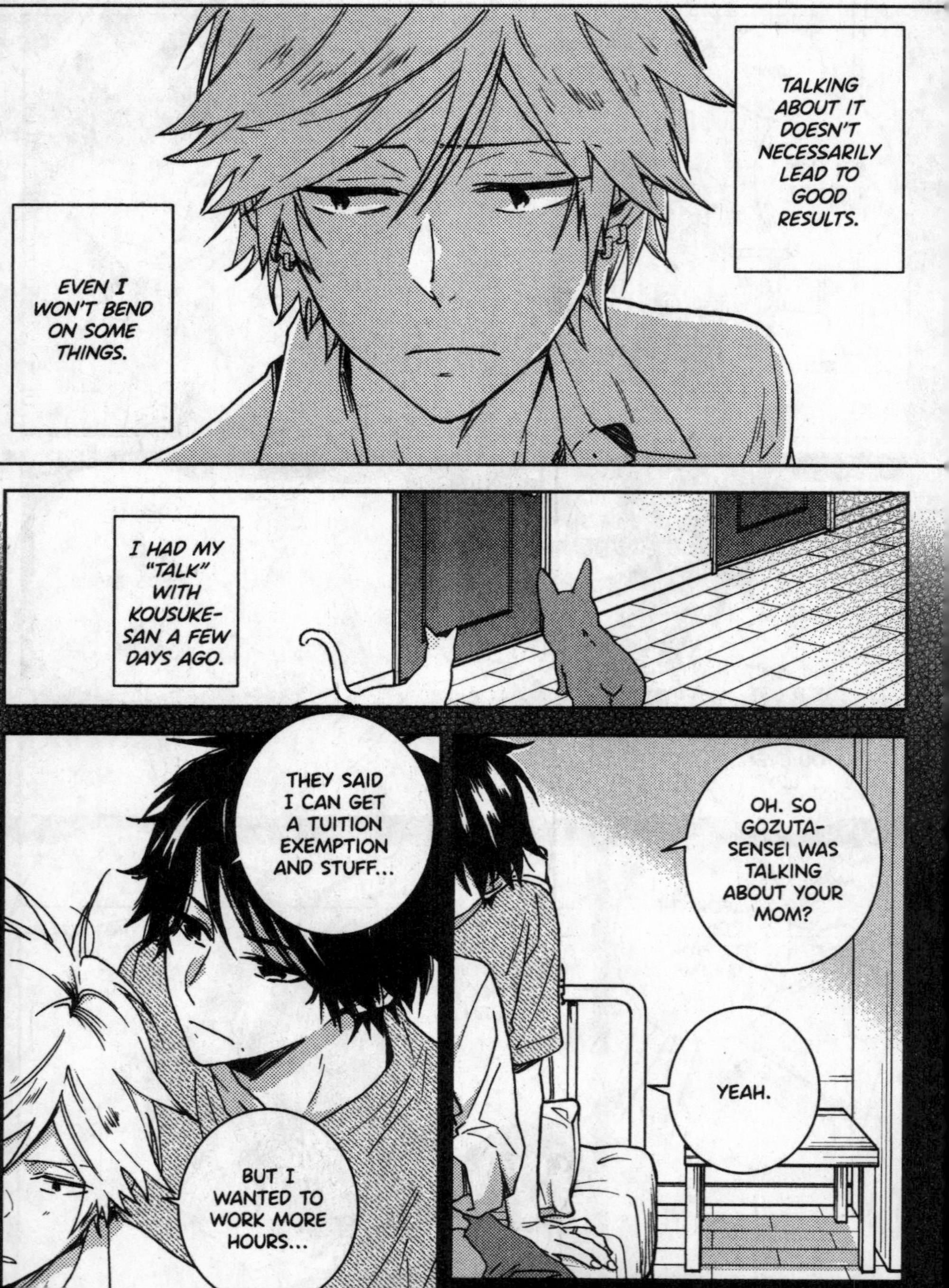
TALKING ABOUT IT DOESN'T NECESSARILY LEAD TO GOOD RESULTS.
EVEN I WON'T BEND ON SOME THINGS.
I HAD MY "TALK" WITH KOUSUKE-SAN A FEW DAYS AGO.
OH. SO GOZUTA-SENSEI WAS TALKING ABOUT YOUR MOM?
YEAH.
THEY SAID I CAN GET A TUITION EXEMPTION AND STUFF...
BUT I WANTED TO WORK MORE HOURS...

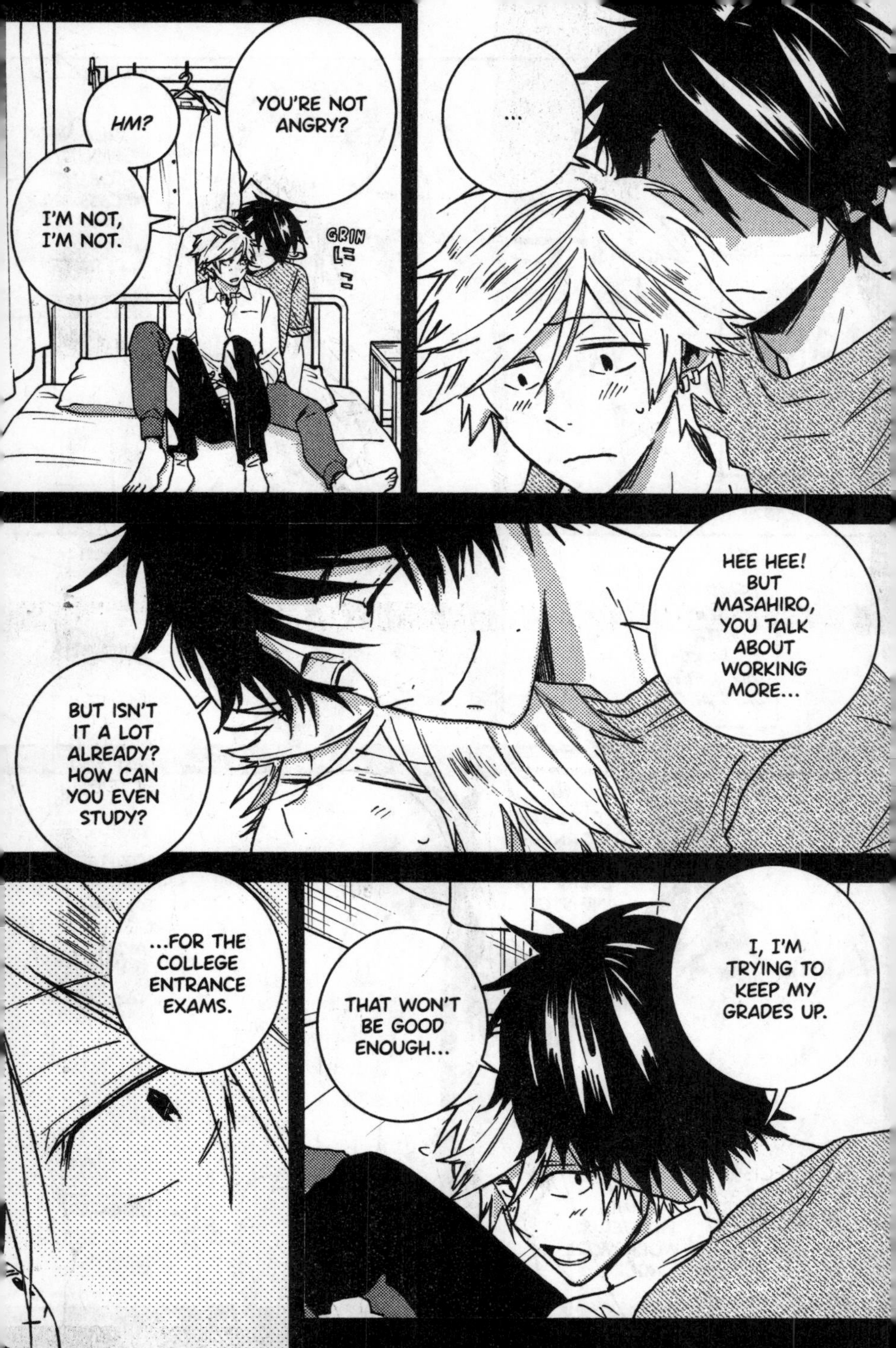
...
YOU'RE NOT ANGRY?
HM?
I'M NOT, I'M NOT.
GRIN
HEE HEE! BUT MASAHIRO, YOU TALK ABOUT WORKING MORE...
BUT ISN'T IT A LOT ALREADY? HOW CAN YOU EVEN STUDY?
I, I'M TRYING TO KEEP MY GRADES UP.
THAT WON'T BE GOOD ENOUGH...
...FOR THE COLLEGE ENTRANCE EXAMS.

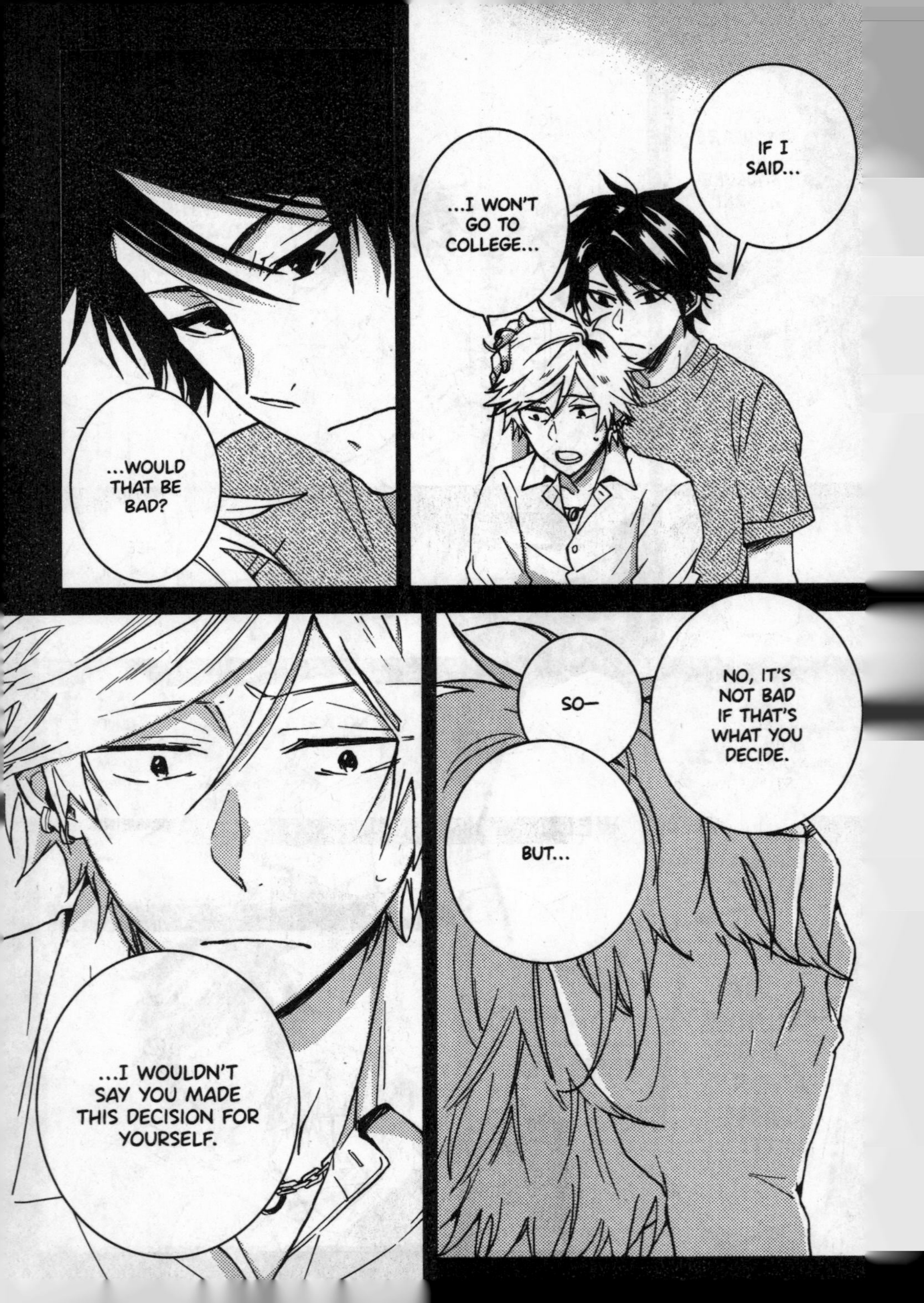
IF I SAID...
...I WON'T GO TO COLLEGE...
...WOULD THAT BE BAD?
NO, IT'S NOT BAD IF THAT'S WHAT YOU DECIDE.
SO—
BUT...
...I WOULDN'T SAY YOU MADE THIS DECISION FOR YOURSELF.

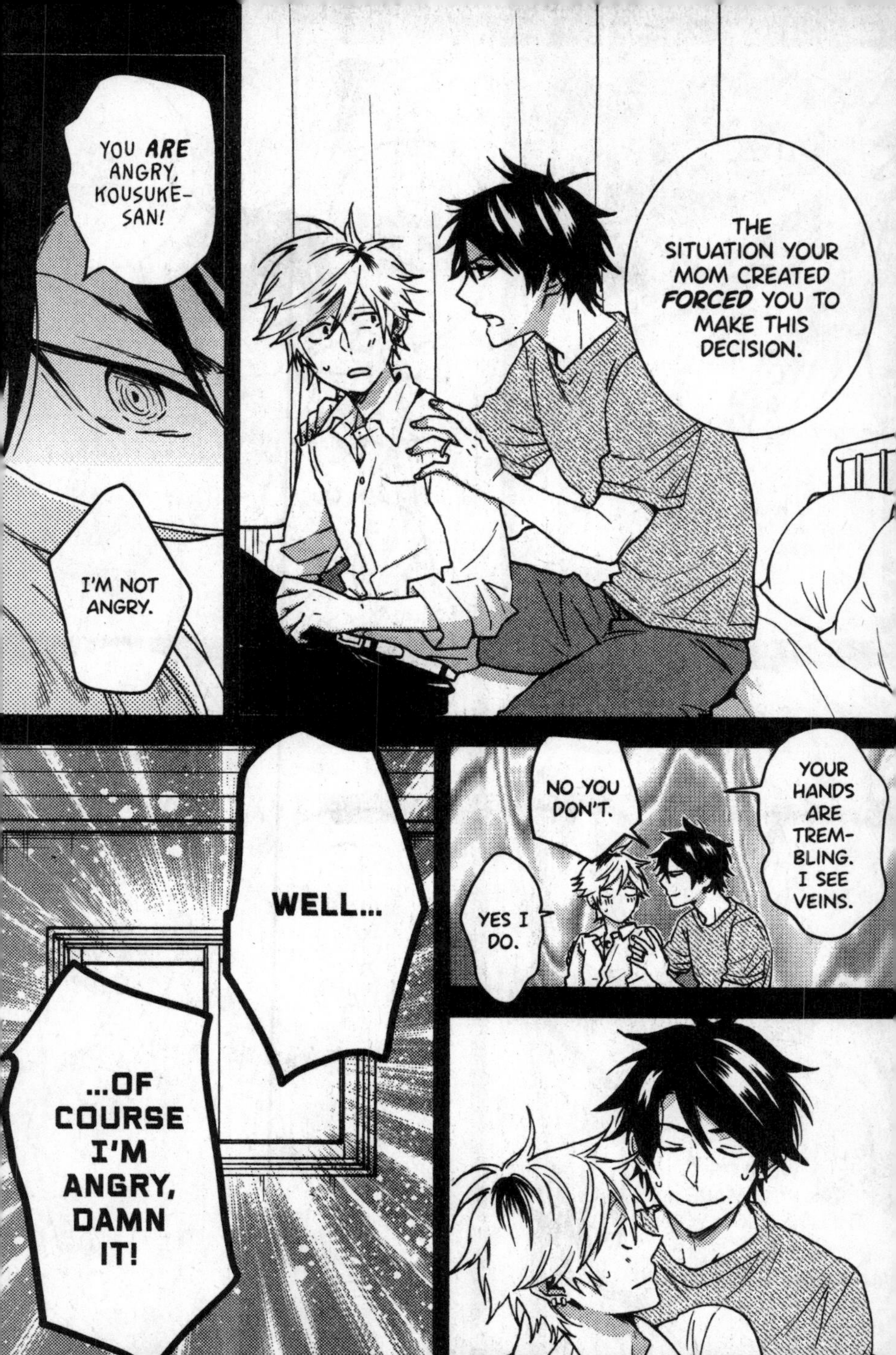
THE SITUATION YOUR MOM CREATED FORCED YOU TO MAKE THIS DECISION.
YOU ARE ANGRY, KOUSUKE-SAN!
I'M NOT ANGRY.
YOUR HANDS ARE TREMBLING. I SEE VEINS.
NO YOU DON'T.
YES I DO.
WELL...
...OF COURSE I'M ANGRY, DAMN IT!

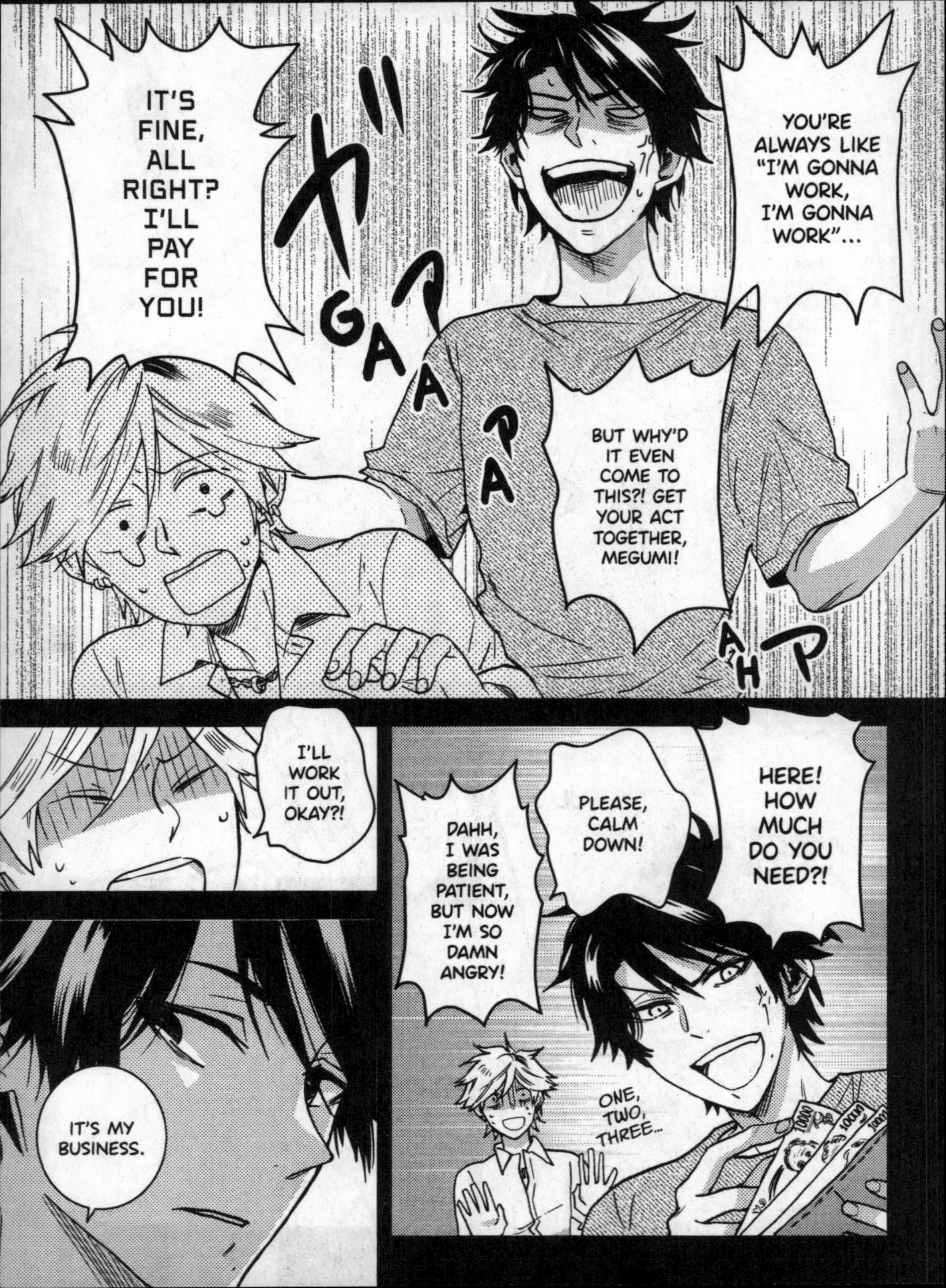
YOU'RE ALWAYS LIKE "I'M GONNA WORK, I'M GONNA WORK"...
BUT WHY'D IT EVEN COME TO THIS?! GET YOUR ACT TOGETHER, MEGUMI!
AH
GAAA
IT'S FINE, ALL RIGHT? I'LL PAY FOR YOU!
HERE! HOW MUCH DO YOU NEED?!
PLEASE, CALM DOWN!
DAHH, I WAS BEING PATIENT, BUT NOW I'M SO DAMN ANGRY!
ONE, TWO, THREE...
I'LL WORK IT OUT, OKAY?!
IT'S MY BUSINESS.

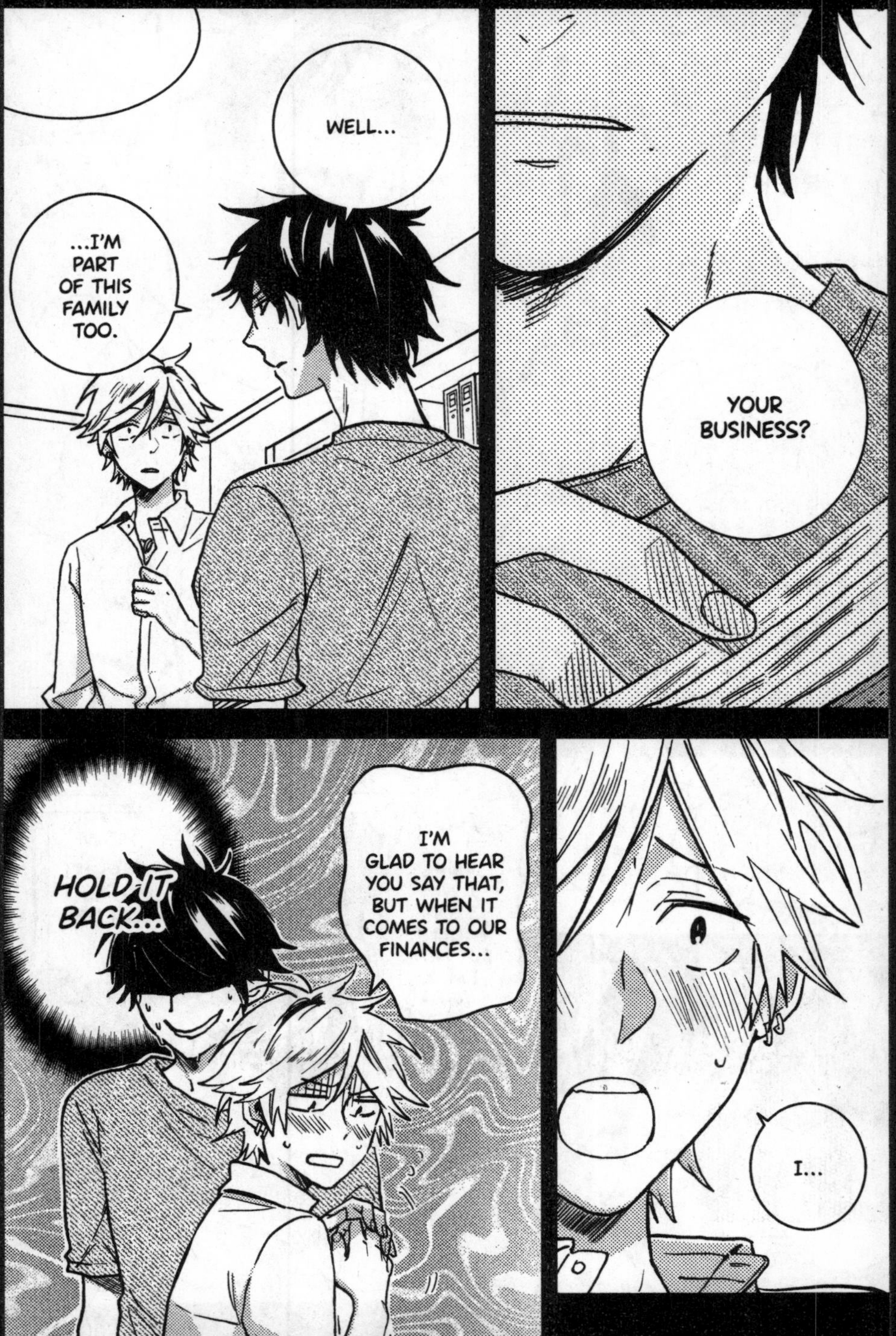
YOUR BUSINESS?
WELL...
...I'M PART OF THIS FAMILY TOO.
I...
I'M GLAD TO HEAR YOU SAY THAT, BUT WHEN IT COMES TO OUR FINANCES...
HOLD IT BACK...

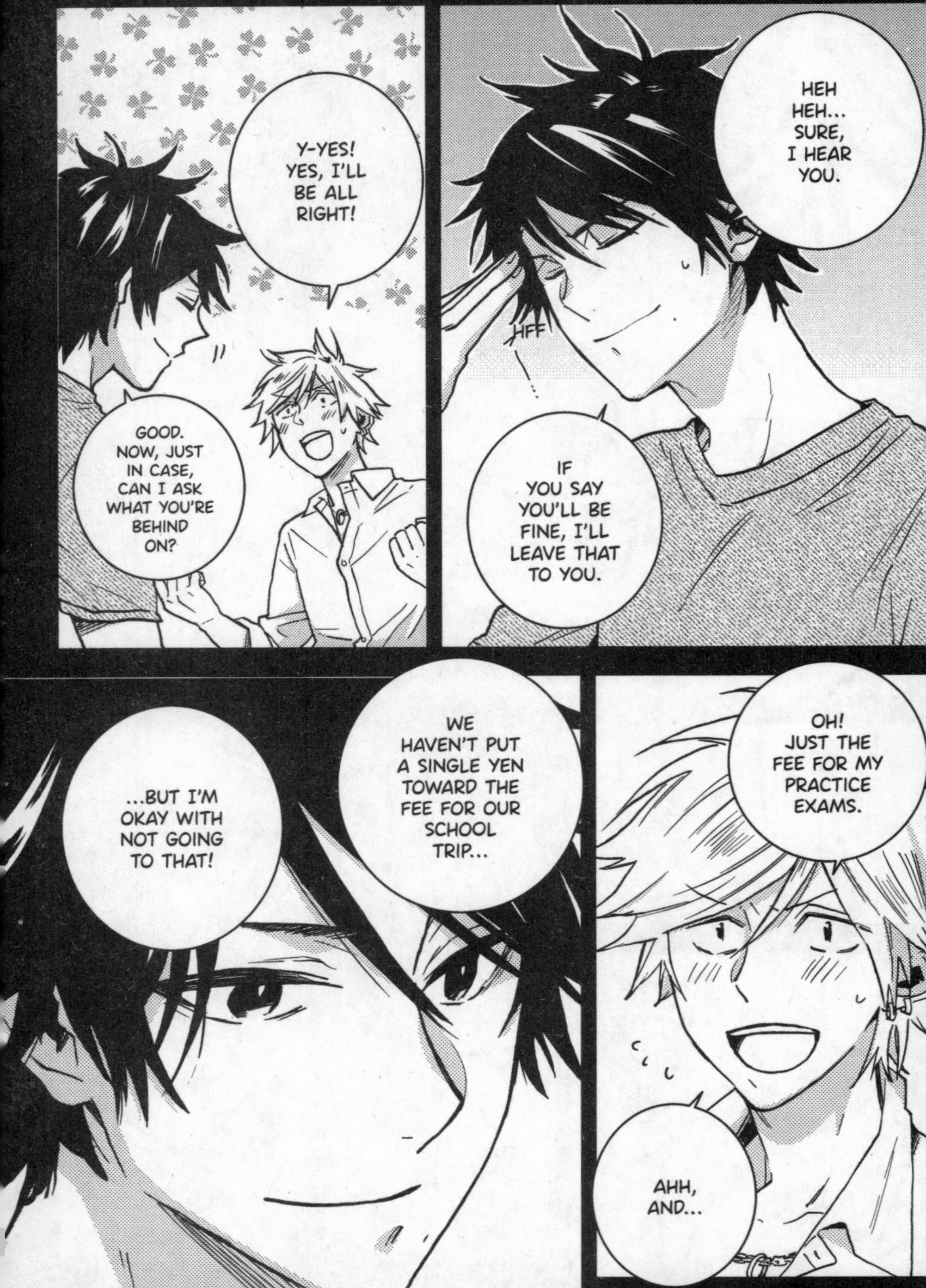
HEH HEH... SURE, I HEAR YOU.
HFF
IF YOU SAY YOU'LL BE FINE, I'LL LEAVE THAT TO YOU.
Y-YES! YES, I'LL BE ALL RIGHT!
GOOD. NOW, JUST IN CASE, CAN I ASK WHAT YOU'RE BEHIND ON?
OH! JUST THE FEE FOR MY PRACTICE EXAMS.
AHH, AND...
WE HAVEN'T PUT A SINGLE YEN TOWARD THE FEE FOR OUR SCHOOL TRIP...
...BUT I'M OKAY WITH NOT GOING TO THAT!

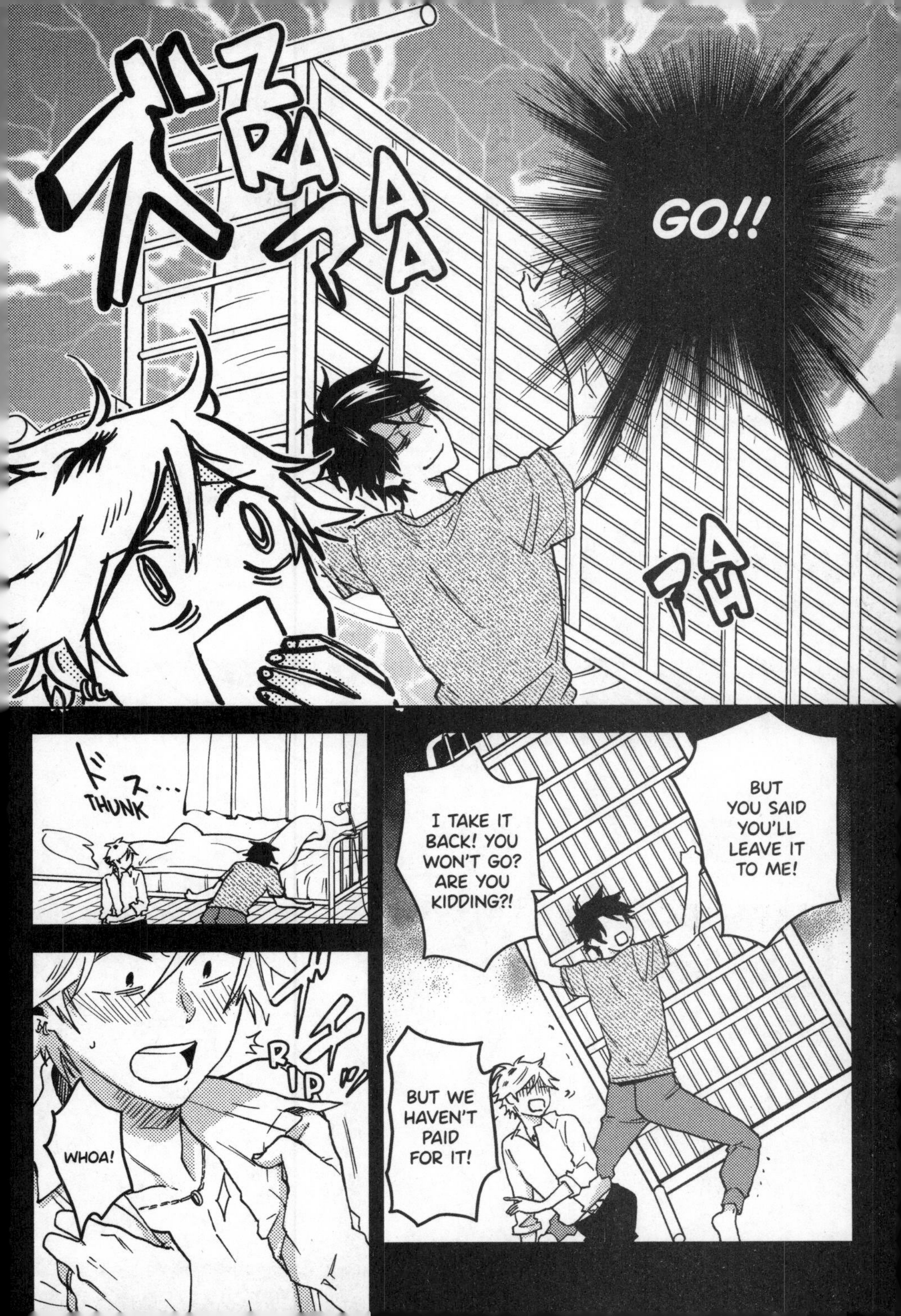
ZRAAA
GO!!
AH
BUT YOU SAID YOU'LL LEAVE IT TO ME!
I TAKE IT BACK! YOU WON'T GO? ARE YOU KIDDING?!
BUT WE HAVEN'T PAID FOR IT!
ドス…
THUNK
RIP
WHOA!

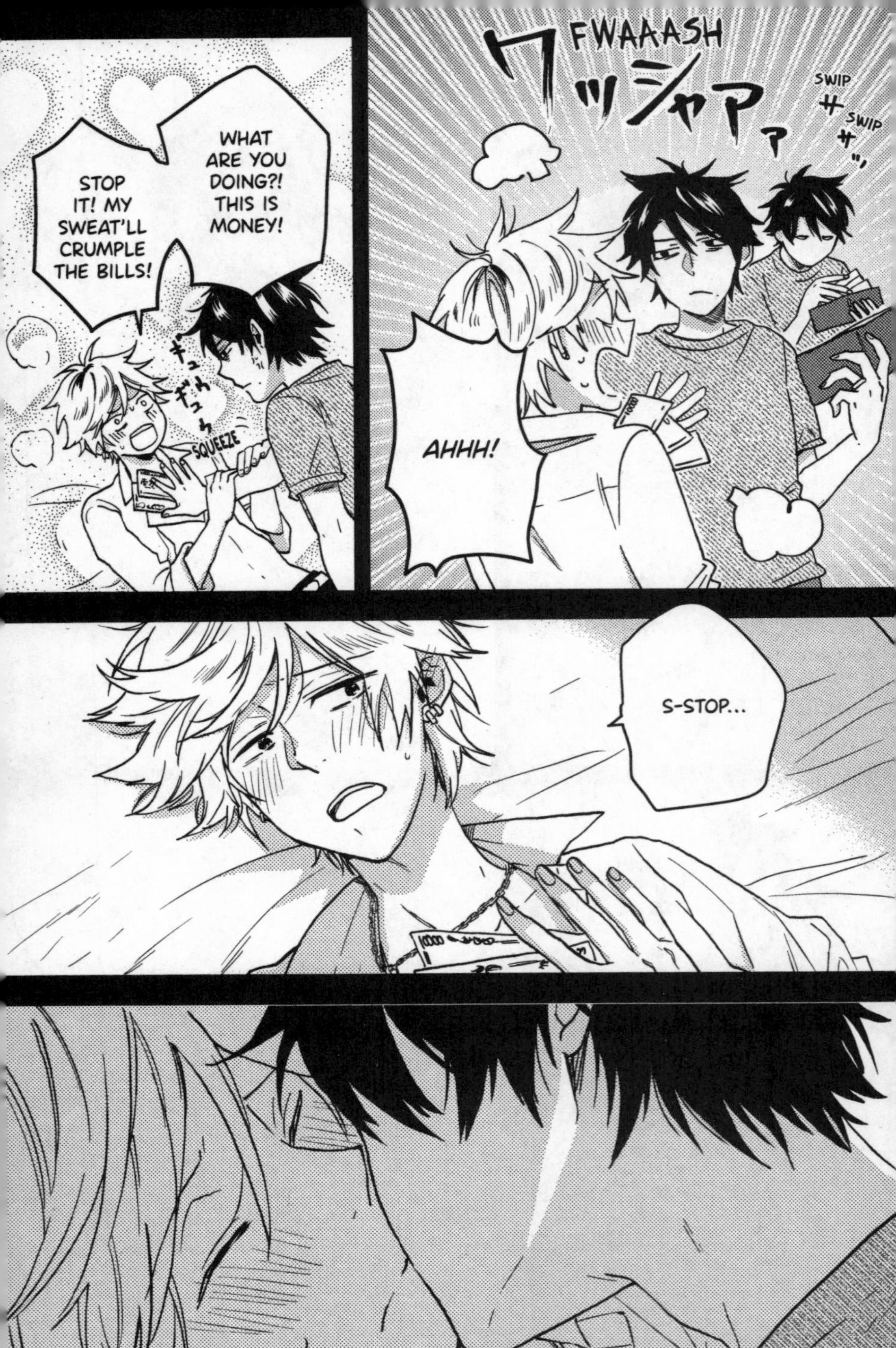
FWAAASH
SWIP
SWIP
AHHH!
WHAT ARE YOU DOING?! THIS IS MONEY!
STOP IT! MY SWEAT'LL CRUMPLE THE BILLS!
SQUEEZE
S-STOP...

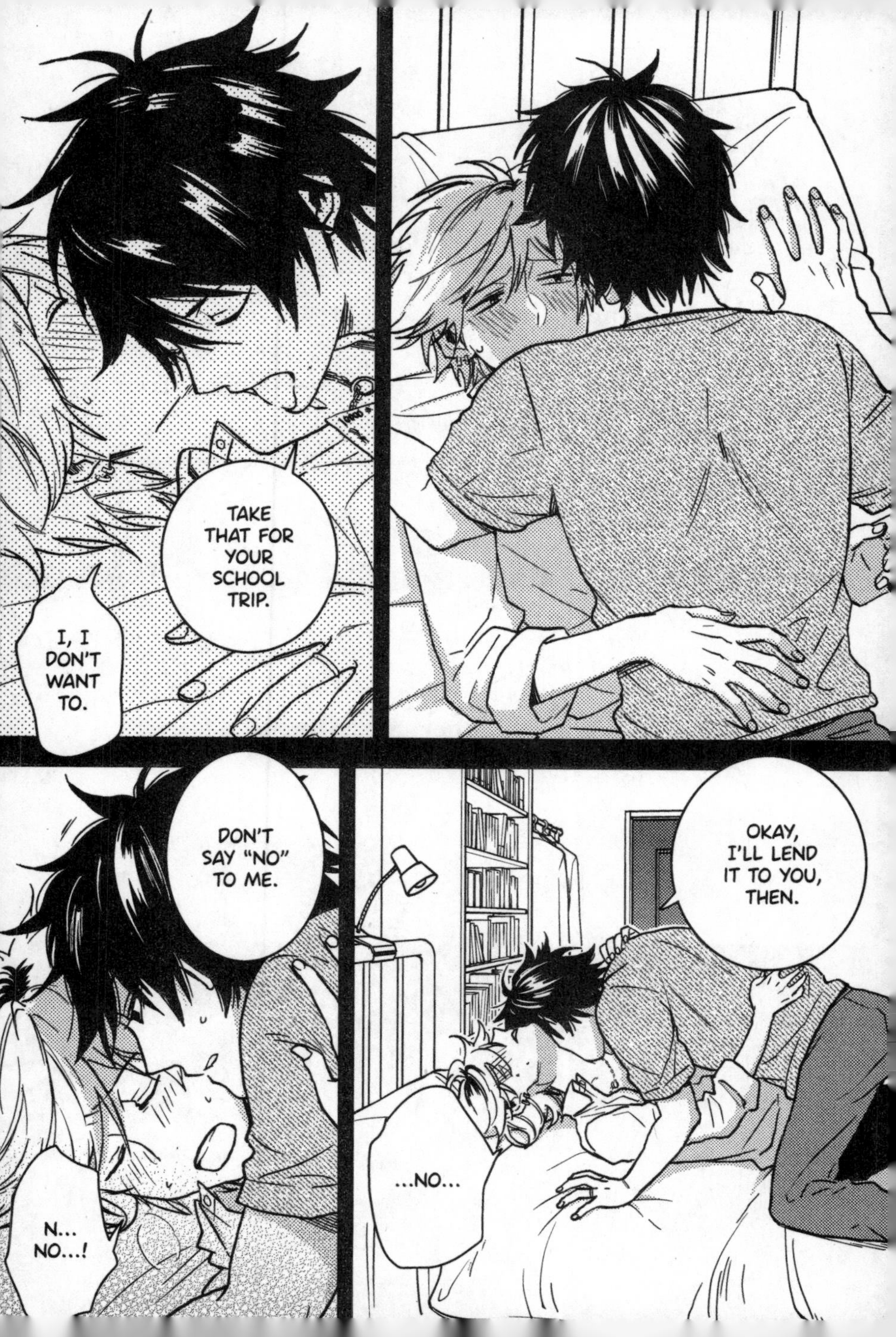
TAKE THAT FOR YOUR SCHOOL TRIP.
I, I DON'T WANT TO.
OKAY, I'LL LEND IT TO YOU, THEN.
...NO...
DON'T SAY "NO" TO ME.
N... NO...!

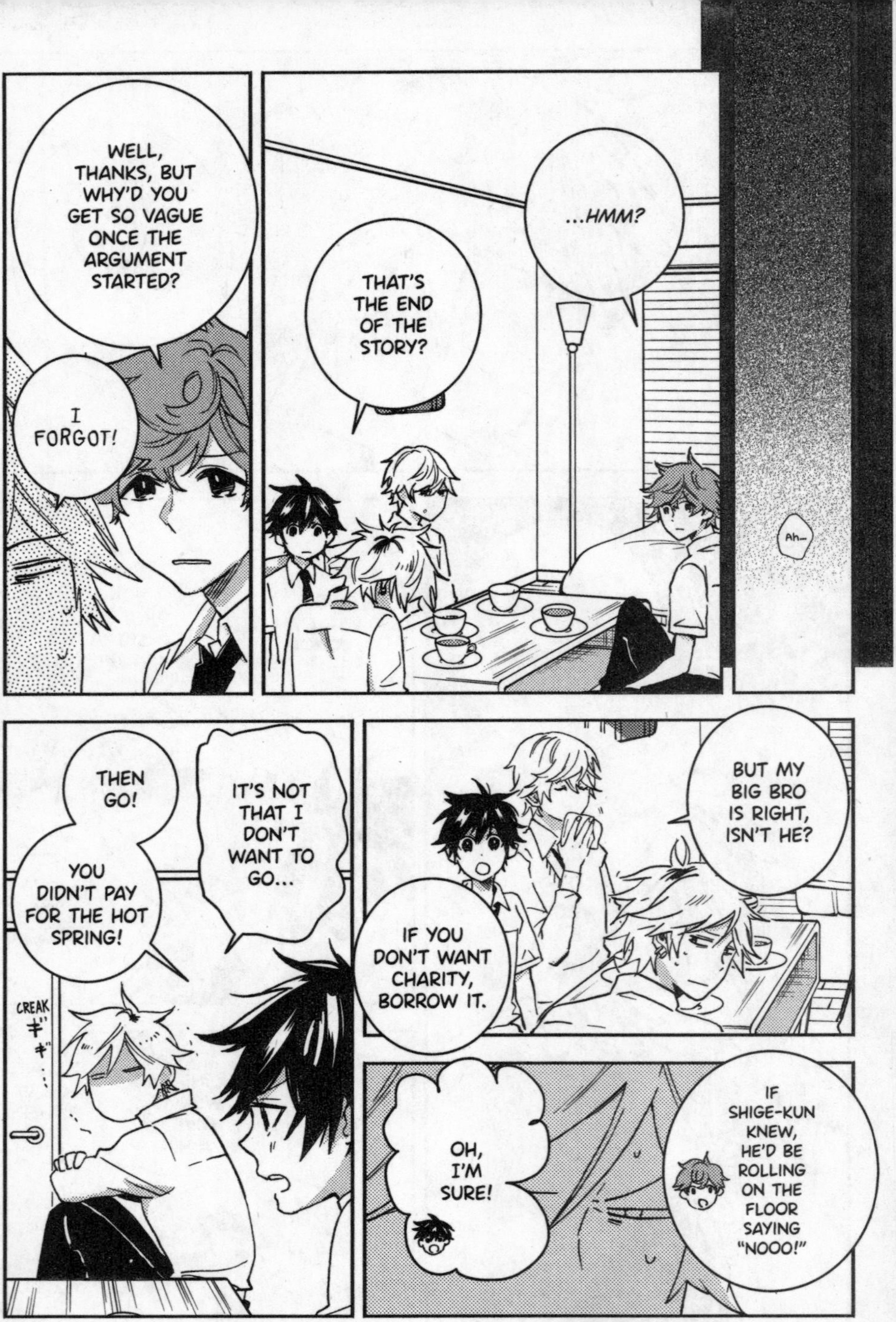
Ah—
...HMM?
THAT'S THE END OF THE STORY?
WELL, THANKS, BUT WHY'D YOU GET SO VAGUE ONCE THE ARGUMENT STARTED?
I FORGOT!
BUT MY BIG BRO IS RIGHT, ISN'T HE?
IF YOU DON'T WANT CHARITY, BORROW IT.
IF SHIGE-KUN KNEW, HE'D BE ROLLING ON THE FLOOR SAYING "NOOO!"
OH, I'M SURE!
IT'S NOT THAT I DON'T WANT TO GO...
THEN GO!
YOU DIDN'T PAY FOR THE HOT SPRING!
CREAK
ギギ

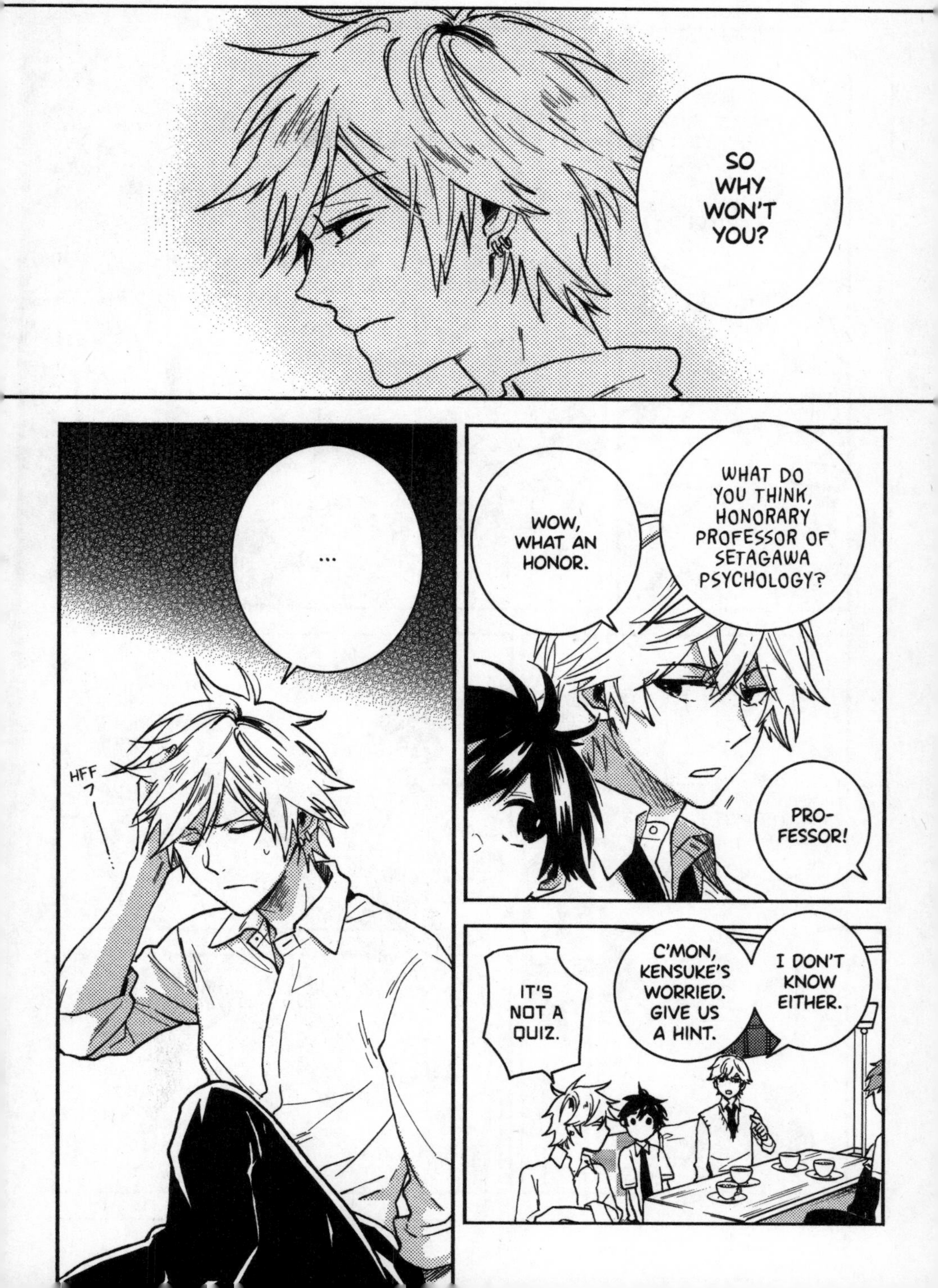
SO WHY WON'T YOU?
WHAT DO YOU THINK, HONORARY PROFESSOR OF SETAGAWA PSYCHOLOGY?
WOW, WHAT AN HONOR.
PRO-FESSOR!
I DON'T KNOW EITHER.
C'MON, KENSUKE'S WORRIED. GIVE US A HINT.
IT'S NOT A QUIZ.
...
HFF

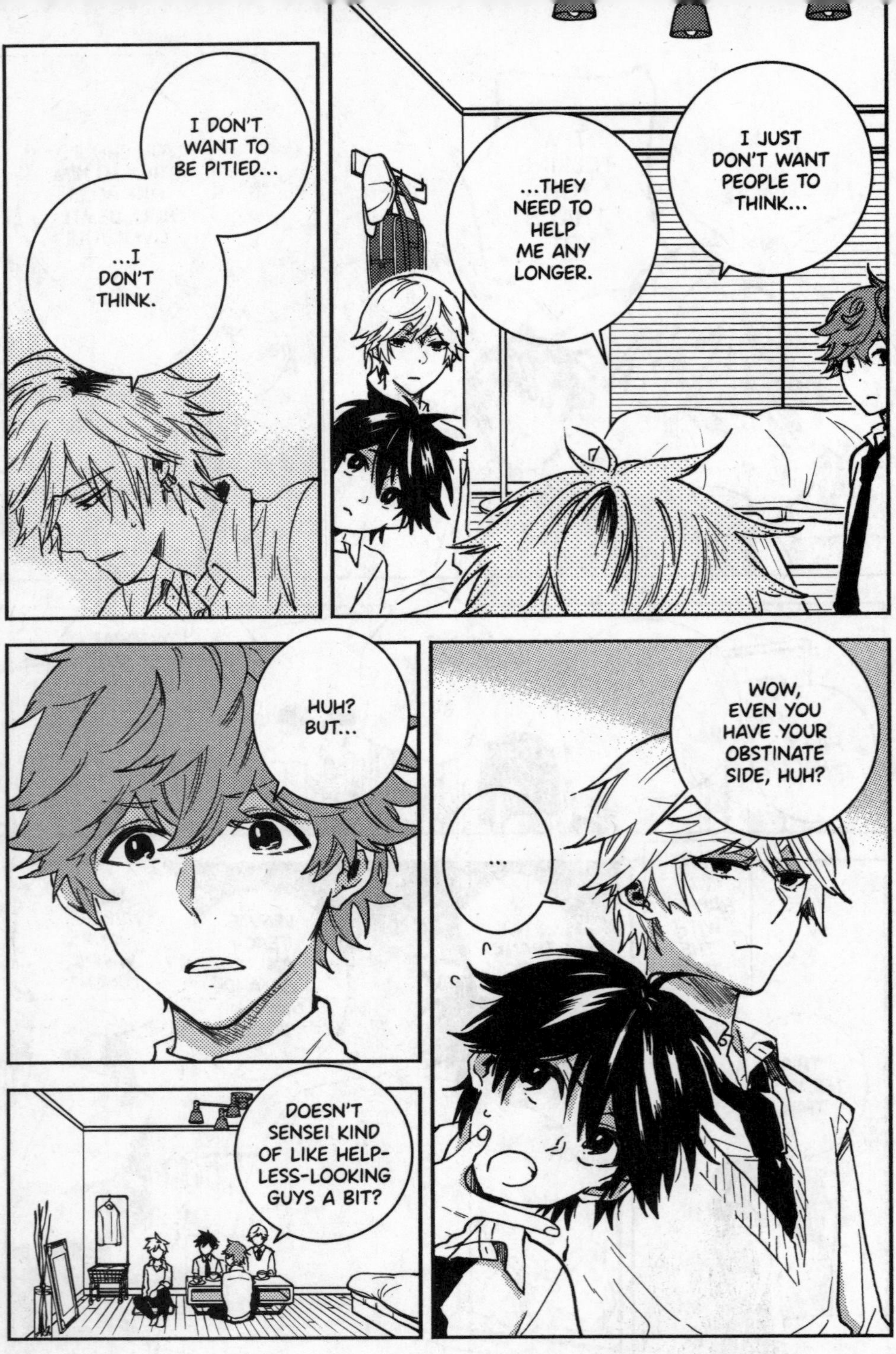
I JUST DON'T WANT PEOPLE TO THINK...
...THEY NEED TO HELP ME ANY LONGER.
I DON'T WANT TO BE PITIED...
...I DON'T THINK.
WOW, EVEN YOU HAVE YOUR OBSTINATE SIDE, HUH?
...
HUH? BUT...
DOESN'T SENSEI KIND OF LIKE HELP-LESS-LOOKING GUYS A BIT?

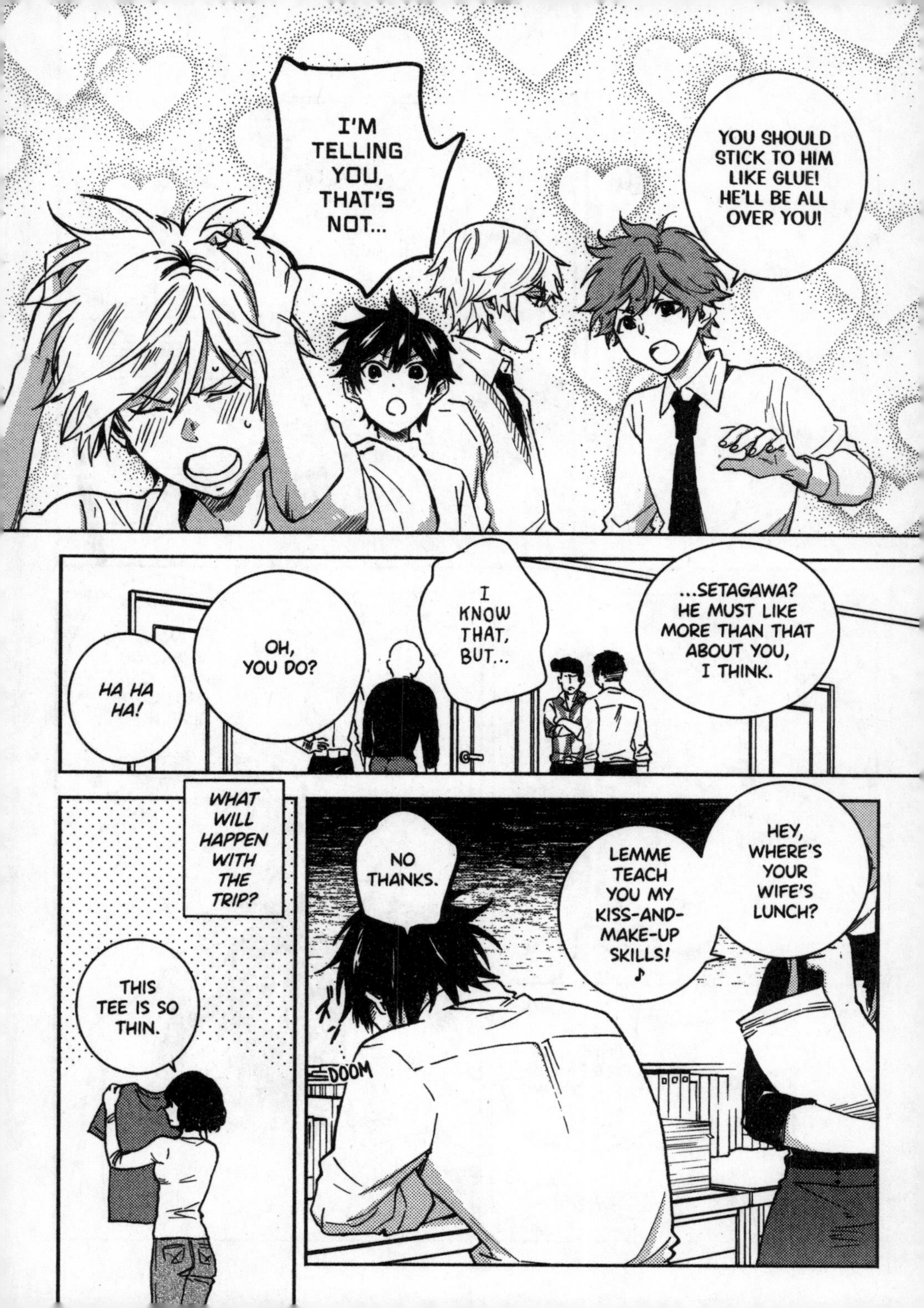
YOU SHOULD STICK TO HIM LIKE GLUE! HE'LL BE ALL OVER YOU!
I'M TELLING YOU, THAT'S NOT...
...SETAGAWA? HE MUST LIKE MORE THAN THAT ABOUT YOU, I THINK.
I KNOW THAT, BUT...
OH, YOU DO?
HA HA HA!
HEY, WHERE'S YOUR WIFE'S LUNCH?
LEMME TEACH YOU MY KISS-AND-MAKE-UP SKILLS! ♪
NO THANKS.
DOOM
WHAT WILL HAPPEN WITH THE TRIP?
THIS TEE IS SO THIN.

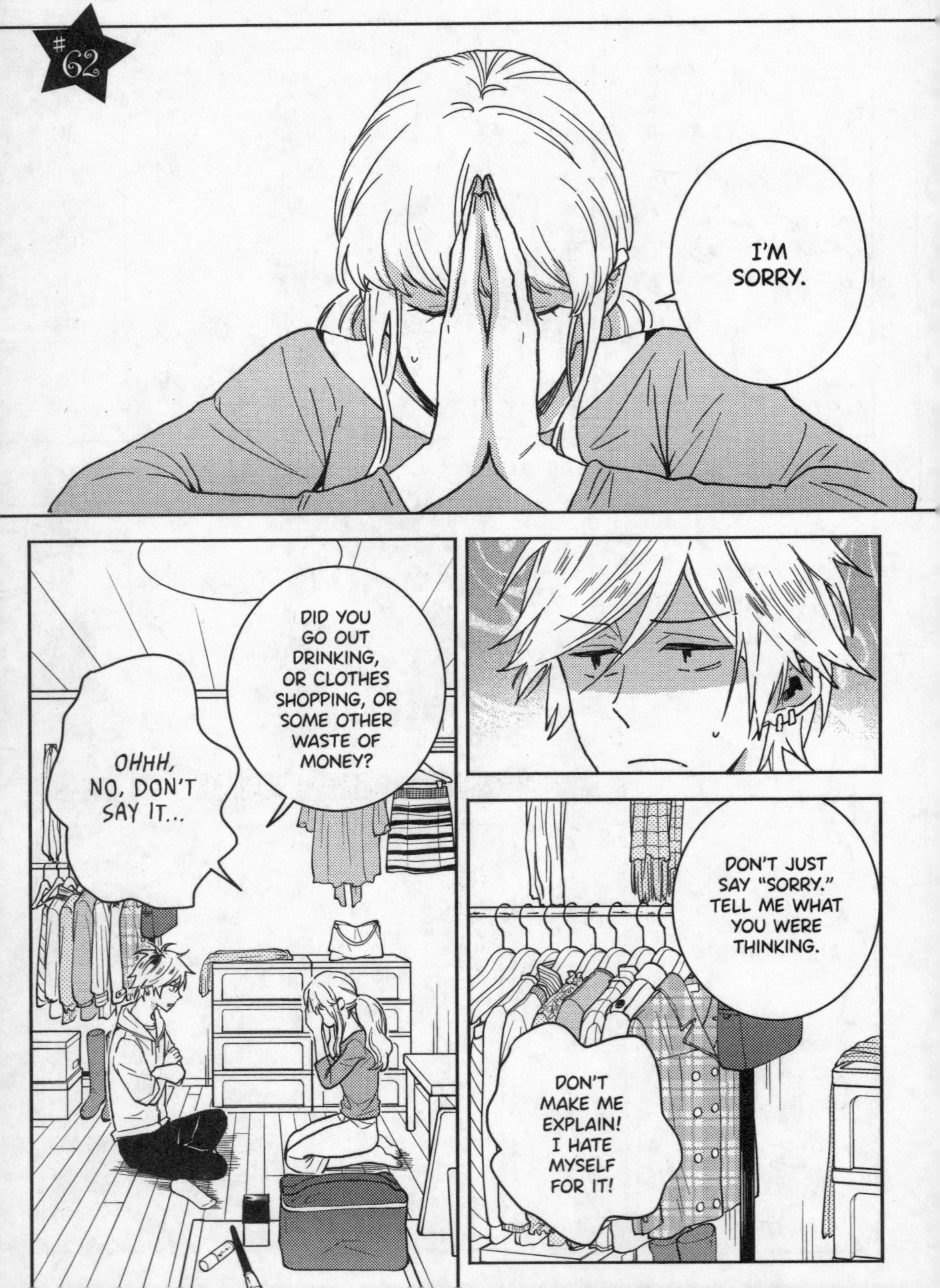
#62
I'M SORRY.
DON'T JUST SAY "SORRY." TELL ME WHAT YOU WERE THINKING.
DON'T MAKE ME EXPLAIN! I HATE MYSELF FOR IT!
DID YOU GO OUT DRINKING, OR CLOTHES SHOPPING, OR SOME OTHER WASTE OF MONEY?
OHHH, NO, DON'T SAY IT...

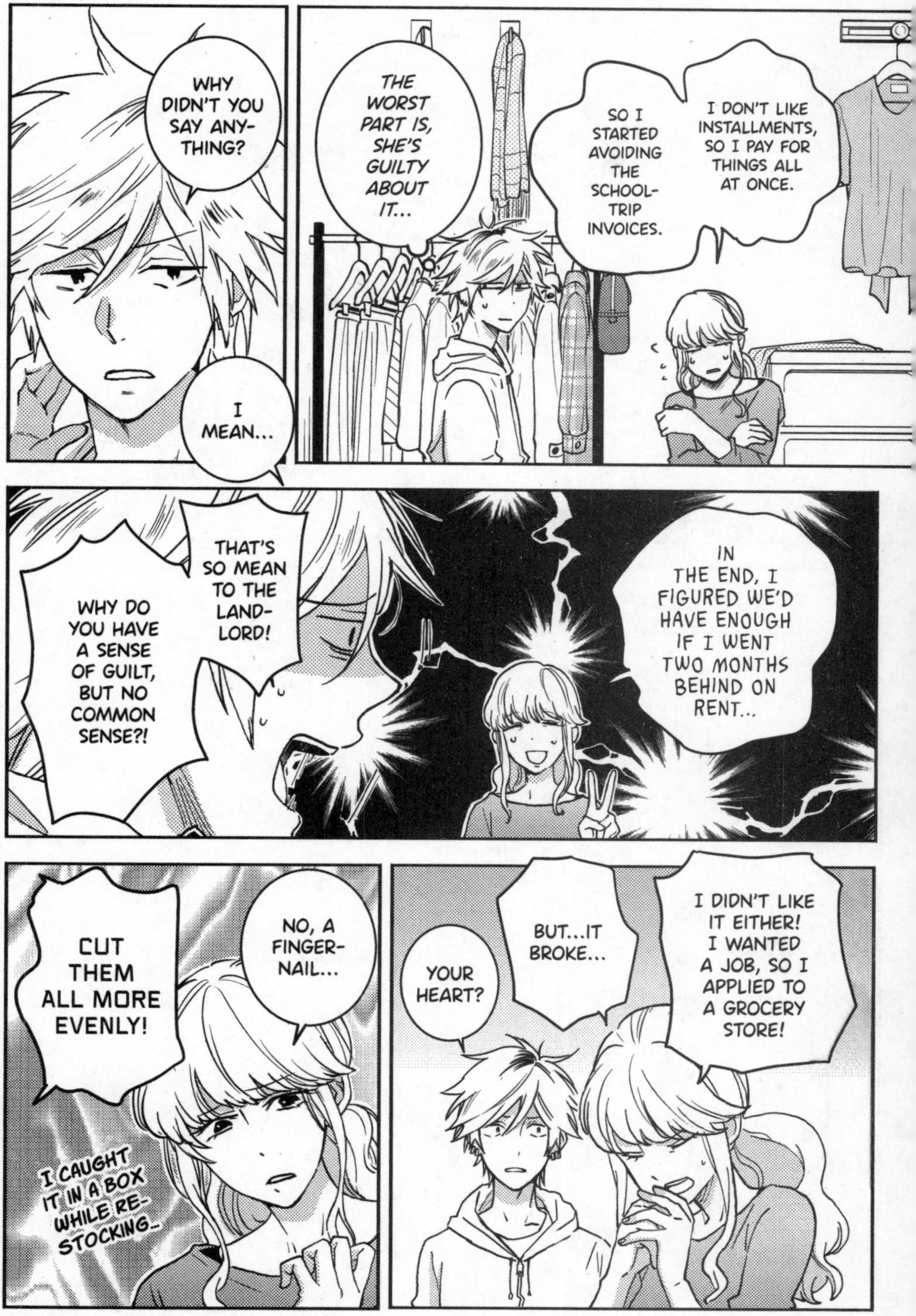
I DON'T LIKE INSTALLMENTS, SO I PAY FOR THINGS ALL AT ONCE.
SO I STARTED AVOIDING THE SCHOOL-TRIP INVOICES.
THE WORST PART IS, SHE'S GUILTY ABOUT IT...
WHY DIDN'T YOU SAY ANY-THING?
I MEAN...
IN THE END, I FIGURED WE'D HAVE ENOUGH IF I WENT TWO MONTHS BEHIND ON RENT...
THAT'S SO MEAN TO THE LAND-LORD!
WHY DO YOU HAVE A SENSE OF GUILT, BUT NO COMMON SENSE?!
I DIDN'T LIKE IT EITHER! I WANTED A JOB, SO I APPLIED TO A GROCERY STORE!
BUT...IT BROKE...
YOUR HEART?
NO, A FINGER-NAIL...
CUT THEM ALL MORE EVENLY!
I CAUGHT IT IN A BOX WHILE RE-STOCKING...

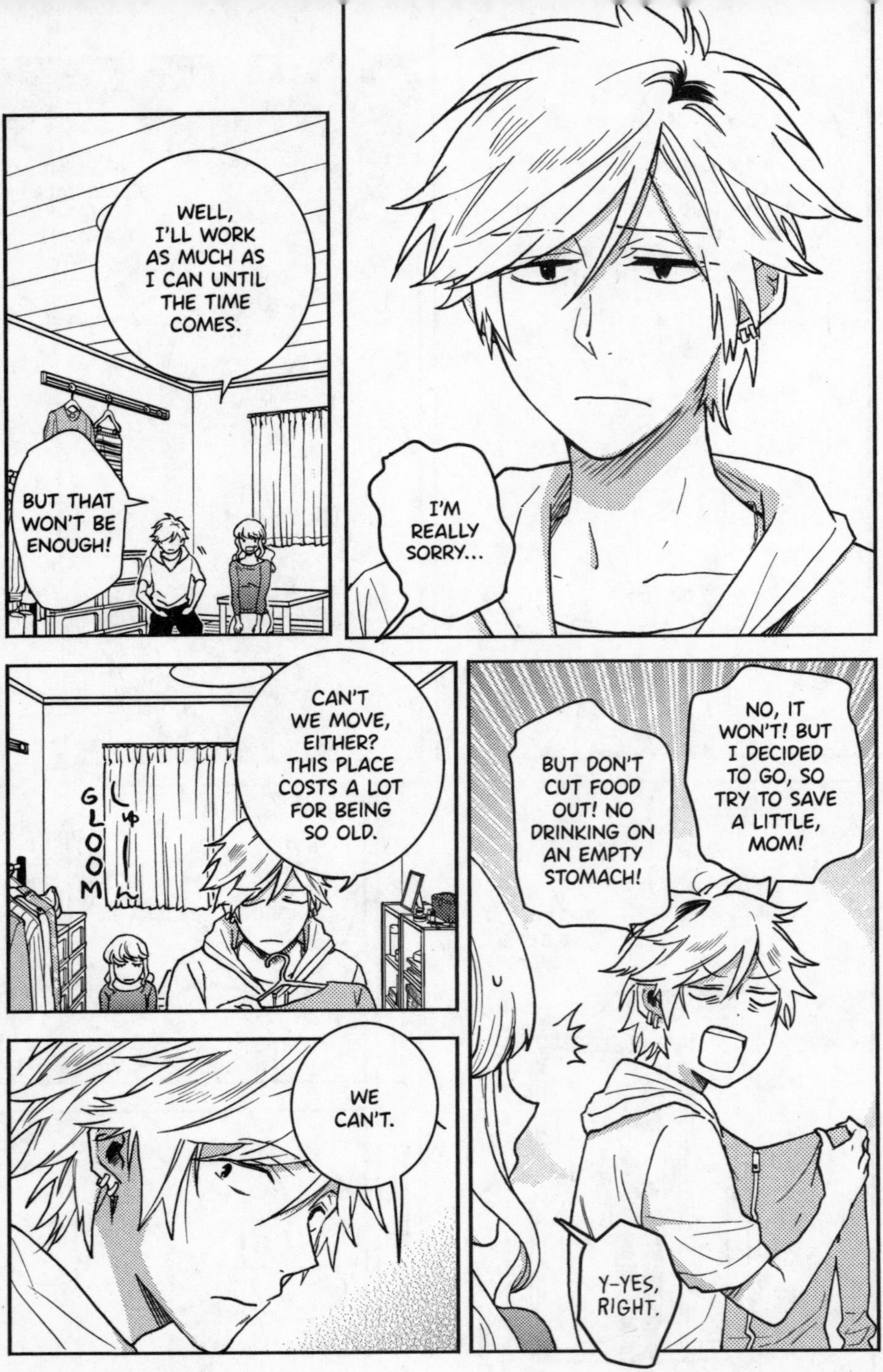
I'M REALLY SORRY...
WELL, I'LL WORK AS MUCH AS I CAN UNTIL THE TIME COMES.
BUT THAT WON'T BE ENOUGH!
NO, IT WON'T! BUT I DECIDED TO GO, SO TRY TO SAVE A LITTLE, MOM!
BUT DON'T CUT FOOD OUT! NO DRINKING ON AN EMPTY STOMACH!
Y-YES, RIGHT.
CAN'T WE MOVE, EITHER? THIS PLACE COSTS A LOT FOR BEING SO OLD.
GLOOM
WE CAN'T.

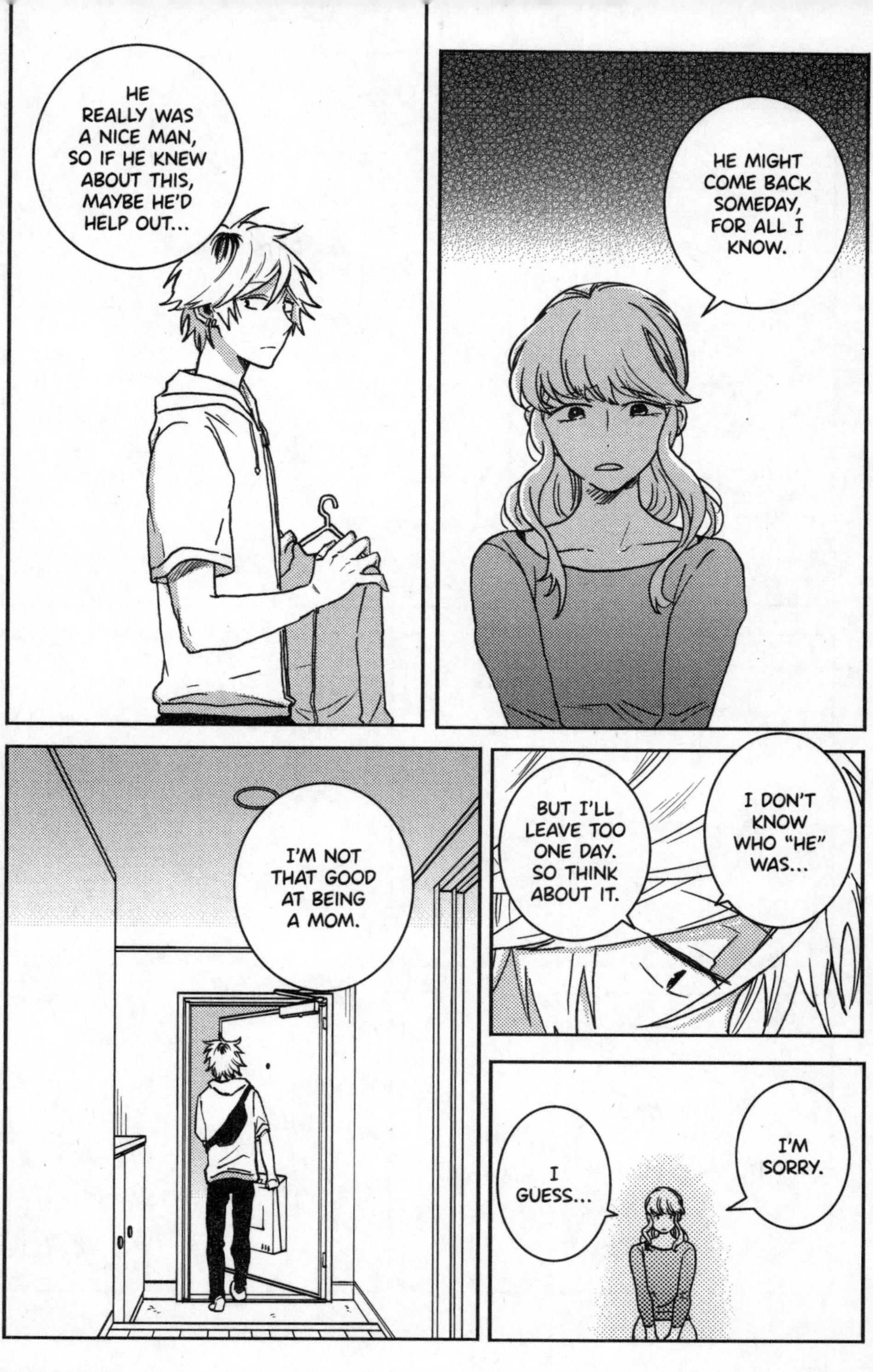
HE MIGHT COME BACK SOMEDAY, FOR ALL I KNOW.
HE REALLY WAS A NICE MAN, SO IF HE KNEW ABOUT THIS, MAYBE HE'D HELP OUT...
I DON'T KNOW WHO "HE" WAS...
BUT I'LL LEAVE TOO ONE DAY. SO THINK ABOUT IT.
I'M SORRY.
I GUESS...
I'M NOT THAT GOOD AT BEING A MOM.

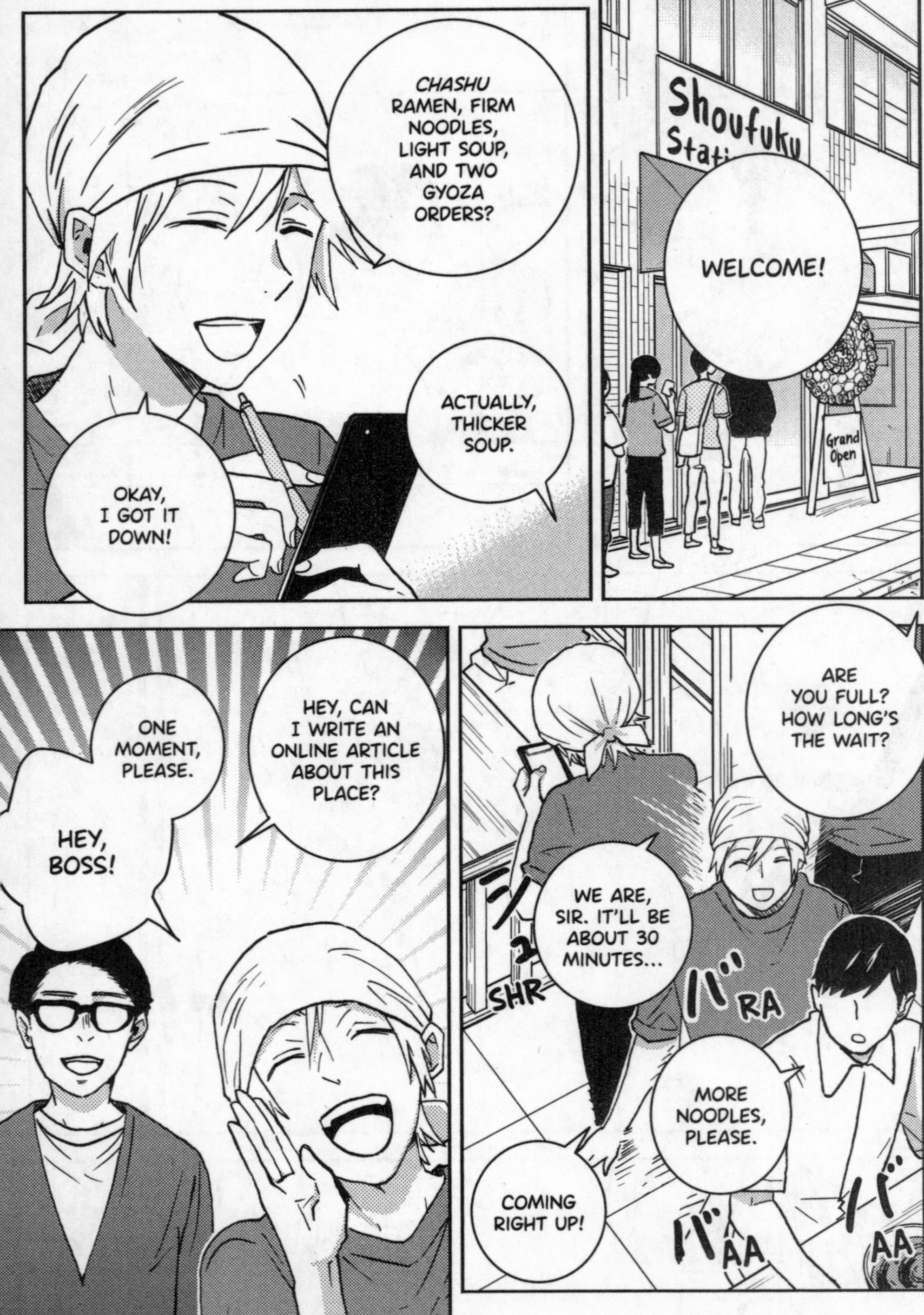
Shoufuku
Stati
WELCOME!
Grand Open
CHASHU RAMEN, FIRM NOODLES, LIGHT SOUP, AND TWO GYOZA ORDERS?
ACTUALLY, THICKER SOUP.
OKAY, I GOT IT DOWN!
ARE YOU FULL? HOW LONG'S THE WAIT?
WE ARE, SIR. IT'LL BE ABOUT 30 MINUTES...
SHR
RA
MORE NOODLES, PLEASE.
AA
COMING RIGHT UP!
AA
HEY, CAN I WRITE AN ONLINE ARTICLE ABOUT THIS PLACE?
ONE MOMENT, PLEASE.
HEY, BOSS!

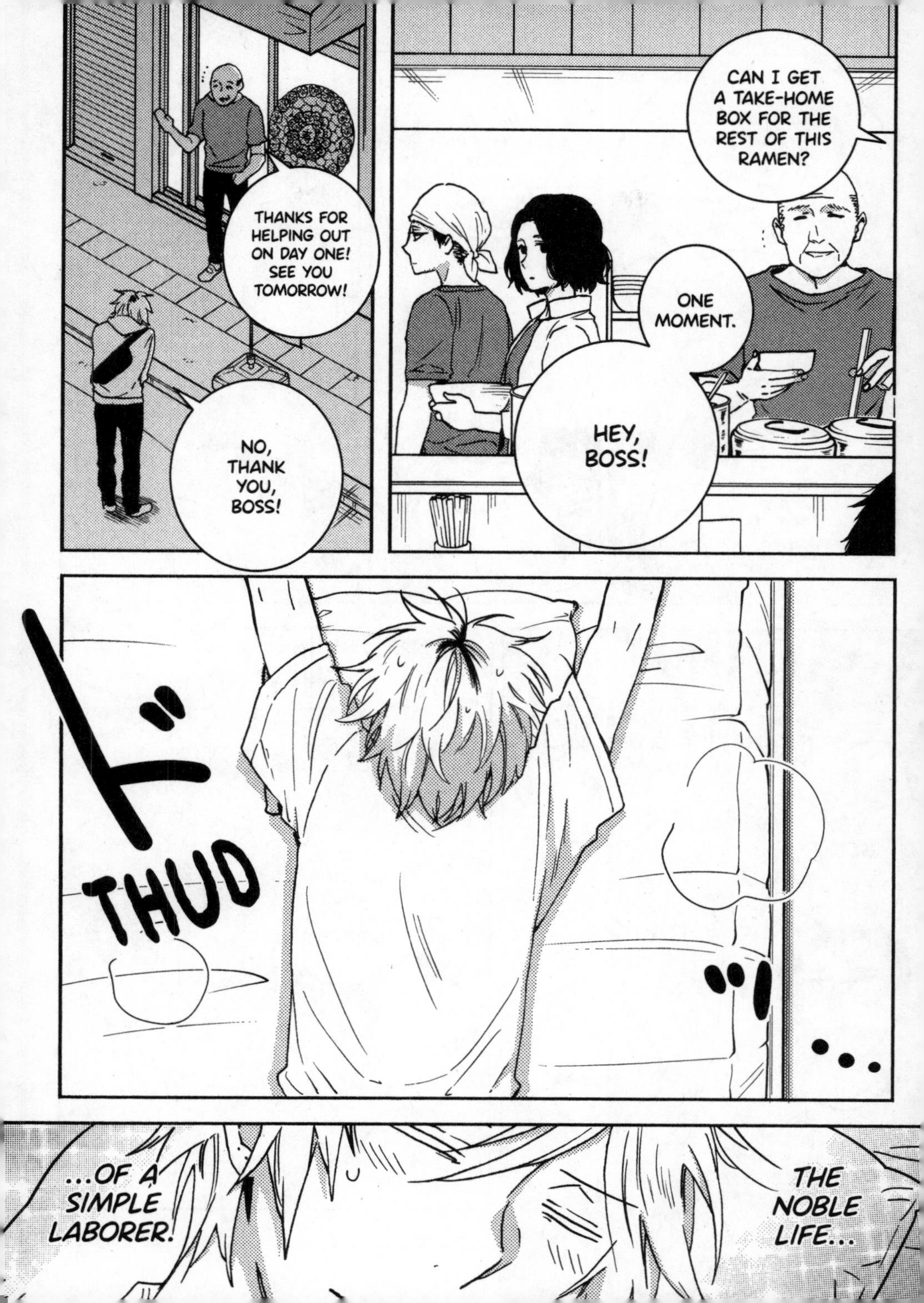
CAN I GET A TAKE-HOME BOX FOR THE REST OF THIS RAMEN?
ONE MOMENT.
HEY, BOSS!
THANKS FOR HELPING OUT ON DAY ONE! SEE YOU TOMORROW!
NO, THANK YOU, BOSS!
ド
THUD
...
THE NOBLE LIFE...
...OF A SIMPLE LABORER.

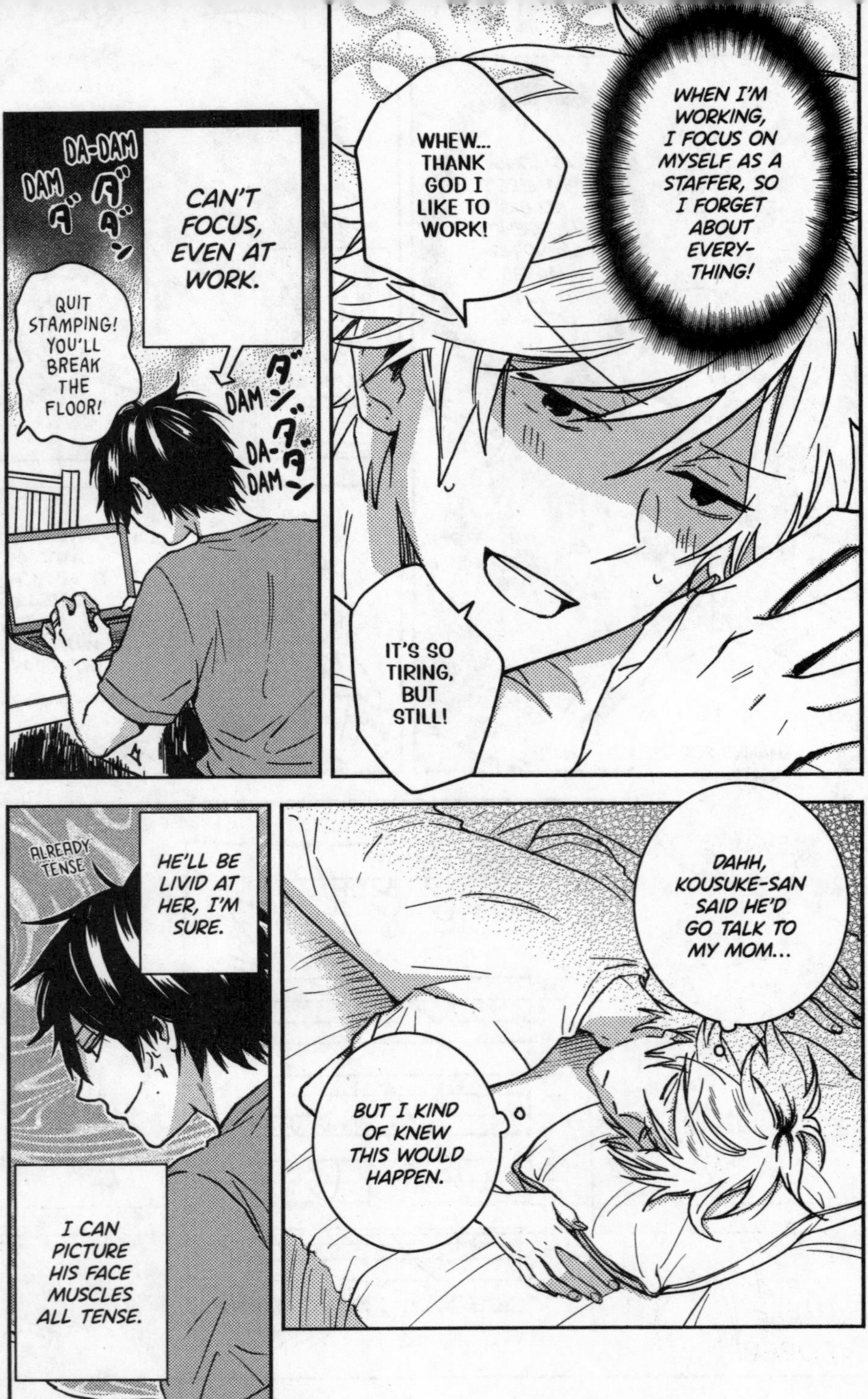
WHEN I'M WORKING, I FOCUS ON MYSELF AS A STAFFER, SO I FORGET ABOUT EVERYTHING!
WHEW... THANK GOD I LIKE TO WORK!
IT'S SO TIRING, BUT STILL!
CAN'T FOCUS, EVEN AT WORK.
DA-DAM
DAM
QUIT STAMPING! YOU'LL BREAK THE FLOOR!
DAM
DA-DAM
DAHH, KOUSUKE-SAN SAID HE'D GO TALK TO MY MOM...
BUT I KIND OF KNEW THIS WOULD HAPPEN.
HE'LL BE LIVID AT HER, I'M SURE.
ALREADY TENSE
I CAN PICTURE HIS FACE MUSCLES ALL TENSE.

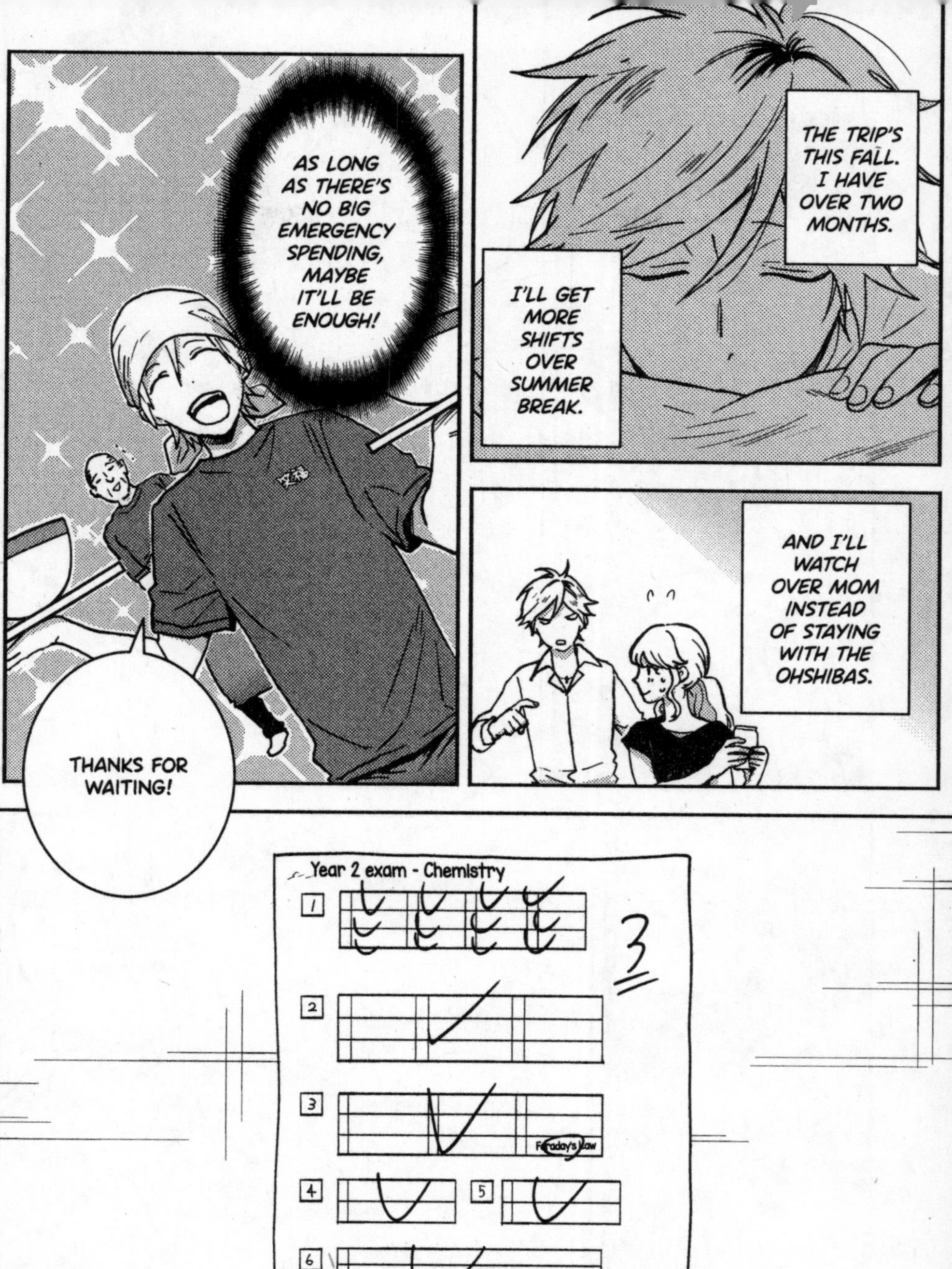
THE TRIP'S THIS FALL. I HAVE OVER TWO MONTHS.
I'LL GET MORE SHIFTS OVER SUMMER BREAK.
AND I'LL WATCH OVER MOM INSTEAD OF STAYING WITH THE OHSHIBAS.
AS LONG AS THERE'S NO BIG EMERGENCY SPENDING, MAYBE IT'LL BE ENOUGH!
THANKS FOR WAITING!
Year 2 exam - Chemistry
1
3
2
3
Faraday's Law
4
5
6
Year 2 Class 3
Masahiro Setagawa

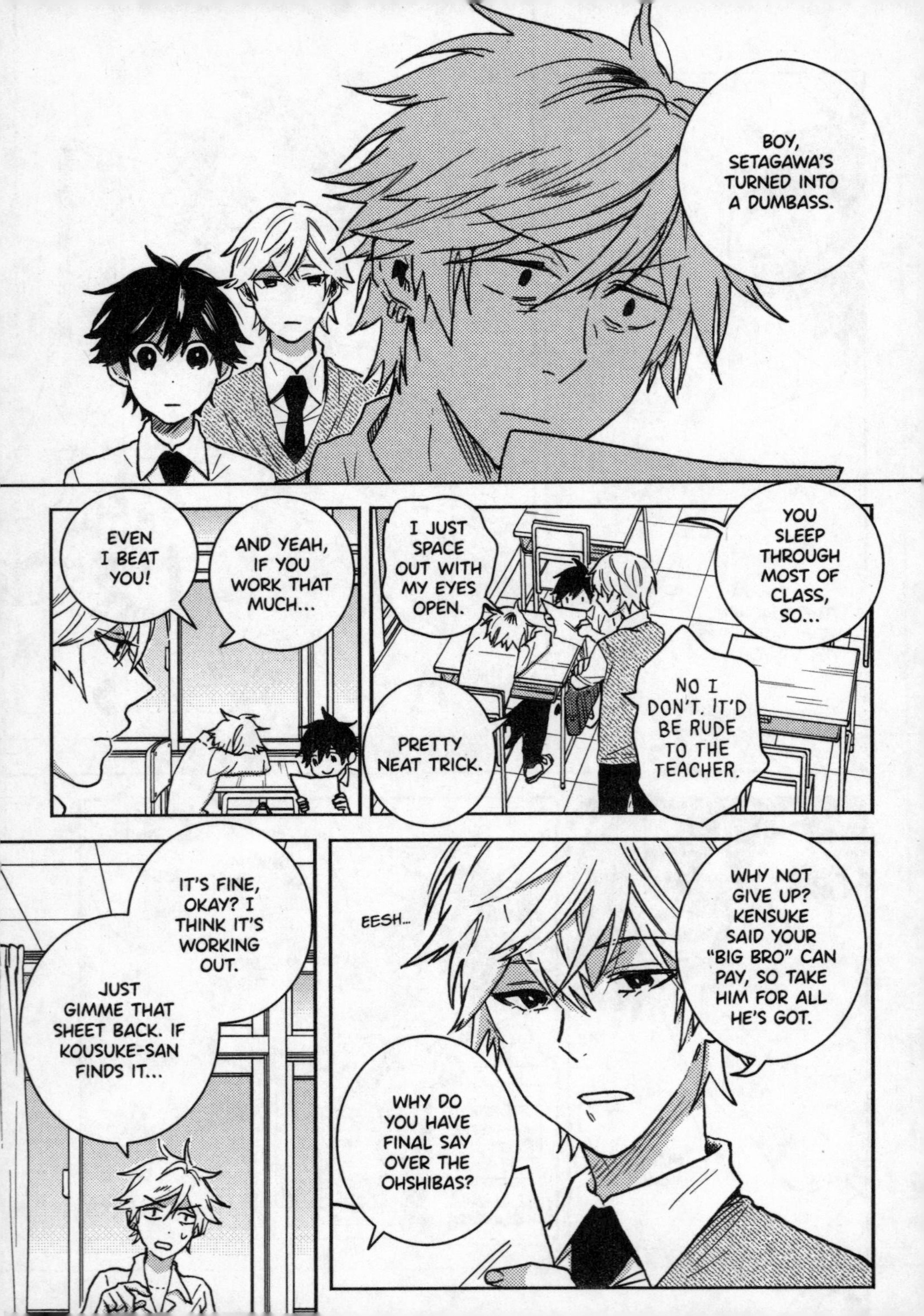
BOY, SETAGAWA'S TURNED INTO A DUMBASS.
YOU SLEEP THROUGH MOST OF CLASS, SO...
NO I DON'T. IT'D BE RUDE TO THE TEACHER.
I JUST SPACE OUT WITH MY EYES OPEN.
PRETTY NEAT TRICK.
AND YEAH, IF YOU WORK THAT MUCH...
EVEN I BEAT YOU!
WHY NOT GIVE UP? KENSUKE SAID YOUR "BIG BRO" CAN PAY, SO TAKE HIM FOR ALL HE'S GOT.
EESH...
WHY DO YOU HAVE FINAL SAY OVER THE OHSHIBAS?
IT'S FINE, OKAY? I THINK IT'S WORKING OUT.
JUST GIMME THAT SHEET BACK. IF KOUSUKE-SAN FINDS IT...

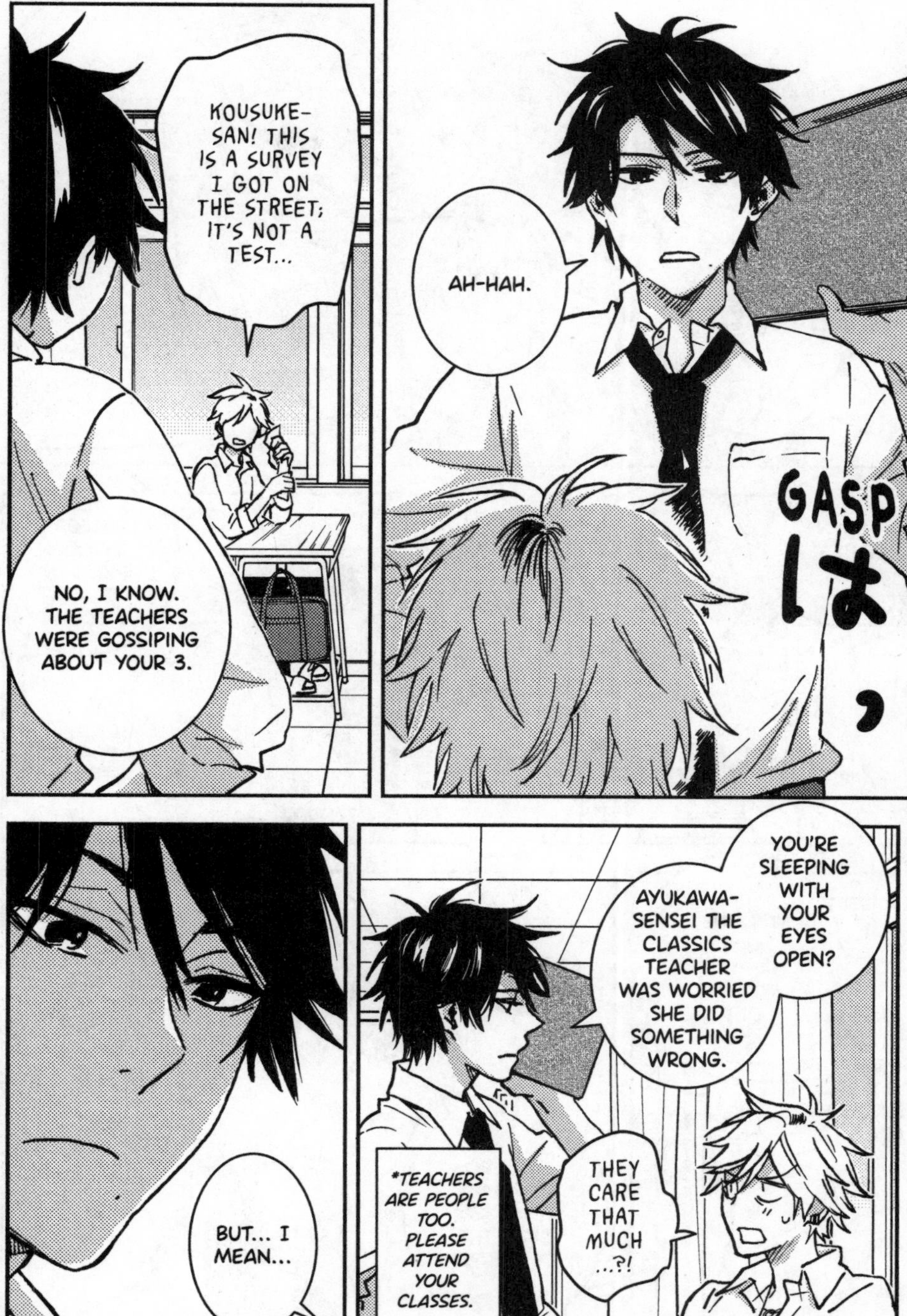
AH-HAH.
GASP
は,
KOUSUKE-SAN! THIS IS A SURVEY I GOT ON THE STREET; IT'S NOT A TEST...
NO, I KNOW. THE TEACHERS WERE GOSSIPING ABOUT YOUR 3.
YOU'RE SLEEPING WITH YOUR EYES OPEN?
AYUKAWA-SENSEI THE CLASSICS TEACHER WAS WORRIED SHE DID SOMETHING WRONG.
THEY CARE THAT MUCH ...?!
*TEACHERS ARE PEOPLE TOO. PLEASE ATTEND YOUR CLASSES.
BUT... I MEAN...

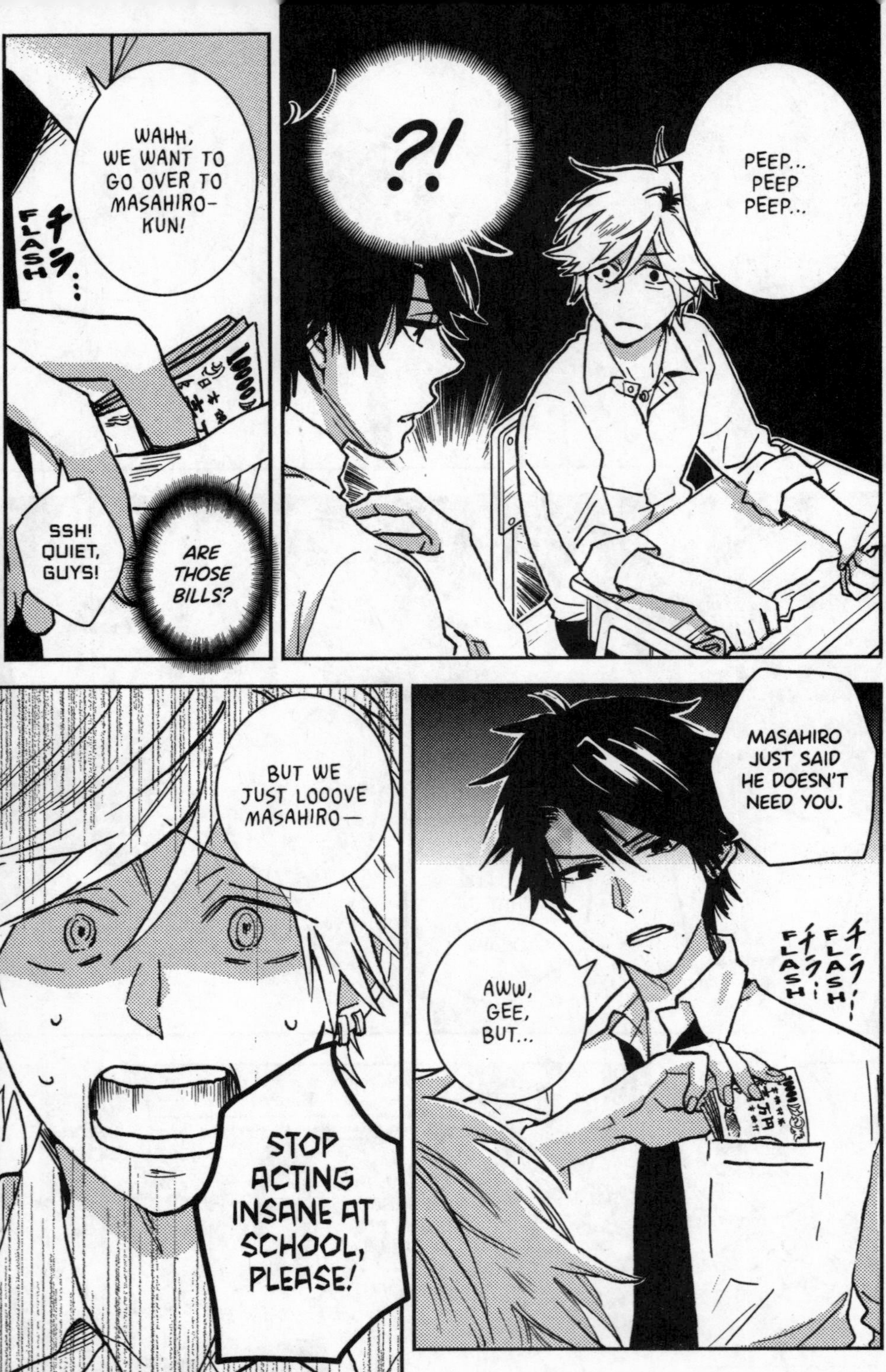
PEEP... PEEP PEEP...
?!
WAHH, WE WANT TO GO OVER TO MASAHIRO-KUN!
チラ… FLASH
SSH! QUIET, GUYS!
ARE THOSE BILLS?
MASAHIRO JUST SAID HE DOESN'T NEED YOU.
チラ! FLASH
チラ! FLASH
AWW, GEE, BUT...
BUT WE JUST LOOOVE MASAHIRO—
STOP ACTING INSANE AT SCHOOL, PLEASE!

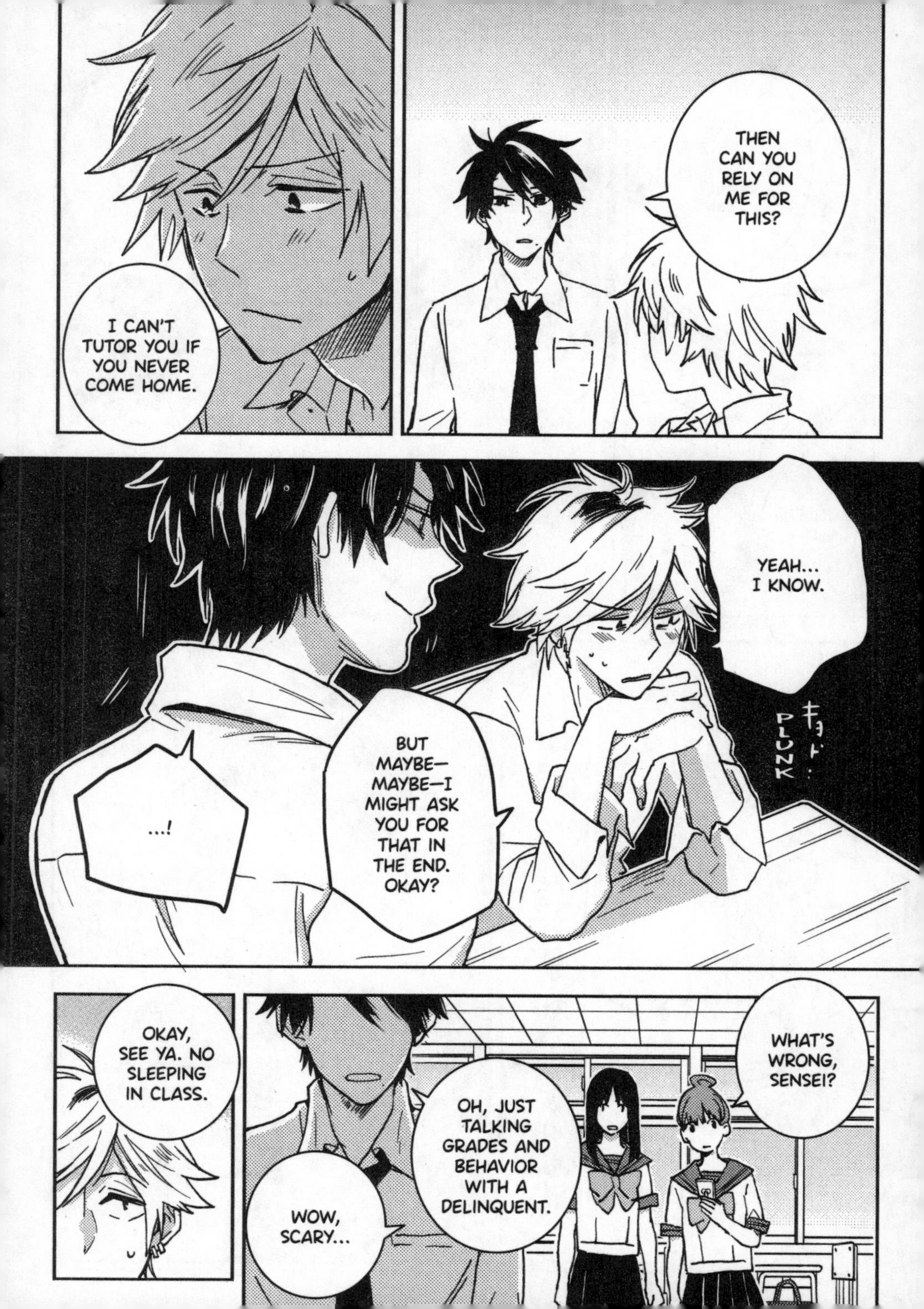
THEN CAN YOU RELY ON ME FOR THIS?
I CAN'T TUTOR YOU IF YOU NEVER COME HOME.
YEAH... I KNOW.
PLUNK
BUT MAYBE—MAYBE—I MIGHT ASK YOU FOR THAT IN THE END. OKAY?
...!
WHAT'S WRONG, SENSEI?
OH, JUST TALKING GRADES AND BEHAVIOR WITH A DELINQUENT.
WOW, SCARY...
OKAY, SEE YA. NO SLEEPING IN CLASS.

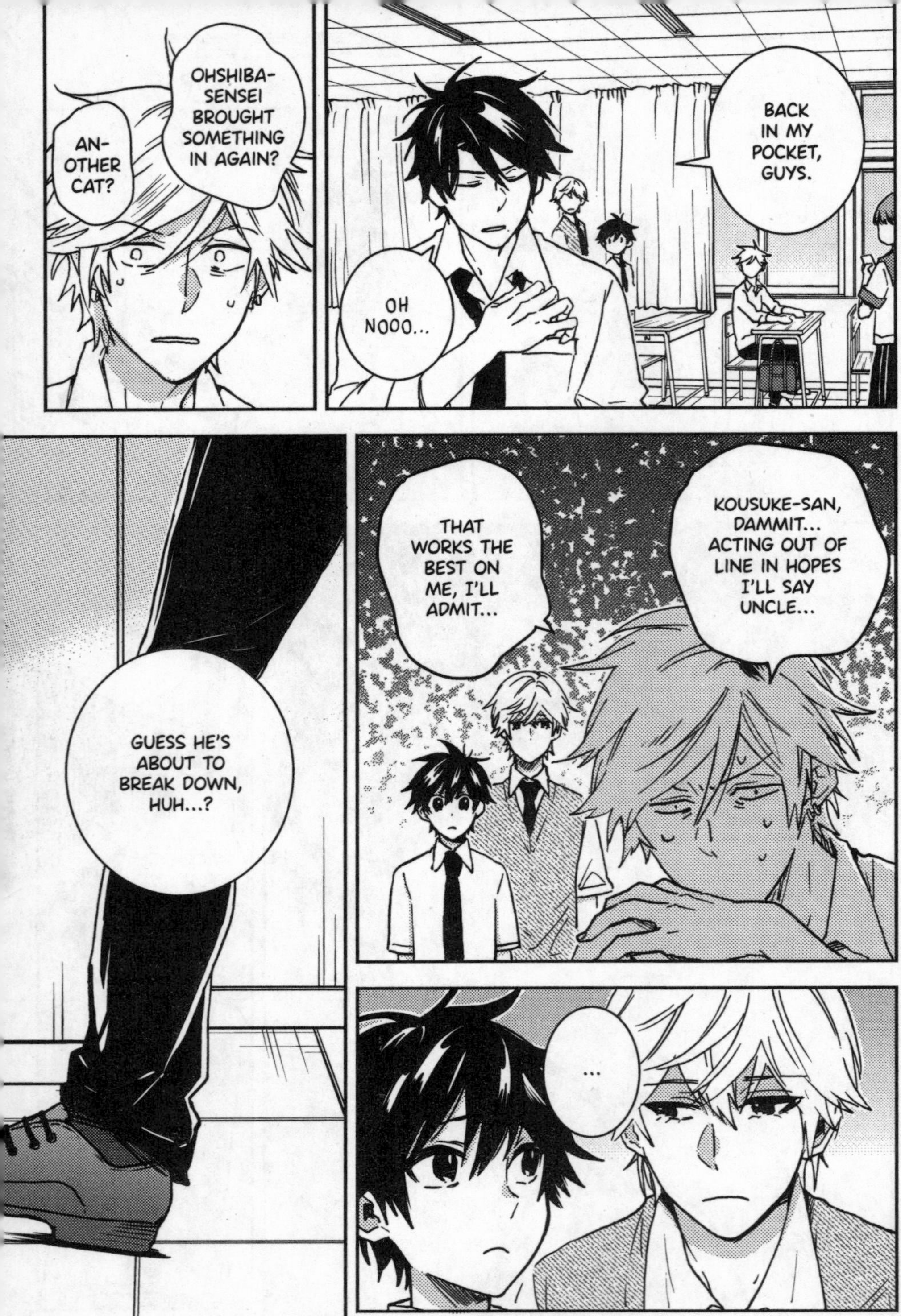
BACK IN MY POCKET, GUYS.
OH NOOO...
OHSHIBA-SENSEI BROUGHT SOMETHING IN AGAIN?
AN-OTHER CAT?
KOUSUKE-SAN, DAMMIT... ACTING OUT OF LINE IN HOPES I'LL SAY UNCLE...
THAT WORKS THE BEST ON ME, I'LL ADMIT...
...
GUESS HE'S ABOUT TO BREAK DOWN, HUH...?

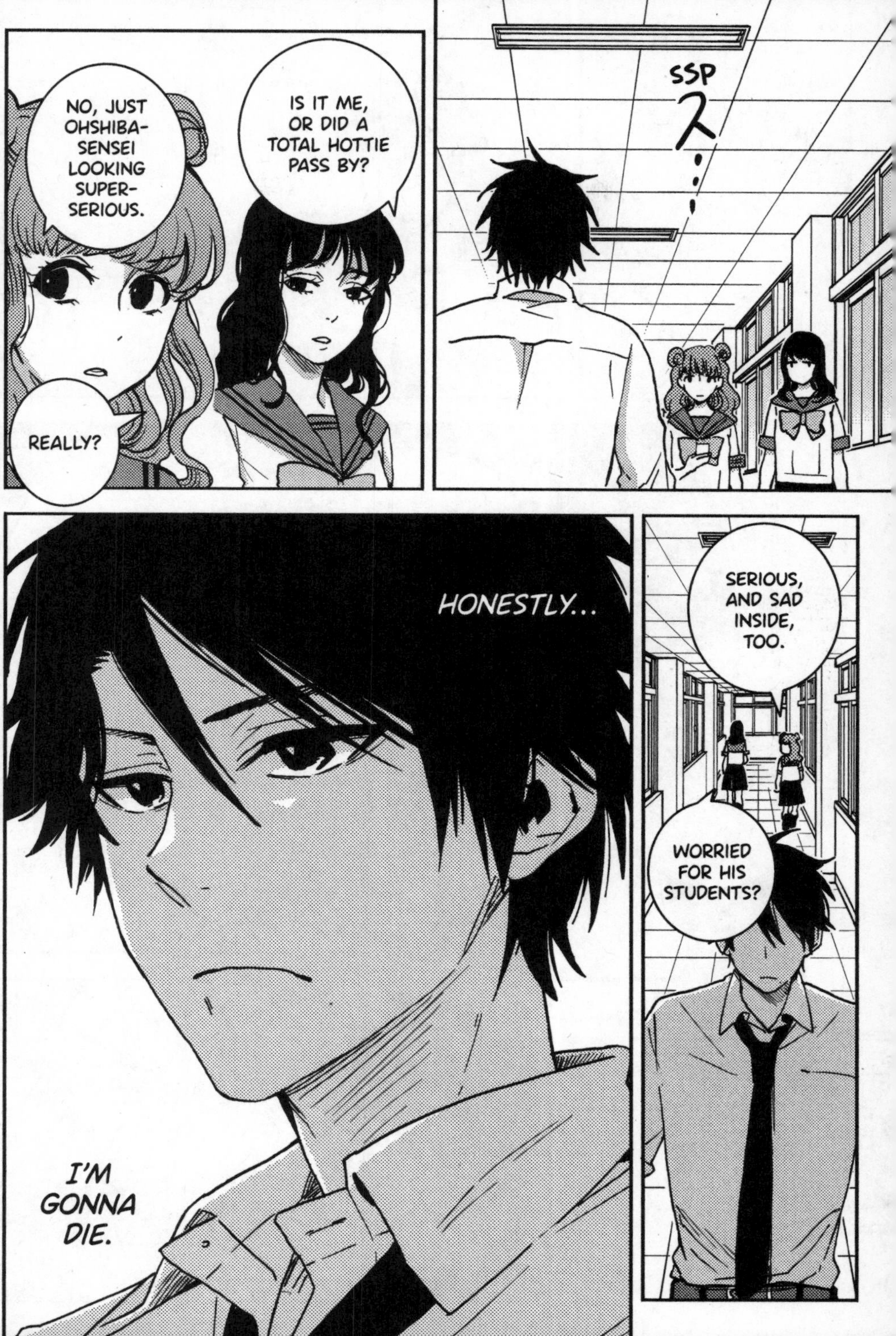
SSP
ス
IS IT ME, OR DID A TOTAL HOTTIE PASS BY?
NO, JUST OHSHIBA-SENSEI LOOKING SUPER-SERIOUS.
REALLY?
SERIOUS, AND SAD INSIDE, TOO.
WORRIED FOR HIS STUDENTS?
HONESTLY...
I'M GONNA DIE.

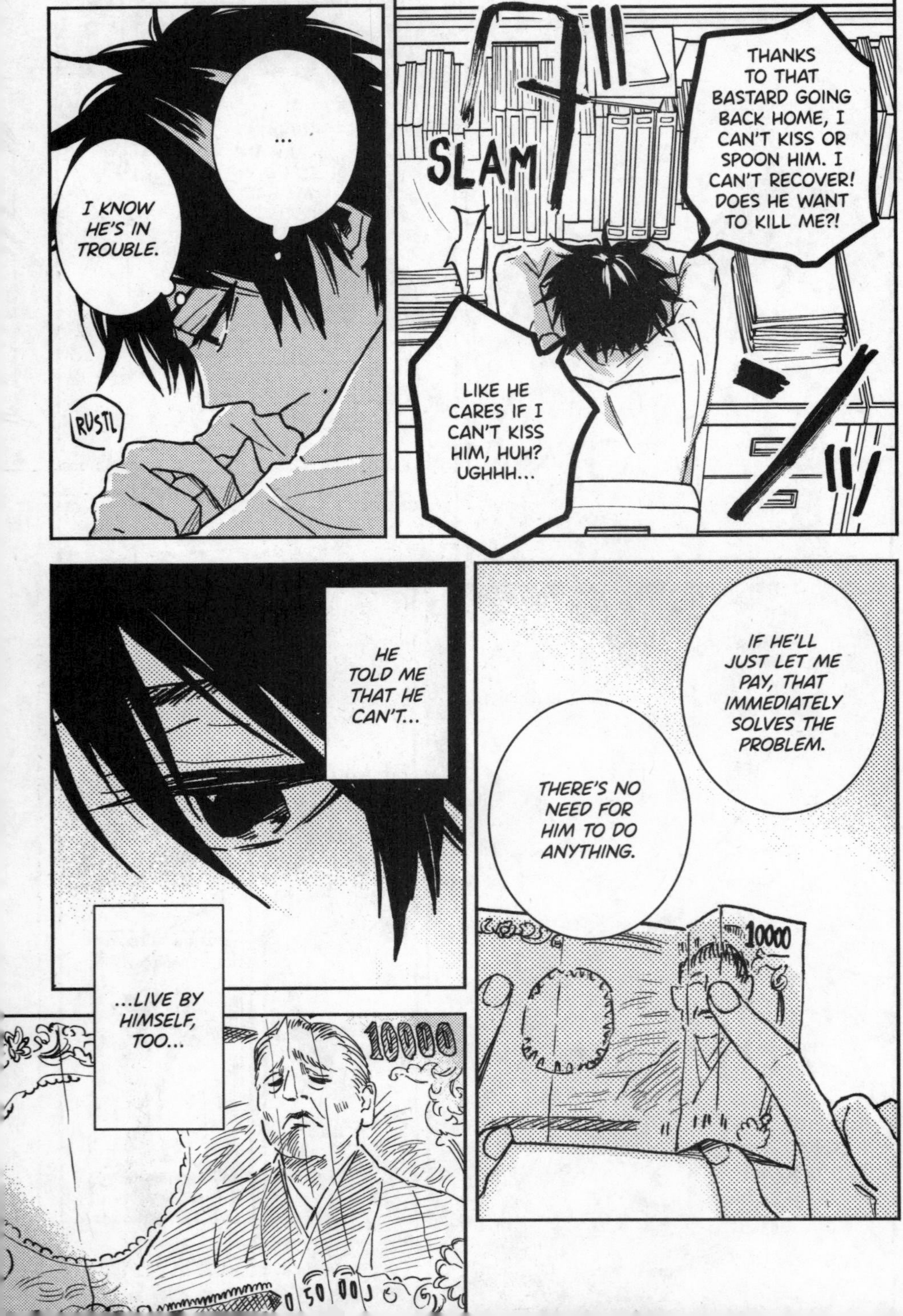
THANKS TO THAT BASTARD GOING BACK HOME, I CAN'T KISS OR SPOON HIM. I CAN'T RECOVER! DOES HE WANT TO KILL ME?!
SLAM
LIKE HE CARES IF I CAN'T KISS HIM, HUH? UGHHH...
...
I KNOW HE'S IN TROUBLE.
RUSTL
IF HE'LL JUST LET ME PAY, THAT IMMEDIATELY SOLVES THE PROBLEM.
THERE'S NO NEED FOR HIM TO DO ANYTHING.
10000
HE TOLD ME THAT HE CAN'T...
...LIVE BY HIMSELF, TOO...
10000

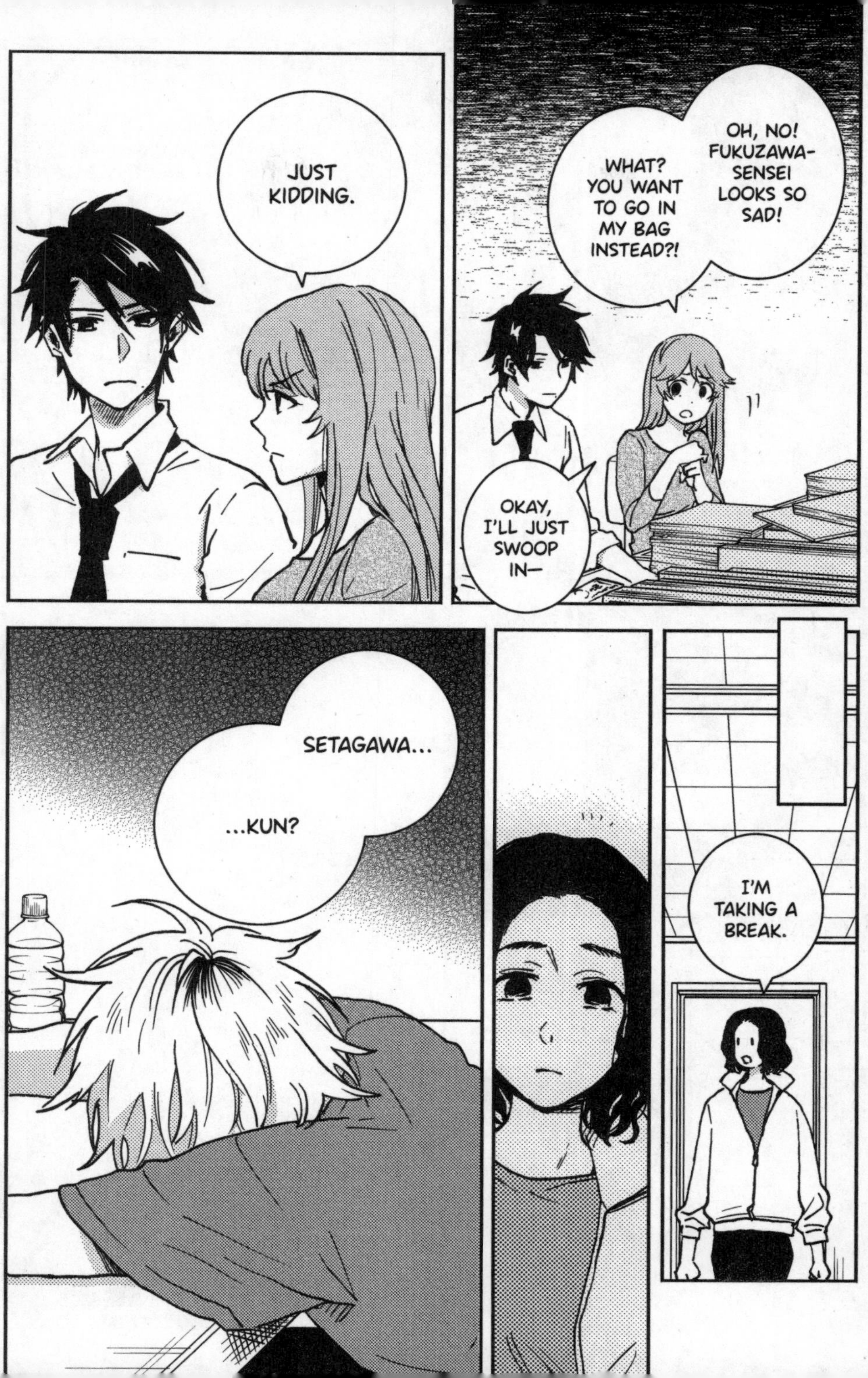
OH, NO! FUKUZAWA-SENSEI LOOKS SO SAD!
WHAT? YOU WANT TO GO IN MY BAG INSTEAD?!
OKAY, I'LL JUST SWOOP IN—
JUST KIDDING.
I'M TAKING A BREAK.
SETAGAWA...
...KUN?

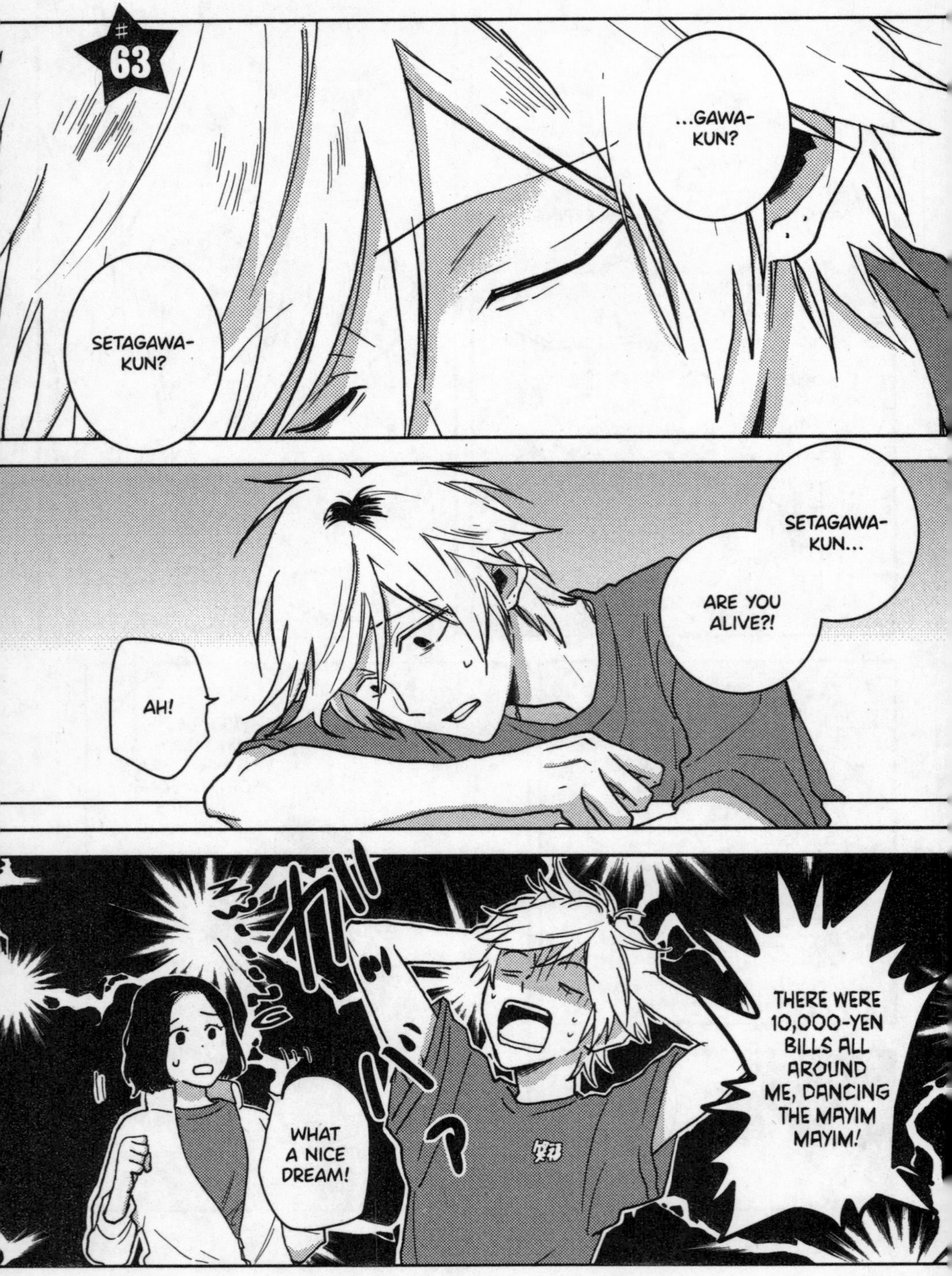
#63
...GAWA-KUN?
SETAGAWA-KUN?
SETAGAWA-KUN...
ARE YOU ALIVE?!
AH!
THERE WERE 10,000-YEN BILLS ALL AROUND ME, DANCING THE MAYIM MAYIM!
WHAT A NICE DREAM!

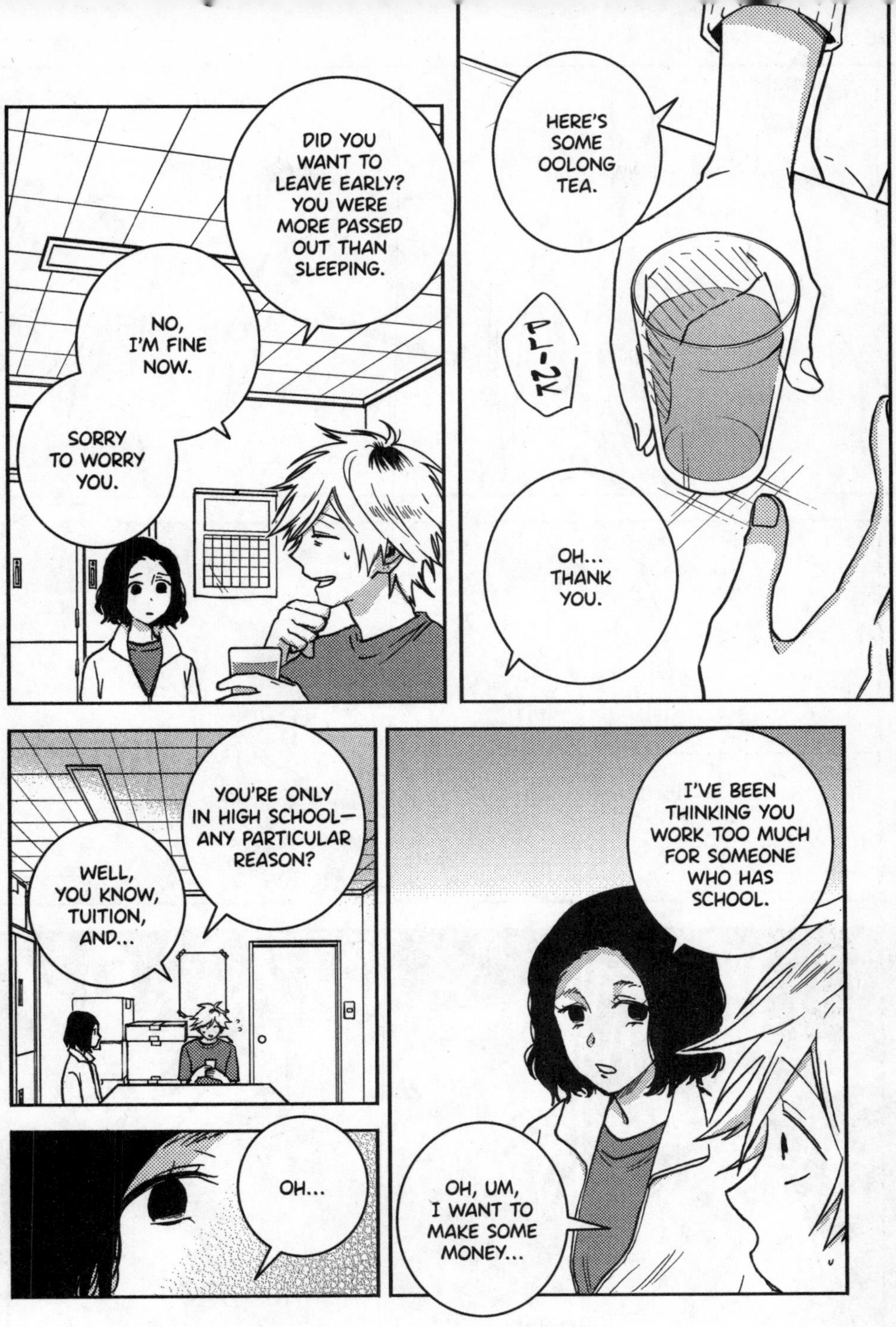
HERE'S SOME OOLONG TEA.
PLINK
OH... THANK YOU.
DID YOU WANT TO LEAVE EARLY? YOU WERE MORE PASSED OUT THAN SLEEPING.
NO, I'M FINE NOW.
SORRY TO WORRY YOU.
I'VE BEEN THINKING YOU WORK TOO MUCH FOR SOMEONE WHO HAS SCHOOL.
OH, UM, I WANT TO MAKE SOME MONEY...
YOU'RE ONLY IN HIGH SCHOOL—ANY PARTICULAR REASON?
WELL, YOU KNOW, TUITION, AND...
OH...

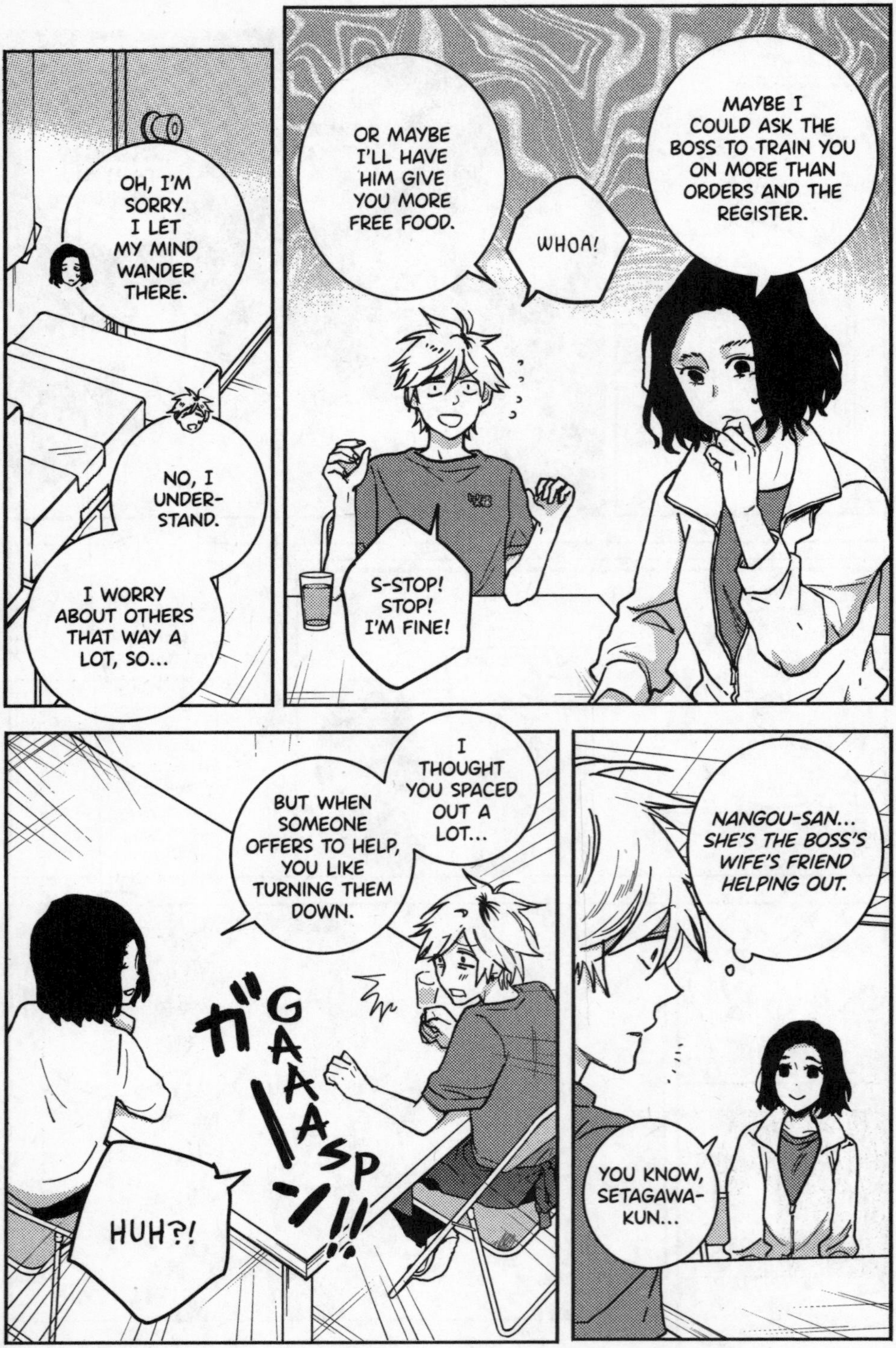
MAYBE I COULD ASK THE BOSS TO TRAIN YOU ON MORE THAN ORDERS AND THE REGISTER.
WHOA!
OR MAYBE I'LL HAVE HIM GIVE YOU MORE FREE FOOD.
S-STOP! STOP! I'M FINE!
OH, I'M SORRY. I LET MY MIND WANDER THERE.
NO, I UNDER-STAND.
I WORRY ABOUT OTHERS THAT WAY A LOT, SO...
NANGOU-SAN... SHE'S THE BOSS'S WIFE'S FRIEND HELPING OUT.
YOU KNOW, SETAGAWA-KUN...
I THOUGHT YOU SPACED OUT A LOT...
BUT WHEN SOMEONE OFFERS TO HELP, YOU LIKE TURNING THEM DOWN.
ガ GAAASP ーン!!
HUH?!

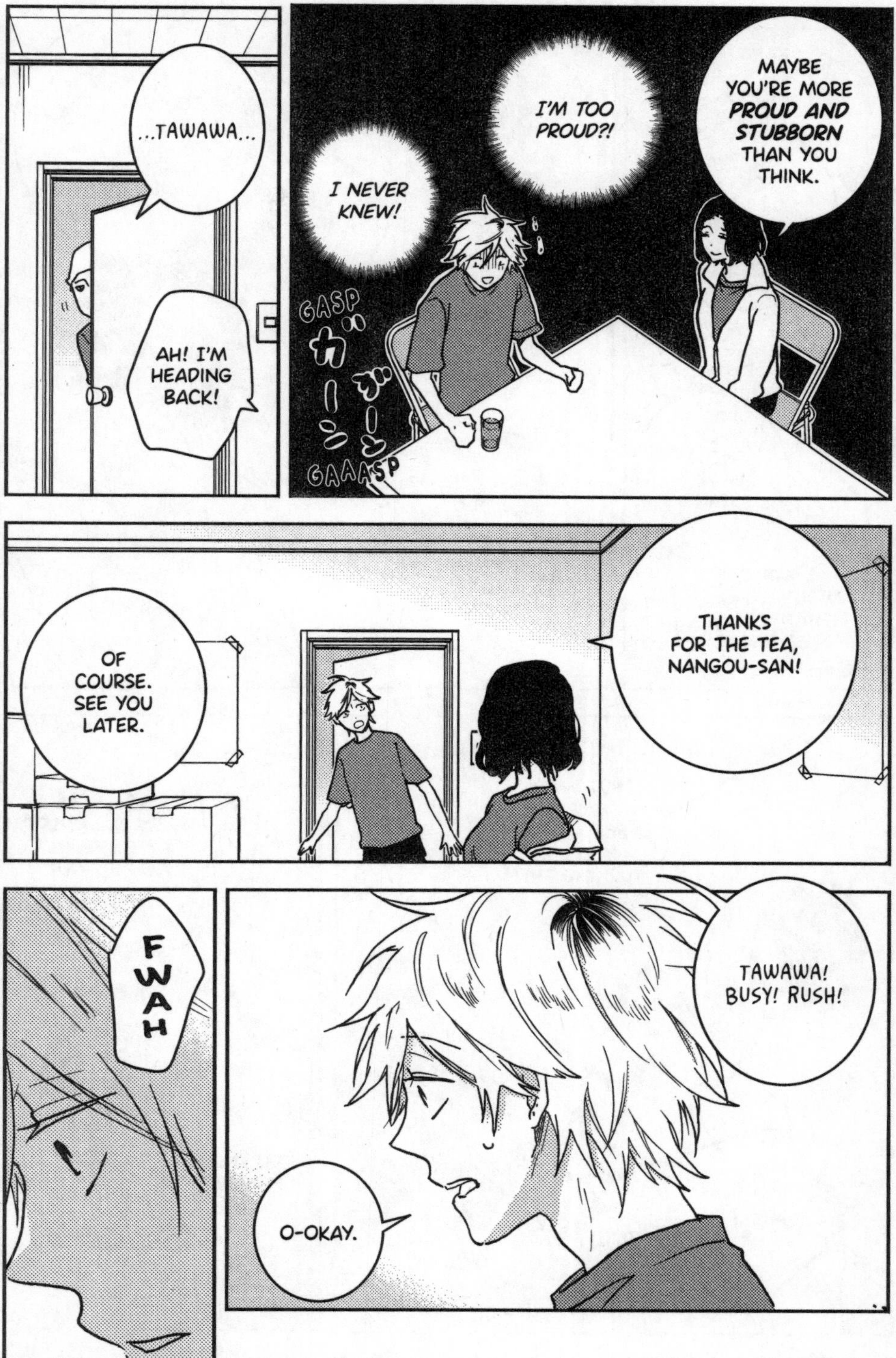
MAYBE YOU'RE MORE ***PROUD AND STUBBORN*** THAN YOU THINK.
I'M TOO PROUD?!
I NEVER KNEW!
GASP
GAAASP
...TAWAWA...
AH! I'M HEADING BACK!
THANKS FOR THE TEA, NANGOU-SAN!
OF COURSE. SEE YOU LATER.
TAWAWA! BUSY! RUSH!
O-OKAY.
FWAH

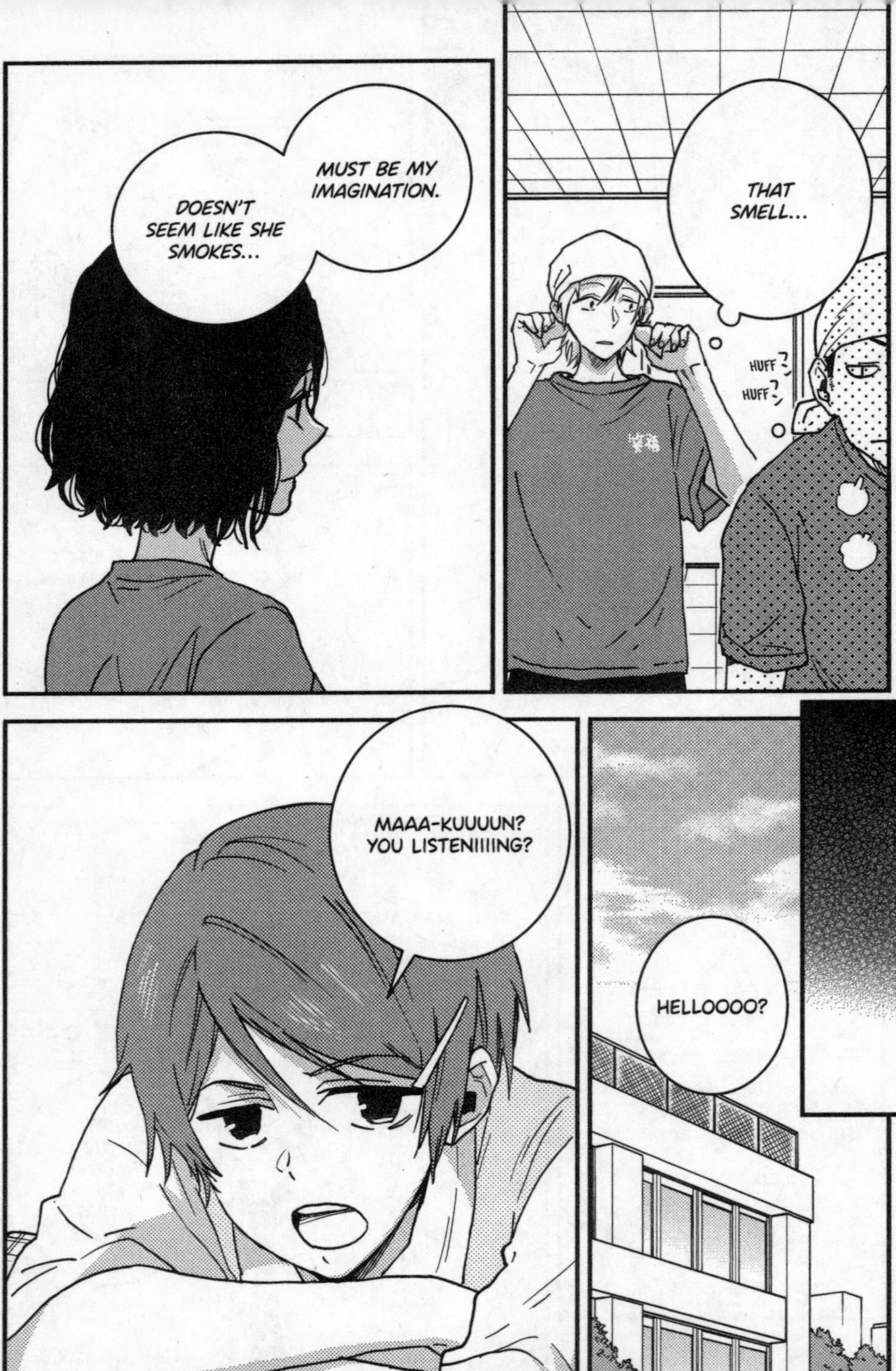
THAT SMELL...
HUFF HUFF
MUST BE MY IMAGINATION.
DOESN'T SEEM LIKE SHE SMOKES...
HELLOOOO?
MAAA-KUUUUN? YOU LISTENIIIING?

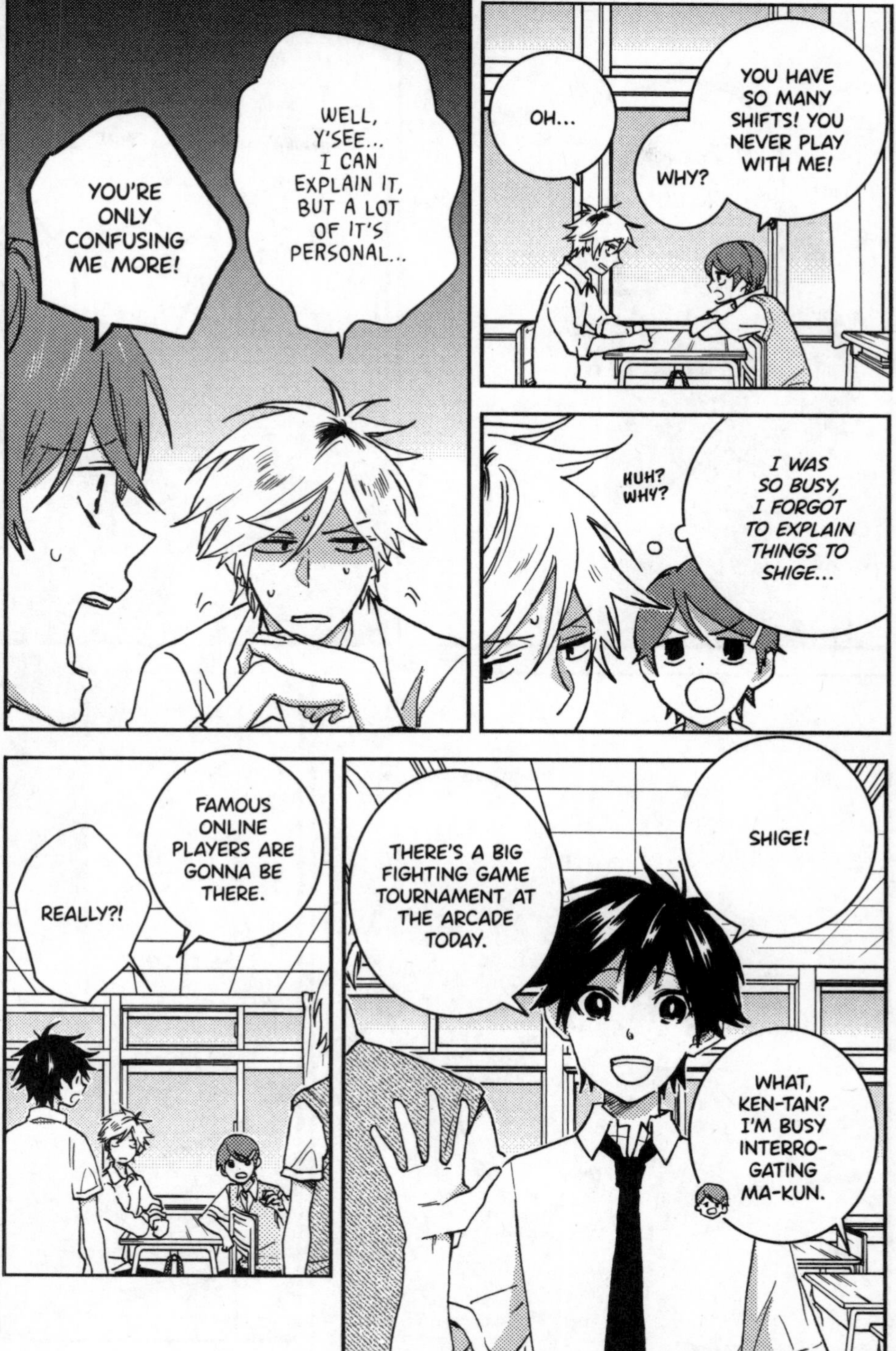
YOU HAVE SO MANY SHIFTS! YOU NEVER PLAY WITH ME!
WHY?
OH...
I WAS SO BUSY, I FORGOT TO EXPLAIN THINGS TO SHIGE...
HUH? WHY?
WELL, Y'SEE... I CAN EXPLAIN IT, BUT A LOT OF IT'S PERSONAL...
YOU'RE ONLY CONFUSING ME MORE!
SHIGE!
WHAT, KEN-TAN? I'M BUSY INTERRO-GATING MA-KUN.
THERE'S A BIG FIGHTING GAME TOURNAMENT AT THE ARCADE TODAY.
FAMOUS ONLINE PLAYERS ARE GONNA BE THERE.
REALLY?!

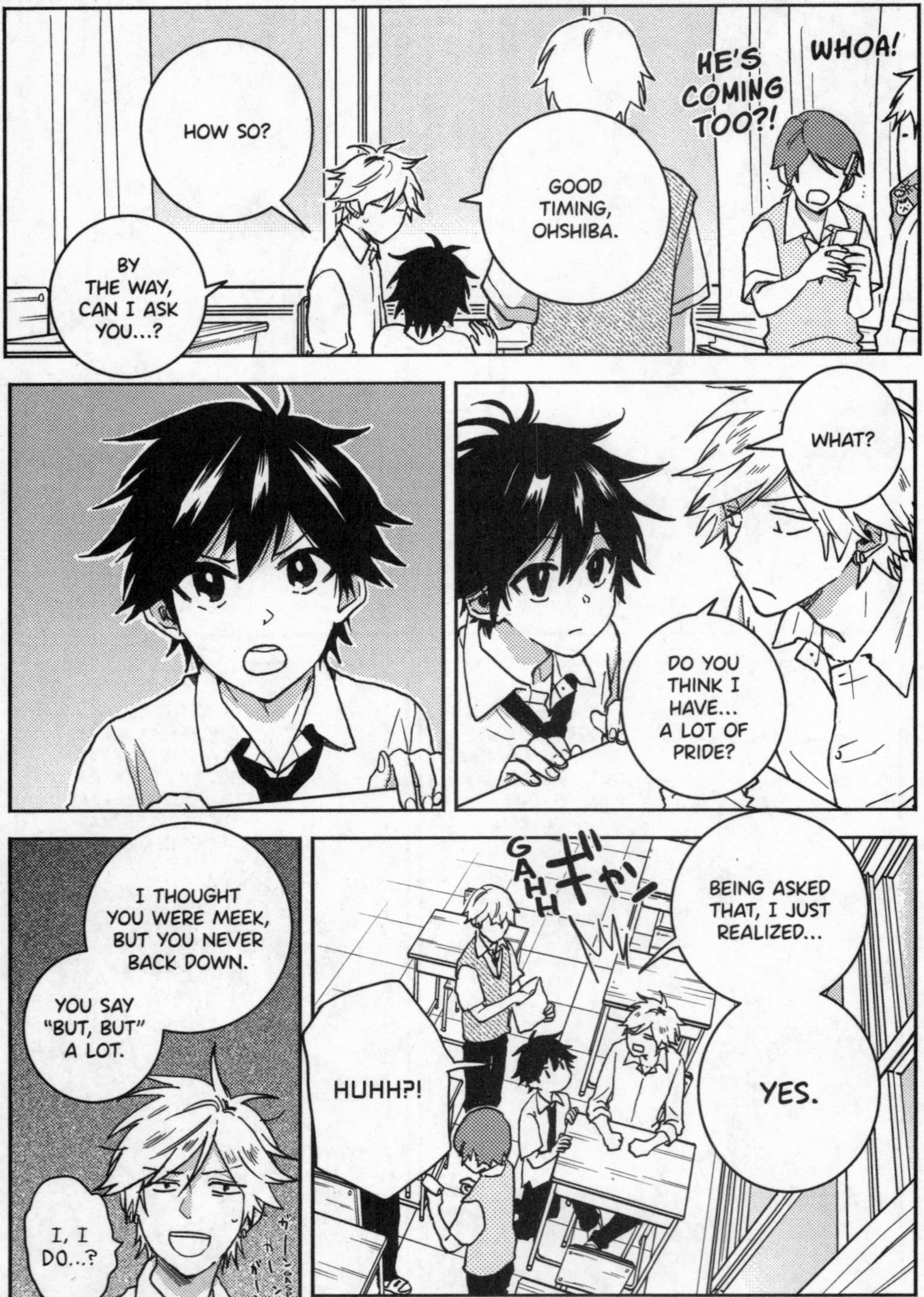
WHOA!
HE'S COMING TOO?!
GOOD TIMING, OHSHIBA.
HOW SO?
BY THE WAY, CAN I ASK YOU...?
WHAT?
DO YOU THINK I HAVE... A LOT OF PRIDE?
BEING ASKED THAT, I JUST REALIZED...
GAHH
YES.
HUHH?!
I THOUGHT YOU WERE MEEK, BUT YOU NEVER BACK DOWN.
YOU SAY "BUT, BUT" A LOT.
I, I DO...?

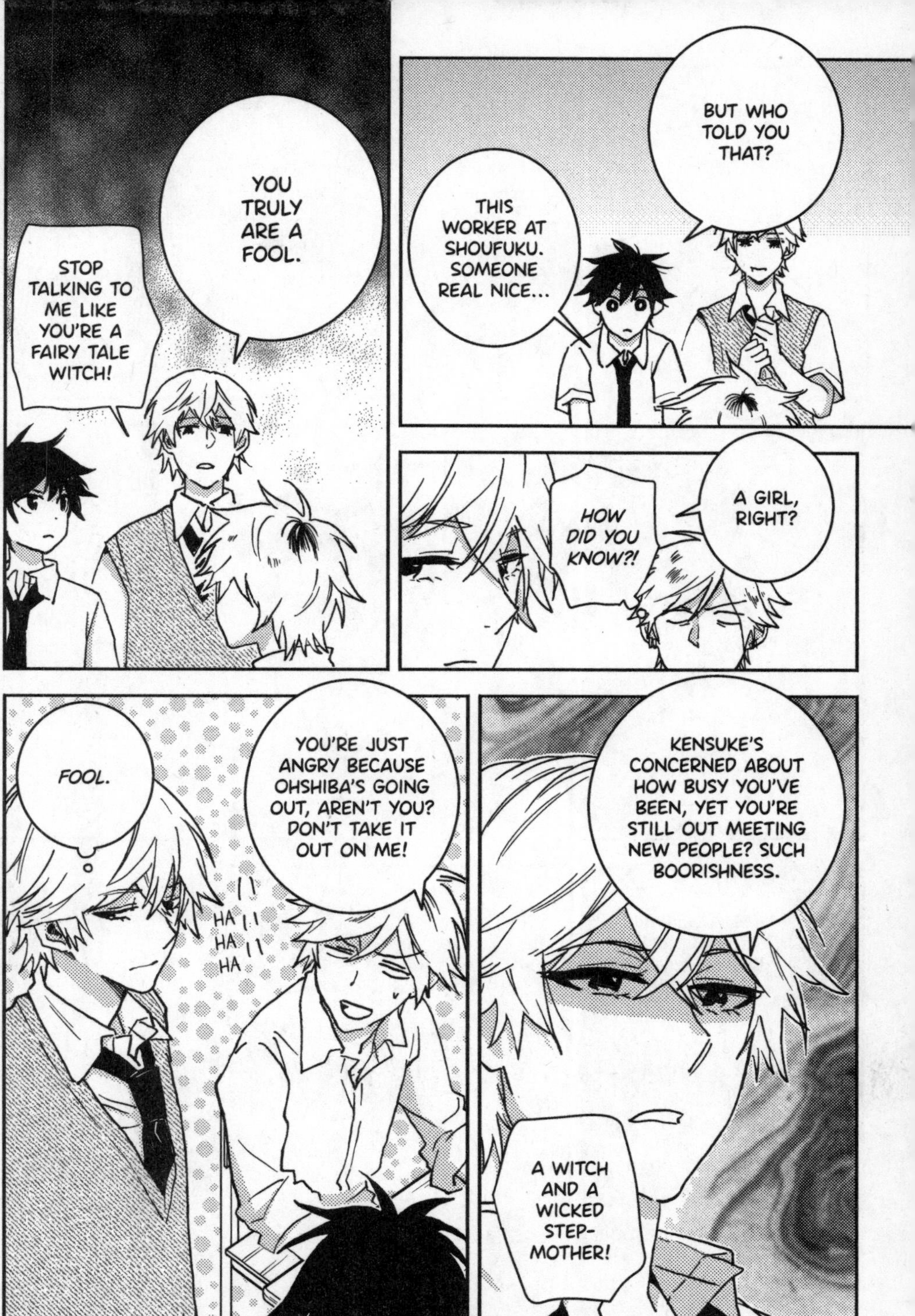
BUT WHO TOLD YOU THAT?
THIS WORKER AT SHOUFUKU. SOMEONE REAL NICE...
A GIRL, RIGHT?
HOW DID YOU KNOW?!
YOU TRULY ARE A FOOL.
STOP TALKING TO ME LIKE YOU'RE A FAIRY TALE WITCH!
KENSUKE'S CONCERNED ABOUT HOW BUSY YOU'VE BEEN, YET YOU'RE STILL OUT MEETING NEW PEOPLE? SUCH BOORISHNESS.
A WITCH AND A WICKED STEP-MOTHER!
YOU'RE JUST ANGRY BECAUSE OHSHIBA'S GOING OUT, AREN'T YOU? DON'T TAKE IT OUT ON ME!
HA HA HA
FOOL.

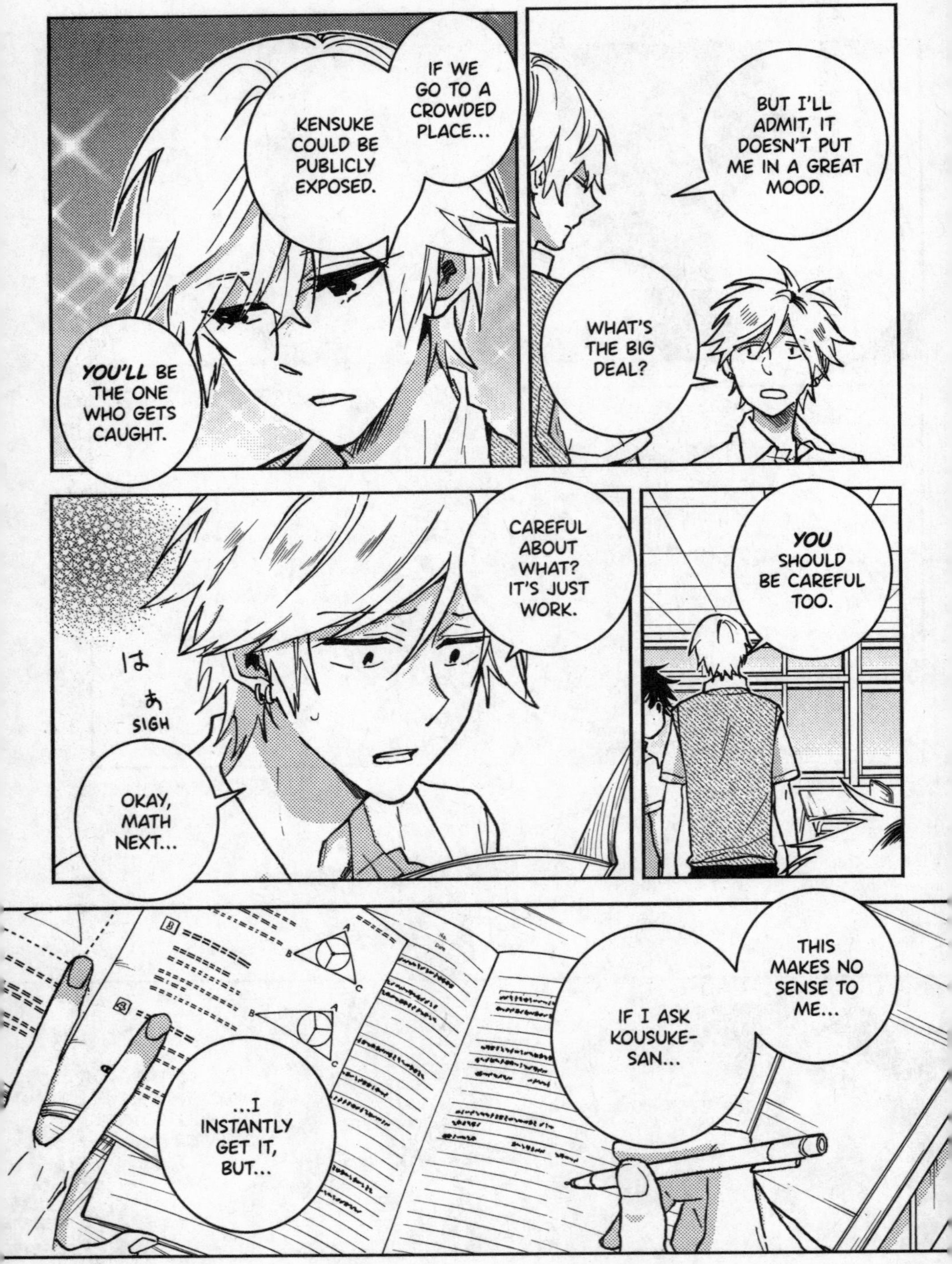
BUT I'LL ADMIT, IT DOESN'T PUT ME IN A GREAT MOOD.
WHAT'S THE BIG DEAL?
IF WE GO TO A CROWDED PLACE...
KENSUKE COULD BE PUBLICLY EXPOSED.
YOU'LL BE THE ONE WHO GETS CAUGHT.
YOU SHOULD BE CAREFUL TOO.
CAREFUL ABOUT WHAT? IT'S JUST WORK.
はあ
SIGH
OKAY, MATH NEXT...
THIS MAKES NO SENSE TO ME...
IF I ASK KOUSUKE-SAN...
...I INSTANTLY GET IT, BUT...

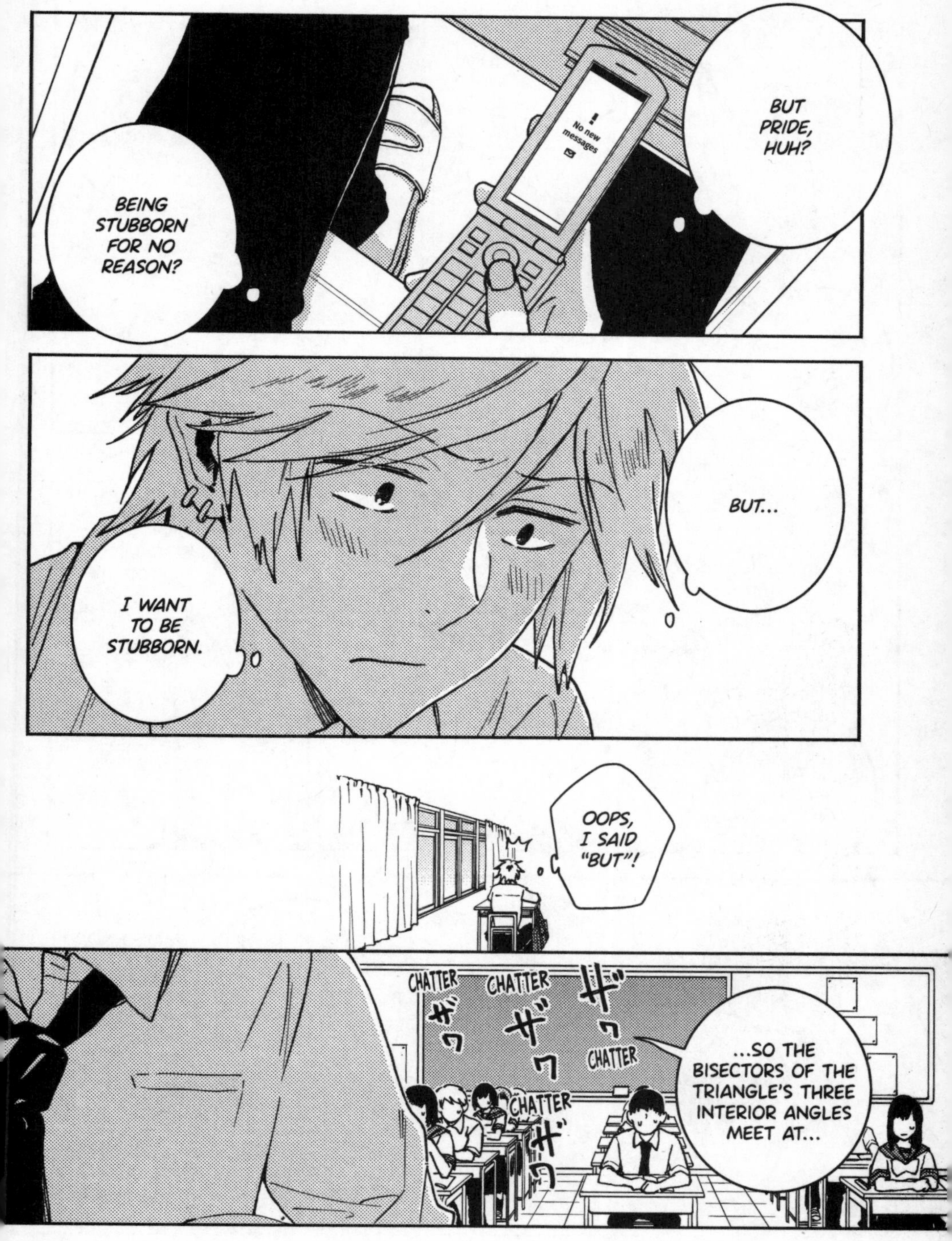
BUT PRIDE, HUH?
No new messages
BEING STUBBORN FOR NO REASON?
BUT...
I WANT TO BE STUBBORN.
OOPS, I SAID "BUT"!
ザワ
CHATTER
ザワ
CHATTER
ザワ
CHATTER
CHATTER
ザワ
...SO THE BISECTORS OF THE TRIANGLE'S THREE INTERIOR ANGLES MEET AT...

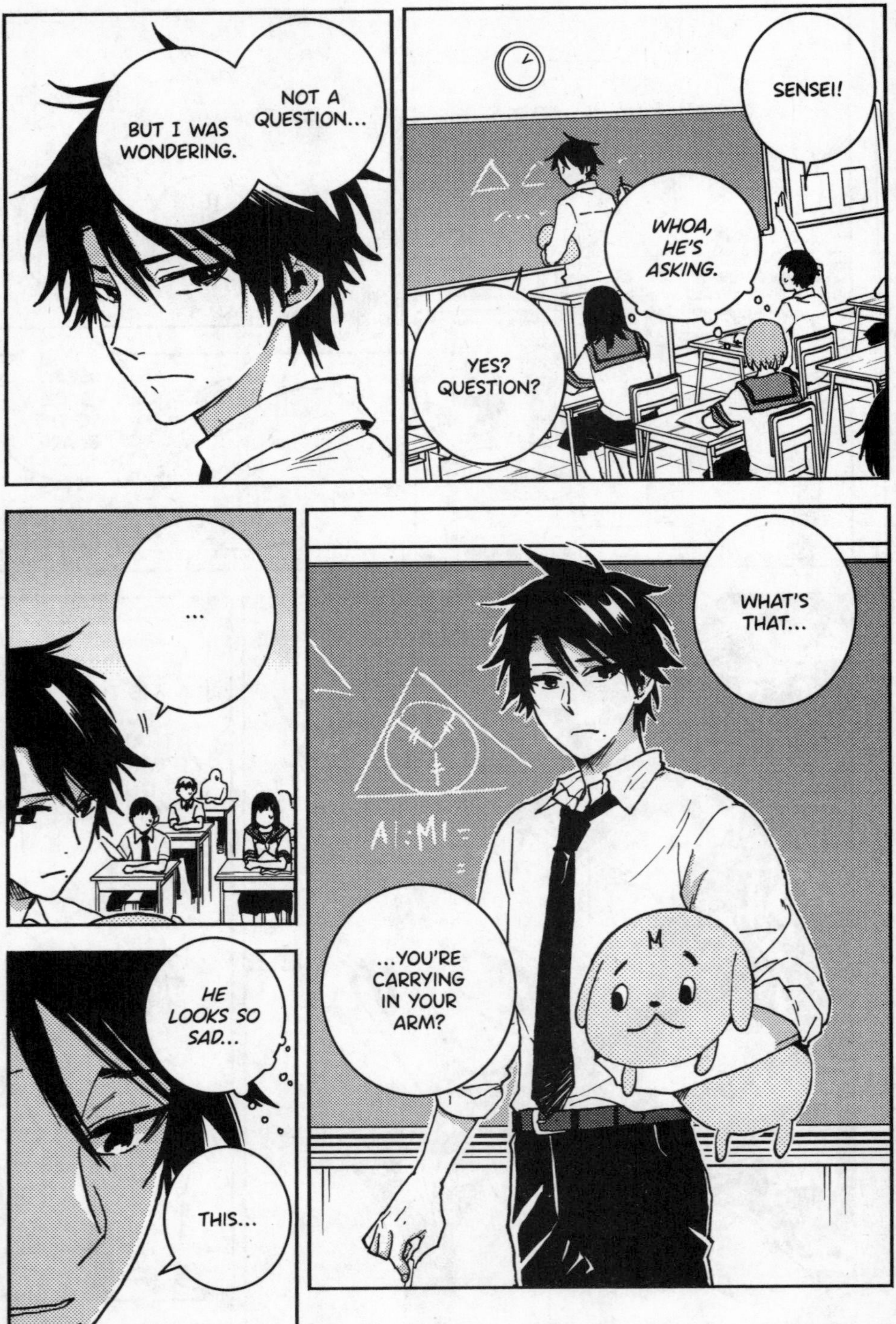
SENSEI!
WHOA, HE'S ASKING.
YES? QUESTION?
NOT A QUESTION...
BUT I WAS WONDERING.
WHAT'S THAT...
...YOU'RE CARRYING IN YOUR ARM?
...
HE LOOKS SO SAD...
THIS...

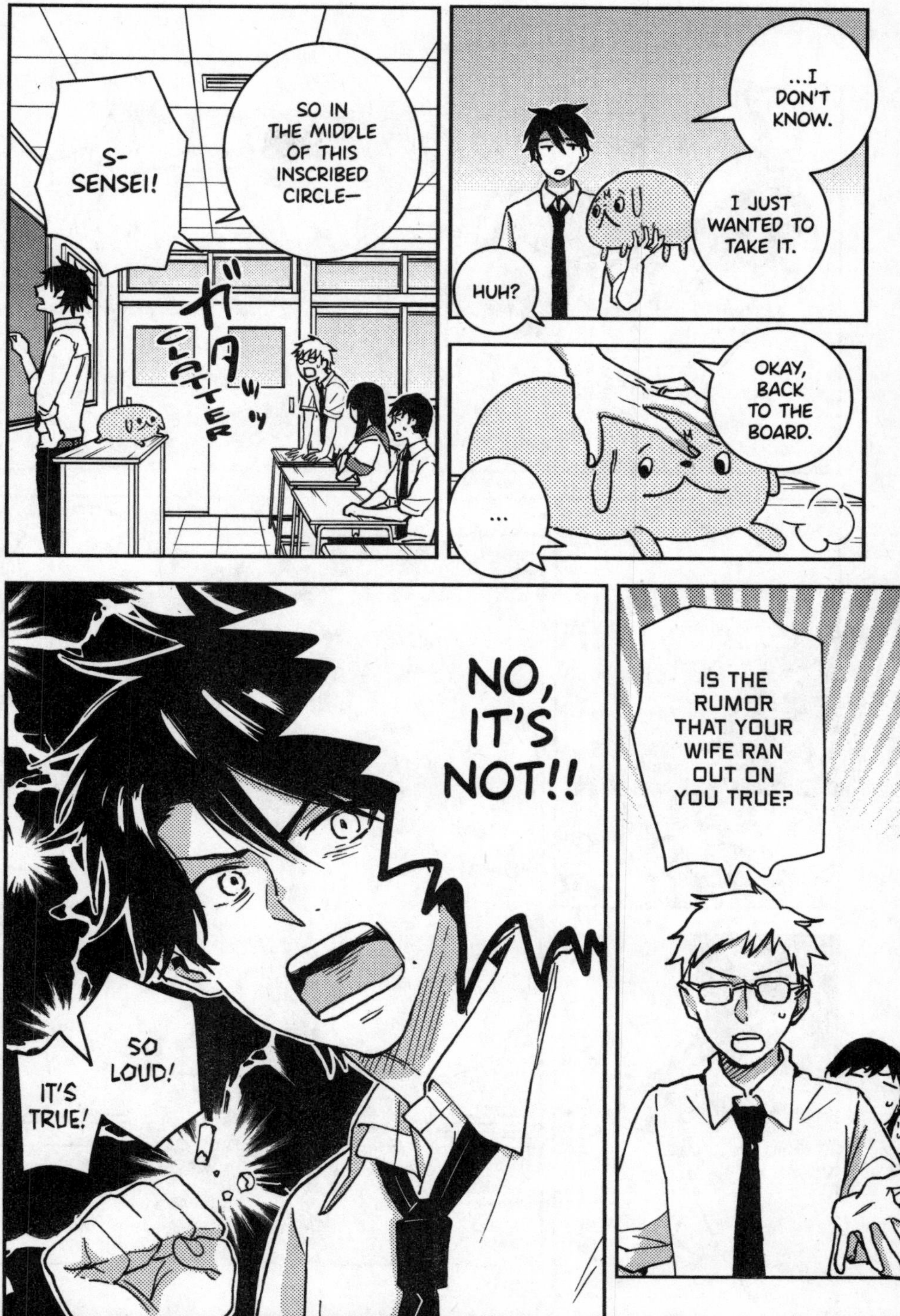
...I DON'T KNOW.
I JUST WANTED TO TAKE IT.
HUH?
OKAY, BACK TO THE BOARD.
...
SO IN THE MIDDLE OF THIS INSCRIBED CIRCLE—
S-SENSEI!
CLATTER
IS THE RUMOR THAT YOUR WIFE RAN OUT ON YOU TRUE?
NO, IT'S NOT!!
SO LOUD!
IT'S TRUE!

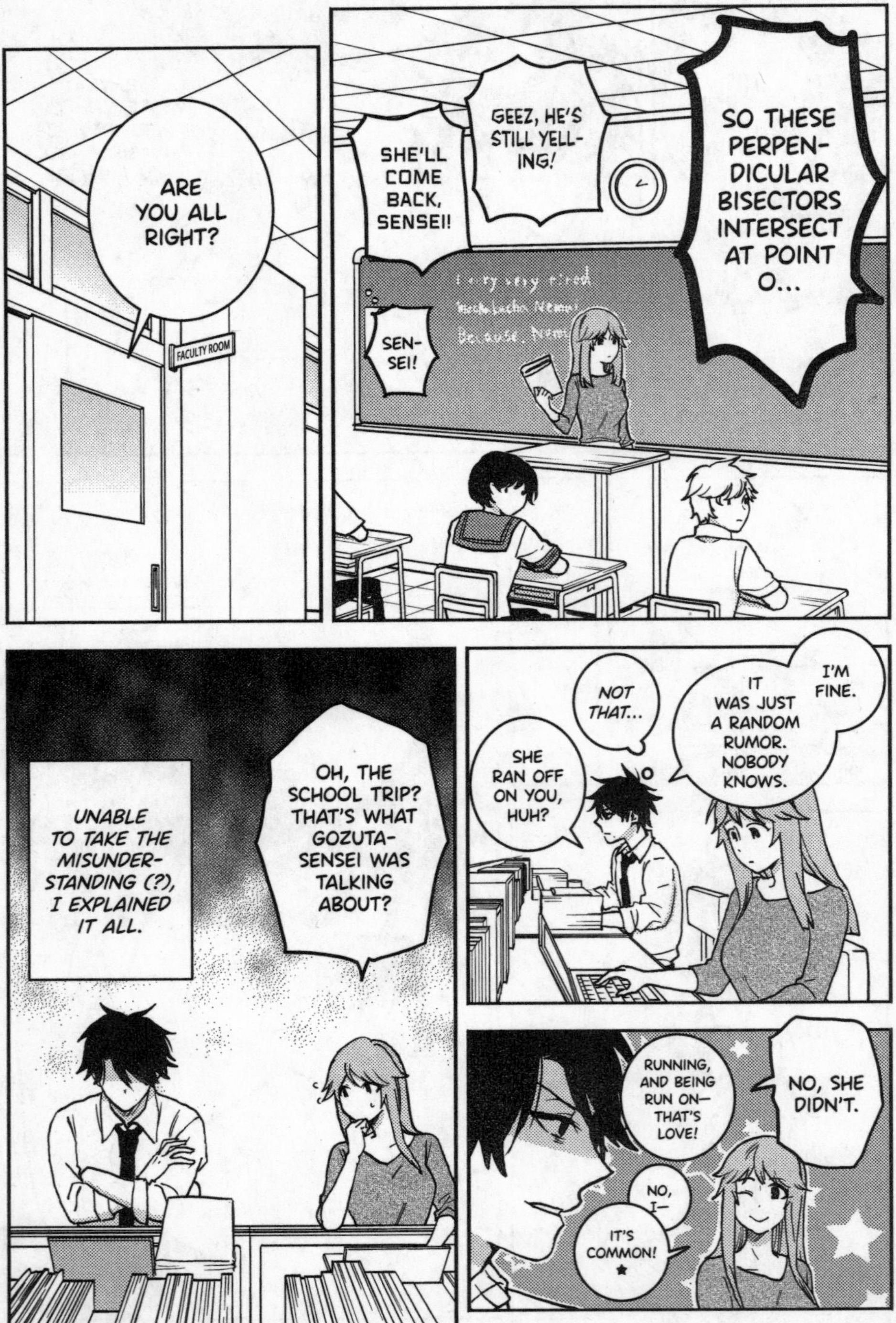
SO THESE PERPENDICULAR BISECTORS INTERSECT AT POINT O...
GEEZ, HE'S STILL YELLING!
SHE'LL COME BACK, SENSEI!
SENSEI!
ARE YOU ALL RIGHT?
FACULTY ROOM
I'M FINE.
IT WAS JUST A RANDOM RUMOR. NOBODY KNOWS.
NOT THAT...
SHE RAN OFF ON YOU, HUH?
NO, SHE DIDN'T.
RUNNING, AND BEING RUN ON—THAT'S LOVE!
NO, I—
IT'S COMMON! ★
OH, THE SCHOOL TRIP? THAT'S WHAT GOZUTA-SENSEI WAS TALKING ABOUT?
UNABLE TO TAKE THE MISUNDERSTANDING (?), I EXPLAINED IT ALL.

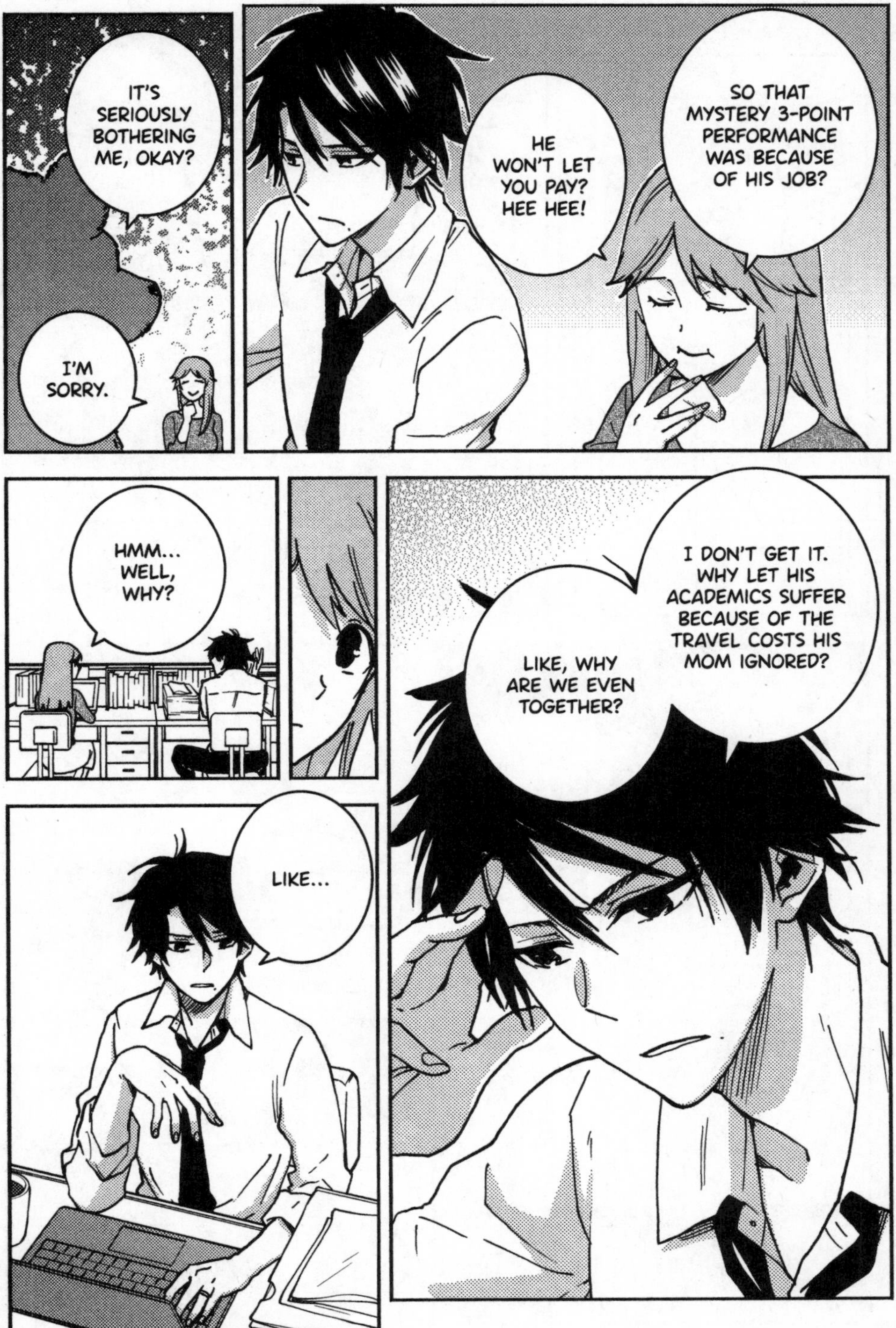
SO THAT MYSTERY 3-POINT PERFORMANCE WAS BECAUSE OF HIS JOB?
HE WON'T LET YOU PAY? HEE HEE!
IT'S SERIOUSLY BOTHERING ME, OKAY?
I'M SORRY.
I DON'T GET IT. WHY LET HIS ACADEMICS SUFFER BECAUSE OF THE TRAVEL COSTS HIS MOM IGNORED?
LIKE, WHY ARE WE EVEN TOGETHER?
HMM... WELL, WHY?
LIKE...

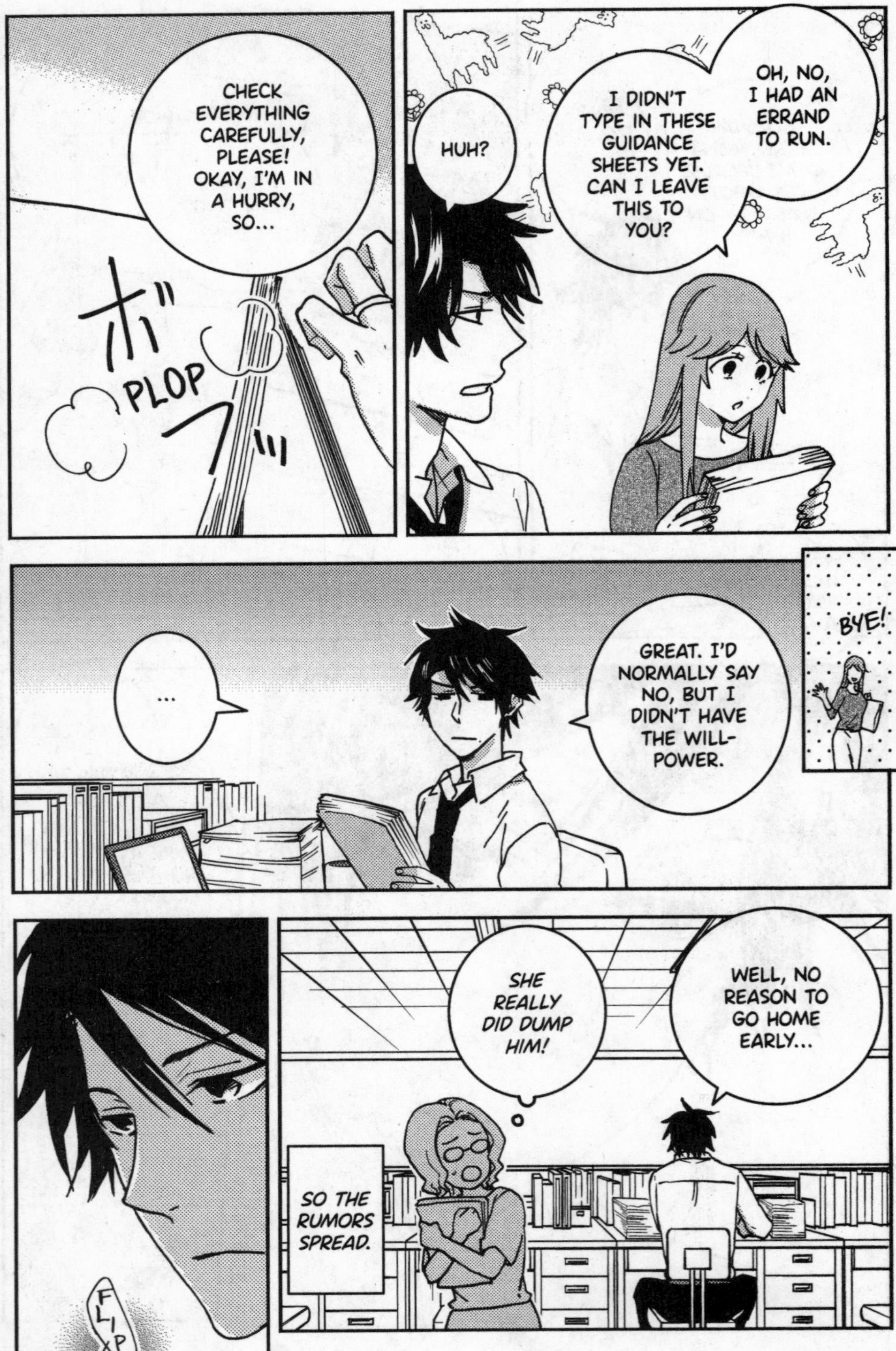
OH, NO, I HAD AN ERRAND TO RUN.
I DIDN'T TYPE IN THESE GUIDANCE SHEETS YET. CAN I LEAVE THIS TO YOU?
HUH?
CHECK EVERYTHING CAREFULLY, PLEASE! OKAY, I'M IN A HURRY, SO...
PLOP
BYE!
GREAT. I'D NORMALLY SAY NO, BUT I DIDN'T HAVE THE WILL-POWER.
...
WELL, NO REASON TO GO HOME EARLY...
SHE REALLY DID DUMP HIM!
SO THE RUMORS SPREAD.
FLIP

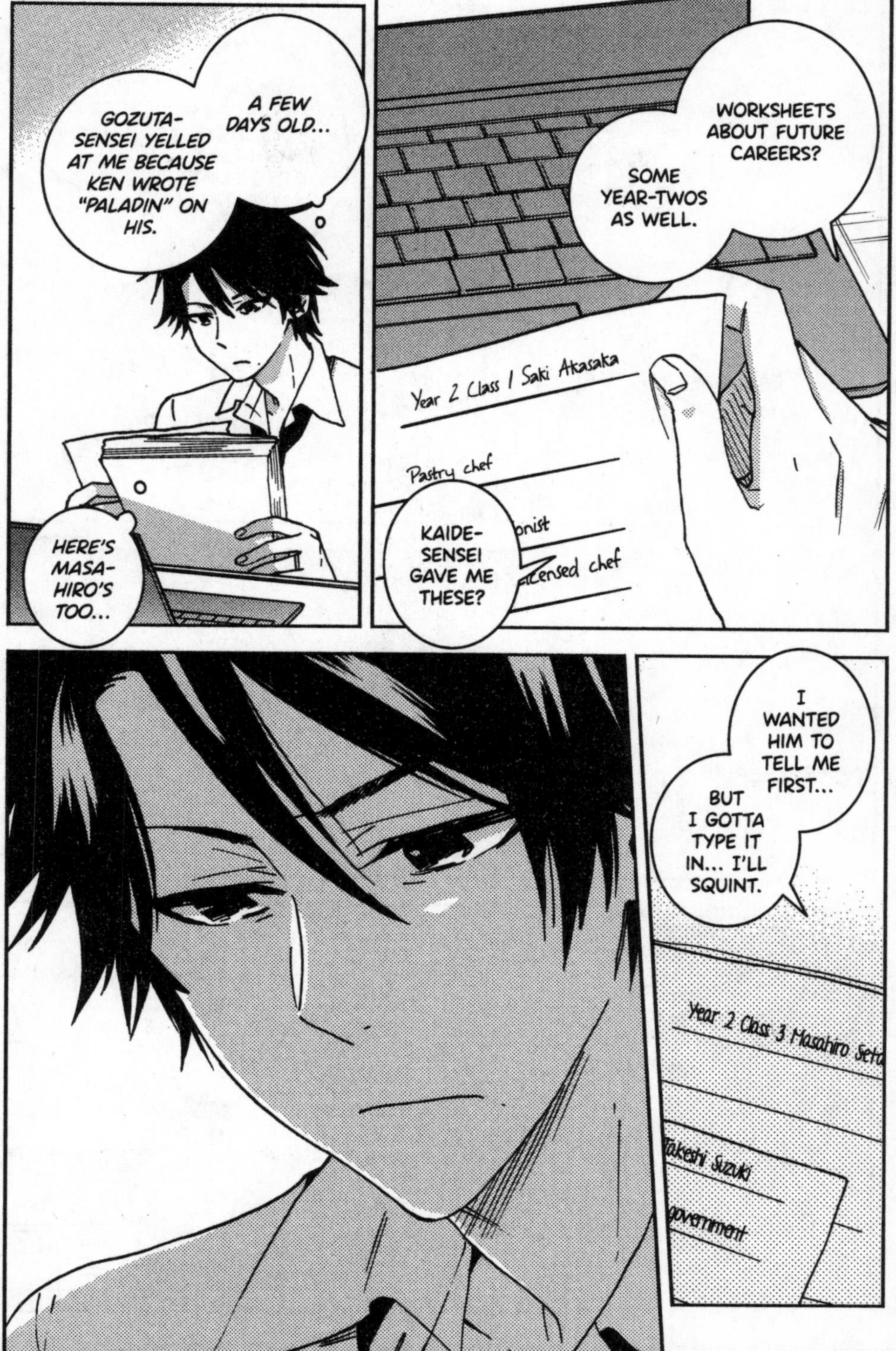
WORKSHEETS ABOUT FUTURE CAREERS?
SOME YEAR-TWOS AS WELL.
Year 2 Class 1 Saki Akasaka
Pastry chef
KAIDE-SENSEI GAVE ME THESE?
A FEW DAYS OLD...
GOZUTA-SENSEI YELLED AT ME BECAUSE KEN WROTE "PALADIN" ON HIS.
HERE'S MASA-HIRO'S TOO...
I WANTED HIM TO TELL ME FIRST...
BUT I GOTTA TYPE IT IN... I'LL SQUINT.
Takeshi Suzuki
government

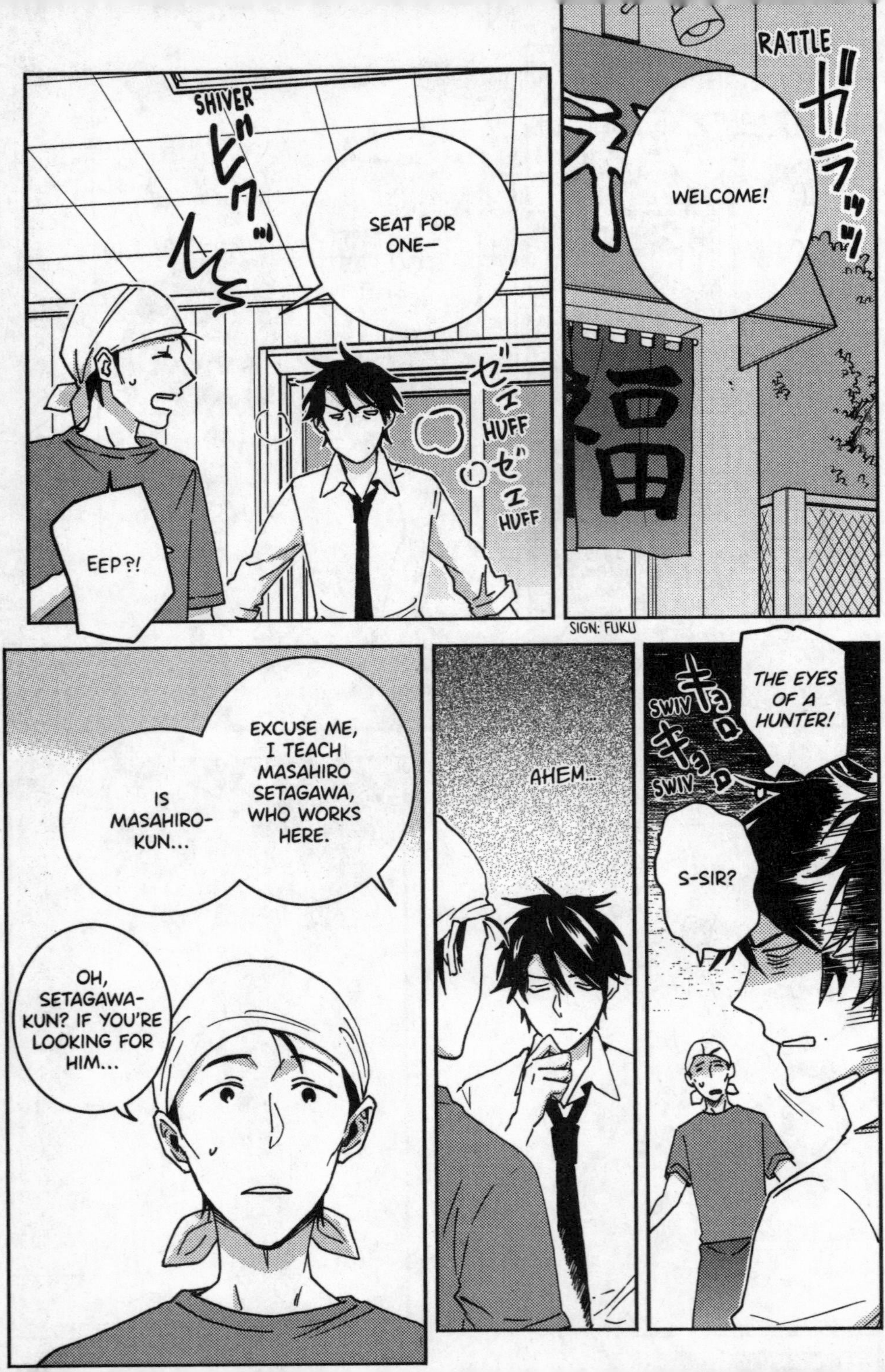
RATTLE
WELCOME!
SIGN: FUKU
SHIVER
SEAT FOR ONE—
HUFF
HUFF
EEP?!
THE EYES OF A HUNTER!
SWIV
SWIV
S-SIR?
AHEM...
EXCUSE ME, I TEACH MASAHIRO SETAGAWA, WHO WORKS HERE.
IS MASAHIRO-KUN...
OH, SETAGAWA-KUN? IF YOU'RE LOOKING FOR HIM...

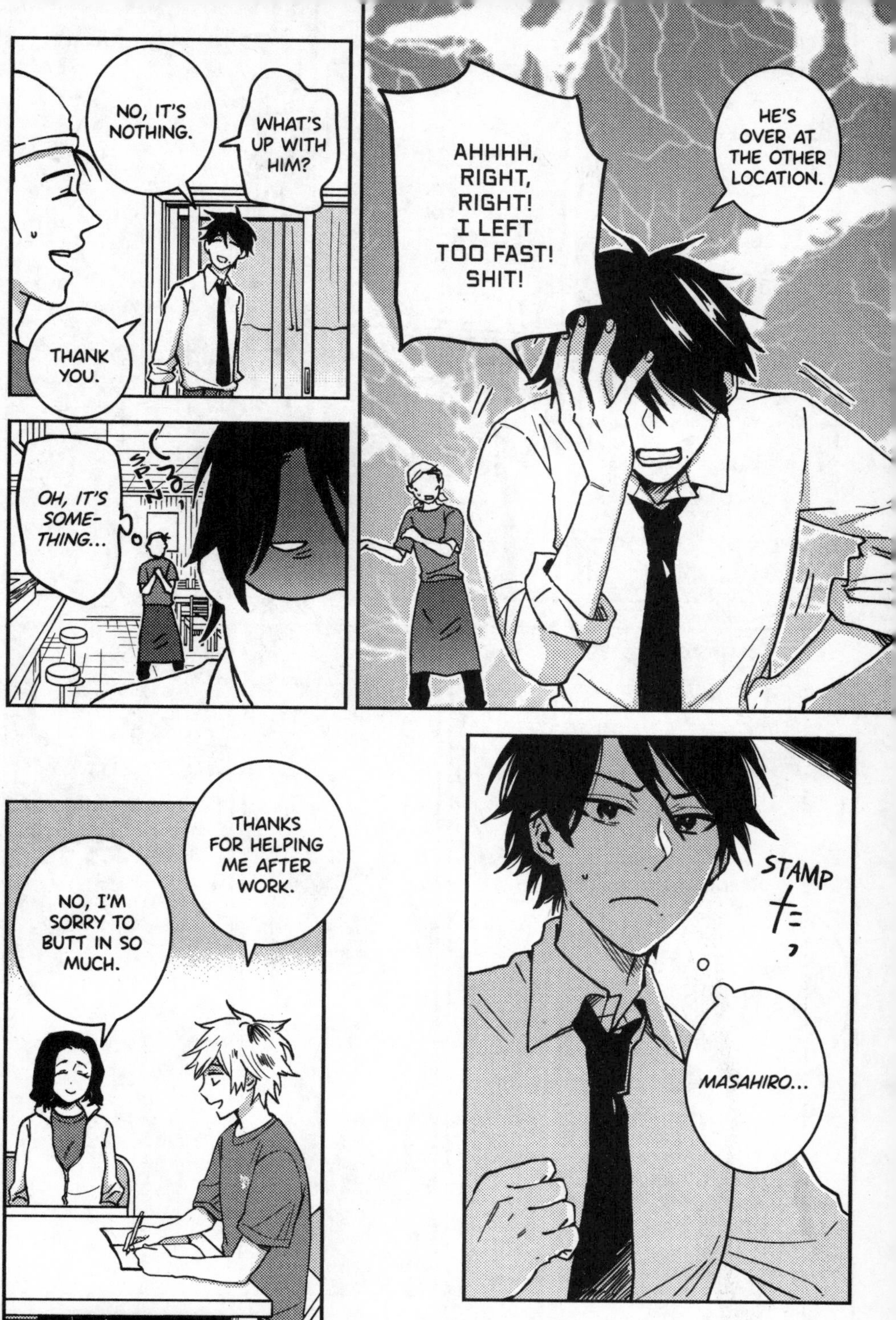

HE'S OVER AT THE OTHER LOCATION.
AHHHH, RIGHT, RIGHT! I LEFT TOO FAST! SHIT!
WHAT'S UP WITH HIM?
NO, IT'S NOTHING.
THANK YOU.
SPIN
OH, IT'S SOME-THING...
STAMP
MASAHIRO...
THANKS FOR HELPING ME AFTER WORK.
NO, I'M SORRY TO BUTT IN SO MUCH.

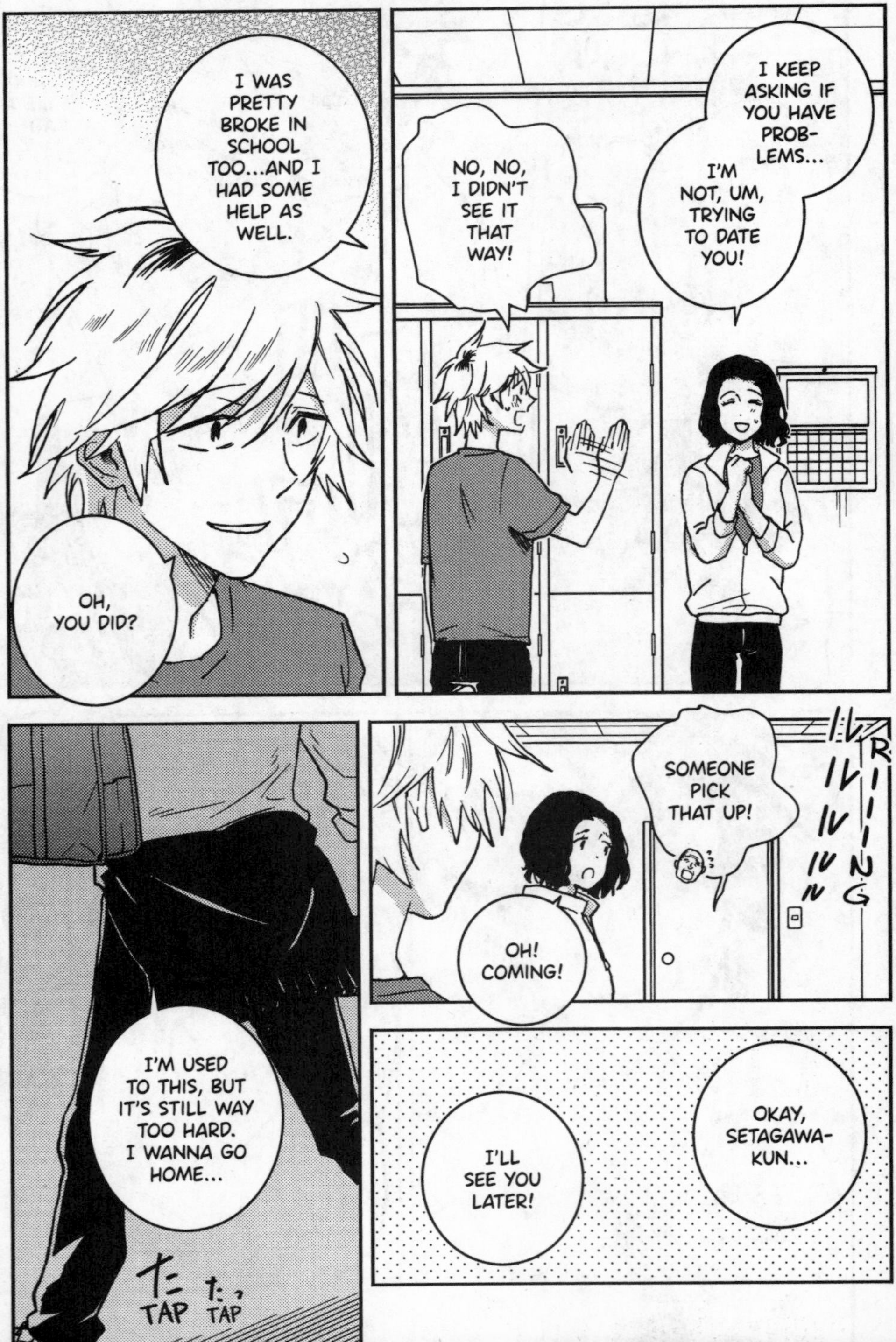
I KEEP ASKING IF YOU HAVE PROBLEMS...
I'M NOT, UM, TRYING TO DATE YOU!
NO, NO, I DIDN'T SEE IT THAT WAY!
I WAS PRETTY BROKE IN SCHOOL TOO...AND I HAD SOME HELP AS WELL.
OH, YOU DID?
RIIIING
SOMEONE PICK THAT UP!
OH! COMING!
OKAY, SETAGAWA-KUN...
I'LL SEE YOU LATER!
I'M USED TO THIS, BUT IT'S STILL WAY TOO HARD. I WANNA GO HOME...
TAP
TAP

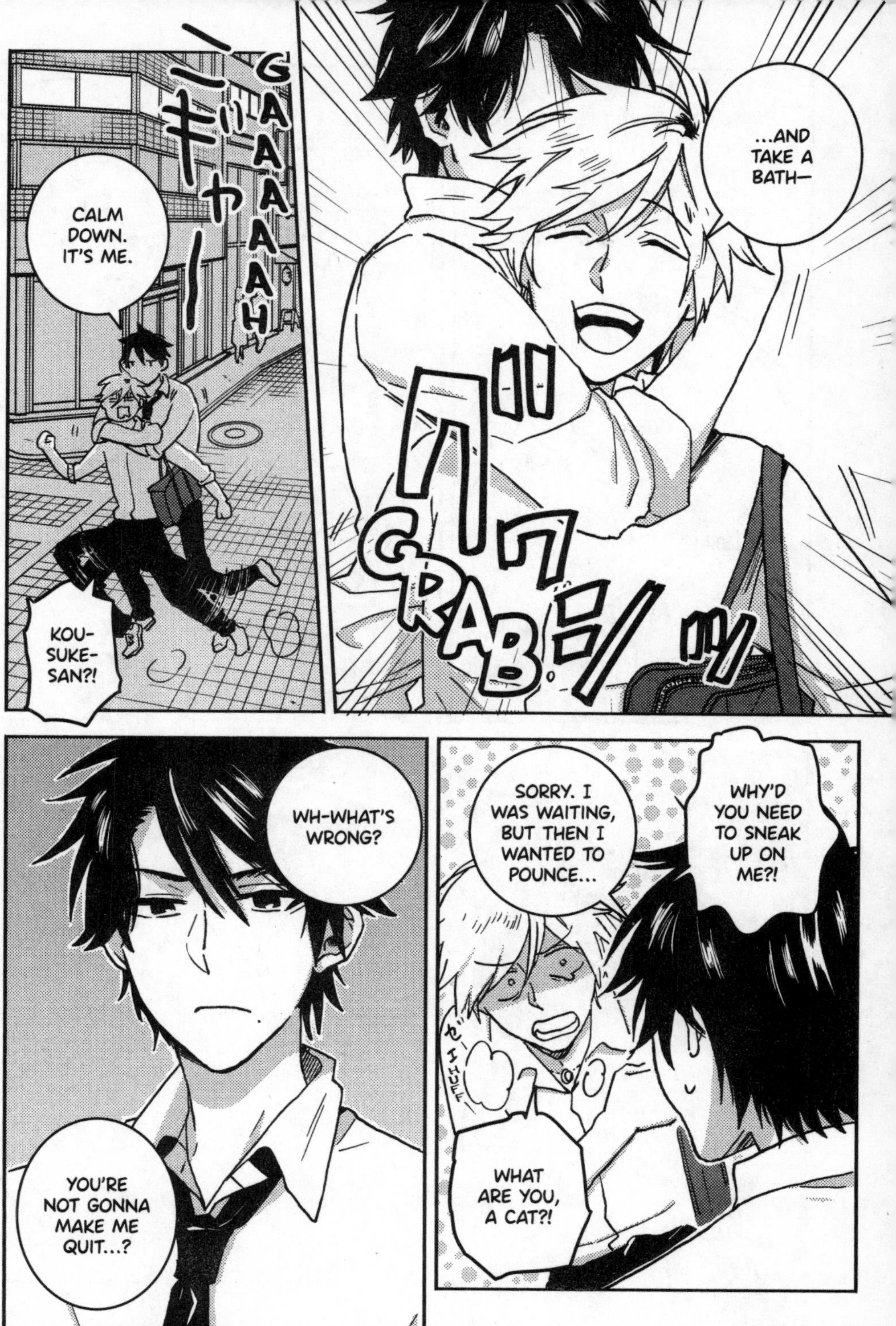
...AND TAKE A BATH—
GRAB!
GAAAAAAH
CALM DOWN. IT'S ME.
KOU-SUKE-SAN?!
WHY'D YOU NEED TO SNEAK UP ON ME?!
SORRY. I WAS WAITING, BUT THEN I WANTED TO POUNCE...
HUFF
WHAT ARE YOU, A CAT?!
WH-WHAT'S WRONG?
YOU'RE NOT GONNA MAKE ME QUIT...?

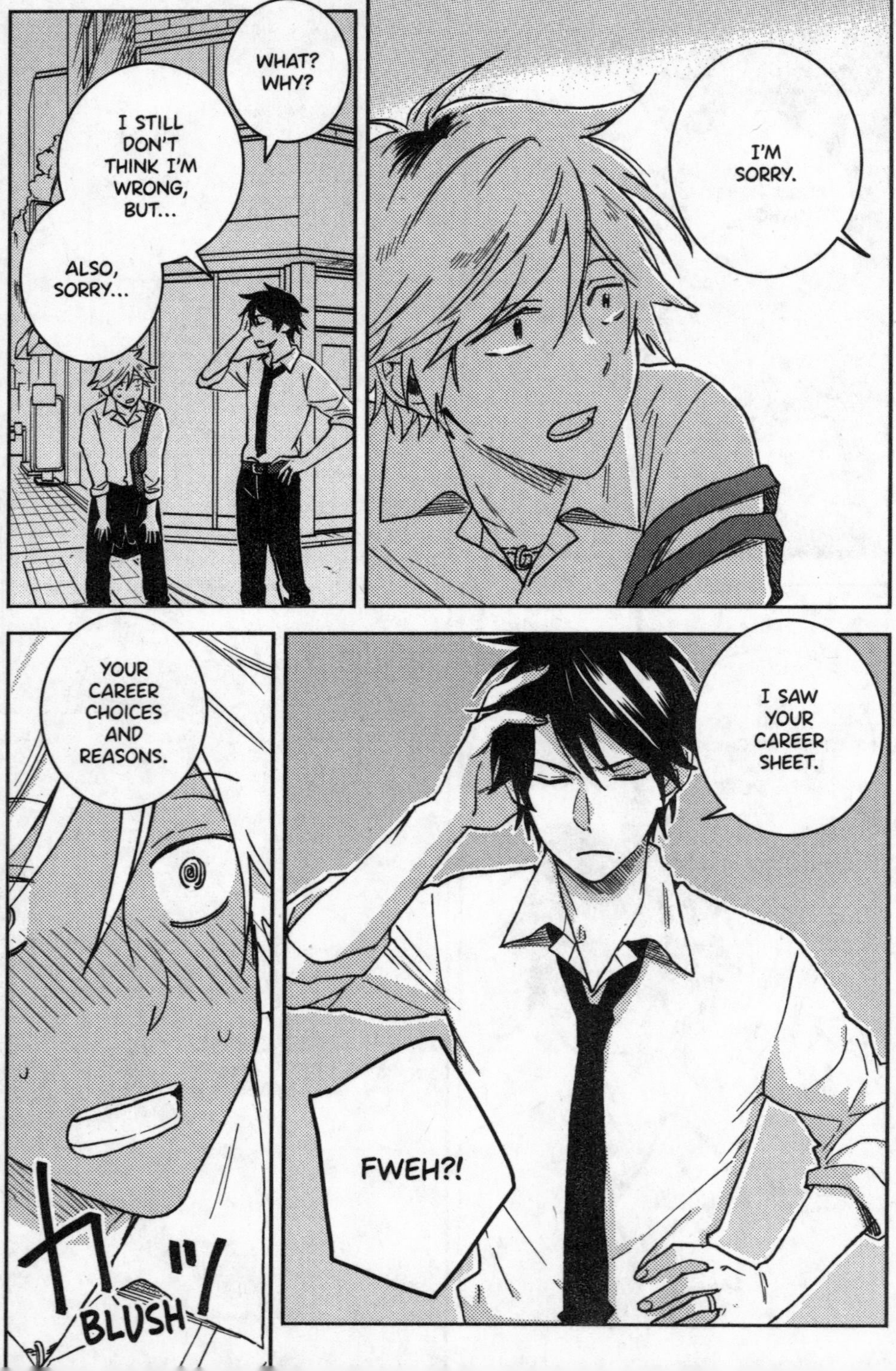
I'M SORRY.
WHAT? WHY?
I STILL DON'T THINK I'M WRONG, BUT...
ALSO, SORRY...
I SAW YOUR CAREER SHEET.
FWEH?!
YOUR CAREER CHOICES AND REASONS.
BLUSH!

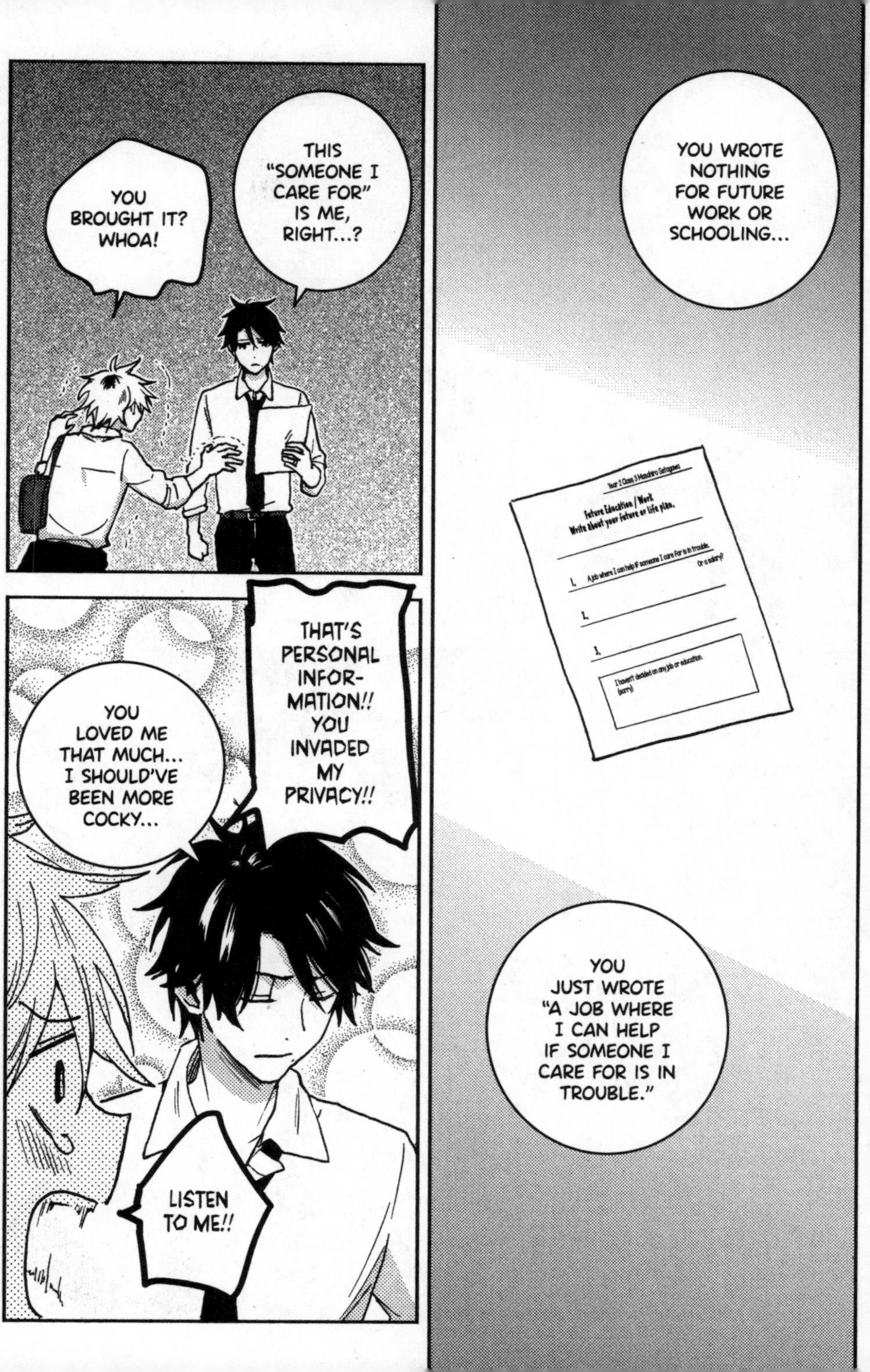
YOU WROTE NOTHING FOR FUTURE WORK OR SCHOOLING...
Year 2 Class 3 Masahiro Setagawa
Future Education / Work
Write about your future or life plan.
1. A job where I can help if someone I care for is in trouble.
Or a salary?
2.
3.
I haven't decided on any job or education.
(sorry)
YOU JUST WROTE "A JOB WHERE I CAN HELP IF SOMEONE I CARE FOR IS IN TROUBLE."
THIS "SOMEONE I CARE FOR" IS ME, RIGHT...?
YOU BROUGHT IT? WHOA!
THAT'S PERSONAL INFORMATION!! YOU INVADED MY PRIVACY!!
YOU LOVED ME THAT MUCH... I SHOULD'VE BEEN MORE COCKY...
LISTEN TO ME!!

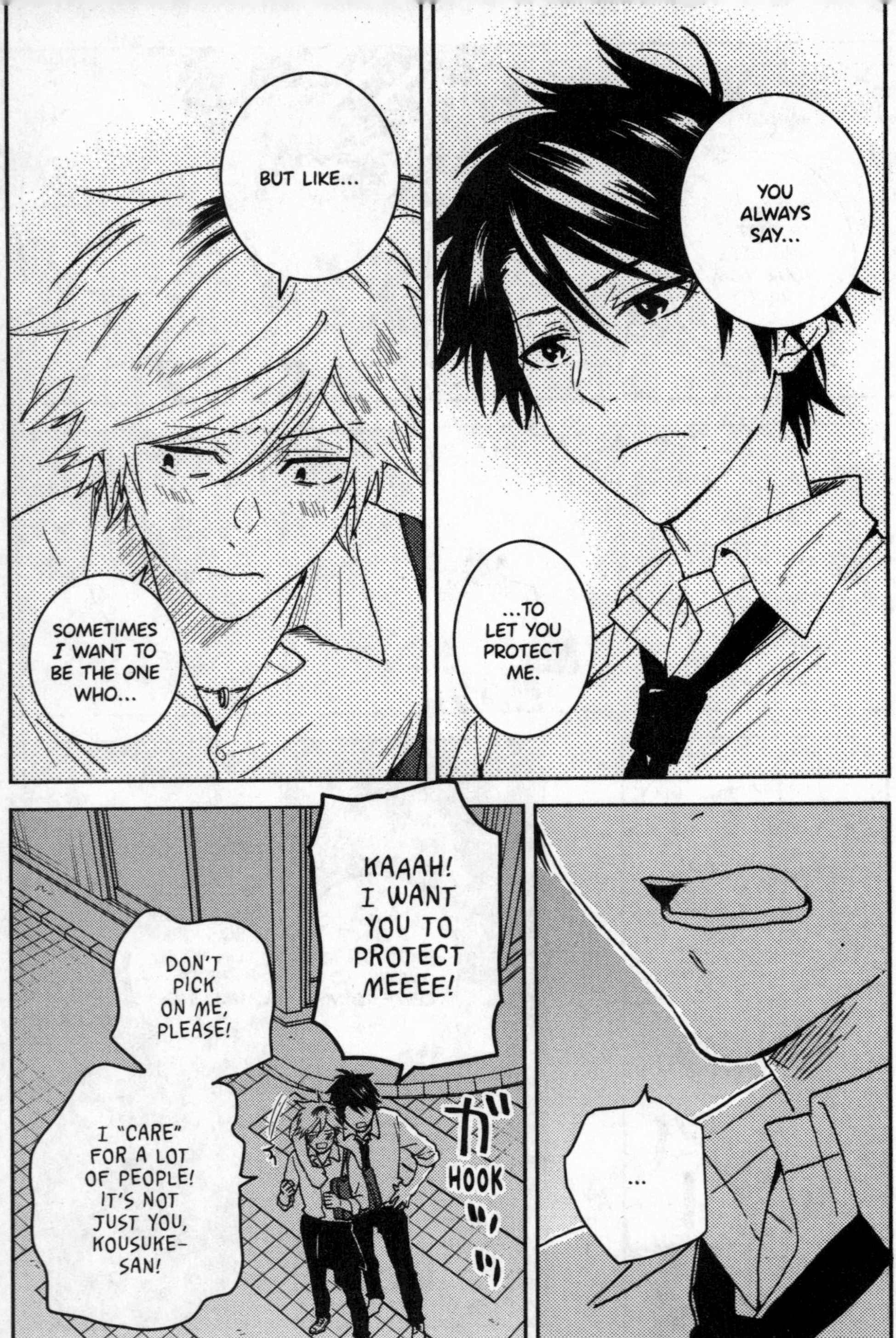
YOU ALWAYS SAY...
...TO LET YOU PROTECT ME.
BUT LIKE...
SOMETIMES *I* WANT TO BE THE ONE WHO...
...
KAAAH! I WANT YOU TO PROTECT MEEEE!
DON'T PICK ON ME, PLEASE!
HOOK
I "CARE" FOR A LOT OF PEOPLE! IT'S NOT JUST YOU, KOUSUKE-SAN!

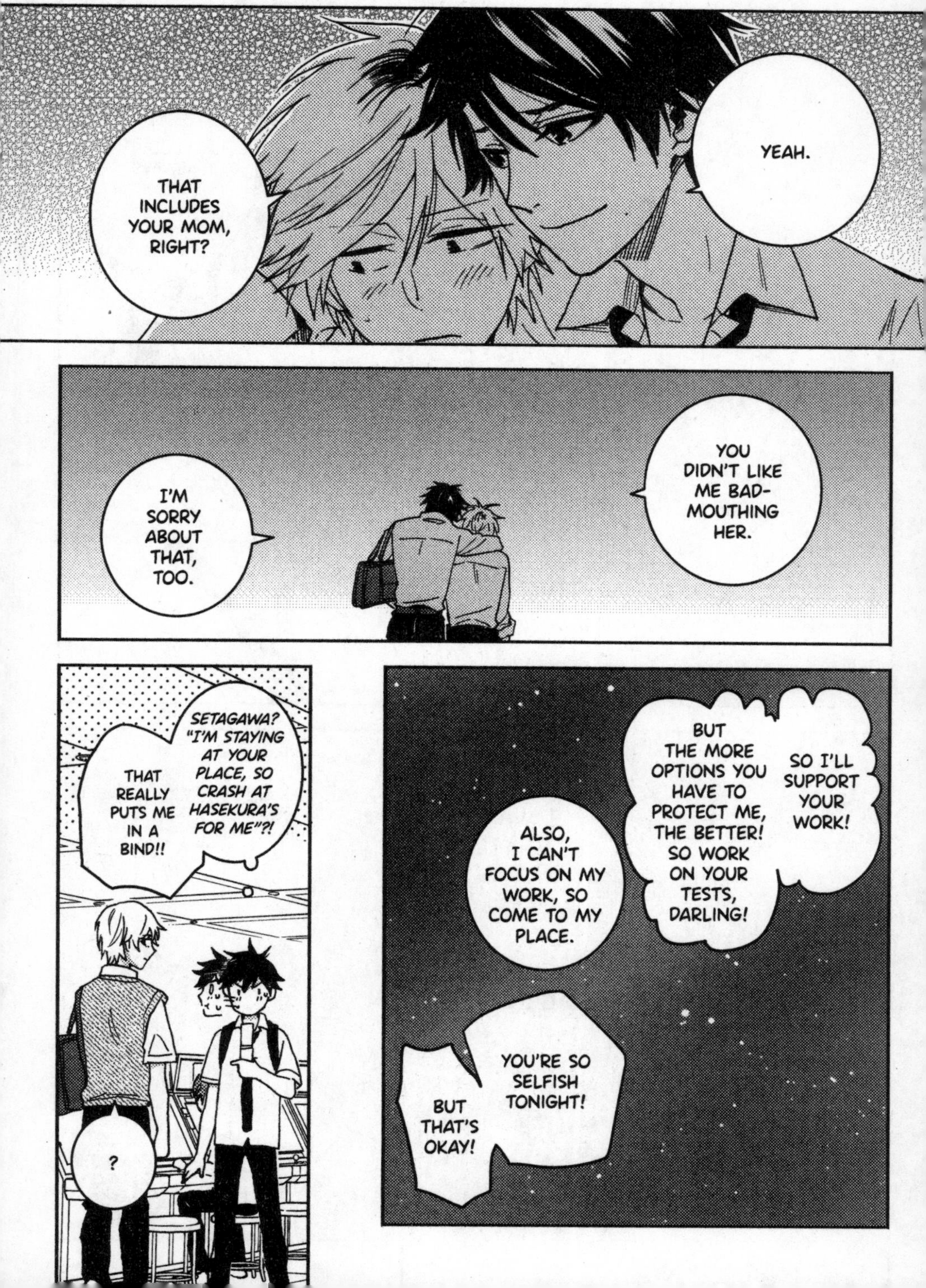
YEAH.
THAT INCLUDES YOUR MOM, RIGHT?
YOU DIDN'T LIKE ME BAD-MOUTHING HER.
I'M SORRY ABOUT THAT, TOO.
SO I'LL SUPPORT YOUR WORK!
BUT THE MORE OPTIONS YOU HAVE TO PROTECT ME, THE BETTER! SO WORK ON YOUR TESTS, DARLING!
ALSO, I CAN'T FOCUS ON MY WORK, SO COME TO MY PLACE.
YOU'RE SO SELFISH TONIGHT!
BUT THAT'S OKAY!
SETAGAWA? "I'M STAYING AT YOUR PLACE, SO CRASH AT HASEKURA'S FOR ME"?!
THAT REALLY PUTS ME IN A BIND!!
?

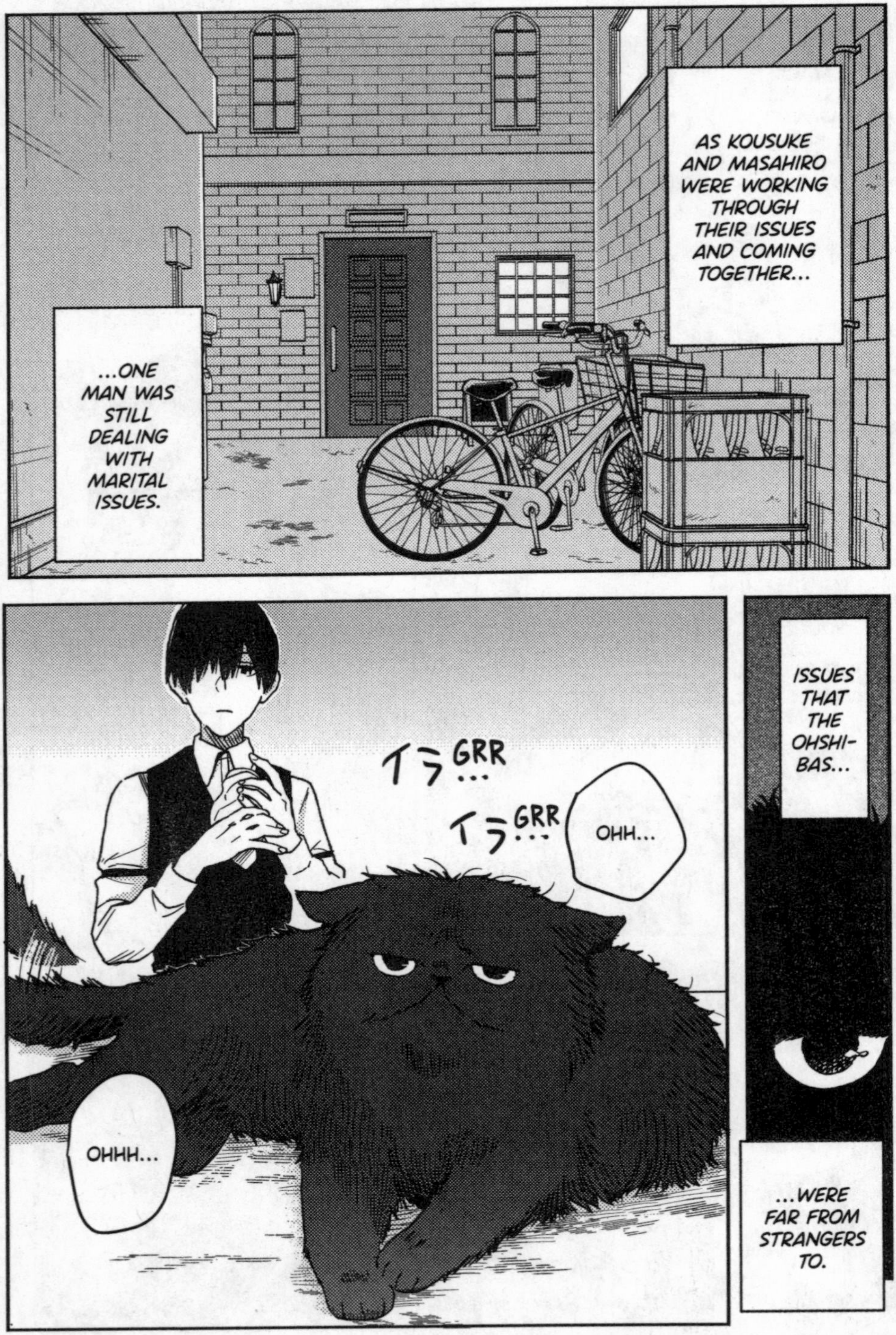
AS KOUSUKE AND MASAHIRO WERE WORKING THROUGH THEIR ISSUES AND COMING TOGETHER...
...ONE MAN WAS STILL DEALING WITH MARITAL ISSUES.
ISSUES THAT THE OHSHIBAS...
...WERE FAR FROM STRANGERS TO.
イラ GRR...
イラ GRR...
OHH...
OHHH...

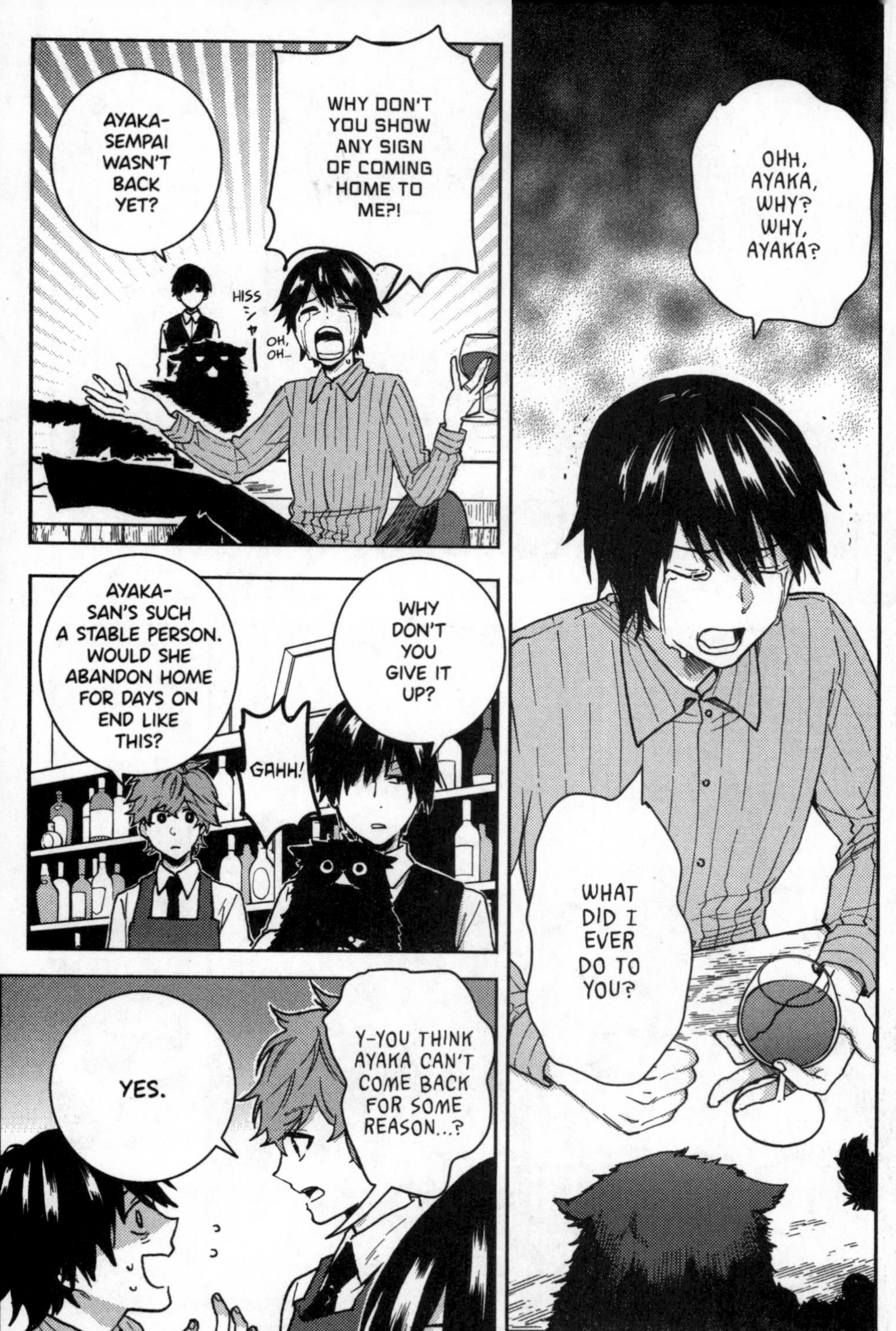
OHH, AYAKA, WHY? WHY, AYAKA?
WHAT DID I EVER DO TO YOU?
WHY DON'T YOU SHOW ANY SIGN OF COMING HOME TO ME?!
AYAKA-SEMPAI WASN'T BACK YET?
OH, OH...
HISS シャー
WHY DON'T YOU GIVE IT UP?
AYAKA-SAN'S SUCH A STABLE PERSON. WOULD SHE ABANDON HOME FOR DAYS ON END LIKE THIS?
GAHH!
Y-YOU THINK AYAKA CAN'T COME BACK FOR SOME REASON...?
YES.

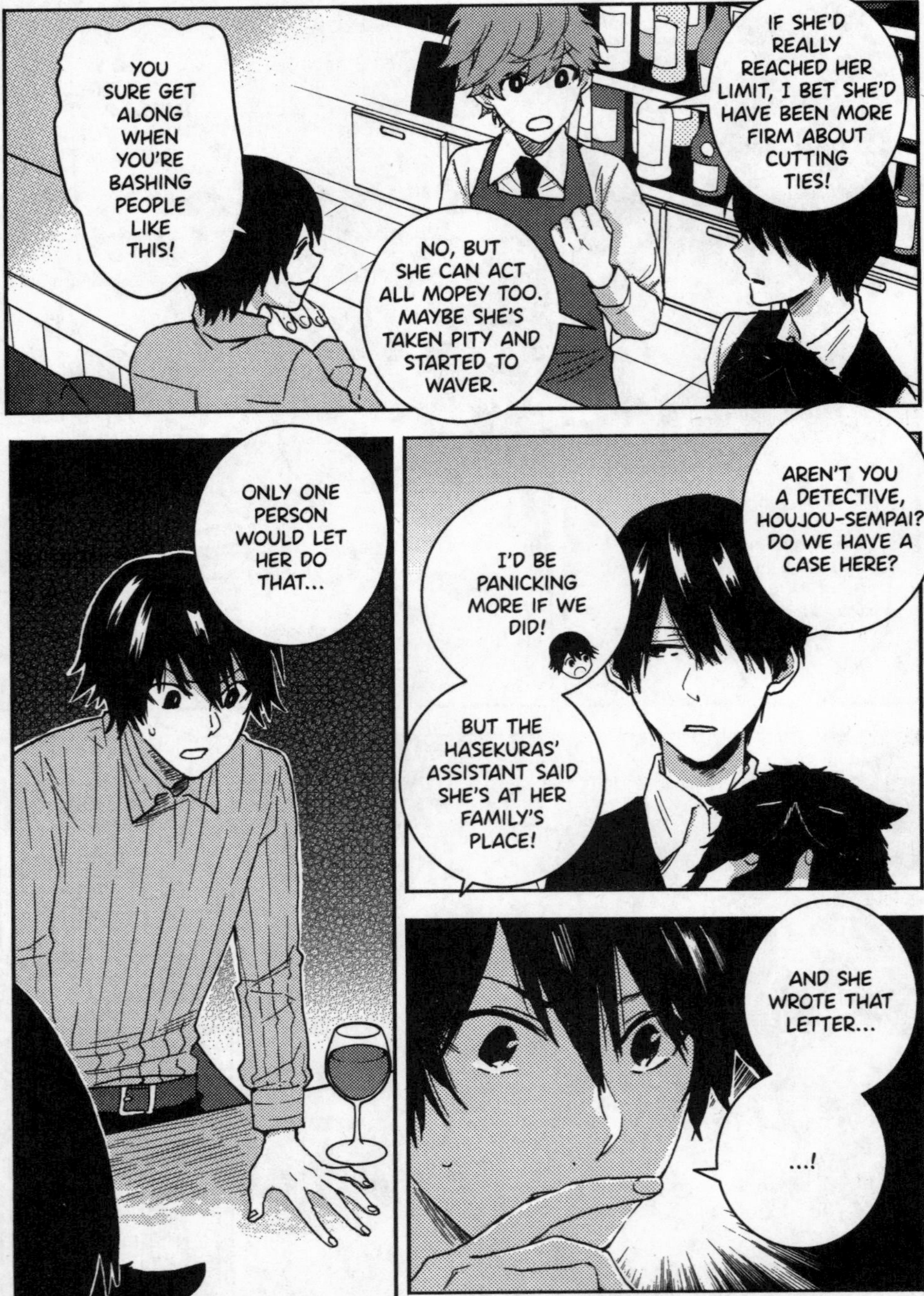
IF SHE'D REALLY REACHED HER LIMIT, I BET SHE'D HAVE BEEN MORE FIRM ABOUT CUTTING TIES!
NO, BUT SHE CAN ACT ALL MOPEY TOO. MAYBE SHE'S TAKEN PITY AND STARTED TO WAVER.
YOU SURE GET ALONG WHEN YOU'RE BASHING PEOPLE LIKE THIS!
AREN'T YOU A DETECTIVE, HOUJOU-SEMPAI? DO WE HAVE A CASE HERE?
I'D BE PANICKING MORE IF WE DID!
BUT THE HASEKURAS' ASSISTANT SAID SHE'S AT HER FAMILY'S PLACE!
AND SHE WROTE THAT LETTER...
...!
ONLY ONE PERSON WOULD LET HER DO THAT...

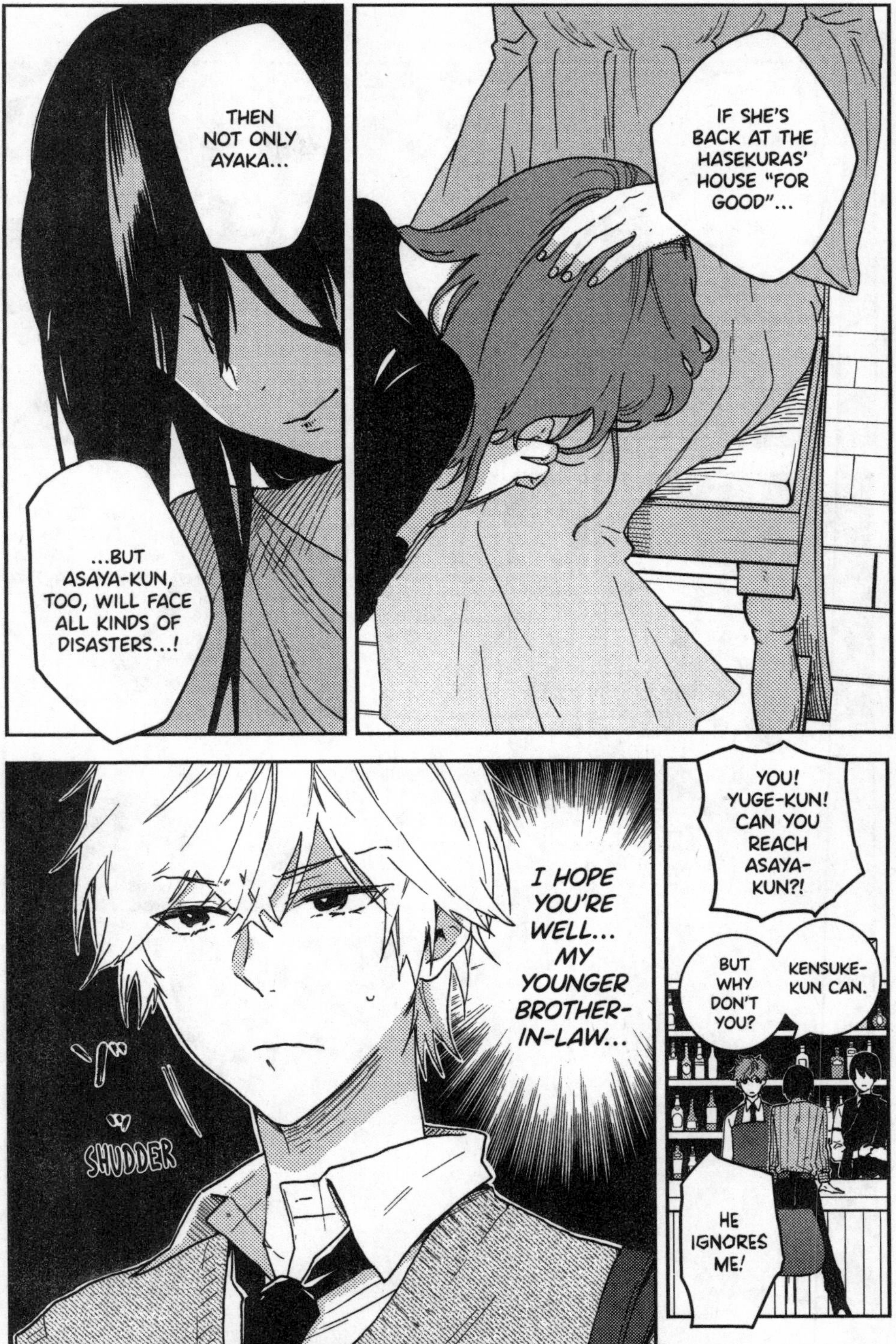
IF SHE'S BACK AT THE HASEKURAS' HOUSE "FOR GOOD"...
THEN NOT ONLY AYAKA...
...BUT ASAYA-KUN, TOO, WILL FACE ALL KINDS OF DISASTERS...!
YOU! YUGE-KUN! CAN YOU REACH ASAYA-KUN?!
KENSUKE-KUN CAN.
BUT WHY DON'T YOU?
HE IGNORES ME!
I HOPE YOU'RE WELL... MY YOUNGER BROTHER-IN-LAW...
SHUDDER

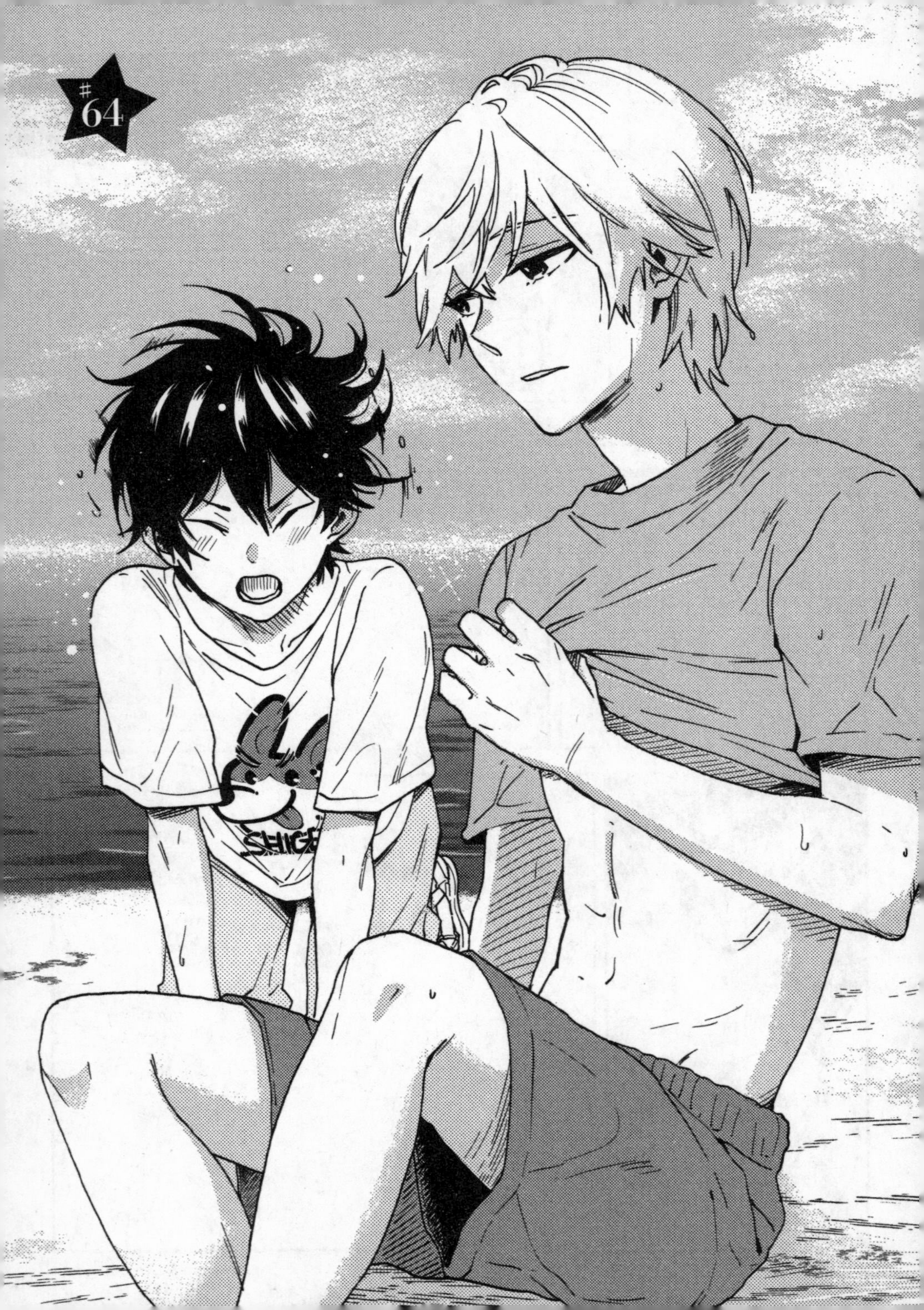
#
64
SHIGE

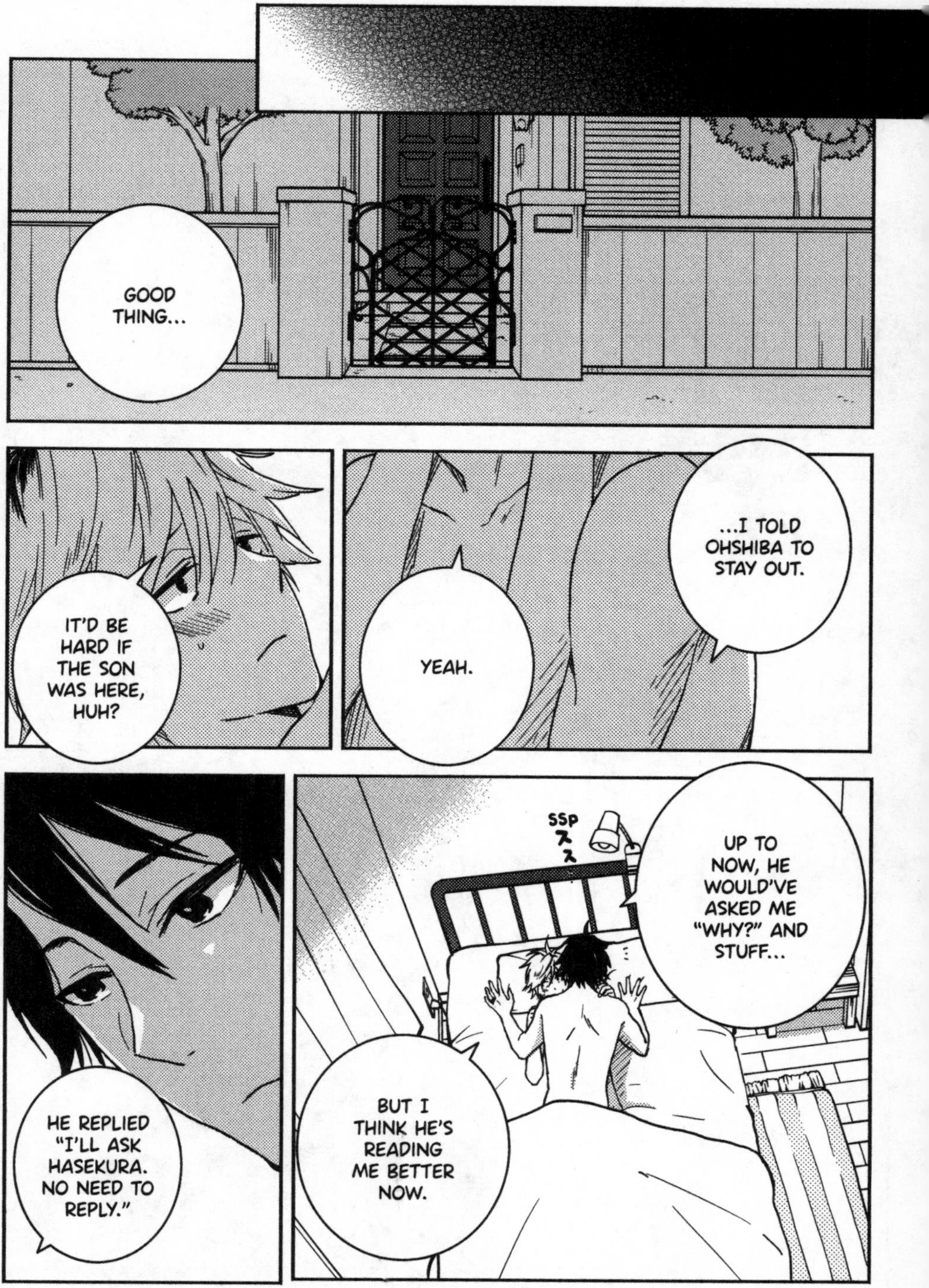
GOOD THING...
...I TOLD OHSHIBA TO STAY OUT.
YEAH.
IT'D BE HARD IF THE SON WAS HERE, HUH?
UP TO NOW, HE WOULD'VE ASKED ME "WHY?" AND STUFF...
SSP
スス
BUT I THINK HE'S READING ME BETTER NOW.
HE REPLIED "I'LL ASK HASEKURA. NO NEED TO REPLY."

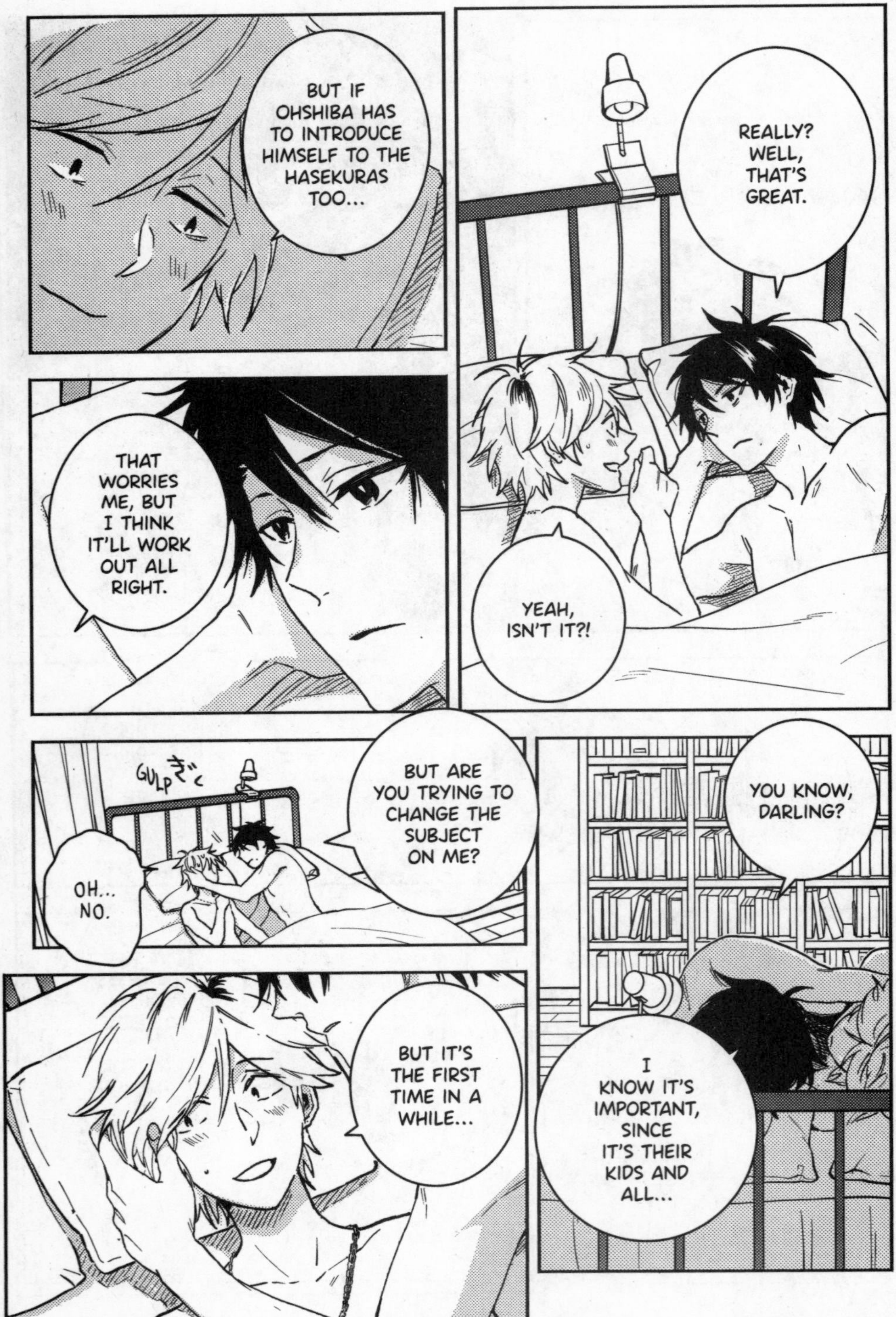
REALLY? WELL, THAT'S GREAT.
YEAH, ISN'T IT?!
BUT IF OHSHIBA HAS TO INTRODUCE HIMSELF TO THE HASEKURAS TOO...
THAT WORRIES ME, BUT I THINK IT'LL WORK OUT ALL RIGHT.
YOU KNOW, DARLING?
I KNOW IT'S IMPORTANT, SINCE IT'S THEIR KIDS AND ALL...
BUT ARE YOU TRYING TO CHANGE THE SUBJECT ON ME?
GULP ぎく
OH... NO.
BUT IT'S THE FIRST TIME IN A WHILE...

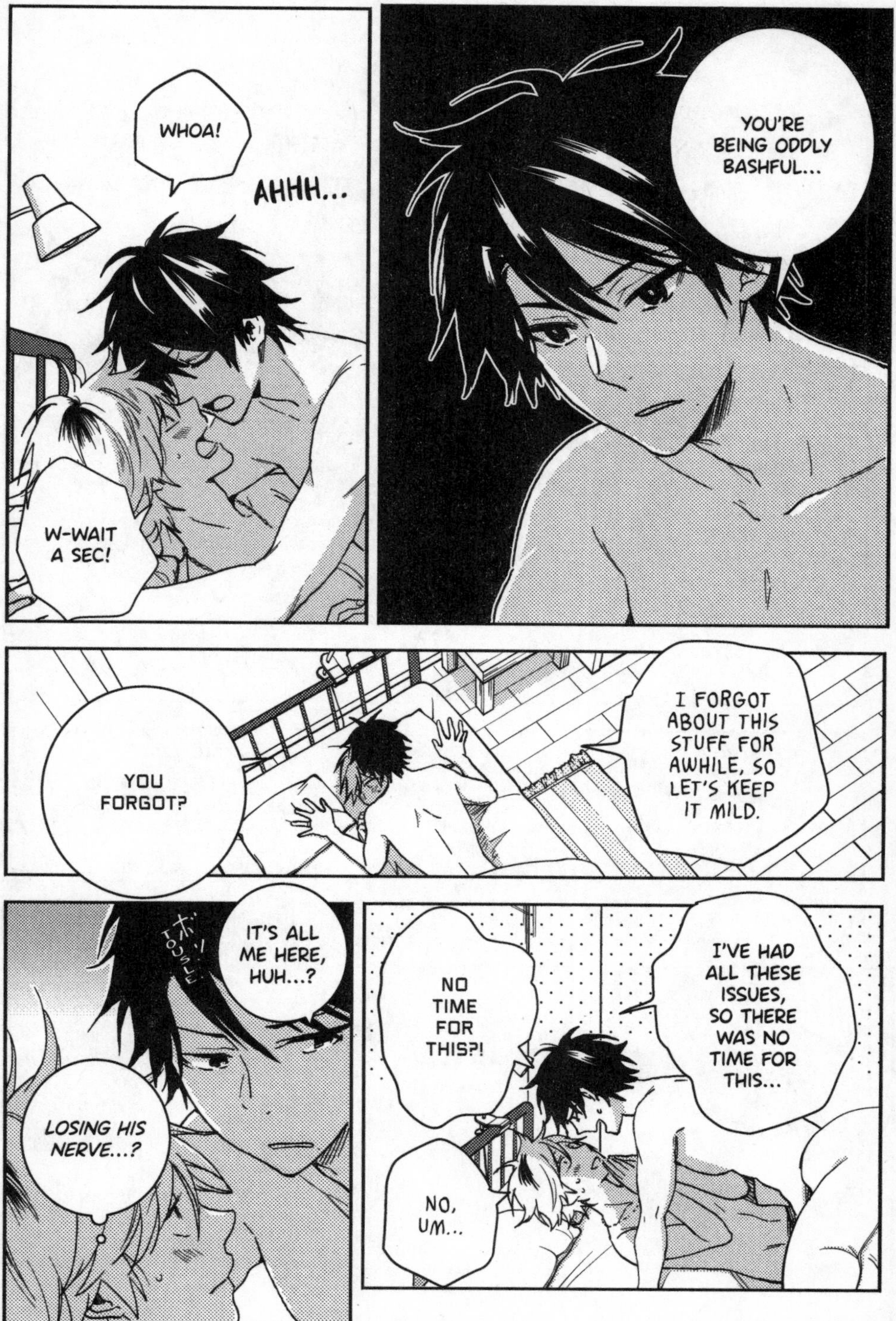
YOU'RE BEING ODDLY BASHFUL...
WHOA!
AHHH...
W-WAIT A SEC!
I FORGOT ABOUT THIS STUFF FOR AWHILE, SO LET'S KEEP IT MILD.
YOU FORGOT?
I'VE HAD ALL THESE ISSUES, SO THERE WAS NO TIME FOR THIS...
NO TIME FOR THIS?!
NO, UM...
IT'S ALL ME HERE, HUH...?
TOUSLE
LOSING HIS NERVE...?

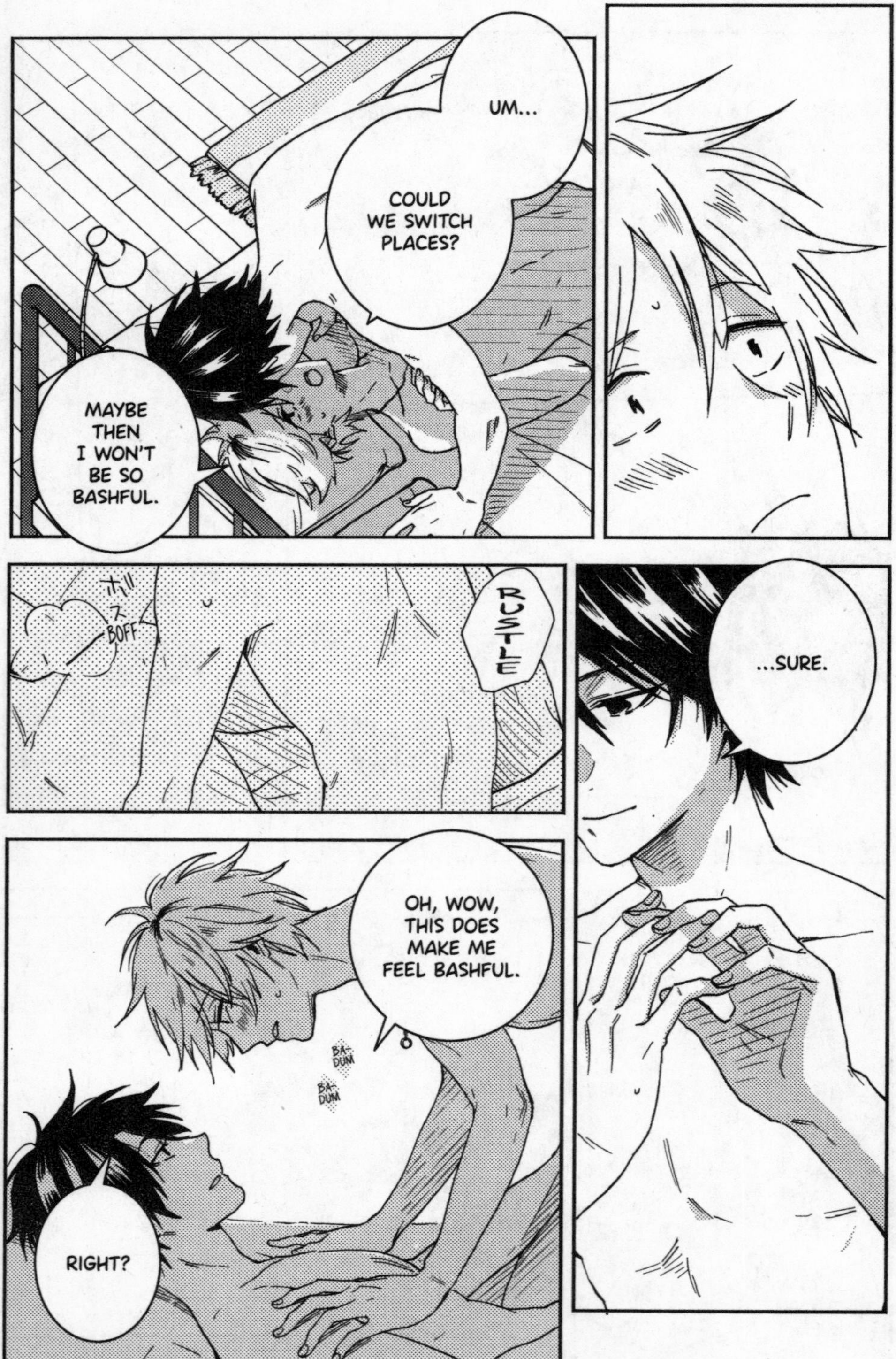
UM...
COULD WE SWITCH PLACES?
MAYBE THEN I WON'T BE SO BASHFUL.
...SURE.
RUSTLE
ホス BOFF
OH, WOW, THIS DOES MAKE ME FEEL BASHFUL.
BA-DUM
BA-DUM
RIGHT?

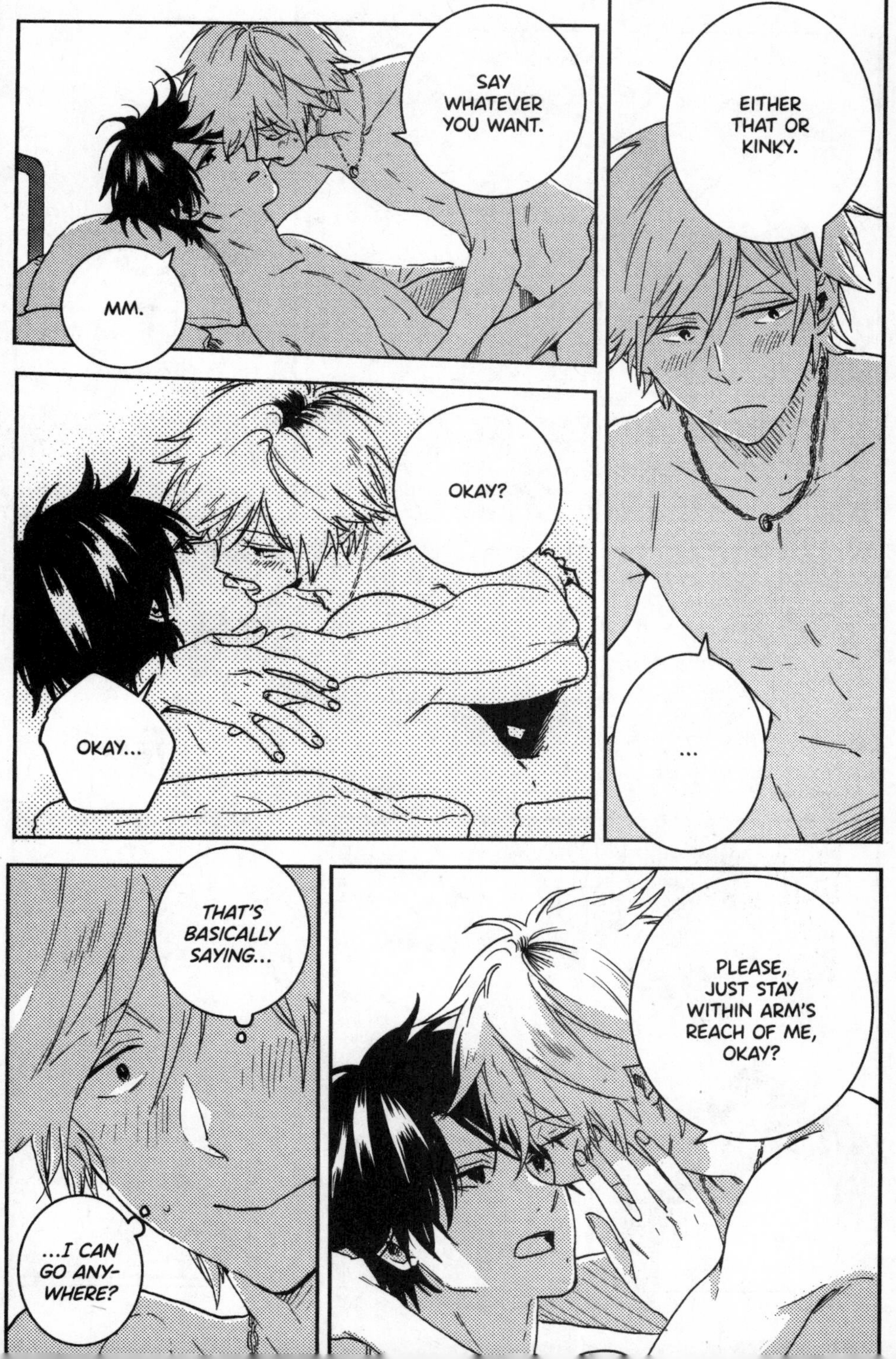
EITHER THAT OR KINKY.
...
SAY WHATEVER YOU WANT.
MM.
OKAY?
OKAY...
PLEASE, JUST STAY WITHIN ARM'S REACH OF ME, OKAY?
THAT'S BASICALLY SAYING...
...I CAN GO ANY-WHERE?

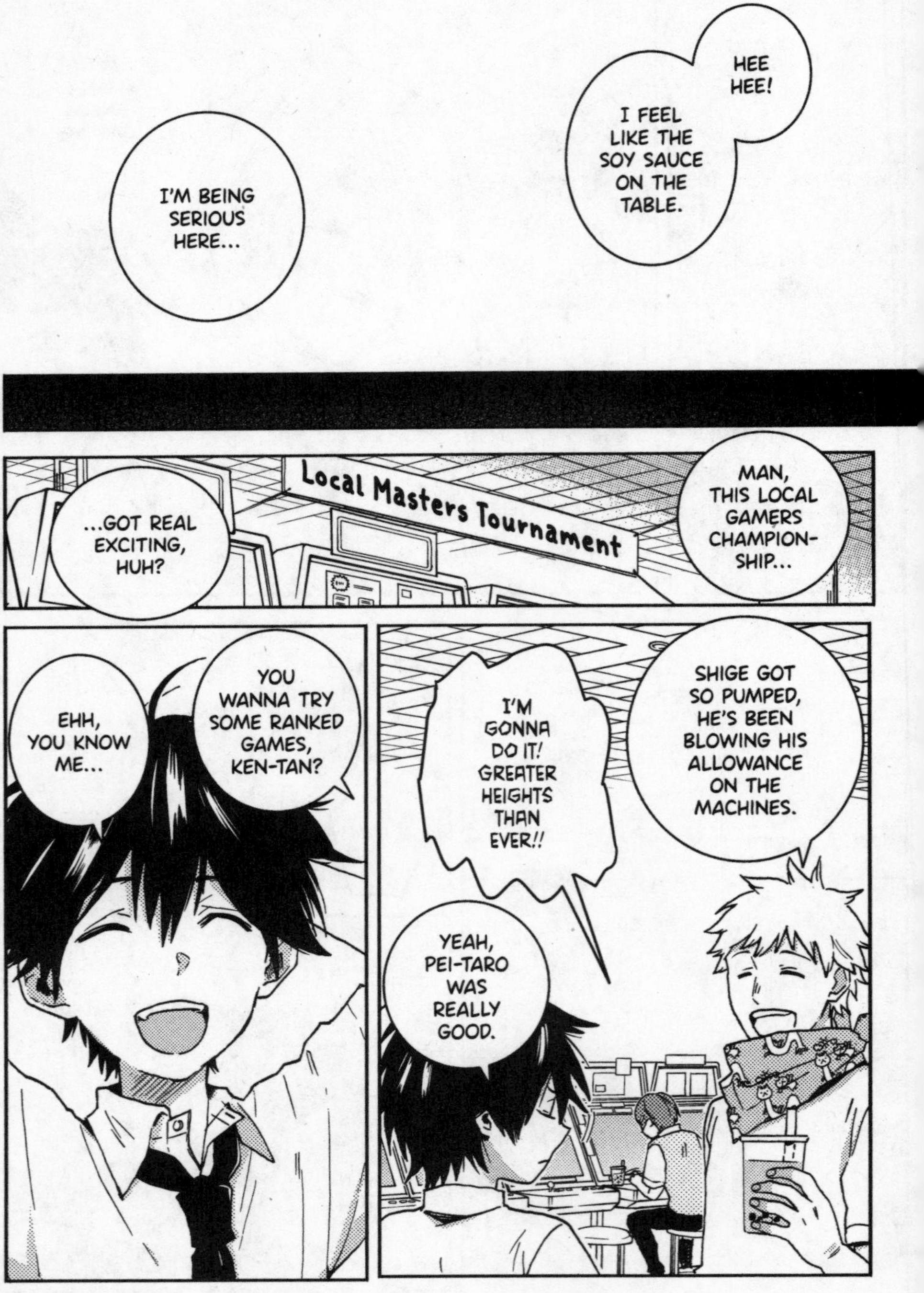
HEE HEE!
I FEEL LIKE THE SOY SAUCE ON THE TABLE.
I'M BEING SERIOUS HERE...
MAN, THIS LOCAL GAMERS CHAMPION-SHIP...
Local Masters Tournament
...GOT REAL EXCITING, HUH?
SHIGE GOT SO PUMPED, HE'S BEEN BLOWING HIS ALLOWANCE ON THE MACHINES.
I'M GONNA DO IT! GREATER HEIGHTS THAN EVER!!
YEAH, PEI-TARO WAS REALLY GOOD.
YOU WANNA TRY SOME RANKED GAMES, KEN-TAN?
EHH, YOU KNOW ME...

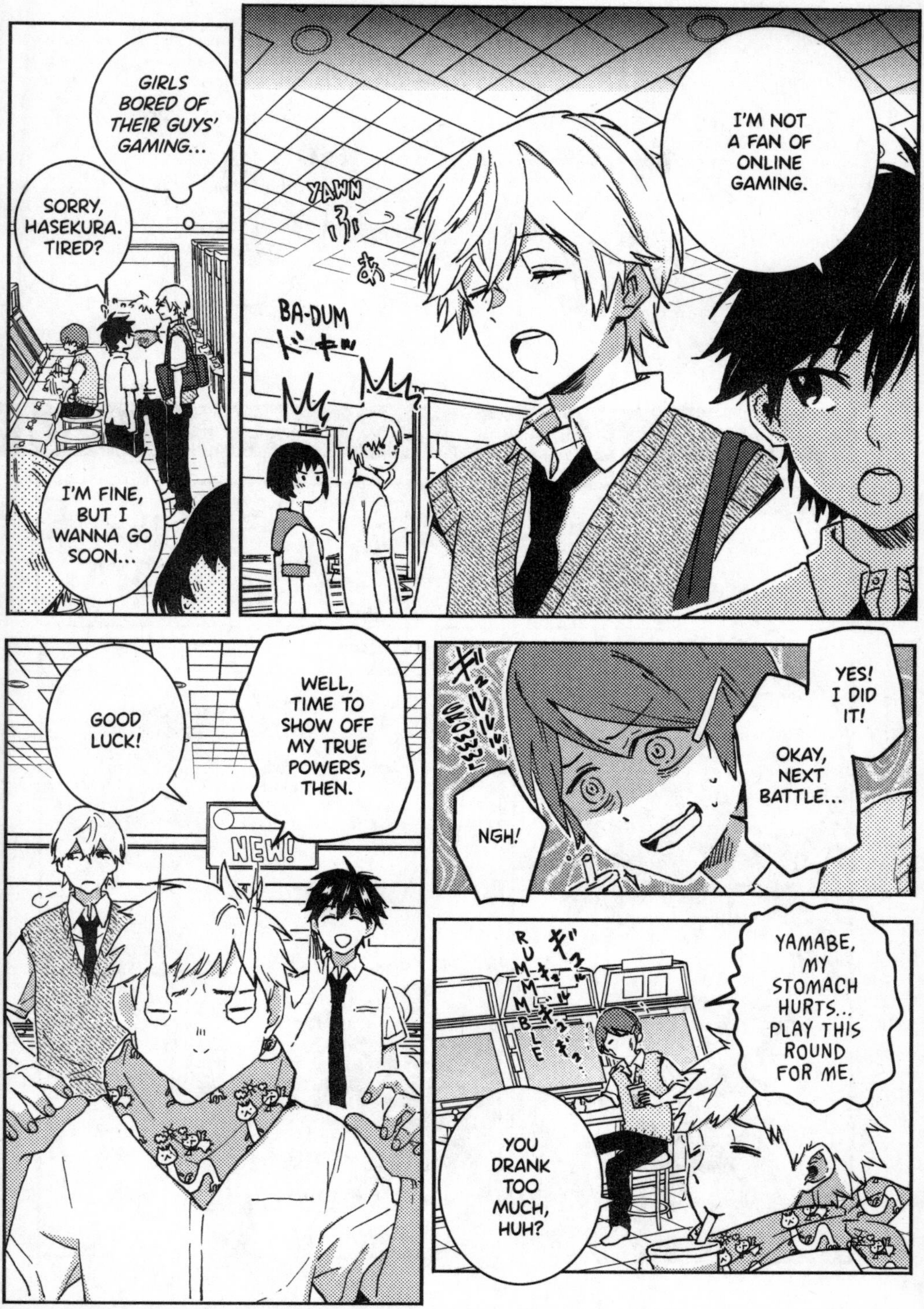
I'M NOT A FAN OF ONLINE GAMING.
YAWN
ふぁ
あ
BA-DUM
ドキッ
GIRLS BORED OF THEIR GUYS' GAMING...
SORRY, HASEKURA. TIRED?
I'M FINE, BUT I WANNA GO SOON...
YES! I DID IT!
OKAY, NEXT BATTLE...
ギュルルルッ
GROWWWL
NGH!
YAMABE, MY STOMACH HURTS... PLAY THIS ROUND FOR ME.
RUMMBLE
ギュルギュル
YOU DRANK TOO MUCH, HUH?
WELL, TIME TO SHOW OFF MY TRUE POWERS, THEN.
GOOD LUCK!
NEW!

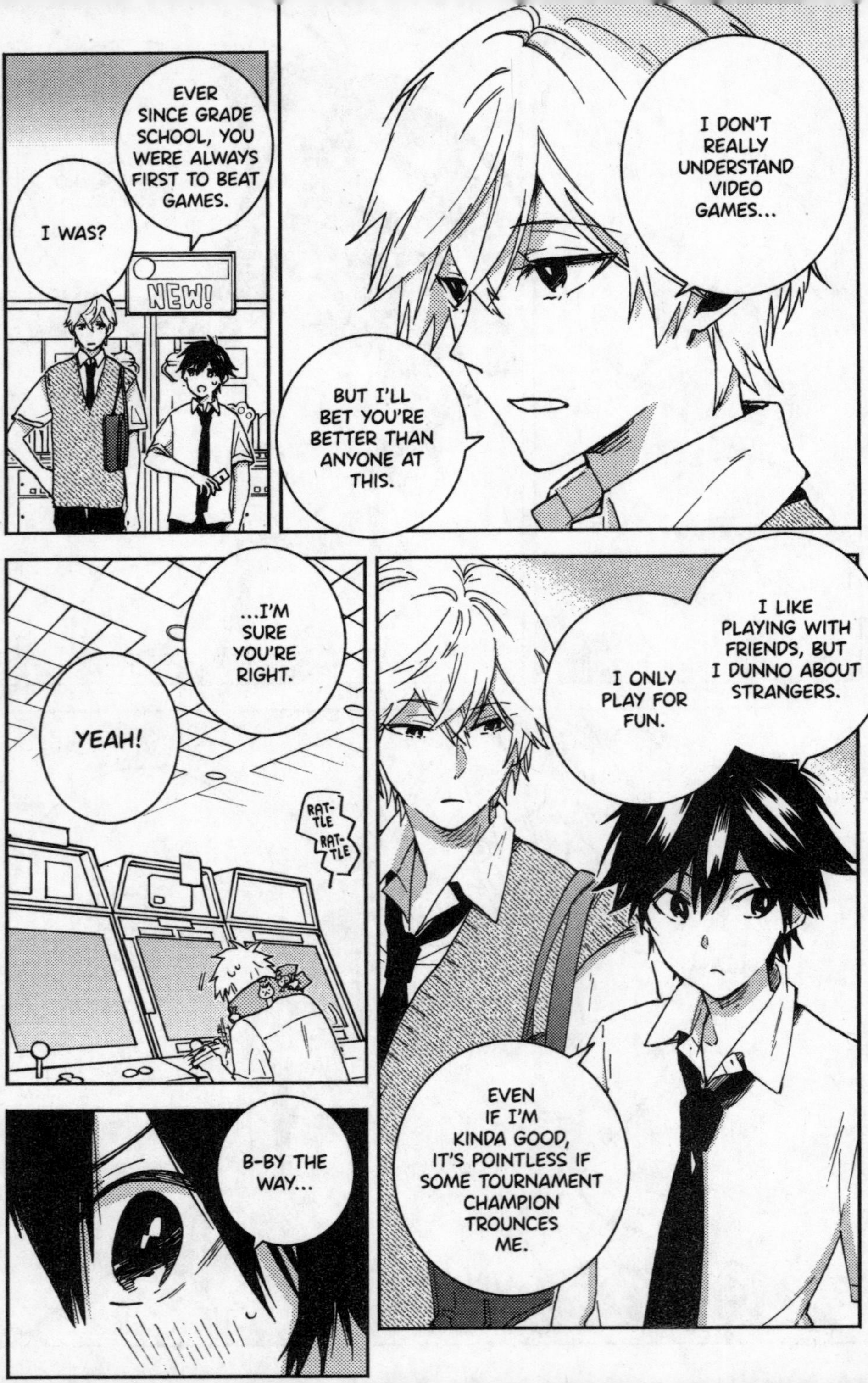
I DON'T REALLY UNDERSTAND VIDEO GAMES...
BUT I'LL BET YOU'RE BETTER THAN ANYONE AT THIS.
EVER SINCE GRADE SCHOOL, YOU WERE ALWAYS FIRST TO BEAT GAMES.
NEW!
I WAS?
I LIKE PLAYING WITH FRIENDS, BUT I DUNNO ABOUT STRANGERS.
I ONLY PLAY FOR FUN.
EVEN IF I'M KINDA GOOD, IT'S POINTLESS IF SOME TOURNAMENT CHAMPION TROUNCES ME.
...I'M SURE YOU'RE RIGHT.
YEAH!
RAT-TLE RAT-TLE
B-BY THE WAY...

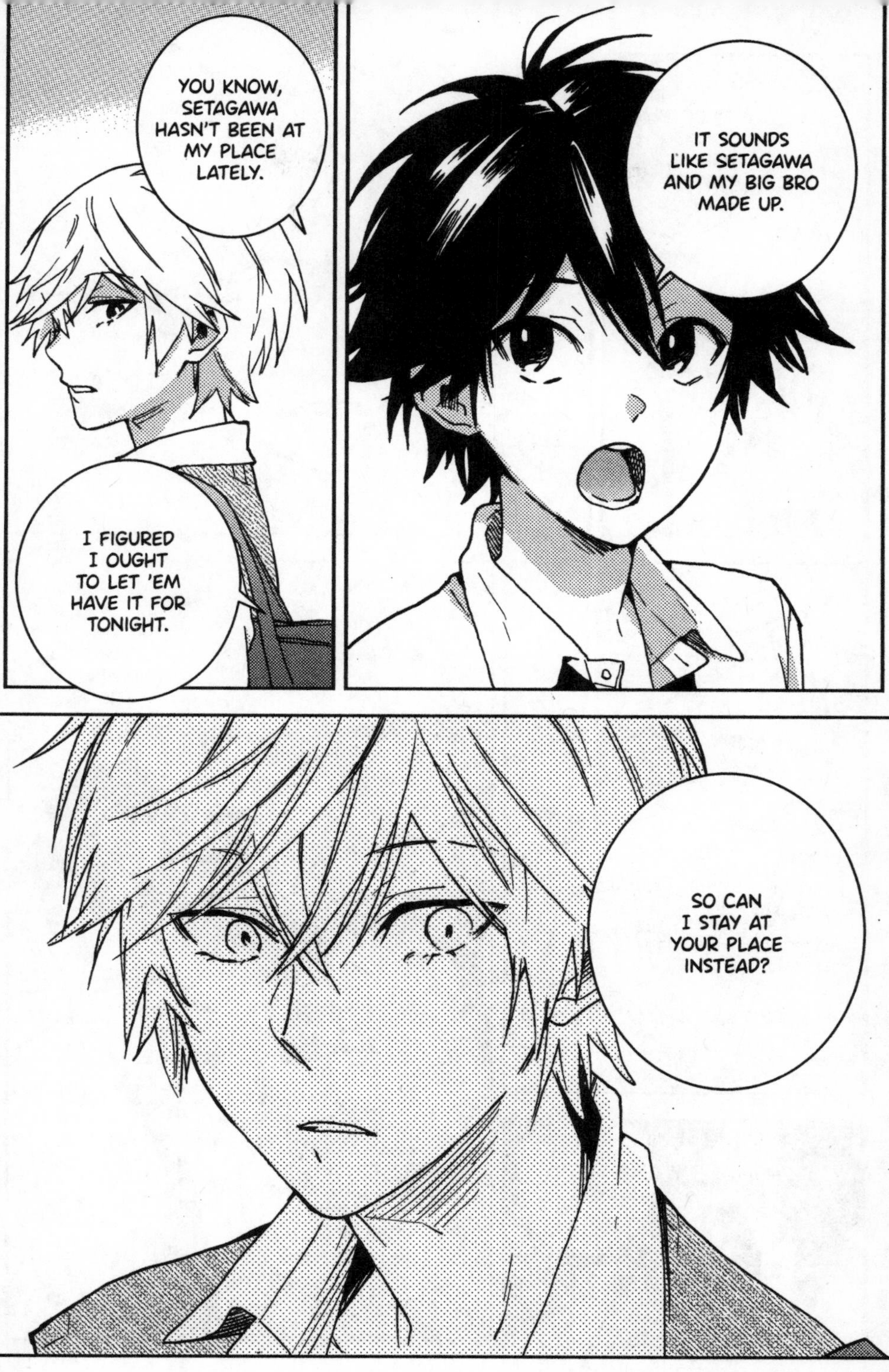
IT SOUNDS LIKE SETAGAWA AND MY BIG BRO MADE UP.
YOU KNOW, SETAGAWA HASN'T BEEN AT MY PLACE LATELY.
I FIGURED I OUGHT TO LET 'EM HAVE IT FOR TONIGHT.
SO CAN I STAY AT YOUR PLACE INSTEAD?

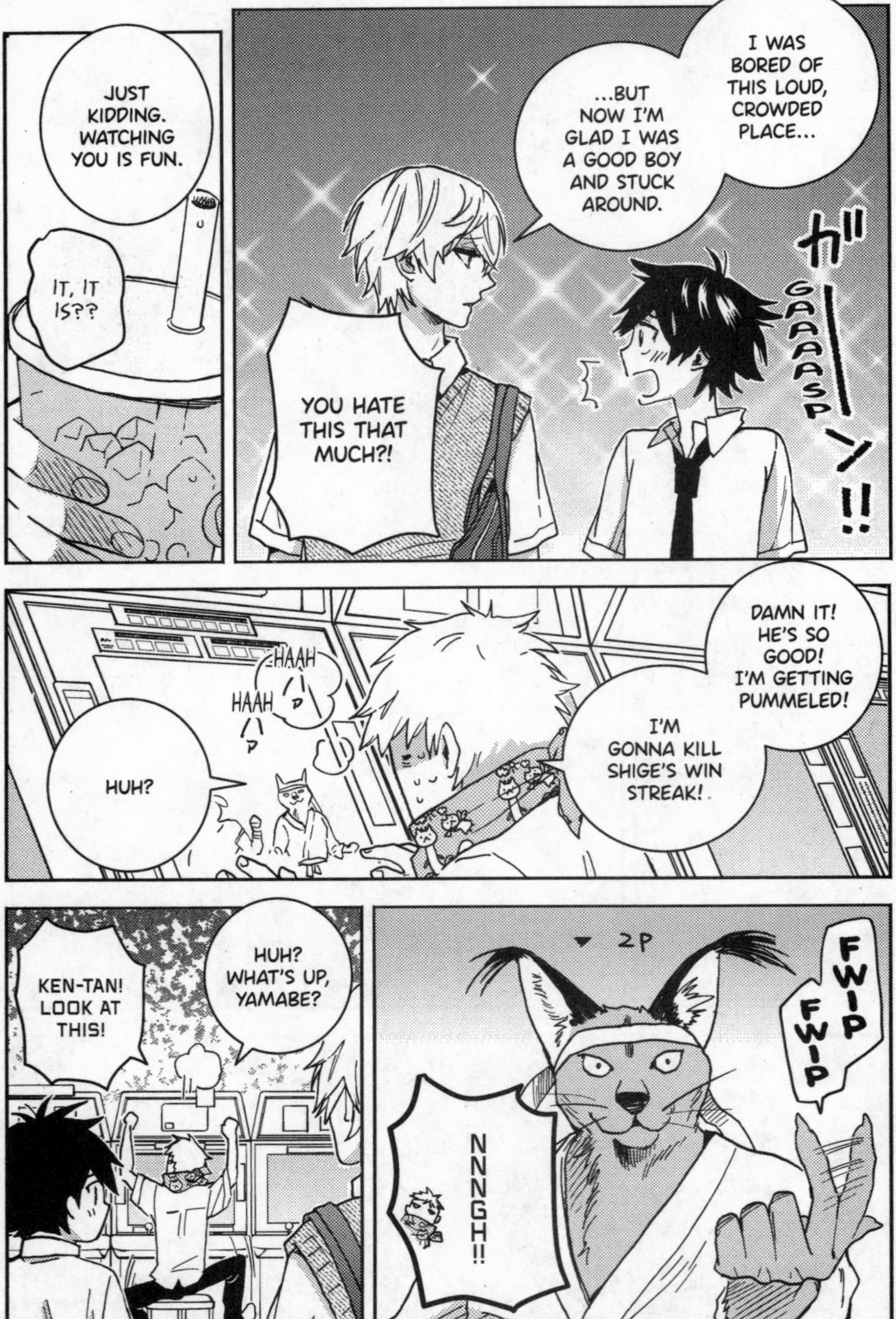
I WAS BORED OF THIS LOUD, CROWDED PLACE...
...BUT NOW I'M GLAD I WAS A GOOD BOY AND STUCK AROUND.
GAAAASP!!
YOU HATE THIS THAT MUCH?!
JUST KIDDING. WATCHING YOU IS FUN.
IT, IT IS??
DAMN IT! HE'S SO GOOD! I'M GETTING PUMMELED!
I'M GONNA KILL SHIGE'S WIN STREAK!
HAAAH
HAAAH
HUH?
2P
FWIP FWIP
NNNGH!!
HUH? WHAT'S UP, YAMABE?
KEN-TAN! LOOK AT THIS!

YOU FIGHT FOR ME, KEN-TAN.

I'M SORRY, MY STOMACH'S IN KNOTS RIGHT NOW TOO...

HUH?

NNGH?!

TAUNTING ME IN THE MIDDLE OF BATTLE...

GROWWWL

...

GET REVENGE FOR ME...

I, I'M OUT OF GAS...

YOU DRANK TOO MUCH JUICE TOO, YAMABE?

IT'S GROWLING HARD...

I CAN'T DO THAT.

MAYBE HE GOT PISSED OFF AND LEFT.

OH, WOW, THE OTHER GUY STOPPED.

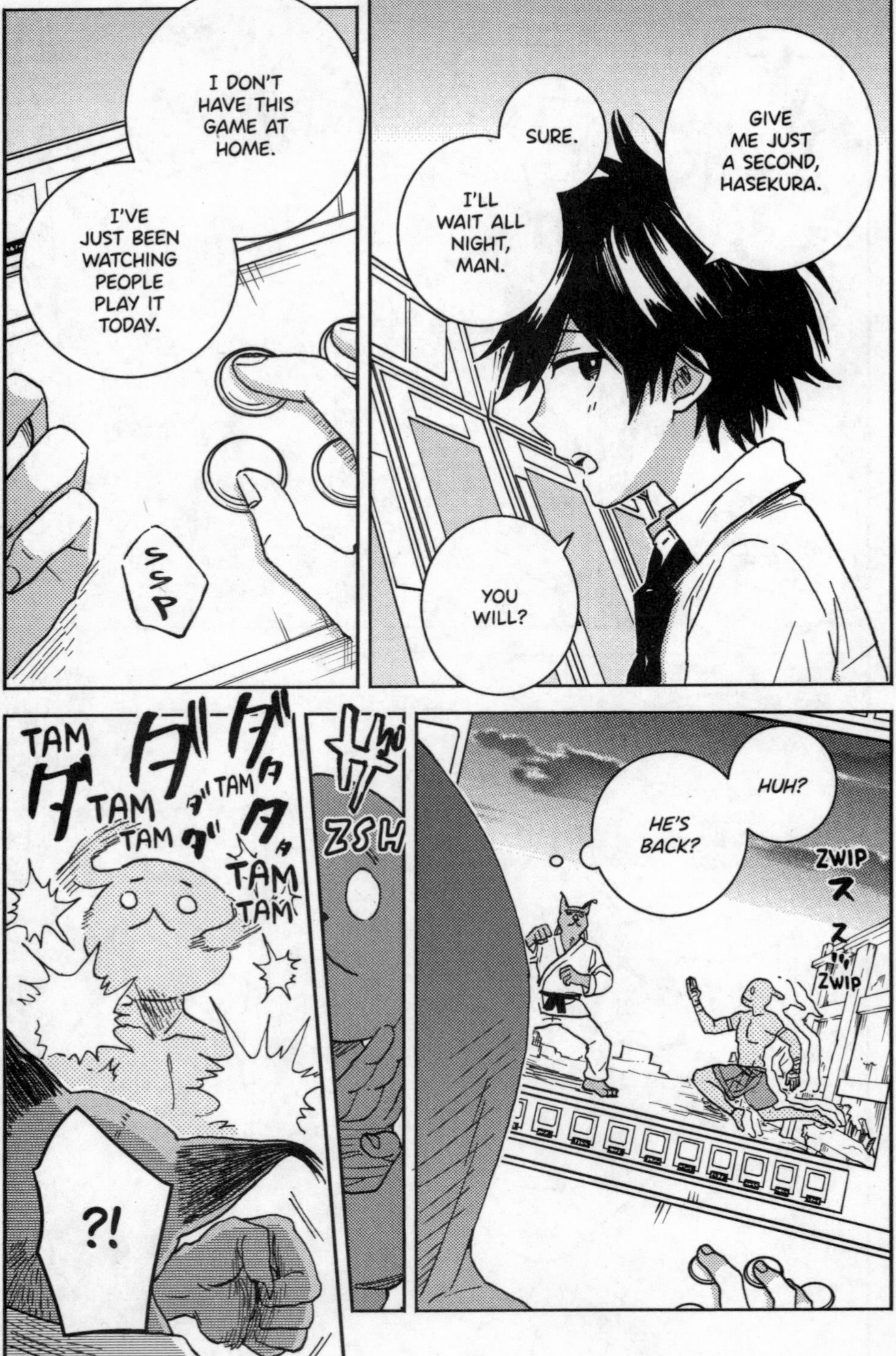
GIVE ME JUST A SECOND, HASEKURA.
SURE.
I'LL WAIT ALL NIGHT, MAN.
YOU WILL?
I DON'T HAVE THIS GAME AT HOME.
I'VE JUST BEEN WATCHING PEOPLE PLAY IT TODAY.
SSP
HUH?
HE'S BACK?
ZWIP
ス
ス
ZWIP
ZSH
TAM
TAM
TAM
TAM
TAM
TAM
TAM
?!

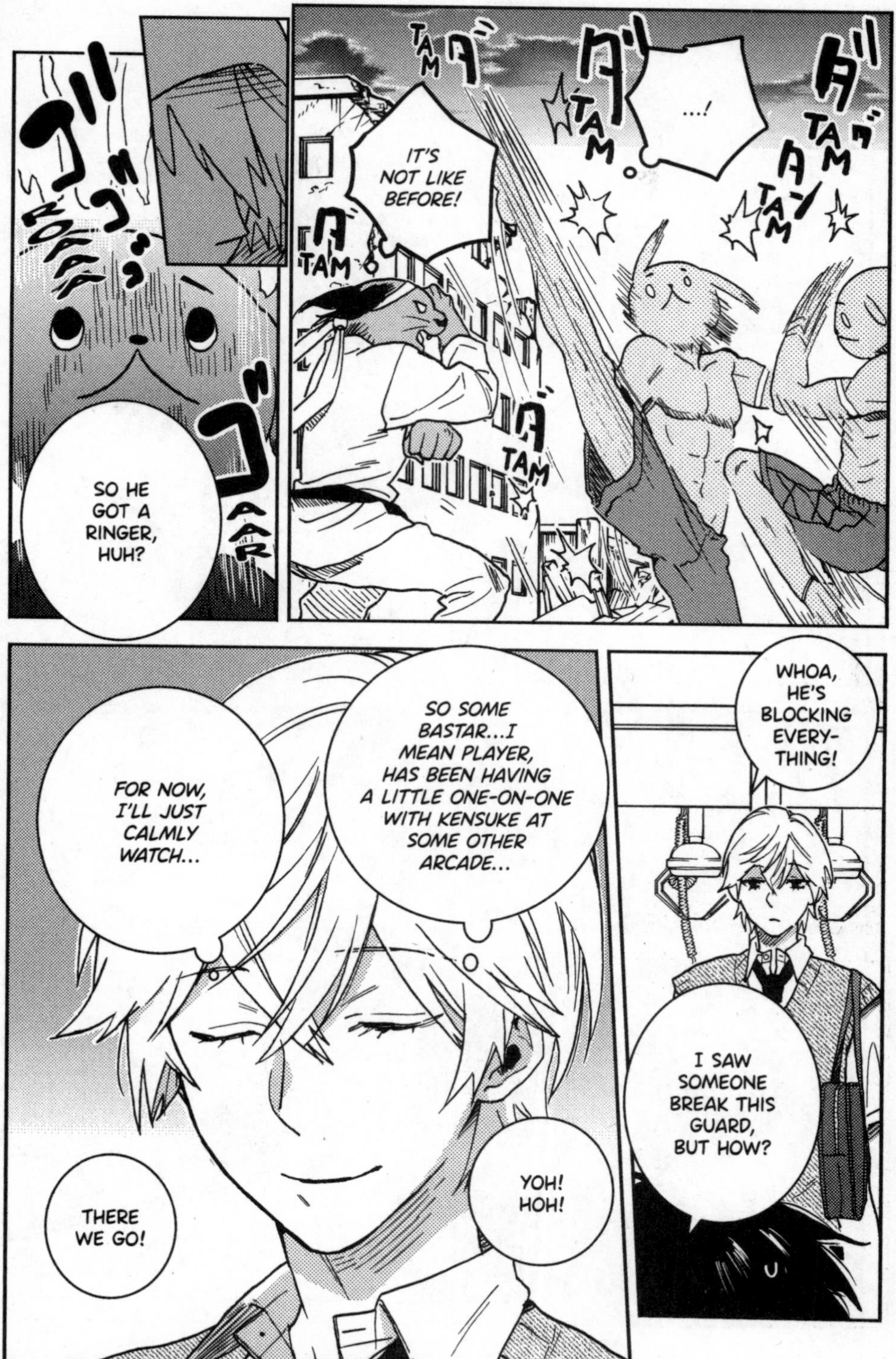
TAM
TAM
...!
TAM
IT'S NOT LIKE BEFORE!
TAM
TAM
TAM
SO HE GOT A RINGER, HUH?
WHOA, HE'S BLOCKING EVERY-THING!
I SAW SOMEONE BREAK THIS GUARD, BUT HOW?
SO SOME BASTAR...I MEAN PLAYER, HAS BEEN HAVING A LITTLE ONE-ON-ONE WITH KENSUKE AT SOME OTHER ARCADE...
FOR NOW, I'LL JUST CALMLY WATCH...
YOH! HOH!
THERE WE GO!

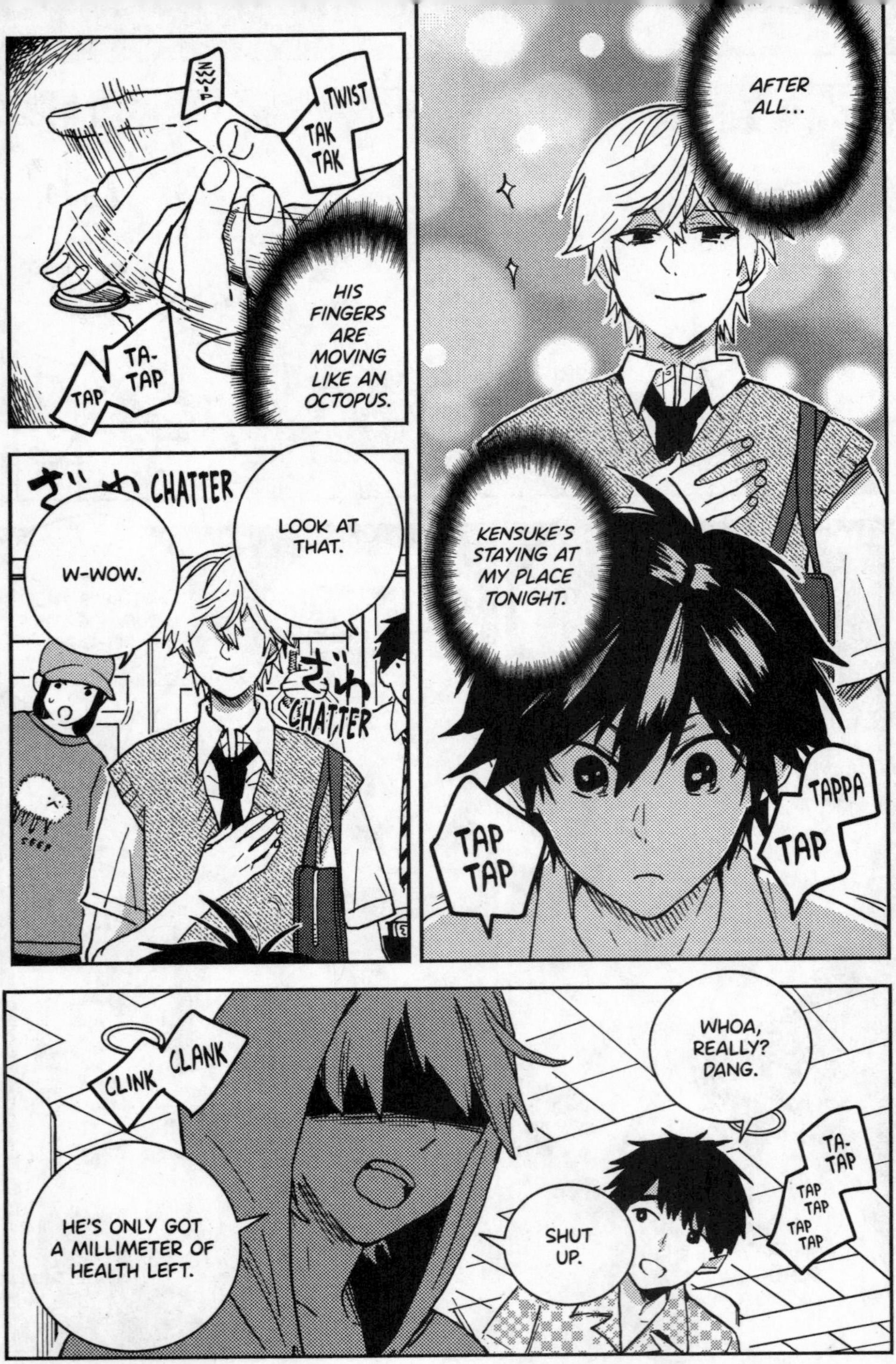
AFTER ALL...
KENSUKE'S STAYING AT MY PLACE TONIGHT.
TAPPA TAP
TAP TAP
TWIST
ZWWIP
TAK TAK
HIS FINGERS ARE MOVING LIKE AN OCTOPUS.
TA-TAP
TAP
LOOK AT THAT.
ざわ CHATTER
W-WOW.
ざわ CHATTER
WHOA, REALLY? DANG.
TA-TAP
TAP TAP TAP TAP
SHUT UP.
CLANK
CLINK
HE'S ONLY GOT A MILLIMETER OF HEALTH LEFT.

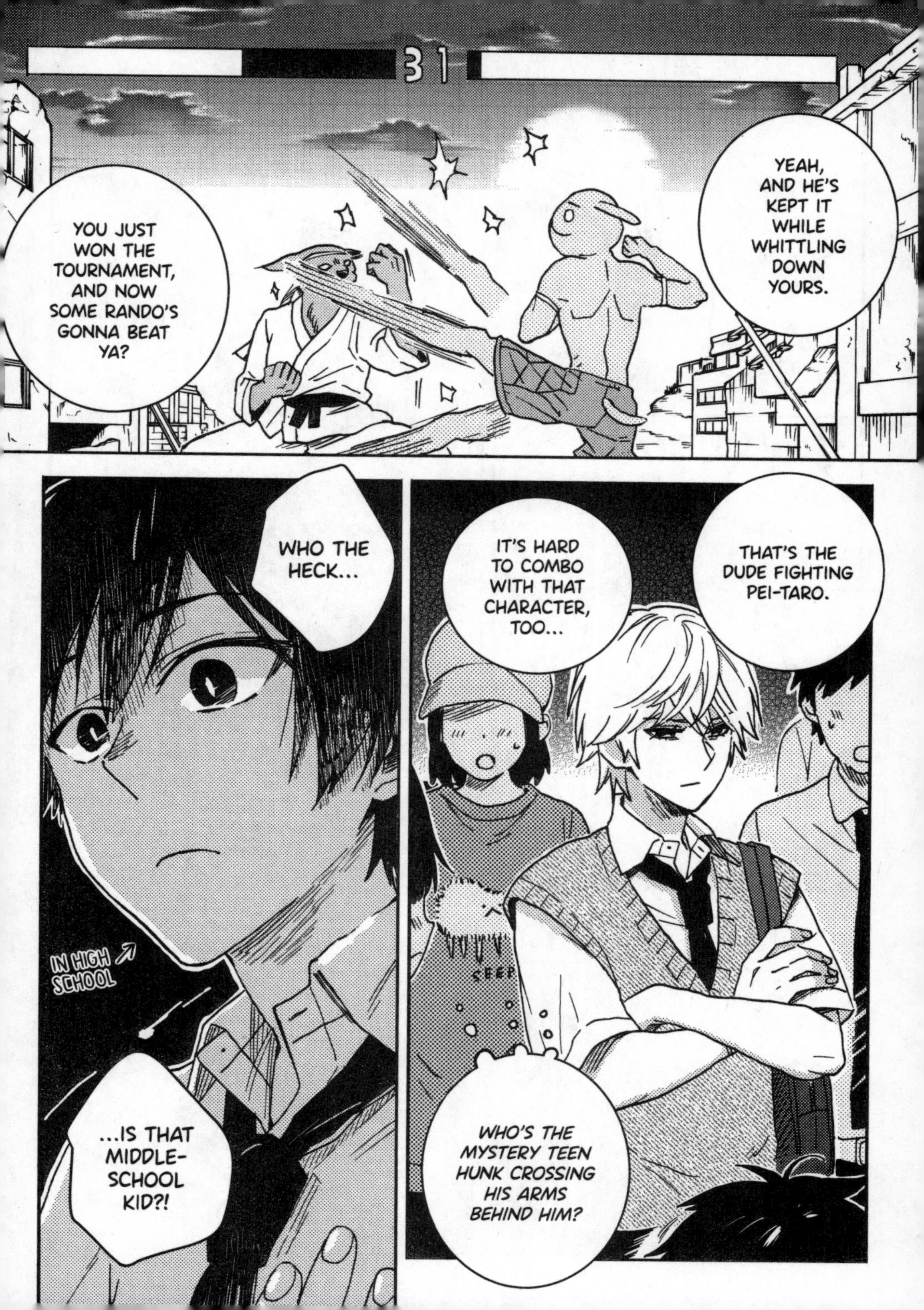
31
YEAH, AND HE'S KEPT IT WHILE WHITTLING DOWN YOURS.
YOU JUST WON THE TOURNAMENT, AND NOW SOME RANDO'S GONNA BEAT YA?
THAT'S THE DUDE FIGHTING PEI-TARO.
IT'S HARD TO COMBO WITH THAT CHARACTER, TOO...
WHO'S THE MYSTERY TEEN HUNK CROSSING HIS ARMS BEHIND HIM?
WHO THE HECK...
IN HIGH SCHOOL
...IS THAT MIDDLE-SCHOOL KID?!

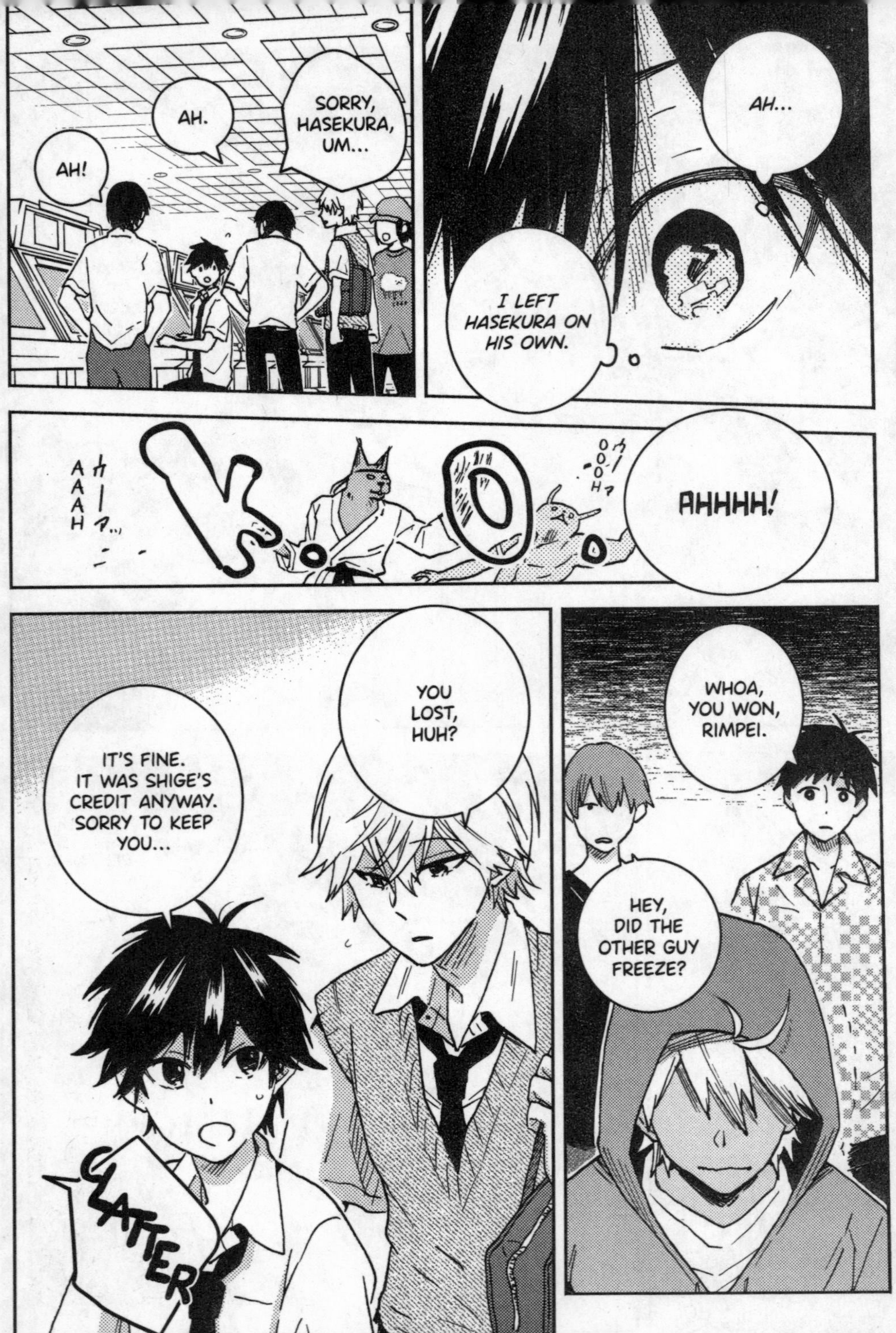
AH...
I LEFT HASEKURA ON HIS OWN.
SORRY, HASEKURA, UM...
AH.
AH!
AHHHH!
OOOOH
KO
AAAAH
WHOA, YOU WON, RIMPEI.
HEY, DID THE OTHER GUY FREEZE?
YOU LOST, HUH?
IT'S FINE. IT WAS SHIGE'S CREDIT ANYWAY. SORRY TO KEEP YOU...
CLATTER

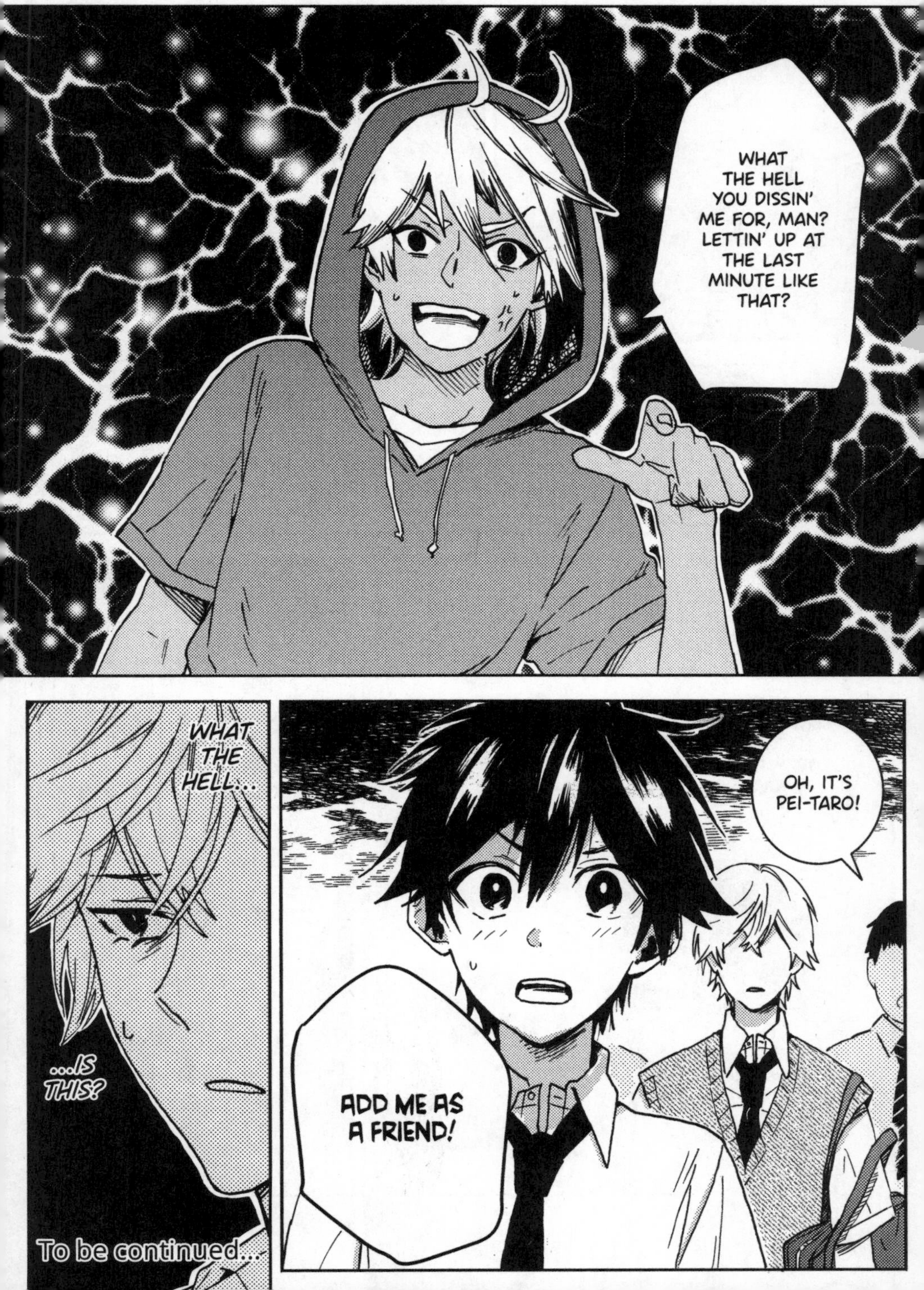
WHAT THE HELL YOU DISSIN' ME FOR, MAN? LETTIN' UP AT THE LAST MINUTE LIKE THAT?
OH, IT'S PEI-TARO!
ADD ME AS A FRIEND!
WHAT THE HELL...
...IS THIS?
To be continued...

★ YUNGE'S TALENT ★

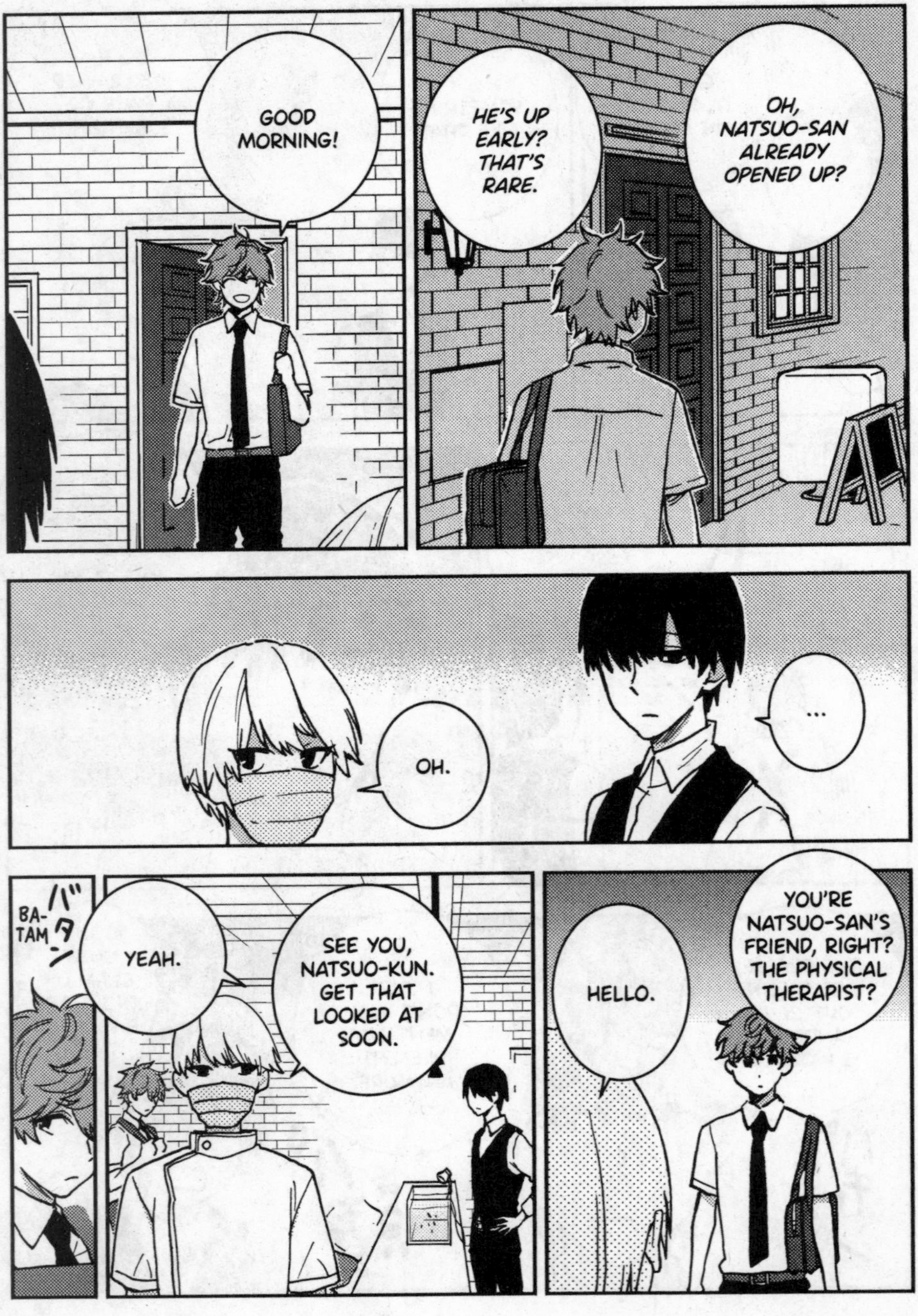

OH, NATSUO-SAN ALREADY OPENED UP?
HE'S UP EARLY? THAT'S RARE.
GOOD MORNING!
...
OH.
YOU'RE NATSUO-SAN'S FRIEND, RIGHT? THE PHYSICAL THERAPIST?
HELLO.
SEE YOU, NATSUO-KUN. GET THAT LOOKED AT SOON.
YEAH.
BA-TAM バタン

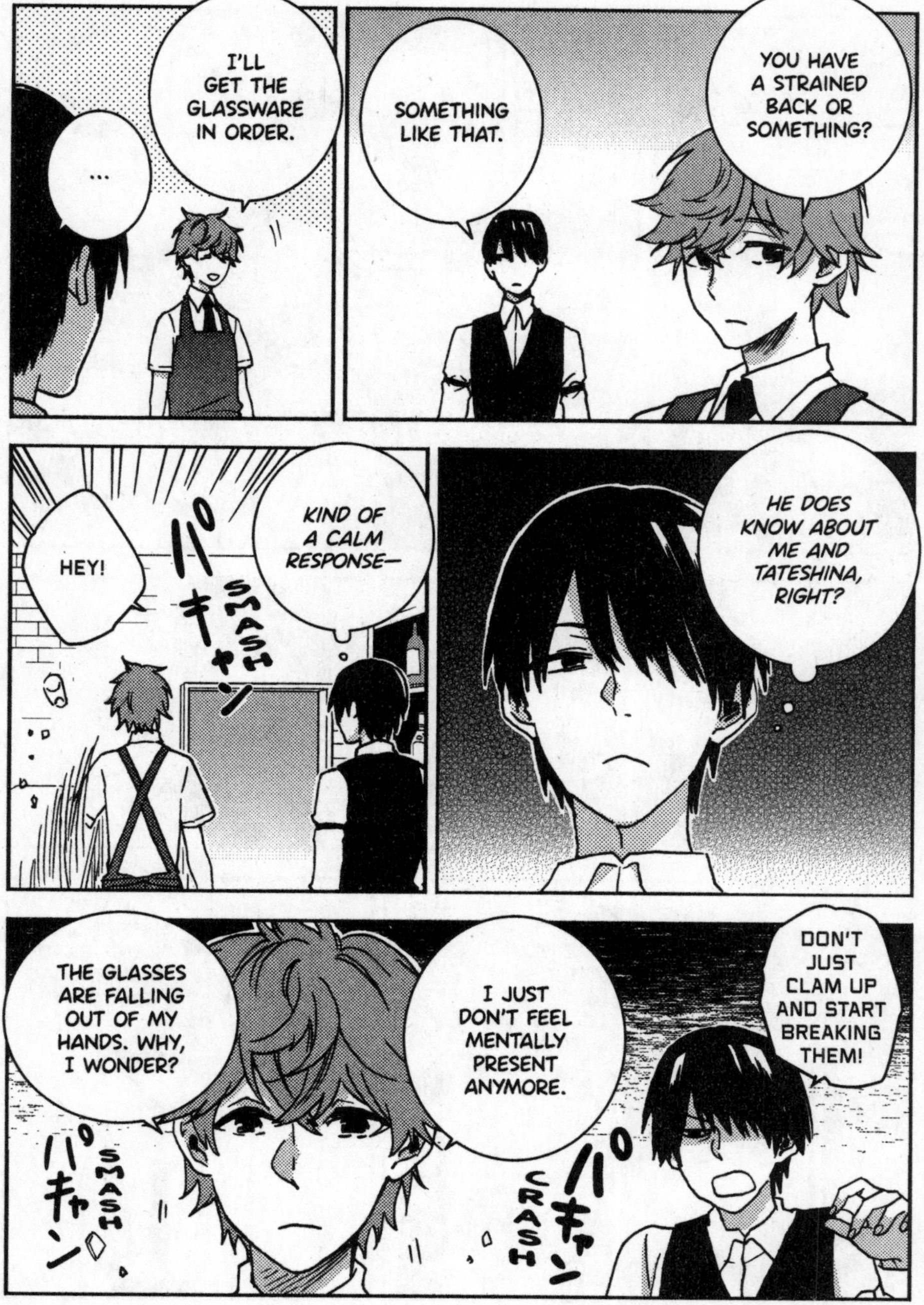
YOU HAVE A STRAINED BACK OR SOMETHING?
SOMETHING LIKE THAT.
I'LL GET THE GLASSWARE IN ORDER.
...
HE DOES KNOW ABOUT ME AND TATESHINA, RIGHT?
KIND OF A CALM RESPONSE—
パキャン
SMASH
HEY!
DON'T JUST CLAM UP AND START BREAKING THEM!
パキャン
CRASH
I JUST DON'T FEEL MENTALLY PRESENT ANYMORE.
THE GLASSES ARE FALLING OUT OF MY HANDS. WHY, I WONDER?
パキャン
SMASH

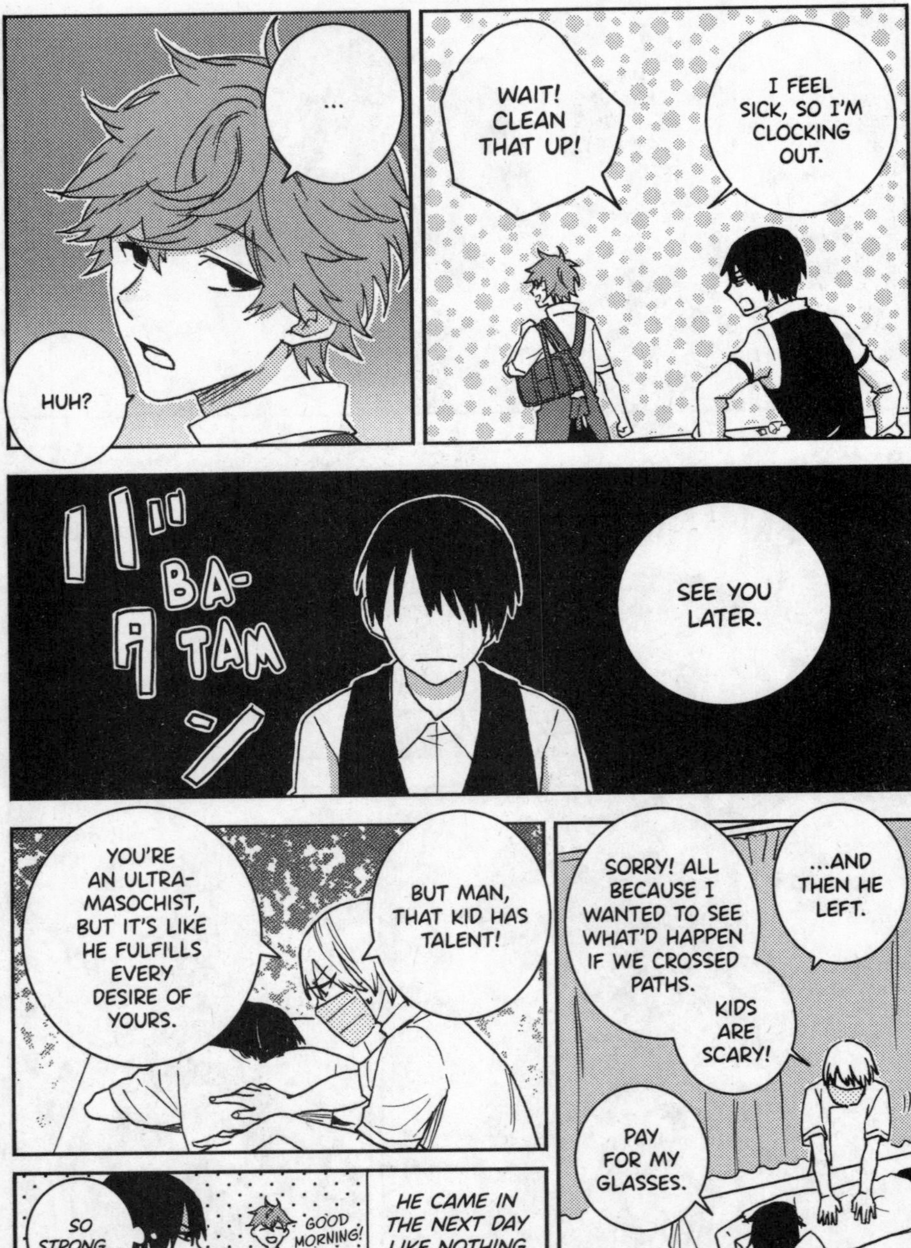
I FEEL SICK, SO I'M CLOCKING OUT.
WAIT! CLEAN THAT UP!
...
HUH?
SEE YOU LATER.
BA-TAM
...AND THEN HE LEFT.
SORRY! ALL BECAUSE I WANTED TO SEE WHAT'D HAPPEN IF WE CROSSED PATHS.
KIDS ARE SCARY!
PAY FOR MY GLASSES.
BUT MAN, THAT KID HAS TALENT!
YOU'RE AN ULTRA-MASOCHIST, BUT IT'S LIKE HE FULFILLS EVERY DESIRE OF YOURS.
HE CAME IN THE NEXT DAY LIKE NOTHING HAPPENED.
GOOD MORNING!
SO STRONG...

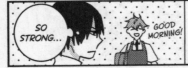

★ GRADUALLY WEAKENING ★

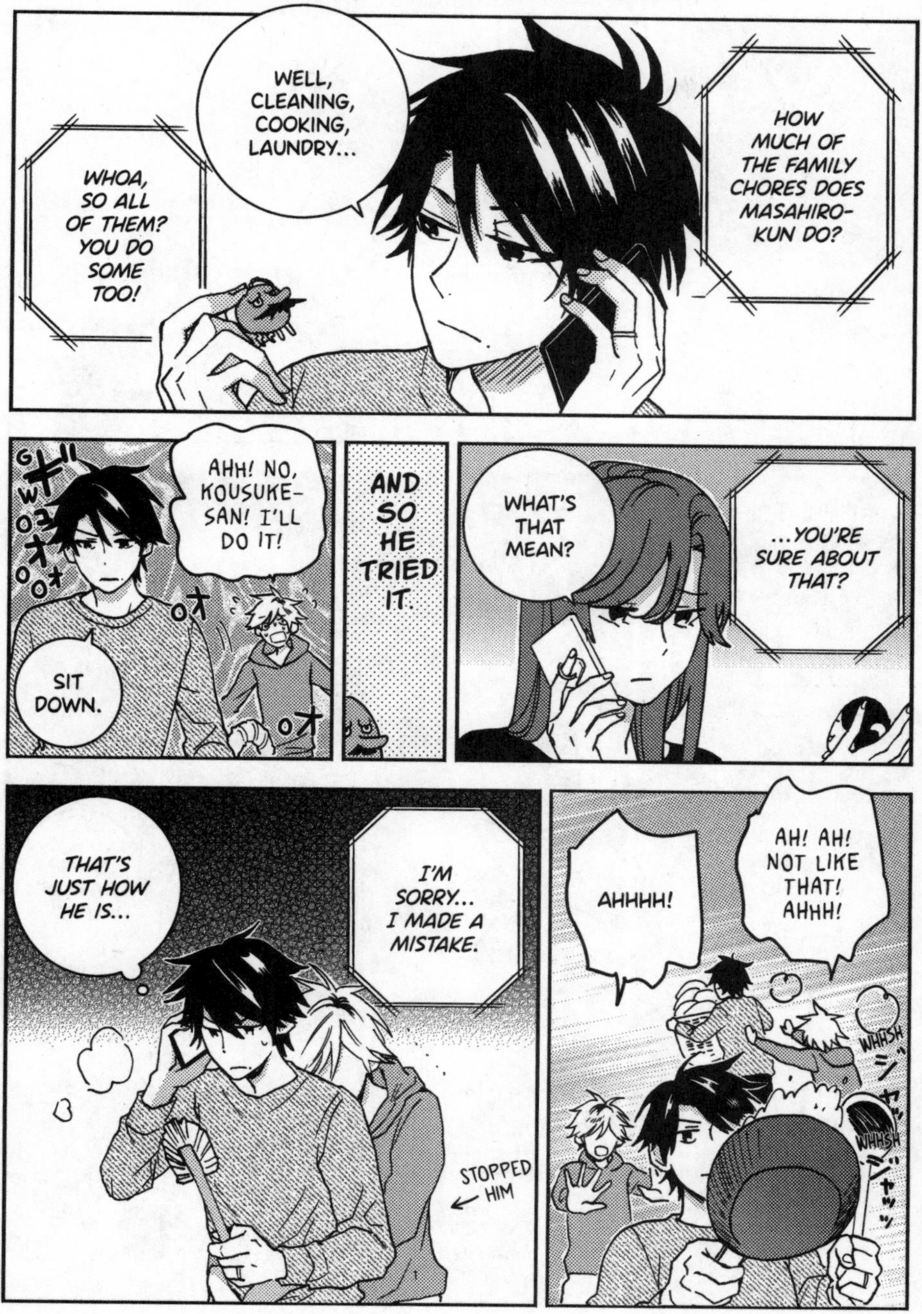
HOW MUCH OF THE FAMILY CHORES DOES MASAHIRO-KUN DO?
WELL, CLEANING, COOKING, LAUNDRY...
WHOA, SO ALL OF THEM? YOU DO SOME TOO!
...YOU'RE SURE ABOUT THAT?
WHAT'S THAT MEAN?
AND SO HE TRIED IT.
AHH! NO, KOUSUKE-SAN! I'LL DO IT!
SIT DOWN.
AH! AH! NOT LIKE THAT! AHHH!
AHHHH!
WHHSH
WHHSH
I'M SORRY... I MADE A MISTAKE.
THAT'S JUST HOW HE IS...
STOPPED HIM

★ THE APRON DISCUSSION ★

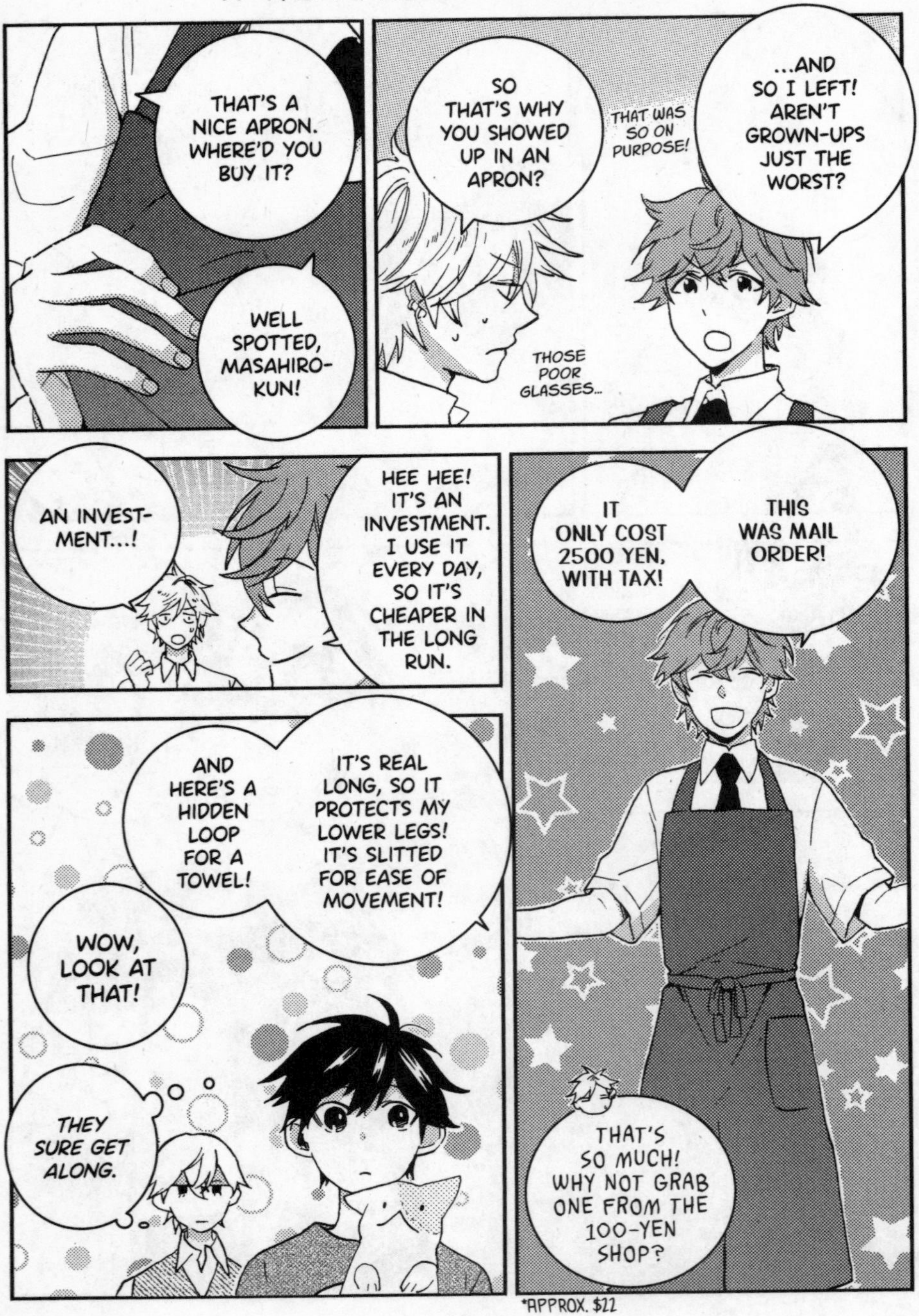
...AND SO I LEFT! AREN'T GROWN-UPS JUST THE WORST?
THAT WAS SO ON PURPOSE!
SO THAT'S WHY YOU SHOWED UP IN AN APRON?
THOSE POOR GLASSES...
THAT'S A NICE APRON. WHERE'D YOU BUY IT?
WELL SPOTTED, MASAHIRO-KUN!
THIS WAS MAIL ORDER!
IT ONLY COST 2500 YEN, WITH TAX!
THAT'S SO MUCH! WHY NOT GRAB ONE FROM THE 100-YEN SHOP?
HEE HEE! IT'S AN INVESTMENT. I USE IT EVERY DAY, SO IT'S CHEAPER IN THE LONG RUN.
AN INVESTMENT...!
IT'S REAL LONG, SO IT PROTECTS MY LOWER LEGS! IT'S SLITTED FOR EASE OF MOVEMENT!
AND HERE'S A HIDDEN LOOP FOR A TOWEL!
WOW, LOOK AT THAT!
THEY SURE GET ALONG.

*APPROX. $22

YOU LOVE THREE-PACKS, DON'T YOU?
SO I LOOKED ONLINE, AND I FOUND A DIFFERENT DESIGN SOLD IN A SET OF THREE FOR 2,000.
HERE, YOU TRY IT ON TOO, KOUSUKE-SAN.
AND CARRY THIS COFFEE POT...
テキパキ
BUSTLE
WOW, YOU LOOK LIKE A GUY RUNNING A WEEKEND CAFÉ AS A HOBBY!
I DO...?
CAN I TAKE A PHOTO?!
GO AHEAD.
MAKES ME WANNA DO CHORES. GUESS I'LL GET ON THE LAUNDRY.
ガシ
GRAB
SO JUST WEAR IT, THEN?

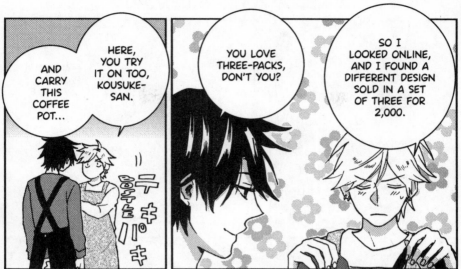

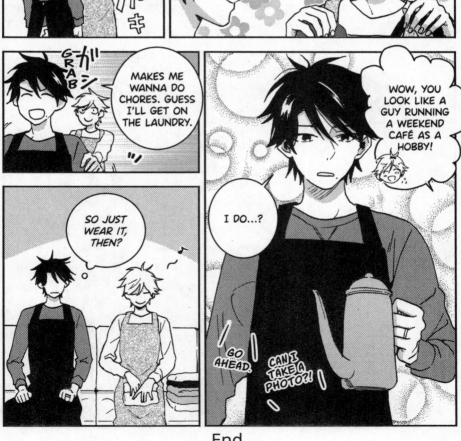

End.

FIRST RUN

Hitorijime My Hero #58 gateau magazine January 2021 issue

Hitorijime My Hero #59 gateau magazine February 2021 issue

Hitorijime My Hero #60 gateau magazine March 2021 issue

Hitorijime My Hero #61 gateau magazine June 2021 issue

Hitorijime My Hero #62 gateau magazine July 2021 issue

Hitorijime My Hero #63 gateau magazine August 2021 issue

Hitorijime My Hero #64 gateau magazine September 2021 issue

AFTER you're done reading this, I'd like a WORD with you

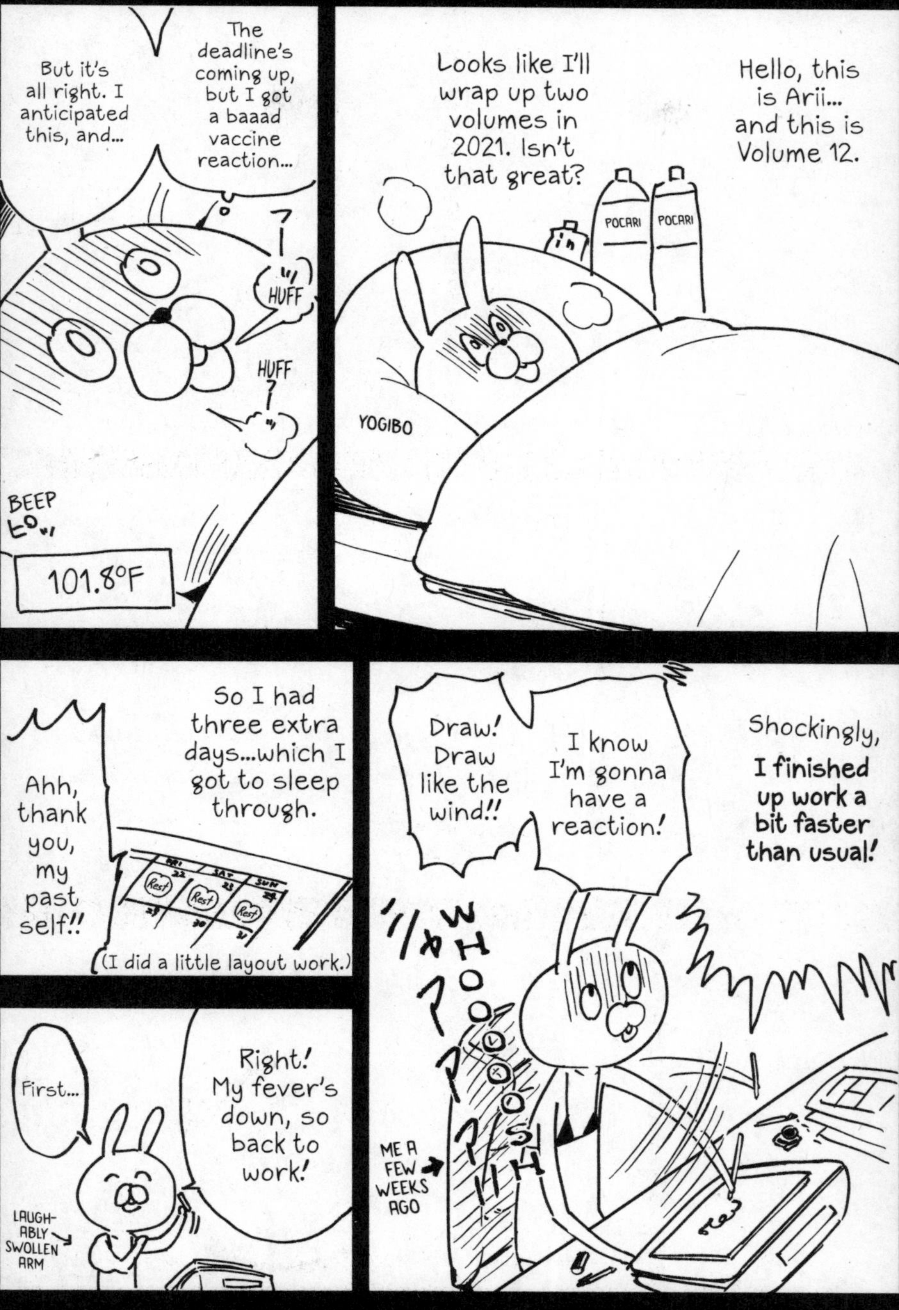
Hello, this is Arii... and this is Volume 12.
Looks like I'll wrap up two volumes in 2021. Isn't that great?
POCARI
POCARI
YOGIBO
The deadline's coming up, but I got a baaad vaccine reaction...
But it's all right. I anticipated this, and...
HUFF
HUFF
BEEP
101.8°F
Shockingly, **I finished up work a bit faster than usual!**
I know I'm gonna have a reaction!
Draw! Draw like the wind!!
WHOOOOSH
ME A FEW WEEKS AGO
So I had three extra days...which I got to sleep through.
Ahh, thank you, my past self!!
Rest
Rest
Rest
(I did a little layout work.)
Right! My fever's down, so back to work!
First...
LAUGHABLY SWOLLEN ARM

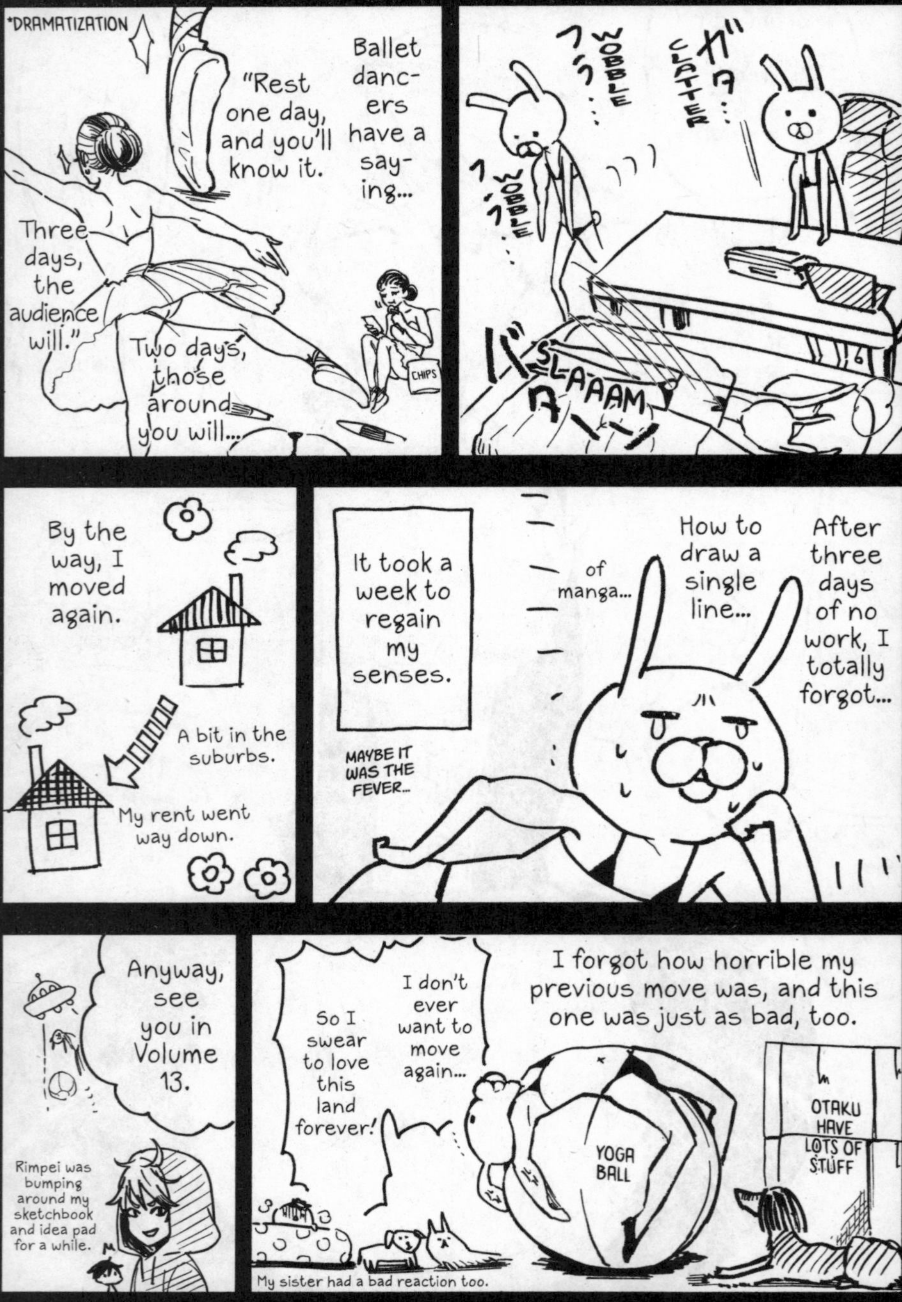
WOBBLE
CLATTER
WOBBLE
SLAAAM
*DRAMATIZATION
Ballet dancers have a saying...
"Rest one day, and you'll know it.
Two days, those around you will...
Three days, the audience will."
CHIPS
After three days of no work, I totally forgot...
How to draw a single line...
of manga...
It took a week to regain my senses.
MAYBE IT WAS THE FEVER...
By the way, I moved again.
A bit in the suburbs.
My rent went way down.
I forgot how horrible my previous move was, and this one was just as bad, too.
OTAKU HAVE LOTS OF STUFF
YOGA BALL
I don't ever want to move again...
So I swear to love this land forever!
My sister had a bad reaction too.
Anyway, see you in Volume 13.
Rimpei was bumping around my sketchbook and idea pad for a while.

Thanks → My editor, the book designer, backgrounds → T-san, filler & tones → my little sister, and you, the readers.

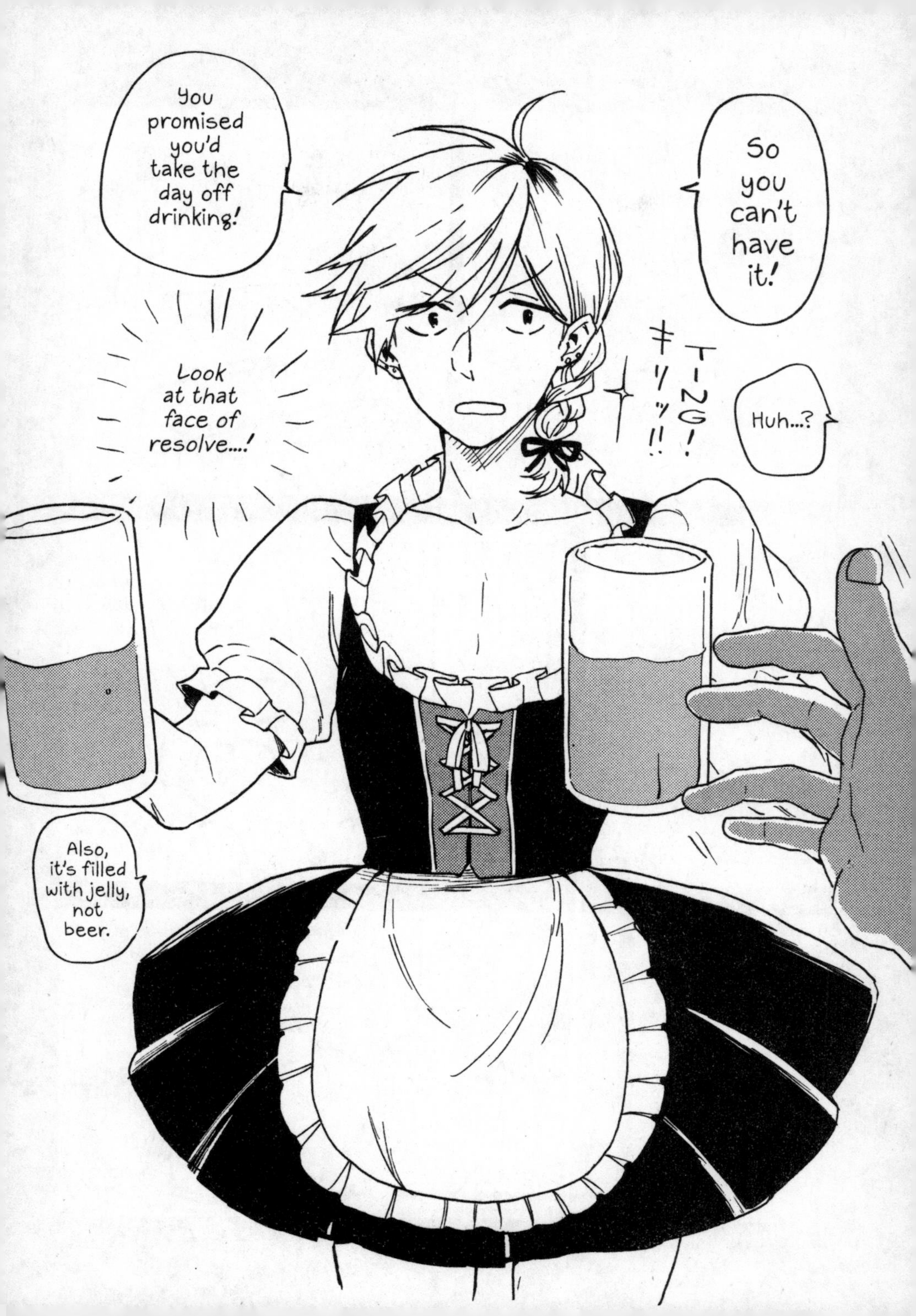
You promised you'd take the day off drinking!
So you can't have it!
TING!
キリッ!!
Huh...?
Look at that face of resolve...!
Also, it's filled with jelly, not beer.

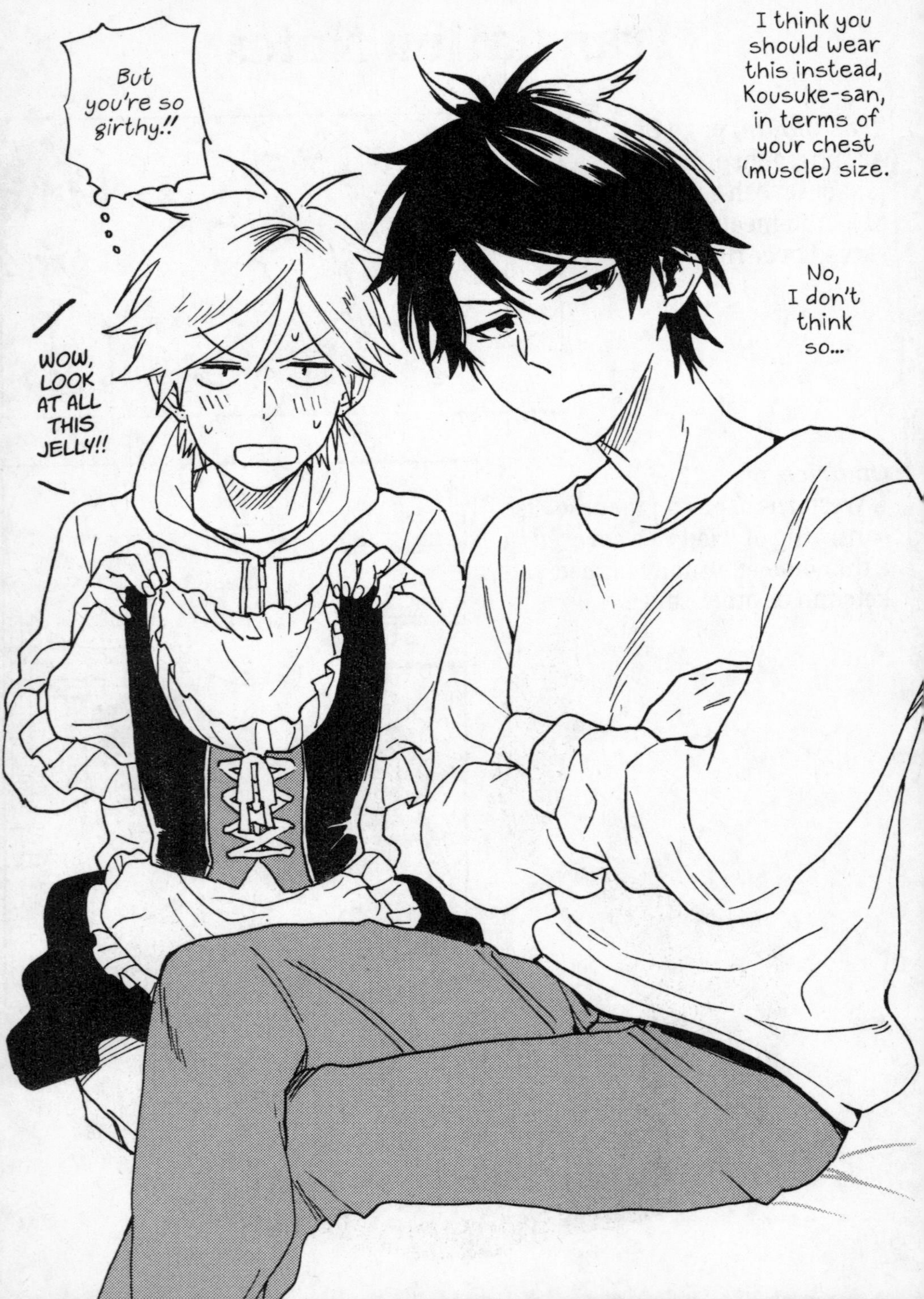

I think you should wear this instead, Kousuke-san, in terms of your chest (muscle) size.
No, I don't think so...
But you're so girthy!!
WOW, LOOK AT ALL THIS JELLY!!

Translation Notes

***Tenshinhan*, page 21**
A Chinese-inspired Japanese dish consisting of a crab-meat omelet served over rice.

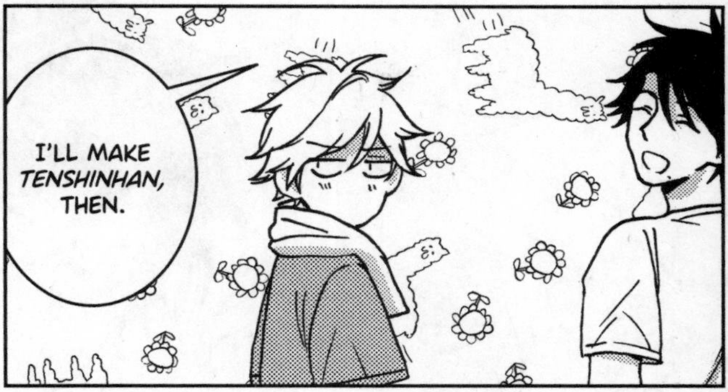
I'LL MAKE *TENSHINHAN*, THEN.

***Omurice*, page 22**
A Western-inspired Japanese dish consisting of fried rice covered in a thin omelet, usually topped with ketchup or other sauce.

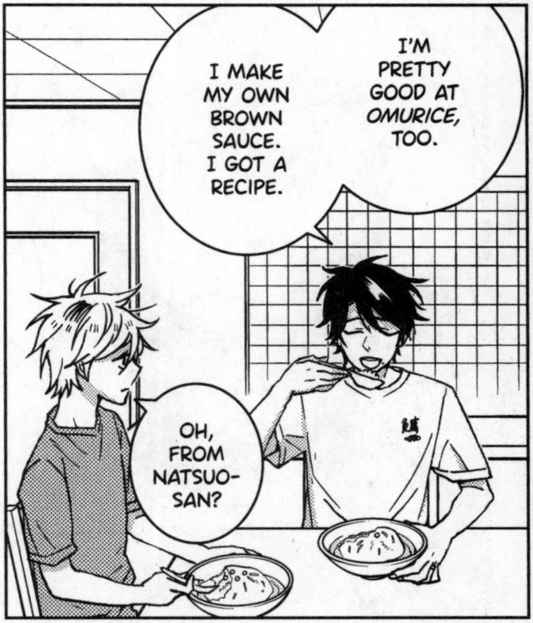
I'M PRETTY GOOD AT *OMURICE*, TOO.
I MAKE MY OWN BROWN SAUCE. I GOT A RECIPE.
OH, FROM NATSUO-SAN?

Young characters and steampunk setting, like *Howl's Moving Castle* and *Battle Angel Alita*

Beyond the Clouds © 2018 Nicke / Ki-oon

A boy with a talent for machines and a mysterious girl whose wings he's fixed will take you beyond the clouds! In the tradition of the high-flying, resonant adventure stories of Studio Ghibli comes a gorgeous tale about the longing of young hearts for adventure and friendship!

One of CLAMP's biggest hits returns in this definitive, premium, hardcover 20th anniversary collector's edition!

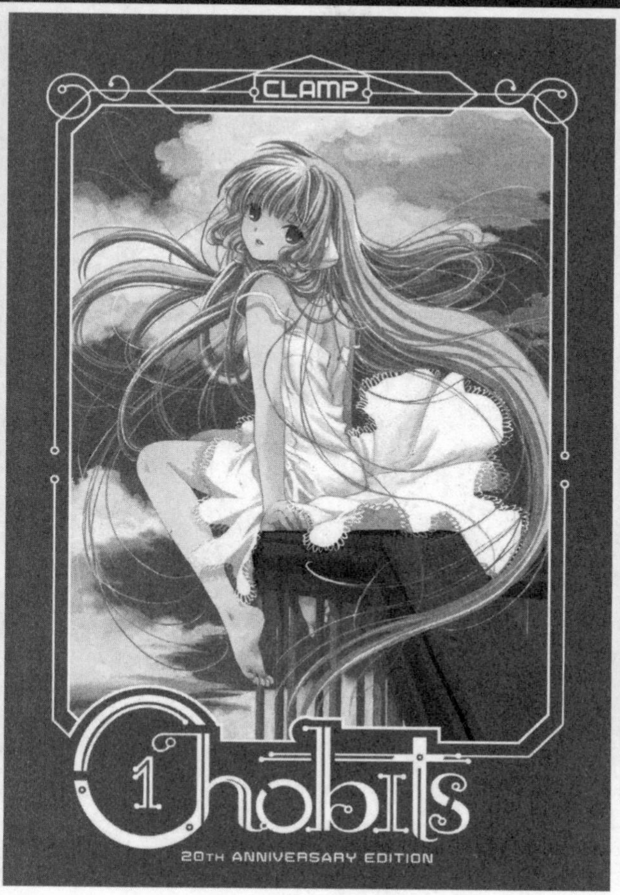
CLAMP
1 Chobits
20TH ANNIVERSARY EDITION

"A wonderfully entertaining story that would be a great installment in anybody's manga collection."
— Anime News Network

"CLAMP is an all-female manga-creating team whose feminine touch shows in this entertaining, sci-fi soap opera."
— Publishers Weekly

Poor college student Hideki is down on his luck. All he wants is a good job, a girlfriend, and his very own "persocom"—the latest and greatest in humanoid computer technology. Hideki's luck changes one night when he finds Chi—a persocom thrown out in a pile of trash. But Hideki soon discovers that there's much more to his cute new persocom than meets the eye.

KC KODANSHA COMICS